CPG Series of Comparative Constitutional Law, Politics and Governance

Edited by the
German-Southeast Asian Center of Excellence for Public Policy and Good Governance

Vol. 1

Prof. Dr. Dirk Ehlers/Henning Glaser/
Dr. Kittisak Prokati (eds.)

Constitutionalism and Good Governance

Eastern and Western Perspectives

Nomos

Die Deutsche Nationalbibliothek lists this publication in the Deutsche Nationalbibliografie; detailed bibliographic data is available in the Internet at http://dnb.d-nb.de.

ISBN 978-3-8329-6987-5

1st edition 2014

Preface

The present volume gathers 19 articles on constitutionalism, good governance and constitutionalization referring to twelve constitutional regimes in Europe and Asia. It is dealing with issues like the rule of law in such different traditions as the British and the German, with federalism in countries like Germany and Nepal, with divided or dividing societies like Nepal, Malaysia and Thailand. Topics are the making and design of constitutions, the effect and emergence of regional governance in Asia and Europe. Other articles reflect on human right issues related to countries like Germany, Malaysia and Thailand as well as the European Convention on Human Rights and its impact on national law. Moreover, the role of courts for constitutionalism and constitutionalization, local self-administration, federalism, the majority principle, and the law on election are further topics addressed here.

With a Privy Councilor of HM the King of Cambodia and former constitutional councilor, statesman and scholar, with the former president of the Judicial Yuan of the Republic of China, the president of the Supreme Administrative Court of Thailand and two German constitutional court justices and former justices respectively, with altogether fifteen legal scholars, two political scientists and one philosopher, the volume presents very different professional perspectives on its issues.

Most of the papers have been presented at the first annual conference of the *German-Southeast Asian Center of Excellence for Public Policy and Good Governance (CPG)* at the end of 2010 at Lebua State Tower Hotel in Bangkok. Others, namely the papers of Føllesdal, Glaser, Grimm, Menzel, Son Soubert and Weng, have been contributed additionally. Particular thanks are owed to them as well as to the other contributors for their time and efforts to make this collection possible. Their points of view, analyses and reflections are most appreciated. We hope to encourage as many of them as possible to be engaged in our future work with the German-Southeast Center of Excellence of Public Policy and Good Governance which is dedicated to the issue of constitutionalism in theory and practice. With the present volume CPG is launching the *CPG Series of Comparative Constitutional Law, Politics and Governance,* with a second one dealing with "Consent and Conflict in the Constitutional Basic Order" coming soon.

The work of our Center of Excellence, CPG, which is formed by the universities of Frankfurt am Main, Münster and Passau as well as Thammasat University, Bangkok, as a joint institute located at Thammasat University, in general as well as the present book in particular is possible due to the support of the German Foreign Ministry, the Federal Foreign Office, and the German Academic Exchange Service (DAAD) as well as Thammasat University as being the host of CPG.

For their contribution to open the first annual conference which gave the initial idea for this book we have to thank HE Peerapan Saleeratthawiphack, Minister of Justice of the Kingdom of Thailand, representing the Prime Minister of the Kingdom of Thailand, Dr. Peter Ammon, State Secretary, German Federal Foreign Office, and Dr. Dorothea Rüland, Secretary General of the DAAD, as well as Prof. Dr. Surasak Likasitwatanakul for hosting the event as the Dean of the Faculty of Law, Thammasat University. Last but not least we thank Duc Quang Ly for supervising the editorial work for this book on its various stages and all the other members of CPG‘s staff who contributed to the editing.

Dirk Ehlers *Henning Glaser* *Kittisak Prokati*

Table of Contents

Part IV: Courts

Part I:

Introduction and Overview

Multiple Constitutionalizations – 'Constitutionalism and Good Governance in European-Asian Perspectives'

Henning Glaser

The present volume collects nineteen interdisciplinary perspectives on fundamental issues of constitutionalism and good governance in Europe and Asia.

Altogether twelve constitutional regimes are serving as points of reference with the constitutional systems of Germany (*Mellinghoff*, *Ehlers*, *Ebsen*, *Esser*, *Pieroth*, *Grimm*, *Grote*) and Thailand (*Warawit*, *Hassavut*, *Boonsri*, *Chen*, *Dressel*) being most strongly represented. Other constitutional systems addressed here are those of Cambodia (*Son Soubert*), Malaysia (*Derichs*), Nepal (*Føllesdal*), the United Kingdom (*Allisson*) and Taiwan (*Weng*), as well as Japan, South Korea and Singapore (*Dressel*). Moreover, *Albert Chen*, in his comparative study, takes all eleven Southeast Asian countries into account, while *Grote*, *Esser* and *Son Soubert* refer to the ASEAN and the European Convention on Human Rights respectively.

As different as the professional backgrounds of the contributors – including fifteen legal scholars, five Justices (*Grimm*, *Hassavut*, *Mellinghoff*, *Son Soubert*, and *Weng*), two political scientists (*Derichs* and *Dressel*), one historian and statesman (*Son Soubert*) and one philosopher (*Føllesdal*) – are the chosen methodological approaches and perspectives. A comparative perspective is taken by *Chen*, *Dressel* and *Menzel*. While *Dressel* compares two Southeast-Asian and two East Asian countries exploring the thesis of a growing judicialization of politics, *Chen* approaches his topic by a historical macro-analysis of the modern constitutional development in Southeast Asia. An essentially historical approach is also taken by *Allison* and *Pieroth* in their accounts on the British and German version of the rule of law respectively, as well as in *Weng's* remarks on Taiwan's constitutional evolution under the guidance of the Constitutional court. *Menzel* finally is reflecting on conditions and patterns of constitutional reform from a practical perspective, an issue which is also touched on by *Son Soubert*.

Two leading theses might help to introduce into this variety of constitutional systems and perspectives; first, the observation of an increasing global tendency of juridification of political power and legal shaping of constitutional regimes, and, second, the assumption that the different constitutional systems are yet representing essentially different answers to the same questions producing an image of multiple constitutionalisms and constitutionalizations.

A. Multiple Constitutionalisms – Between Unity and Difference

An initial point of reference for this observation of multiple constitutionalisms is presented by *Albert Chen's* thorough reconstruction of the post-colonial spread of constitutionalism in Southeast Asia.

Chen understands constitutionalism as a product of modern Western civilization which despite its origins in Western modernity "has found homes in all corners of the earth." However, beyond this adherence to globalized patterns of governance, Southeast Asia, besides all its cultural diversity, is also characterized by a broad range of diverse legal and constitutional cultures and political systems. The latter are ranging from socialist people's republics, to presidential and parliamentary systems, to not less than four different kinds of monarchies while the legal systems are shaped by such different influences like the British, Dutch, French, German, Spanish, socialist and US-American. *Chen* tries to order these patterns of unity and difference according to their relation to Western constitutionalism, which thus serves as the unifying band to analyze and compare them. Doing so, he suggests a typology of constitutionalism which is consequently developed from the perspective of Western constitutionalism as the common denominator and appears in three different forms: the 'pure' Western one called "*liberal constitutionalism*", the *"hybrid"* and lastly the *"Marxist-Leninist"* form of constitutionalism. The latter two forms are modifications of the Western basic model each combined with one additional characterizing feature. That is the "socialist one-party rule" and such authoritarian elements respectively, which derive either "from traditional or indigenous notions, norms, institutions and practices of politics, or [as] a result of deliberate attempts by rulers or ruling elites" (*Chen*). These variations reflect different degrees of approximation (or deviation) in relation to the basic model. Here, *Chen* is drawing on *Karl Loewenstein's* conceptual distinction between "nominal", "semantic" and "normative" constitutions, assuming that liberal constitutions as the Western 'pure type' are normative ones and as such fully entrenched in the political realm. Hybrid constitutions are then either "normative" or "nominal" while Marxist-Leninist constitutions are either "nominal" or only "semantic" ones. This model, derived from a concise recapitulation of Southeast Asia's constitutional history, follows and cultivates a classical tradition of constitutional and comparatist thinking, which could be labeled as "universalist version of constitutionalism." Used by *Chen* rather as a heuristic tool to approach the variety of his subject under a common denominator, it is, in its application, sated with a range of distinct normative implications. In this latter sense universalism claims the existence of one right answer to the quest how societies should be governed, leading to a dichotomy of success (in principle) and (gradual) failure from a teleological perspective. The underlying assumption is a Manichaean distinction of chaos and order, justice and injustice, the good and the bad which is persistently recurring in the model of a global governance standard of Western origin, which is presumed to be achieved in different grades of convergence by non-Western states. This perspective still represents a Western standard view on non-Western states, which are perceived as either deviating from the Western model – even with a promising tendency sometimes – or failing. This view is widespread and practically important. It is also not easy to contradict, because originally Western elements of law and governance are indeed constantly diffusing on a global scale encountering often conditions which are less favorable for them than those of the Western world. Yet, it is unsatisfying to reduce the relevance of non-Western otherness merely to pure deviation and will inevitably result in justified resistance on the one side and distorted perceptions on the other. Instead, it is suggested here to modify this standard view providing for a partly different model, which might be described under the label of "multiple constitutionalism".

However, in accordance with *Chen's* heuristic approach, to provide a comparative perspective, there has to be a certain element of unity to enable any comparison at all. This common denominator of contemporary constitutionalism is – following *Chen* – indeed a model of governance originated in the West. Acknowledging its factual global influence too, the difference to the standard view is marked by the denial of its automatic implication of superiority sating both, the perception of and the communication with this otherness, sorting the latter in a one-dimensional way and depriving it from its own characteristics beyond the unnecessary notions of deviation or failure where it comes to respect and understanding first. The approach to multiple constitutionalisms thus assumes that only the initially unbiased view on the very characteristics of any single constitutional system enables an adequate analysis of facts and does prepare the ground for meaningful dialogue instead of establishing a definitional regime of presumed knowledge.

I. Unity in Diversity

Asking on this basis for the element of unity in global constitutionalism, it might be sufficient to stress a notion of commonalities across the regions by indicating how much the topics presented here touch, overlap, and complement each other, revealing a shared background of patterns of constitutionalism as well as the need for differentiation which, however, is not at all restricted to a simple East-West-dichotomy.

Federalism for instance, addressed here by *Ehlers* and *Føllesdal* for Germany and Nepal respectively, is mentioned as a basic feature of the Malaysian constitution also by *Derichs*. The reflections on the majority principle by *Ebsen* are not only concretized by *Mellinghoff's* account on the German law on elections but point to one of the core issues in Thai constitutionalism presented by *Boonsri*: a different, sceptical perception of majority rule where it comes to *electoral* democracy and party rule which is, however, very much reminiscenting experiences of early American and French constitutionalism as well the predominating view during the first German republic from 1919 to 1933. This issue is implicitly addressed also in *Hassavut's* analysis of the judicial mandate in Thailand which can be perceived as aiming at disciplining democratic mechanisms, and furthermore echoed by *Dressel's* account on judicial activism in comparative perspectives. *Ebsen's* plea in favor of the majority principle also touches on persisting problems in shaping a Nepalese federal state (*Follesdal*) as well as on Malaysia's constitutional core principle of a "Malay supremacy" (*Derichs*), cases which are useful to be compared to Canada´s Quebec-question or the political aspirations of the Lega Nord as one of the major political parties in Italy.

The necessity to locate constitutional features in their historical context is exemplified by *Allison* and *Pieroth* who are presenting the historical development of the German and English version of the rule of law respectively, while *Grimm* is asking for its exportability, a question partly answered by *Chen*. *Weng*, *Hassavut* and *Dressel* are addressing constitutional courts as major actors of constitutionalization from different perspectives. *Weng*, as a pioneer of the rule of law in Asia[1], offers insights how constitutionalization works at the coal-face of judicial interpretation, while *Dressel* asks for the

1 See Lee, "The Advocate and Practitioner of the Idea of Guardian of the Constitution," 2011.

conditions and processes leading to more active or passive judicial performance where it comes to politics, an issue which is also addressed by *Hassavut* whose remarks from an 'internal' perspective can be partly read as an answer to critics of an alleged undue judicialization of politics in Thailand, drawing a line between acceptable and unacceptable criticism on the basis of the predominant view in Thai constitutionalism. This is leading to the topics of *Grote* and *Warawit*, both writing about the exercise of political basic rights, the freedom of expression and assembly in particular. Even these few examples indicate that constitutionalism is indeed globally about the same problems and offering the same tools, and yet enables quite different solutions and perspectives.

II. Difference

Variety in constitutionalism in terms of essential differences has been acknowledged by a newer perspective on legal comparison which was developed especially in public law. This newer approach is looking beyond the older search for unity in comparing law and achieves to overcome any "axiomatization of similarity" as implicit vantage point.[2] However, as the universalistic stance still forms the standard view on non-Western constitutionalism, it is useful to pay some attention to its underlying normative and teleological assumptions. An integral part of them is the idea of a steady civilizational progress against which all concepts of political power beyond liberal constitutionalism have to be classified either as transitory steps or temporary failures of an eventually linear development towards the final goal

---

2 See for instance Legrand, "What 'legal transplants'?," 2001, p. 67: "Comparison must not have a unifying, but a multiplying effect: it must aim to organize the diversity of discourses around different (cultural) forms and counter the tendency of the mind toward uniformisation. Comparison must grasp legal cultures diacritically. Accordingly, the comparatist must emphatically rebut any attempts at the axiomatisation of similarity [...]." For a good description of the universalistic concept see Choudhry, "Globalization in Search of Justification," 1999, p. 833: "At the opposite end of the spectrum from particularists stand scholars who posit that constitutional guarantees are cut from a universal cloth, and that all constitutional courts are engaged in the identification, interpretation, and application of the same set of principles. (...) Courts working in this interpretive mode regard themselves 'as giving meaning to liberties that transcend national boundaries.' A universalist view of the law is an important strain in comparative law scholarship."

of this "one right constitutionalism" whose terms are totally defined by the West – including the 'acceptable' exceptions if necessary.[3] Moreover, the universalistic perspective on constitutionalism might be seen as an expression of a kind of political faith which is not only serving vested interests and preserving power relations but often also comes with the best intentions. If it is true that Western constitutionalism essentially reflects the secularization of the ideas of state and human rights, it is also true that it inherited a quasi-religious visionary belief in a progress towards an utopian end from its Christian roots[4] which does not only support the notorious self-assertion of a superior Western knowledge about the right political order but often also underlies Western assessments of non-Western constitutional systems as being "on the way" (to heaven or hell). Even done with good intentions, these classifications are hardly convenient for the assessed and often misleading for the assessing. However, the practice is as old as approved, producing recurring patterns in the production of an epistemic "power-knowledge" (*Foucault*) which has been reinforcing global power structures for centuries. An early version of these alternating assessments of either non- or not yet mature political communities is reflected by one of the earliest disputes of the problem how to treat non-Western societies according to international law in early modern Western history, the dispute of Valladolid (1550-1551). Here, the main adversaries, *Las Casas* and *Sepulveda*, finally agreed on the question how to handle the peoples in America with the compromise that the *Indians would be treated as being free and ready to be missionized while the Africans had been lost and could be taken to be treated and traded as slaves* (a fate they often shared with their theoretically favored Indian brothers if those lost their appeal as allies of the Spanish against other Indians).[5] The pattern prevailed. Following it, 'transitional states' are those states which are already on a 'good way' requiring just some support and guidance, while the judgment of a state as being 'failed' inclines to end its

3 See Scheuner, "Die Funktion der Verfassung für den Bestand politischer Ordnung," 1979, p. 116.

4 *Kant* for instance described the religious faith as the continuous approximation to the invisible kingdom of God in world history. See Kant, "Die Religion innerhalb der Grenzen der bloßen Vernunft," 1793, 3, 2. This kind of faith, inevitably linked with the idea of a continuous approximation to an utopian end, which is yet happening in this world and being supposed to develop and improve it, has been secularized as a political faith.

5 See Trouillot, "Undenkbare Geschichte," 2002, p. 87.

sovereignty.[6] This whole discourse structure which is still influential in Western perceptions of non-Western political realities is possible due to a persisting lack of acknowledgment of differences *on their own terms*. Thus, the respective modes of the encounter are shaped by a tendency to ignore or damn deviating traditions, ideologies and narratives, be it with good or bad intentions.[7] This grand universalization which is denying meaningful differences on a conceptual level is currently facing a deep and growing resistance, coinciding with interest in and respect of Western achievements and the fact that the originally Western *form* of governance is indeed enjoying an increasing importance as a model to be used, but to be used on the own terms of each respective country (see for the latter also *Ehlers*).

Notwithstanding this critique, it is not suggested here to correct the own moral and political assumptions and the right to stand for them on the side of the West but just to engage in adequate cross-cultural discourse and analysis with a realistic understanding of the Other where academic or political communication is produced. Insofar, *Jullien's* question is justified, if the West is even aware of the problems of other cultures to be forced to operate on the basis of discourses, norms and concepts having been developed in the West to analyze their own particular constitutional systems.[8] Nevertheless, the imposition of denial and patronization is often not leading to a blunt refusal of Western constitutionalism as such but its underlying assumptions[9]: "What is called into question is the implicit belief that we have here in the West about the *knowability* of Others, and the assumption that they can be *predicted through knowledge*."[10] Similarly difficult are the simplifications: "[…] moreover, this assumption of knowability and representational practice of knowing through self-interested and self-referential categories were compounded by the assumption that once known [...] these representational truths can be taken, once and for all, as the final designator and

---

6 That the assessment of the respective "way" of a country is very much dependent on its utility to serve as an ally, be it in Cold War or a War on Terrorism, is evident.

7 See Loomba, *Colonialism/Postcolonialism*, 1998, p. 17.

8 See Jullien, *Das Universelle, das Einförmige, das Gemeinsame*, 2002, p. 198 f.

9 See Son Soubert's account on the Non-Aligned Movement, the 1955 Bandung Declaration and the "Five Principles of Peaceful Coexistence". Find the Bandung Declaration on http://franke.uchicago.edu/Final_Communique_Bandung_1955.pdf.

10 Chio, *Malaysia and the Development Process*, 2005, p. 188.

predictor of – and for – whole cultures, societies and nations."[11] On the other hand, the practical use of the "distorting lenses of vested political interests and ideological positions" of a standard Western view leads also to false impressions on the side of the observer.[12] This whole architecture of the cross-cultural constitutional discourse, which forces non-Western scholars to play according to Western standards, narrowly frames even the heuristic potential of those Western scholars, which try to do justice to the "multiplicity of ways constitutionalism manifests itself around us."[13] They often face the flipside of the asymmetrical relations which are created on the basis of this discourse structure which is leaving not enough space for independent and autochthon perspectives on the one side and, on the other side, do not encourage Western scholars to learn enough about the Other to contribute substantial material for comparative analysis. For both sides it is too costly to leave the well prepared and defined terrain of constitutional analysis and comparison. Thus, as it had been described for Southeast Asian constitutionalism, even the benevolent Western scholar faces the lacking of any "suitable, flexible and sophisticated grammar of discourse" and a huge lack of "real knowledge and understanding of law and society […], which has been hampered by a comparative lack of empirical and socio-legal research."[14]

Nevertheless, while it proves indeed to be a difficult task for the comparative lawyer to deal with the diversity and individuality of non-Western constitutional systems, the perspective on multiple constitutionalisms is at least *in principle* already developed on an interdisciplinary level. Corresponding to the standard account on constitutionalism, it is equally rooted in a wider world-view, namely the perception of "multiple modernities" as being analyzed in post-colonial, cultural and subaltern studies. This epistemic model of modernity strives to deconstruct the overarching model of a uniform and unilinear process towards an already fixed development goal, a particular and exclusive governance model defined by the West, its idea

11 Chio, *Malaysia and the Development Process*, 2005, p. 188. See also Jacobsen and Bruun, "Introduction: Human Rights and Asian Values," 2000, p. 13: "For centuries, Western academics have been gigantic producers of sweeping universalisms in all fields, while Western political and economic dominance have facilitated their march ahead in. Considerable arrogance arose from the implicit appropriation, through terminology and language, of shared intellectual creations of the world."

12 See Reuter, "Indonesia's political and cultural transformation," 2010, p.3.

13 Albert, "The Cult of Constitutionalism," 2012, p. 374.

14 Harding, "Comparative law and legal transplantation," 2001, p. 203.

of governance and free market economy.[15] The perception of a single modernity is instead replaced by the paradigm of a pluralist and fragmented one. Methodological consequence for legal comparison is the demand for a *contextual analysis* of constitutions. The latter "[...] emphasizes the fact that constitutional law is deeply embedded in the institutional, doctrinal, social, and cultural contexts of each nation, and that we are likely to go wrong if we try to think about any specific doctrine or institution without appreciating the way it is tightly linked to all the contexts within which it exists."[16]

Anyway, beyond any preparedness of the constitutional doctrine to redefine its heuristic assumptions, an increasing importance of essentially non-Western visions of constitutionalism in form and substance has already been noted[17] and one does not have to look to contemporary Beijing to find it. An older – critical – study of Thai constitutionalism originated in 1979 for instance is introduced with the following confession of the author: "I began to view 'Thai democracy' on its own terms, and not as something to be dismissed as a political ploy of conservative forces, or as messy, inferior hybrid for which one must apologize to outside observers."[18] And in the context of the making of the present Thai constitution of 2007 *Andrew Harding* acknowledged the Malaysian constitution as an autochthonous one with the following words:

> In this constitution it is relatively easy to identify such elements, despite what we may call the Anglo-Indian origins of the 1957 Constitution: the special privileges of Malays […]; and the restriction of rights of freedom of expression in a way that is designed to protect the social fabric from being rent by racially or religiously divisive pronouncements. Moreover the Constitution provides for

15 See Eisenstadt, "Die institutionellen Ordnungen der Moderne," 2005, p. 338; Moore, *Soziale Ursprünge von Diktatur und Demokratie*, 1968, pp. 475 ff. See also the works of *Edward Said, Homi Bhaba, Dipesh Chakrabarty, Gayatri Chakravorty Spivak.*

16 Tushnet, *Weak Courts, Strong Rights*, 2008, p. 10; see also Harding and Leyland, *The Constitutional System of Thailand*, 2011, p. XXXII.

17 Hirschl, "Constitutionalism in a Theocratic World," 2010, speaks about a growing importance of 'constitutional theocracies' and 'ethnic democracies' (see in particular pp. 266 f.).

18 Thak Chaloemtiarana, *Thailand*, 2007, p. XXIII. See also Thak on page p. XIV: "I do not subscribe to the idea of a singular democracy. Thai democracy is a distinct entity – no better or worse than others. It arises in a certain time and place, and we need not make excuses for it looking different from Western models (which are also many)." Exemplary, separating is and ought, Thak states further: "However, this does not mean that we should accept what is. There is always room for improvement […]."

> the position of Islam [...]; provides for traditional elements of governance such as the monarchies and the Conference of Rulers; and the Malay states themselves within the federal structure. In these matters, whether or not we describe them as 'Asian' constitutional features, they are certainly ones based on local, distinctively Malaysian values, political and economic factors, and also cultural traditions. [...] Malaysia is a good example [...] of a country with an autochthonous constitution.[19]

The differences to be acknowledged are manifold. They may be found in specific institutional settings, the respective societal context, worldviews, values and norms. Concerning Southeast Asia, to give an example for the latter aspects, the first president of the Constitutional Court of Indonesia, *Jimly Asshiddiqie*, circumscribed the concept of law to be applied by the Asian courts as being based not only on written law but a whole plurality of relevant normative orders to be taken into account. Moreover, – according to *Jimly* – the existing rational Western originated or Western-type laws would have to be "synergized with the transcendental beliefs of Asians whose base resource lies upon the norms and values of religion and culture".[20] For Islamic constitutionalism, to give a last example, it is noteworthy that even an explicitly secular political leader like *Ahmed Ben Bella* has stated about the postcolonial emerging Arab nationalism: "It's an error to believe that our nationalism is the nationalism of the French Revolution. Ours is a nationalism fertilized by Islam. [...] All our political formulation is Koranic formulation. [...] Thus Algerian nationalism and Arab nationalism is a cultural nationalism essentially based on Islam."[21]

B. Constitutionalism and Constitutionalization: Concepts, Meanings & Tendencies

As most of the contributions in this volume do not conceptualise the key terms it is useful to reflect briefly on them, namely on the terms 'constitution', 'constitutionalism', 'constitutionalization', and 'good governance'.

---

19 Harding, "New Asian Constitutionalism," 2006, p. 29.

20 Asshiddiqie, "Conflict of Interest between different Basic Rights," 2006.

21 *Ahmed Ben Bella* quoted by Kaiwar and Mazumdar, "The Coordinates of Orientalism," 2009, p. 35. Similarly, it has been stated for India that any similarity between Indian and Western ideas of constitutionalism is no argument against the originality of Indian political theories. See Behr, "Moderne Theorien der Demokratie," 1999, p. 39, 56.

I. Meanings

'Constitutionalism', to start with this term, shall be understood broadly as the *project to rest political power on a constitution*, a term which requires clarification itself. Indeed, the "term 'constitution' is a demanding concept which can be understood only as an overall constellation of numerous components" and which can hardly be brought in a complete and consistent terminological system which offers a uniform approach.[22] First of all, the term 'constitution' can be understood in both basic modes of is or ought, considering the constitution either as the *empirical fact* of a given ordered structure of the political or as the *distinct norm* achieving to do so. Primarily, the term 'constitution' might be understood here in the latter meaning, while the former is taken into account by the methodological request for a contextual analysis of the constitution as norm. In functional terms constitutions as norms might be understood by their task to establish, define and convey state powers, to legitimate and channel their exercise and to regulate both, the relationship among the state powers and between them and the citizen.[23] Thus, if it is said, that "constitutions tame politics" because they limit political power and separate it in agencies which check and balance each other, this is only one side of the medal.[24] On the other side constitutions also *make politics*, namely by organizing, stabilizing and channeling power – something what other governance-models like personal rule, ad-hoc coordination based on force or conviction or central-authoritative planning could not do with the same sustaining effectiveness. Moreover, if constitutions tame politics, this is true not only for the sake of the ruled but also of the ruling. A particularly important feature of the constructive function of constitutions is the fact, as *Chen* notes, that constitutions serve as symbols to express and stabilize a national identity and the collective aspirations of the political community.

What the constitution itself is and has to be in fulfilling these functions seems to be more difficult to say. One (yet not conclusive) ideal-typical set of definitional elements may identify the constitution as a *legal* norm regulating political power, claiming to be the *supreme* (legal) norm in most of

22 See Wahl, "In Defense of 'Constitution'," 2010, p. 241.

23 See also the definitions of Tamanaha, *On the Rule of Law*, 2004, p. 56; McIlwain, *Constitutionalism*, 1947, p. 15; Aristotle, *Politics*, Book IV, 1289 a 15-20.

24 See Kautz, Melzer, Weinberger and Zinman, "Introduction: The Idea of Constitutionalism," 2011, p. 3.

the systems[25], and inclining even to be the *exclusive* one in the whole political realm in some systems – at least as a normative fiction.[26] Finally, the constitution is normally, even if not necessarily, founding and organizing a political community by a particular *foundational act*, which is made visible and being embodied by a *written document* and which is often reflected particularly by the preamble and supported by some constitutional myths, narratives and symbols.

This constitutional blueprint, put in power once by the sovereign as an expression of the project called 'constitutionalism', has to be permanently unfolded then in view of changing circumstances leading to the phenomenon being described by the third term 'constitutionalization'.[27] It is understood here as the *process* of entrenching the constitution (as supreme norm) within the legal and political order.[28] This process serves the purpose to reinforce and reproduce the constitution and to create a dynamic, ever emerging and differentiating system of ordering. As a historical process it is developing contingently and not foreseeable by its founders: not unilinear but complex and open to external influences and evolving in varying speeds, circles, spirals and loops including contradictions and setbacks.[29] Its basis is the con-

---

25 Different are those systems which are governed by the principle of parliamentary supremacy as it is known for some common law systems but which was also been prominent in 'continental' constitutional thinking. See for the German empire of 1871 Laband, *Das Staatsrecht des Deutschen Reiches*, Vol. II, pp. 38 ff. Is the constitution acknowledged as the supreme norm as it is the case of most contemporary constitutions, it will have to *stabilize* itself against easy changes and sometimes even exempt essential parts of the constitution from amendment. Moreover, the supremacy of the constitution inclines to require *judicial review*, an issue which will be discussed below. See for constitutional stability (or rigidity) the empirical-comparative overview of Lorenz, "How to Measure Constitutional Rigidity," 2005.

26 Interesting is the Austrian constitution which carefully combines the idea of a supreme legal norm and exclusive norm of the political in the language of the constitution by avoiding even the term '(state) power'. See Wiederin, *Österreich/ HIPE*, 2010, § 7, margin no. 127.

27 See Badura, "Verfassungsänderung, -wandel, -gewohnheitsrecht," 1992, margin no. 7.

28 See M. J. C. Vile who stresses the importance of 'the concept of process' as a major explanatory concept of constitutionalism alongside the "older concepts of function and structure." See Vile, *Constitutionalism and the Separation of Powers*, 1967, pp. 347 and 377 ff.; see from a British point of view also Bogdanor, *The New British Constitution*, 2009, p. 272.

29 See generally for the nature of societal processes Luhmann, "Geschichte als Prozess," 1981.

stitutional text whose potential impact has been put in the following words: "Hitherto unknown powers are slumbering in the letters of the constitution to be discovered by the legislator and called into being by the judge."[30] This process is normatively limited and channeled by the original constitutional blueprint while being exposed to new interpretations and shifting balances of powers and always exposed to changes of the direction, which might be ordered also by amendments or even the replacement of the constitution. Constitutionalization is furthermore dependent on the influences and conditions set by the cultural deep structure it operates in, the given institutional and human resources, extra-constitutional forces and so on. One of the most significant driving forces of constitutionalization is judicial decision making. However, judicially driven constitutionalization is not confined to final decision making by constitutional courts and the particular case but continues in scholarly debate and the sensitization of law- making and enforcement bodies as well as (lower) courts.[31] The *patterns* of constitutionalization are sometimes paradox when the attitudinal and behavioral dimensions are taken into account. This is the case for instance where constitutional achievements are supported by those powers which formerly opposed them because they realize that they are now – under changed political circumstances – useful for them. In such a scenario, the motivation for support of constitutional achievements may partly contravene their underlying logic in the attempt to control or co-opt their institutional impact. However, this reflects a general pattern of any societal development as processes of change often seem to integrate resisting elements belonging to the order they start to change. *Luhmann* described this phenomenon as the use of "evolutionary crutches". Major regime changes for instance may probably not occur – at least not non - violent - without participation of some elements of the ruling elites. Another example is the increasing role of constitutional review being supported and propagated by those political elites who face a deprivation of their power in the near future, before they resisted the introduction of constitutional review as long as their position was unchallenged.

While constitutionalism describes the decision to *make* a constitution rule, constitutionalization means the entrenched *making* of that rule in an ongoing

30 Jellinek, *Verfassungsänderung und Verfassungswandlung*, 1906, p. 20, loosely translated by the author.

31 See Gerhardt, "Verfassungsgerichtliche Kontrolle der Verwaltungsgerichtsbarkeit," 2008, pp. 737 ff. This is particularly important where decisions of the constitutional courts have no effect *erga omnes*.

process. Constitutionalism in a wider sense might also be understood as the concerted efforts serving the project to bind political power to a constitution, which is including the adherence to a certain constitutional structure, the existence of accompanying narratives and symbols, supportive discourses and contributions of scholarly and public debate, as well as the shared experiences and values of the political community. While constitutionalism refers then more to the entirety of the constitutional order, constitutionalization again is the process to unfold the given model of constitutional governance in legal terms, the endeavor to set the model in motion and action.[32]

'Good governance', as the last term to be explained, seems to be both, a practice and a goal, the former justified by the latter. Its 'good' appears simply as being induced by the procedures it justifies, creating a perfect circle. This is no accident. Term and concept of 'good Governance' have indeed been purportedly designed to appear as neutral as possible, when they gained popularity claiming to reflect an allegedly universal form of reason in governance which was introduced and strongly promoted by the Bretton-Woods institutions during the 1990 s. The trick with this concept is that it offers a seemingly undisputable 'good' which is yet precisely describable merely *as practice*, while this praxis itself is justified by the undisputable end it serves *and defines*. Good governance appears as a naturally given, universal aim whose necessary conditions just have to be fulfilled and which itself is put out of discussion claiming to be substantially approachable solely via its procedural conditions which itself are supposed to form a universal standard. In fact, good governance according to this concept is not value-neutral or reinforcing universally accepted values and policies at all. It has, on the contrary, been very much an instrument to achieve a particular political vision, namely a (neo-) liberal one. As such it is only at the surface solely an economic approach but effectively represents a distinct, fully-fledged worldview. Being not different than humanist, socialist or Islamic constitu-

32 This process rather than the constitutional text makes all the difference. See for instance Rosenn, "The Success of Constitutionalism in the United States," 1990, p. 1: "If the world were destroyed today, and archaeologists of the future were to discover only the constitutions of the United States and the Latin American Republics, they would probably conclude that constitutionalism was far more developed in Latin America than in the United States. Compared to Latin American constitutions [...] the US constitution appears undeniable underdeveloped. Yet this brief, frequently omissive charter has worked extraordinary well [...], while the more elaborated charters in Latin America have generally worked poorly."

tionalism in this respect, it is unique in denying this fact, claiming instead value neutrality for its end and procedure. Different to them, it pretends to enforce a positive development due to a set of governance instruments without any connotative, normative, historical and discursive sub- and context, while effectively transporting a distinct governance purpose which is by no means neutral or a universally accepted norm. This standard meaning is refused here. Instead of using good governance as a covert ideological term it might be used heuristically as a starting point in search of a substantial description of those processes and techniques which are suitable in relation to a certain normative end. Thus, good governance is necessarily to be concretized as Buddhist, Islamic, secular humanist, socialist, neoliberal or whatever kind of (good) governance.[33]

II. Tendencies

To introduce into contemporary constitutionalism as increasingly important source of governance it is helpful to reflect on some actual tendencies displaying notions of unity and difference as well as some limits or shadowsides of the overarching trend of juridification.

1. Countervailing Tendencies Concerning the Relative Impact of Constitutionalism

According to the relative impact of constitutionalism in "East and West" it is noteworthy that the trend of an increasing importance of constitutional law as a steering tool of public order on the national level is particularly pronounced by the developments in Asia. One might even observe a somehow countervailing tendency in relation to Europe with respect to the fact that national constitutions in Western countries seem to have lost some ground to both other constitutional regimes beyond the state as well as extra-constitutional regimes penetrating spaces formerly occupied by tighter constitutional rule. Even where these developments are global ones – this is

33 Noteworthy, the Thai translation of the term 'good governance', *thammaphiban*, refers to the cosmic rule of *dhamma* or *dharma*, thus linking good governance to a distinct set of norms and requirements in the context of a (religious) Buddhist understanding of righteous rule.

especially true for the latter – do European countries look stronger affected than others, notwithstanding the fact that these tendencies might hit the Western constitutional project on an already highly developed level.

Generally, the relevance of national constitutions is exposed to three global developments affecting their impact, firstly the emerging *multi-level* governance structures leaving the state embedded in an environment of surrounding, intervening and reshaping legal regimes on different levels and of different sources. This tendency is partly overlapping with a growing *economic impact* on the shape and fate of law and governance and the massive shift towards a dominant role of national and international security regimes challenging constitutional core values in the *post-9/11 world*.[34]

All these tendencies seem to affect Western constitutions relatively stronger for a number of reasons. They have, first of all, been so differentiated and entrenched that interventions have unavoidably strong effects on the established system as a whole. Secondly, and partly even a success story, national constitutions are nowhere so exposed to competing constitutional regimes which are partly regulating the same issues with a rapidly emerging impact like in Europe as exemplified by *Esser* and *Grote* here. While this partly competing regional governance level is following widely the same core values like the national constitutions the globally growing security regime is – in terms of law as well as extra-legal, if not outright illegal practices – a massive challenge for the substance core of Western constitutionalism as being essentially based on fundamental rights and representative democracy.[35] A variation of the threat to these core values is the threat to the particular extended rule of law and the claim that the constitutional is not only the supreme but the exclusive norm in the realm of political power

34 See Scheppele, "The Migration of Anti-constitutional Ideas," 2006.

35 Where security regimes are established by law they pose a challenge of the universalistic substance of constitutionalism which can be resolved according to the benchmarks of constitutional law and doctrine. However, the extent of security law regimes after 9/11 raises serious concern if this can still be done with respect to the universalist core values of the constitution. The widespread extra-legal practices of national security policy are definitely contravening them. Tushnet called this new regime tellingly a "political constitution", a term which will be explained more detailed below. See Tushnet, "The political constitution of emergency powers," 2008.

(see *Grimm* and *Pieroth*) as typical features of European constitutionalism, especially in Germany.[36]

Another reason for the relative decline of European state constitutions looms in the sphere of global politics. The US for instance, while also deviating from some constitutional core values of their own to a more national security-ridden governance structure domestically and abroad, are actively preserving global strategic interests by reinforcing their hegemonic political power in doing so. In the same time the believability and attractiveness of those core values which are shared by Western constitutionalism is declining. Thus, the appeal of European grown constitutionalism as a universal benchmark for good governance seems to come increasingly under stress with America increasingly deviating from these core values and countries like China challenging the conceptual superiority of Western constitutionalism with a supposed impact in the coming years.

In sum, being far away from a critical condition, the *relative* decrease of the constitutionalism as a national project in Europe and growing irritations of European core values coincide with a *tendency* of an increasing appeal of constitutionalism in some Southeast Asian countries as an expression of multiple constitutionalizations.

2. From Cultural to Legal Constitutionalism: The Thai example

An example for the Southeast Asian trend of an increasing impact of the constitution as predominantly *legal* rule is Thailand, where the constitution was merely a stepchild of political practice and thinking until it started to receive a "normative" (even if not exclusive) meaning (see *Chen referring to Loewenstein*). Two developments are underlying this process, firstly the shift of the established political system from a preference of a so-called "cultural constitution" to a growing willingness to steer politics in terms of legal rules in form of Western constitutionalism and secondly the need to deal with an emerging challenge of the substance core of this Thai constitutionalism which itself remained unchanged during the transition from the

36 The roots of this typical Western view are deep and famously expressed by *Locke* when he states: "Where-ever law ends, tyranny begins." (See Locke, *Second Treatise of Government*, 1689, p. 103 (s. 202)). Contrary, non-Western countries are more used to tolerate and operate normative pluralism including non-legal norms and are thus inclined to be less vulnerable against disappointments in this respect.

predominantly cultural to the Western constitutional form. It is in this sense and understood "on its own terms" first and foremost offering a distinct and differentiated concept of governance centered around the reigning king (rather than the monarchial institution as such).[37] In the period before the 1990 s, when the written constitution merely served as a minimum-set of rules to organize the set-up and interplay of democratic institutions which were not supposed to play a steady and dominant role in governing the country, the unwritten and the written part in the encompassing system of ordering the political were mainly seen as opposites on unequal terms.[38]

One of the basic assumptions of the "cultural constitution" forming the dignified *and* the effective part[39] of this "Thai-style democracy" with elections, political parties and parliaments as merely technical tools is the direct link between a father-like king and his people, perceiving good governance in general as resulting rather from morally 'good' people than formal rep-

37 Since the 1990 s, with the shift to a more legal understanding, the term "democratic regime with the King as head of state" gradually replaced the older term "Thai-style democracy".

38 See Tongnoi Tongyai, "The Role of the Monarchy in Modern Thailand," 1990, p. 155: "Consider even a lifeless thing like the [written] Thai Constitution [as legal document]. It has been shifted and changed so much [...] that no-one can say what its basic tenets are. The Thai monarchy on the other hand, is the only thing that remained all the time closely identified with the basic interests of the Thai nation and people, and although highly personalized at any single time, it is the only thing in Thailand which people readily accept as an institution. As such, the Thai monarch stands on a par with, for example, the Constitution in the United States or Marxism in communist countries." The parallelism between the monarchial regime and the written constitution is still resonated by the preamble of the 2007 constitution, where his Majesty is "graciously pleased to proclaim that the President of the National Legislative Assembly addresses royally that the democratic regime of government with the King as Head of State has been evolved in Thailand for more than seventy five years and, through this period of time, the Constitutions had been promulgated, repealed and amended for the compliance with the situation of the nation and the changing circumstances [...]."

39 See Bagehot, *The English Constitution*, 1867, pp. 61 ff.

resentative institutions, institutionalized rights and judicial safeguards of such rights.[40]

Especially since the mid-1990 s the attitude of a critical mass of elite segments towards modern constitutionalism which was formerly considered as an alien and unsuitable plant to the Thai soil changed. Among the manifold reasons were complicating balances of power, uncertainties about the future of the Throne after the natural end of the reign of the present king, and finally accelerating social dynamics in the wake of the Asian economic crisis catalyzing the making of the 1997 constitution, which was perceived in an unprecedented manner as a supreme law of the land to be applied on a daily basis. Its most appealing quality was its impact on rationalization and stabilization of governance in legal terms. Many of the accompanying substantial features – a growing role of electoral democracy and rights – were considered with more skepticism and countered by arranging a differentiated and rigid system of checks and balances. Especially mechanisms of representative democracy were embedded in a legally shaped system of scrutiny and disciplining to prevent any challenge to the established constitutional core.[41] The abstract fear became reality with an unprecedented electoral success of one single party and the populist politics of its leader who claimed to possess the democratic mandate of the people as the decisive basis of his

---

40 See for instance Thak Chaloemtiarana, *Thailand*, 2007, p. XIII: "The idea of access and accountability is modified to mean that the leader/father visits his children to listen and observe their needs directly." See also Baker and Pasuk Phongpaichit, *A History of Thailand*, 2009, p. 235. Exemplary are the words of Seni Pramoj, former Prime Minister and leader of the Democrat Party, warning that a new constitution envisioned for the 1990 s would not change anything. He counters the observation that "today, people are loud in their demands for [Western-style] democracy" with lessons drawn from a century old stone inscription of the ancient kingdom of Sukhothai which is still considered as the first Thai constitution of the first Thai democracy: As long as the direct bond between the people and their fatherly ruler was intact, it was supposed to be a perfect become demanding and misusing their rights and forgetting their duties: "the free democratic people of Sukhothai were abusing their rights and liberties" and "the greater rights and liberties, the greater the degree of corruption" as: "[...] freedom corrupts: absolute freedom corrupts absolutely". Contrary, the non-legal constitution of Sukhothai is not only considered as an older democracy than the Western ones but also the better, superior to the Magna Charta or the documents of the American and French revolution, all evolving from misuse, rebellion and revolution, granting rights as a mirror of the general moral decline of their societies. See Seni Pramoj, "Stone Inscriptions of Father King Ram Khamhaeng," 1990, pp. 18, 26, 31 f., 39 f., 43 f., 46 f.

41 See Tamada, *Myth and Realities*, 2009, p. 166.

legitimacy. When he continuously increased his influence, partly by circumventing some of the tight mechanisms of scrutiny and constitutional safeguards which had been established against the unleashed powers of electoral democracy, a constitutional crisis was triggered which finally resulted in his ouster by the coup of 2006 and the present constitution of 2007. This constitution even increased and tightened the mechanisms of legal control and containment of electoral democracy particularly by a more active role of the judiciary as the most important guardian of the basic structure beside the military.[42] A far-reaching expression of this shift are the decisions of various Thai courts which are disciplining major politics (see *Hassavut* and *Dressel*). Furthermore, civil rights and elements of direct democracy are now used to be mounted against the government and its parliamentary majority causing the formation of a mass movement which is effectively challenging key elements of the old system. This movement and the re- emerged political forces of the Thaksin camp are now at odds with the legalistic notion of the present constitution and the influences of its watchdog bodies on politics leading to the next issue, namely the reemergence of the idea of the political constitution.

3. Political Constitutionalism in Favor of a Better Democracy?

While not only Thailand but Southeast Asia in general is currently marked by an ongoing trend of juridification and Western-style constitutionalism at least in form, there are counter-movements not only in Thailand but also in the Western world orienting their focus away from a predominantly legal and even formal understanding of the constitution claiming for a 'political constitutionalism'.[43] It has to be remembered so far, that the extent to which the constitution was supposed to operate as a legal more than a political instrument has been disputed since the beginnings of modern constitutionalism in the West.[44]

---

42 Similar to the German Weimar Republic for instance, judges are considered to represent one of the most system-loyal elite segments of the society.

43 See Alexander, "Constitutionalism and Democracy," 2011; Bellamy, "Political Constitutionalism," 2007.

44 Typical positions have been the opposing understanding of rights as merely legal rule or merely political aspiration in the French declaration and the US constitution

An instructive articulation of such a 'political constitutionalism' as a counter-tendency to juridification came up in France during the 1990 s. The criticism was fundamental, targeting the concept of the constitution as a legal document as endangering the constitution's substantial core as well as the 'real' constitution. The latter was supposed to be represented by the effective political order and to be reflected by the written constitution as predominantly enshrining a political promise.[45] This view, above all, expresses a specific reaction against the growing influence of constitutional law and constitutional interpretation in the wake of an emancipating constitutional council since 1971.[46] The accompanying renaissance of a merely legal understanding of the constitution and its entrenchment by means of legal interpretation prompted heavy criticism against a supposed precarious domi-

---

respectively, or, even more general, the liberal and conservative preference of judicial safeguards against the 'dictatorship of the majority' vis-à-vis the claim of progressive democrats and socialists to respect the people's will in 19th-century constitutionalism in Europe and the Americas.

45 See, also for the following, Guenaire, "La Constitution ou la fin du politique," 1991. For a critical overview see D. Rousseau, *Questions de Constitution*, 2000; D. Rousseau, "Constitution ou la politique autrement," 1991.

46 The *Conseil Constitutionel* started its emancipation from its nearly complete domination by the authority of the president *De Gaulle*, who died in 1971, only with a famous decision about the law on associations in the same year and received a major push with a constitutional reform in 1974 (see Shapiro and Stone Sweet, *On law, Politics and Judicialization*, 2002, pp. 184 ff). Culturally this view reflects the classical French role-conflict between judges and political representatives and the traditional fear of a government of judges, while it follows methodologically *Michel Foucault*, regarding law as just one disciplining discourse of the society among others – a result which would also be supported by an adoption of *Niklas Luhmann's* 'system theory'. The layers of conflict are furthermore comprising a certain distrust towards a claimed rigidity of the legal methodology which is considered by critics as unable to adjudicate the political will appropriately on the ongoing stream of societal and political life and strong professional rivalries between political scientists and lawyers in France (see for the strategic influence of certain professional communities on discourses about a predominately legal or political mode of the constitution also Sadurski, "Constitutional Justice, East and West," 2002 and for the historical role of the French lawyers in the formation of the French constitution C. Schmitt, "Die Formung des französischen Geistes durch den Legisten," 1942). Finally, the dispute is also related to two versions of the *Rousseauan* concept of legitimacy which are – while normally competing with each other – united in their aversion of too much judicial influence on politics. This is firstly the Gaullist one, focused on *national sovereignty* which is represented by strong political leadership of the president, and secondly the *parliamentary one* which is focused on parliamentary supremacy.

nance of constitutional law. The latter, according to *Michel Guenaire* for example, establishes a stifling control regime on the realm of politics, paralyzing the legislator, destroying political debate as the most significant and substantial expression of the general will and undermines a constructive confrontation of opinions. The vivid representation of society by parliament is thus replaced in this view by abstract juridical principles, establishing a government of dead letters over the living presence. Consequently, the "anti-juridical philosophy" of these critics, called the 'politicals', demands a return to the dominance of politics which is subordinating constitutional law and the activity of judges under a political regime of legitimate democratic representation.[47] In another, more fundamental attempt to subordinate the legal mode of the constitution under politics, *Pierre Avril* argues that even the constitution itself is not able to represent the political will and has therefore nothing to say in the realm of politics.[48] – Even if the battle seems to be lost in favor of a *predominantly* legal understanding of the constitution in the wake of the progressed emancipation of the constitutional council and the increasing influence of the European Court on Human Rights,[49] the critical discourse favoring a political understanding of the constitution is still a considerable counter-force.[50]

A similar line of debate favoring a more political understanding of the constitution is influential in actual Anglo-Saxon constitutional theory. *Mark Tushnet* for example suggests that a weaker form of judicial review would serve as a sound foundation for a stronger advocacy of social welfare rights,

---

47 D. Rousseau, "Questions de Constitution," 2000, p. 19 (*la philosophie antijuridique des partisans du tout politique*).

48 See Avril, "Le juge et le représentant," 1993; Avril, *Les Conventions de la Constitution,* 1997. According to him, it is the performance of political key actors and their practical definitions of what the constitutional regime is, what is for the government. This is the real source of governance as being manifested in speeches, public announcements and decisions altogether forming the unwritten conventions, the real constitution which is just using the constitutional text to establish its respective regime. – In the moment this regime is giving constitutional law a more dominating place it is supposed to decline.

49 See Wachsmann, "Die Europäische Menschenrechtskonvention und innerstaatliches Recht," 2008.

50 The project to limit the influence of constitutional law on the domestic political power even leads to the suspicion that individual rights could be could be pitted against the political rights of the representatives of the sovereign power. In consequence, some 'politicals' are even skeptical about a constitutional jurisprudence which is realizing an active human rights enforcement.

namely if the politically accountable legislative and executive power would be able to reject contrasting constitutional rulings by the judiciary.[51] This view is complemented by the interesting claim of *Richard Bellamy* that "courts have proved unreliable protectors of individual rights" in the context of the growing security paradigm post 9/11.[52] A more fundamental account is taken by *Joel Colón-Ríos* referring to the constituent power which, according to him, demands a more profound participation of ordinary citizens at least when it comes to constitutional change.[53] This is directly leading to the currently widely discussed concepts of *monitory-* or *counter-democracy.*[54] Influential with his concept of counter- or negative democracy is here a French author again, *Pierre Rosanvallon.* He attempts to restore the dignity and functionality of the democratic project by describing the extra-formal counter-part to representative democracy as its necessary antagonism. This counterforce to the expressions of the represented people's power means in particular the rise of *informal, direct democracy.*[55] This "negative democ-

---

51 See Tushnet, *Weak Courts, Strong Rights*, 2008. Striking is the similarity to the New Deal constellation in the relations between judiciary and the governing political majority concerning the question of social rights.

52 See Bellamy, *Political Constitutionalism*, 2007, p. 250.

53 See Colón-Ríos, *Weak Constitutionalism*, 2012.

54 See Keane, "Monitory democracy?," 2011.

55 The most visible symbol of critical tensions between the concepts of representative and negative democracy respectively, are occupations of parliaments as it happened 1990 in Romania, 2000 in Serbia, 2003 in Georgia, 2008 in Thailand and 2011 in Chile and Kuwait. More moderate was the occupation of the green facing the British House of Commons since 2001 for 10 years, with the demonstrators' tents becoming a permanent presence of protest at the heart of Westminster. However, in the same time this very allusive and powerful sign of negative democracy may in the course of events easily emerge into a more radical situation in which the borderline between a mere antagonism (still based on an integrative basic consent and the constitutional core reflecting it) on the one hand and a friend–foe split of society (like in Thailand or Georgia) on the other starts to blur. Another symbolically charged expression of negative democracy which is prone to emerge into a serious division is the boycott of elections as in Thailand 2011, when the People's Alliance for Democracy (PAD), a street- based protest movement, boycotted the national elections with effect to their political party arm, the New Politics Party. The demarcation between negative–democracy of informal citizen groups and formally organized structures which emerged in the very context of representative democracy coalesces at this point where political parties themselves are resorting to such means normally attributed to

racy" is conceptualized as the expression of a "dual sovereignty" and the antagonist to the exclusive exercise of sovereignty by the legally constituted representatives of the people.[56] As the genuine exercise of social power against the misuse of delegated political power it serves the aims of preventing and vetoing any kind of misuse of formal power. The means to realize this end is a *culture of insurrection* as the most radical form of negative politics.[57] Thus, negative democracy is not at all passive but active in a direct, unrepresented form of civil commitment to rejection up to an essentially hostile form of this kind of public participation.[58] For *Rosanvallon* this is basically, even if not always good: a necessary resource of a good democracy in principle. Passive consent of the populace on the opposite is supposed to make any democracy weak.[59]

While some of the more cautious voices against predominantly legal constitutionalism echo notions of parliamentary supremacy, the more recent and radical versions exemplified by *Rosanvallon* define an additional and *permanent constitutive function* of the sovereign besides its function to create the representative organs or to participate in the channeled forms of plebiscite. Are the latter understood here as merely controlled, limited and singular acts of public participation, does *Rosanvallon* describe an alternative, complementary governance concept to formal constitutionalism,

---

negative democracy of the unrepresented. Parliament occupations and election boycotts by political parties are thus indicating a deep crisis within the constitutional system. See for instance the boycott of national elections in Thailand 2006 by the opposition (the Democrat Party) followed by a coup d'état in the same year and the occupation of the parliament in South Korea in 2006 by the oppositional Democratic Party (DP).

56 See Rosanvallon, *Counter-Democracy*, 2008, p. 107.

57 See Rosanvallon, *Counter-Democracy*, 2008, pp. 179 ff., 182, 185. Forms of negative democracy or negative people´s participation have become somewhat institutionalized in countries like France or Thailand, while they served as a more sporadic phenomenon of protest movements culminating in system change in many European countries like Poland, Hungary, East Germany or Romania burying the Cold War. These movements stand in a line with previous mobilizations of this kind in Asia and Africa in form of the various civil resistance movements leading to major constitutional change from *Gandhi* in India to the Thai protest movement of 1973 to the anti-Marcos demonstrations in Manila. Contemporary, protest movements in the wake of the sub-prime crisis and European fiscal crisis as 'Occupy Wallstreet' or the various Arab spring movements in North Africa and the Middle East are expressions of counter-democracy in favor of a wide range of very different governance ideas.

58 See Rosanvallon, *Counter-Democracy*, 2008, pp. 186 f.

59 See Rosanvallon, *Counter-Democracy*, 2008, p. 186.

which, however, is in the last instance yet linked to the underlying core ideas of the constitution and attempting to enabling them in dialectical moves. At this point the alternative form and the established substance are linked: the non-formal form of participation corresponds directly with the supreme ideal democratic sovereignty. However, counter-democracy can be claimed from quite different constitutional vantage points: as the *expression of (real) majority* rule but also as an *instrument against* it, to be exercised in both cases against the electively constituted representative bodies and existing legal restraints. This critical endeavor may favor either a vision of real democracy but might also be dedicated by a minority to "higher" constitutional values or a claimed better understanding of them. Especially in this latter sense, techniques of counter-democracy are forming the opposite side of the topic addressed by *Ebsen* here, the majority principle in its formal, legal understanding.

4. Universalistic Constitutionalism vs. Reason of State-Based Governance

If it is true that "the strength of the constitutional fabric consists in the interweaving of different threads [...]"[60], it is also true that some of these threads may represent competing normative concepts, more or less co-existing or conflicting in the framework of the same constitution. The most significant expression of this phenomenon is the tension between universalistic and reason of state-centered elements of the constitution.[61] In the Western tradition constitutionalism is a product of a distinct historical experience which is bound to a set of normative and institutional structures – in particular a certain understanding of human rights and democracy – expressing an *inherently universalistic stance* in perceiving governance.[62] Is this specific universalistic notion of governance historically charged and rooted in Western trajectories, is the reason-of-state approach of governance the universal one. While it is the universalistic impact of this constitution-

60 Tully, *Strange Multiplicity*, 1995, p. 197.

61 Similar is the above mentioned observation that the development of rights might be seen in the context of the emergence of the state's monopoly of power.

62 Differently accentuated *universalistic norms* and concepts of governance can derive from a wider range of cultural settings like the Islamic ones for instance, while the emergence of the *constitution* as *universalistic*, *secular*, *legal* norm as supreme (if not exclusive) order of the political is historically product and expression of Western constitutionalism.

alism which gave the constitutional endeavor of the modernity its particular vigor leading to a constantly expanding constitutional rule, it is encountering inevitably the conflicting claims of the reason of state, which are thus forming its natural counter-discourse and -practice which is always inclining to limit, suspend or overrule the universalistic substance of constitutionalism. Doctrinally especially elaborated in ancient China, India or Rome as well as during the period from the European renaissance to the early modernity, reason of state might be understood as a ubiquitous notion of governance aiming at the state's active and ever aware self-preservation, the acquisition and conservation of its power as supreme purpose and end.[63] Committed to this substantially empty supreme norm, reason-of-state governance perceives all other kinds of laws, rules and values including the constitution as merely instrumental and always being subordinated to the possibility of suspension if it deems it necessary for the sake of the state. This latent possibility defines the reach of any constitutional claim to command the realm of political power *in principle*. It is generally subordinating the constitutional norm under the sufficient interest of the state. Paradigmatic for Western reason-of-state reasoning are certain Roman thoughts, rules and practices embodied for example in principles and key words as *salus populi suprema lex, securitas* and *necessitas*.[64] Significant is also the governance principle enshrined in the formal phrase which has been used to enact the *senatus consultum ultimum*, the state of emergency: *videant consules, ne quid res publica detrimenti capiat*, loosely translated as: "may the government protect the country from damage." The *senatus consultum ultimum* is particularly interesting for our purpose because, different to other emergency powers in the Roman Republic (as the *dictatorship*), it created an extra-constitutional, extra-legal emergency power of the government for the time it had been empowered, constituting a kind of prototype in Western political think-

---

63 See Frankenberg, *Staatstechnik*, 2010, p. 21; Isensee, "Gemeinwohl im Verfassungsstaat," 2006, margin no. 83.

64 It is interesting to note that Roman political thought influences the contemporary American discourses on governance much more than it does in Europe. Insofar, one could say slightly simplified, that Europe has been shaped during the Middle Ages merely in terms of *legal* consideration by the Roman heritage, contributing to the evolving concept of the rule of law, while the US, after gaining independence, due to the widespread interest in Roman political thought at that time and the appealing example of a powerful republic also have been strongly and continuously interested in that heritage of the Antiquity, but much more in *political* terms being reflected by key institutions and symbols of the founding period as the senate, capitol or pentagon.

ing.[65] This example exemplifies most importantly the fact that the demands and policies of internal and external security are immediate expressions of a reason-of-state order.[66] The effect of this kind of security regime towards the constitution has been described by a German constitutional scholar as exerting their effect as nothing less than a "demolition block" within the regime of constitutional law.[67] Thus, the more a constitution is dedicated to the described universalistic stance the more it has to contain the inevitable notions of reason of state.[68] However, both concepts derive their normative appeal from the fact that they are claiming validity beyond the written constitution. Thus, reason-of-state order is influencing the constitution (like universalistic norms) from inside and outside, as an integral part and an external order, the latter mostly as an extra-legal order.

---

65 See Lazar, *States of Emergencies in Liberal Democracies*, 2009, pp. 147 ff. The *senatus consultum ultimum* devolved the complete state power to the consules allowing even the violation of fundamental constitutional principles.

66 Actually it is especially the post-9/11security paradigm which represents the strongest reason-of-state based counter movement against the spirit of Western constitutionalism. However, reason-of-state approaches manifests themselves not only in matters of national security but are also often populist and performance-orientated when the preservation of the state is supposed to demand that the government provides the 'masses' with a certain level of social security or subsistence to prevent a critical level of dissatisfaction (see Bloch, *Vorlesungen zur Philosophie der Renaissance*, 1972, p. 133).

67 See Isensee, "Verfassungsrecht als 'politisches Recht'," 1992, margin no. 94; the opposition between the claim of a reason of state-prone governance approach and the universalistic substance core of the present German constitution has been exemplified by a critic of this constitution by *Ernst Forsthoff*, one of the leading conservative constitutional scholars in the early years of this constitution who drew a gloomy scenario of the obliviousness of the constitutional state abandoning its supreme duty of self-preservation by its "fixation" on basic rights and parliamentarian procedures. See Forsthoff, "Zur heutigen Situation der Verfassungslehre," 1968, p. 208.

68 The former is strongly exemplified for the example in the German constitution which adheres to the *absolute* integrity of human dignity vis-à-vis the state as its first and foremost rule, binding all state powers and, different from all other basic rights, is ruling non-restrictable (see art 1 Basic Law). Consequently, *any* violation of the human dignity of an individual makes the respective exercise of state power – be it a law, administrative act or court decision – inevitably invalid, *at all costs* (see the *Aviation Security Act* Case of the Federal Constitutional Court of Germany with explicit reference to the 9/11 incident, file no. 1BvR 357/05; online on http://www.bverfg.de/entscheidungen/rs20060215_1bvr035705en.html).

As an example for the impact of a reason-of-state approach as an inherent limitation limit of the constitution as supreme law located not in any written rule but the attitude of constitutional actors, it is intriguing to realize how consequent the veritable father of the constitution of one of the most inspiring nations for the development of Western constitutionalism confessed to adhere to a sheer reason-of-state approach:

> Three things count in constitutional matters. First, the higher interest of the country [...] and of that I alone am judge. Second, far behind, are the political circumstances, arrangements, tactics. [...]. Third, much further behind, there is legalism. [...] I have accomplished nothing in my life except by putting the welfare of the country first and by refusing to be entrapped by legalisms. Questioned by his biographer he responded: Do you really believe I am bound by the constitution?[69]

These words of *Charles de Gaulle* reflect a typical combination of charismatic leadership and populism based on a dominant reason-of-state orientation towards political ordering and a corresponding rejection of constitutionalism.

After decades of constitutionalization continuously entrenching the reach of (universalistic) constitutional law to contain and fill the spaces of power previously open to reason-of-state decision making and forming the attitudes of constitutional actors in Western democracies, it is the global security regime post 9/11 which creates a new major thrust towards a dynamic structure of anti-constitutionalization.

C. Constitutional Rule – Structures, Features & Actors

Most of the articles presented here highlight a particular constitutional feature or actor. However, if they are read together an outline of a common structure emerges which itself may serve as a heuristic tool for comparison. In this sense some of them might be reflected on.

What most modern constitutions share first of all is that they presume a certain *substance core*, an "unquestionable" or "basic structure" of the con-

69 Charles de Gaulle quoted by Stone Sweet, *The Birth of Judicial Review in France,* 1992, p. 64.

stitution[70], expressing in the words of *Carl Schmitt* the "fundamental political decision" of the political community.[71] It can be understood as the *neutral point* in the center of the constitutional coordinate system with its *x-axis* constituted by the *power allocation between state and citizens* (the question of rights) and its *y-axis* constituted by the *power allocation within the state structure itself* (among the representations of state power).

I. The Basic Structure and the Organization of State Power

The basic structure of the constitution is the starting point and fundament of the constitution, expressing a particular vision of good governance as final goal and directing the paths of constitutionalization towards this normative horizon. Challenges of the basic structure can express critical deviations from the basic consent underlying the political system as such, possibly resulting in constitutional crisis.[72] This seems to be the case in varying grades in Malaysia (*Derichs*), Nepal (*Føllesdal*) and Thailand (*Boonsri*, *Hassavut*, *Dressel*). In Malaysia, an increasing shift along ever latent frictions of the basic consent since independence created an unprecedented challenge for the existing system in the wake of the Asian financial crisis of late 1990 s which has lingered on since then. Division in Thailand has emerged as a phenomenon of critical size since the 2006 coup and has been constantly deepening since then. There are a number of reasons mentioned with respect to the crisis for both countries. For Thailand a conflict between elites and "masses" or different regions has been identified while the division in the cases of Malaysia and Nepal is explained partly, though not exclusively as ethnically and culturally-driven.[73] However, in all three countries the con-

70 See also Albert, "The Cult of Constitutionalism," 2012, p. 390; v. Simson, "Zur Theorie der Legitimität," 1971; the term "basic structure" became especially popular in Indian constitutional law.

71 See Schmitt, *Constitutional Theory*, p. 77 ff.

72 See Isensee, "Verfassungsrecht als 'politisches Recht'," 1992, margin no. 104; Frankenberg, *Die Verfassung der Republik*, 1997, p. 193.

73 A classical distinction between culturally homogenous and culturally divided (not only diverse) societies has been made by *Arend Lijphart* (see Lijphart, *Democracy in Plural Societies,* 1977, pp. 71 ff.). It should be complemented by the often overlapping distinction between politically rested and politically divided societies (see

flict is more complex but lastly always about the societal consent on the constitutional basic structure with respect to competing concepts of the same.

Whether constitutional law, single constitutional actors or the society – or another actor, for instance a foreign power as exemplified by *Son Soubert's* account on the Cambodian tragedy – has to be blamed for the failure of creating a legitimate order is often impossible to answer and never by an either-or. Yet, it is one purpose of the constitution "to take certain questions 'off the table' and thereby limit normal [...] politics to questions that do not challenge that fundamental consensus."[74] Necessary consent, however, is not a comprehensive state of consensual harmony but a practicable construct for which the sufficient conditions are difficult to define. Latent discord between major societal forces and institutionalized conflict is therefore no problem in principle. For ancient Roman constitutionalism permanent conflict has even been identified as its very matrix of success by *Machiavelli* who perceived constitutionalism in general as a kind of "continuation of civil war by other means."[75]

Beyond the question how the constitutional basic structure is finally fabricated and preserved, the issue may serve as an often overlooked, yet crucial aspect for the comparative analyses. Taking one of the classical elements of any constitutional substance core, the sovereign power, it is striking how different the ways are to represent and exercise it. The sovereign power according to the German constitution for example is exercised by the people, mainly in elections which are therefore the "foundation of the democratic state" because they mean nothing less than the "transfer of sovereign power" (see *Mellinghoff*). It is evident from this point of view that citizens' rights and people´s sovereignty are mutually linked (see below and *Grimm* and *Pieroth*). The Thai constitution, similar to most other Southeast Asian constitutions, is based on a different concept of sovereignty and thus provides for a different understanding of elections, political parties and parliament. In art 3 it is stating that it is the King who *exercises* the sovereign power of the people through the three state powers. Consequently, they are differently

Choudry, "Bridging comparative politics," 2008, p. 4 f.). In fact, most but not all culturally divided societies will be politically divided, while many politically divided societies are not culturally divided on a fundamental level in terms of religious or ethnical division.

74 See Choudry, "Bridging comparative politics," 2008, p. 4 f. See also the contributions of *Follesdal* and *Menzel* here.

75 Tarcov, "Ideas of Constitutionalism," 2011, p. 20.

perceived, constructed and balanced than by the German constitution. In particular the elements of representative democracy are not perceived as being the dignified centre of the Thai constitution but rather the contrary. Based on the mentioned concept of constitutionalism placing the "democratic regime with the King as the head of state" in the very centre, elements of representative democracy have been viewed as merely instrumental and even inclined to be dangerous for the constitutional integrity if they are not sufficiently disciplined reflecting a perceived dichotomy of moral statesmanship on the one side and corrupted party politics on the other. This is shown by *Boonsri's* thorough analysis of the Thai constitution of 1997 and reflected in the present constitution of 2007 distributing significant powers to institutions which are not or partly not legitimated by an uninterrupted chain of democratic legitimacy based on elections. The 2007 constitution is therefore marked by a shift of responsibilities for preserving constitutional integrity towards the judiciary, an impressive ensemble of so called 'watchdog bodies'[76], the change from a fully elected to a half appointed Senate and a very tight control regime concerning political parties and politicians with draconian consequences for misbehaviour. Accordingly different is *Ebsen's* topic, the majority principle, perceived: What is the indispensable basis of a moral and reasonable rule for him, looms as an unapt or dangerous principle from the perspective of the Thai (or Malaysian) constitution where it is not controlled sufficiently. Noteworthy is the fact, that this deeply critical notion of electoral democracy runs throughout the whole constitutional discourse of the 19th and early 20th century in the West, starting with *Washington's* fear of mass democracy (and contemplation to introduce a monarchy) and being reflected by the constitutional ideas of leaders and scholars like *Simon Bolivar*, *Benjamin Constant*, *John Stuart Mill*, *Walter Bagehot*, *Woodrow Wilson*, *Gustave Le Bon*, *Carl Schmitt*, *Ludwig v. Mises*, *F. A. Hayek*.

Another central feature of state organization which is evolving from the basic structure in some systems is subject of *Ehlers'* account on federalism and local self-administration in Germany. Both features are part of the German constitutional basic structure and interesting also as typical expressions of the historical roots of German constitutionalism. Since the Middle Ages, elements of federalism and local self-administration have influenced con-

76 See for the watchdog bodies like the Election or the Counter Corruption Commission Leyland, "Thailand's Constitutional Watchdogs," 2007.

stitutional thinking with significant impact on the theory and practice of governance in Germany and beyond. *Føllesdal* for instance is highlighting the importance of federal and communal ideas in the work of *Johannes Althusius* as one of the fathers of modern international public law. In the 19th century *Otto von Gierke* drew heavily on the century-old traditions of local self-administration in developing his legal and constitutional theories which influenced not only the constitution of the first German republic of 1919 whose 'father' *Hugo Preuss* was his student but also the constitutional thinking in England and France represented for instance by scholars like *Frederick Maitland* and *Léon Duguit*.

This is leading to the comparative aspect and the question of a migration of these constitutional features raised in *Ehlers'* conclusion and being subject of *Føllesdal's* account on the Nepalese constitution making process (see also *Grimm* and *Menzel*). Even if an answer to this question is not possible here it is interesting to point to *Ehlers'* distinction of *competitive and cooperative federalism*, with the German one as being a comparatively cooperative and successful type.[77] However, constitutional institutions – this is exemplified by *Ehlers'* account – are determined to a high degree not only by legal design, but by a supportive culture, tradition and political/social practice. Many of the problems concerning efforts of decentralization and devolution of state power – be it with respect to provincial, regional or local levels in Southeast Asia – seem to be caused by a lack of such a supportive environment even if major legislative efforts have been made since the 1990 s and in the beginning of the 21st century.[78] Particularly interesting is the Malaysian case, in which federalism, against the odds seems to function as a successful feature in many respects, in particular with positive effects on the balance of powers in terms of ethnical and ideological cleavages, while local self-gov-

---

77 In the German case this reflects a general 'formula' of the German constitution according to which all constitutional actors are similarly empowered in a way which supports their cooperation rather than it facilitates antagonistic politics.

78 See the Local Government Code of the Philippines (1991), the Law No. 22, 1999 Regarding Regional Governance of Indonesia, the Decentralization Act (1999) and the Law on Administration of Communes in Thailand (2001) as well as the Law on Election of the Commune Councils of Cambodia (2001), combining issues of decentralization and democratization. See for Thailand Nelson, "Thailand," 2001; Aspinall and Fealy, *Local Power and Politics in Indonesia*, 2003; Van Klinken and Barker, "Introduction: State in Society," 2009, p. 5; Schmit, "Decentralization and legal reform in Indonesia," 2008; Sedara and Öjendal, "Decentralization as a strategy for State Reconstruction in Cambodia," 2009.

ernment is not effectively organized at all, still suffering the abolition of local elections since the 'emergency' of the 13 May 1969.

II. Rights

A central feature of contemporary constitutionalism are rights, might they be understood as human or civil rights.[79] However, the dominant tendencies in the development of this important field are slightly different in Europe and Southeast Asia. While the most significant dynamics in Europe are coming from the regional level, namely through the growing influence of the ECHR and the ECJ, the issue of rights in Southeast Asia is still predominantly emerging in the national framework, even if the implementation of the ASEAN Intergovernmental Commission on Human Rights in 2009 and the ASEAN Human Right Declaration from 2012 signal a careful beginning also on the regional level. It is true, Asian constitutional systems while mostly guaranteeing similar sets of rights like the European ones – if not even more when it comes to social and cultural rights – seem still to be more reluctant or unable to cope fully with the normatively promised when it comes to constitutional practice, notwithstanding the numerous improvements which have been made. In fact, human rights have become an integral part of Southeast Asian constitutionalism with Indonesia, the Philippines and Thailand paving the way. A crucial difference to Europe, however, is that the link between rights and the constitution's substance core is practically weaker than it is in the West – this is the case for Indonesia and the Philippines – or conceptually hardly existing. The latter is the case in Thailand where rights are forming an increasingly important and integral part of the constitution, yet not an inevitable and robust element of its substance core.

To further explore the difference[80] – given the fact that rights are an integral and dynamic part of constitutionalism in East and West – it is useful to ask about origin, context and deep structure of the respective concept of rights, especially as the differences often do not become visible in positive law. Rights, similar to constitutionalism, can be understood in both ways, as

79 See in this volume the contributions of *Boonsri*, *Derichs*, *Esser*, *Grote*, *Warawit* and *Weng*.

80 See also *Warawit's* statement on rights in this volume that "it is the attitude towards the law that distinguishes the Westerners from the Easterners".

an expression of a particular historical experience which is rooted in the West and having evolved into a globalized normative concept and regime claiming universal appreciation and effect on the one hand and as a product of this process which has grown in non-Western environments and undergone substantial modifications emerging as an autochthon type in form and substance.

The 'original' Western concept in this ideal-typical distinction has developed in three different historical thrusts which interweave and shape both, its form and substance. These are: the *Christian formulation* of universalistic, individual and legally defined rights with the inherent potential to transcend the sphere of worldly power, their *secularization* during the Enlightenment and their connection to *democracy* and people's sovereignty by the great revolutions of the Western modernity.[81] Even if not all Western con-

81 The Christian formulation of universalistic and thus state-transcending, individually centered and legally defined rights is theologically based on the assumption of the human creation as an *imago dei*, the incarnation of God as human being and the redemption through *Jesus Christ*. It was elaborated and differentiated since the late antiquity in essentially legal terms and emerged into a kind of international law supervised by a burcaucratized central authority with the Papal Church in Rome and its jurisdiction during the High Middles Ages (see Tierney, *Religion, law, and the growth of constitutional thought,* 1982). With the secularization of this rights concept, which, despite some rationalist precursors, was starting with the Enlightenment, it was disconnected from religion, a process drawing on other European legal traditions and concepts like "possessive individualism" rooted in feudal law or in the ancient philosophy (see Blumenberg, *Die Legitimität der Neuzeit*, 1966; Macpherson, *The Political Theory of Possessive Individualism*, 1962). This secular rights concept is also an expression of an antagonistic development to the emergence of the modern state with its unprecedented monopoly of power serving as the latter's downside and complement (see Tetzlaff, "Das Demokratieverständnis in Afrika und Asien," 1997, p. 349). Remarkable for the resistance against the secularization of rights is the fact, that it took until the Second Vatican Council (1962-65) to reconcile officially with the modern concept of secular human rights for the Catholic Church (see Philpott, "The Catholic Wave," 2005, p. 105). Comparably long time was needed for the finalization of the last stage, the inevitable connection of rights and democracy. See for the latter *Grote* in this volume pointing out the vital role of the 'political' rights for the stabilization of representative democracy and especially Starck, "Grundrechtliche und demokratische Freiheitsidee," 2005, margin no. 4. Interesting is an early commitment to this idea from the founding period of modern constitutionalism by a critic of the majority opinion during the drafting of the US constitution which was initially noticeably reluctant in the rights issue: "There are certain unalienable and fundamental rights which, in forming the social compact, ought to be explicitly

stitutions adopted this concept of rights immediately and explicitly with the same ease and effect, it is forming an essential element of Western constitutionalism, placing rights at the top of the normative hierarchy. As such it has been spreading over the world. However, this happened not always on the basis of its inherent appeal but also as a result of power-related discourses dominated by the West and reflecting the Western aspiration to universalize its own understanding of good governance. Consequently, there is an international rights discourse and there are interrelated international rights regimes which are inherently linked to the Western concept, notwithstanding the fact that its global diffusion meets alternative views as well as resistance. The latter is often raised particularly against the claimed discursive hegemony of the West as such, may the claim be accompanied by idealistic conviction or self-interest. In fact, rights discourses are – wherever they are touching political realities – *inevitably* linked to policies or as *Shapiro* puts it: "[…], rights, no matter how defined or sourced, are favored interest".[82] Leaving this problem aside – the double nature of rights as highly idealistic aspirations sometimes leading to disappointment and as particularly powerful type of norms sometimes seducing to misuse – we may ask for the non-Western version of rights. Suggested as a common denominator beyond the Western origins of the concept is a type of universalistic rights of the individual, which are enforceable against the state and enjoying superiority in relation to normal laws. Given furthermore the assumption that there is no irreducible ethical knowledge[83], it is only plausible to expect indeed more in the normative world of today than the Western pure type, its globalized appearance including and domestic reproduction 'abroad' which often in-

---

ascertained and fixed. A free and enlightened people, in forming this compact, will fix limits to their legislators and rulers […]." See *Federal Farmer Letters II, III, IV and XII, 9., 10., and 12. October 1787, 12. January 1788*, in: Allen and Lloyd, *The Essential Antifederalist*, 2002, pp. 149, 151. Noteworthy again is to see how careful the founding fathers treated the issue even where they supported the cause: "I do not think it is impossible, that we may yet form a federal constitution, much superior to any form of government, which has ever existed in the world: but, whenever this important work shall be accomplished, I venture to pronounce, that it will not be done without a careful attention to the framing of a bill of rights." *Old Whig Essay, IV October 1787*, in: Allen and Lloyd, *The Essential Antifederalist*, pp. 171, 172; for the long time from recognition to enforcement in US constitutionalism see Shapiro, "Some Conditions for the Success of Constitutional Courts," 2002, pp. 52 f.

82 Shapiro, "Judicial Review in Developed Democracies," 2004, p. 18.

83 See Putnam, "Werte und Normen," 2001, p. 308.

clines to be conceptually looser, less stable and institutionally less supported than the 'original'[84] and outright counter-concepts like state-centered norms (reason of state) or traditional, equally non-universalistic norms and values like those claimed with the so called "Asian values debate".

Most important among autochthon rights conceptions is the Islamic one. It shares with the Western type the guarantee of universalistic, subjective rights which shall be legally enforceable according to a transcendent principle of justice, even against the interests of the state. However, while the Western rights concept claims normative superiority not only in its older version presupposing a divine source of rights but also in its contemporary secular one, the Islamic rights concept is doing so *exactly because it is not secular*.[85] This sacral derivation and its implications form the most important criterion for demarcation in the Islamic understanding of rights barring for example *certain* notions of personal autonomy[86] or a strong link between rights and people´s sovereignty (of the Western type). The Islamic concept is also more rigid concerning substantial change through interpretation, shielding some traditional values from those contents which would mirror a Western way of life and claim undisputable recognition according to the dominating Western understanding. On the other hand the Islamic rights concept can often claim a more dedicated support of the people adhering to it and will at least claim to be less hypocritical in practice than Western rights

84 If "history is the science of things which are never repeated" (see Paul Valery, *Varieté IV*, quoted in Dunleavy, "New Worlds in Political Science," 2010, p. 251), and if the 'thick' version of rights is evolving from an European historical experience of a *longue durée*, it is indeed quite natural that the globalization of culturally deeply sated concepts like human rights can hardly mean their unmodified diffusion in a comparatively short time, especially where it lacks the supportive historical experiences including the normative, institutional and social settings of its origin.

85 See for the religious character of Islamic rights Sadeghi, "The Position and Function of Judges in Islamic Law," 2007; Abou El Fadl, "The Centrality of Shari'ah," 2012.

86 The specific Western notion of personal autonomy is one of the most important differences not only in relation to the Islamic right concept but also to the so called African- or Asian values, while not for all Southeast Asian countries to the same extent (less problematic for Thailand for instance). However, individualism in the context of rights marks an element of the Western concept´s deep structure whose evidence is often taken too much for granted: "The West is not sufficiently aware of its cultural presuppositions to explain itself clearly. The Western discourse on rights often detours serious discussions on human rights. It is full of arrogant and ignorant claims about the individual. Historically, after all, it is *groups* that have been excluded." See Friedman, "Since There Is No East and There Is No West," 2001, pp. 21, 27.

discourses. In sum, it is a hybrid on its own terms and as such typologically different from mere reproductions of the Western original in the sense that it can claim authenticity while comprising autochthon Islamic elements and those emerging from the globalized Western type.

Shifting the focus on Southeast Asia, some of the typical simplifications – the reduction of rights regimes to deviant reproductions of the Western type or the accordingly undifferentiated counter-claim of dominating Asian values – prove to fall equally short when it comes to contemporary realities. In other words: Southeast Asian rights discourses serve a bigger cause than the interest to find vague excuses for people in power to avoid being scrutinized and they represent also more than the gradual failure to comprehend Western rights standards. How differentiated and heterogeneous rights discourses on the national level are and how dynamic the competing rights conceptions interact cannot be sufficiently explained here. However, some glimpses using the examples of Thailand and Malaysia might give an impression.

For Malaysia, two aspects shall be pointed out here. First, the basic structure of the Malaysian constitution contains a normatively paramount guarantee of the Malay supremacy among the Malaysians expressed by the huge, decade-lasting national project to enable, entrench and protect this ethnical predominance described by *Derichs'* here. This, according to the dominant understanding, *requires* a kind and degree of limitations of rights that results in a significant deviation from any thick notion of rights. This includes a massively *unequal treatment* of non-Malay citizens solely based on ethnical belonging and harsh reactions against any opposition against it based on a collection of tight security measures restricting the freedom of expression and assembly "to protect the social fabric from being rent by racially or religiously divisive pronouncements" (*Harding*). This domestic notion of rights establishes rights distant from and even weakened by the substantial core of the constitution. This is leading to the second aspect, the rights discourses which are challenging the official view. In fact, not even all Malays are satisfied with the described social contract. The overarching project to preserve the Malay supremacy and appease the other ethnical groups in particular by co-opting enough minority elite support in the framework of the traditional coalition arrangement of UMNO, Malaysia' s leading governing party since independence 1957, with its Chinese and Indian junior partners, alienated not only non-Malay Malaysians but also Malay.

During the founding years of post-colonial Malaysia this was leading to "the insurgency" with a great number of Chinese supporting the communists cause as offering a universalistic and anti-colonial rights concept.[87] Today many Chinese and Indian, but also Malay Malaysians are supporting Western-style constitutionalism and rights even if often "on their own terms" whose precise contours remain yet to be outlined. Another challenge is emerging with another universalistic rights claim which grew among those Malay who adhered to Islamic constitutionalism and rights.[88] Thus, the particularistic (ethnically differentiated) rights concept of the Malaysian constitution as a major subject of national security is facing a double challenge by two competing universalistic rights conceptions, one Islamic and one secular, all three presently locked in a stand-off. Paradox is that both, the universalistic Islamic as well as the parochial pro-Malay concept of governance are drawing on Islam, expressing a serious rivalry of two major interpretations of political Islam, one state-sponsored and -controlled and one independent and universalistic.[89]

Similar to Malaysia, the protection of human rights is no integral part of the *fundamental core* of the present Thai constitution. However, as *Boonsri* and *Warawit* exemplify, civil rights are theoretically extensively protected by the constitution. More importantly, the possibility to limit these rights is itself subject to limitations.[90] Furthermore, the protection of human rights is, compared to Malaysia, less restricted by emergency powers and security laws in theory and practice, while the level of rights protection especially through the Thai administrative courts is exemplary for the region.

---

87 It is noteworthy, that Singapore's legendary founding father *Lee Kuan Yew* also started as a pro-socialist human rights attorney in British Malaya to build his political support base which enabled him to take over power in Singapore and turn to the promulgation of a completely different understanding of rights after achieving its independence from Malaysia in 1965.

88 While challenging the particularistic and parochial interpretation of Islam in the framework of the Malaysian constitution the advocates of the Islamic rights and governance concept are, however, approaching the universalistic application of rights with respect to religious belonging finally limiting the universalistic stance in a similar way like Western constitutions with their model on rights and citizenship.

89 See Ahmad Fauzi Abdul Hamid, *Islam and Violence in Malaysia*, 2007, pp. 7 ff.; Liow, *Piety and Politics*, 2009, pp. 37 ff.; Means, *Political Islam in Southeast Asia*, 2009, p. 129. This dispute about the power of definition on Islamic governance among Malay has been influencing public life heavily since more than three decades and has established a second front line of contested rights standards resulting in a parallel constitutionalization of plain law which is driven not by secular constitutional but by Sharia-law

90 See especially art 29 of the Thai constitution.

This altogether is hinting to the fact, that civil rights play indeed a role for what could be called reminiscent to *Bagehot* the *effective part* of the constitution.[91] Enforceable rights are however granted only to the Thai people, at least according to the dominating and methodologically more convincing scholarly opinion[92], an anti-universalistic notion which reveals some general difficulties to accept the full concept on a broader base. Moreover, rights, despite the tempered appreciation by the constitution and notwithstanding the manifold attention the legal system pays to them, do not constitute the substance core of the constitution. To comprehend this, it is helpful to remember the above mentioned traditional perspective on rights, merely focusing on mutually existing moral obligations in the framework of a hierarchical social fabric (addressing the individual mildly) which is prevailing while it has somehow merged with notions of the modern rights concept as the constitution provides it. While both concepts marked predominantly opposing positions during the making of the 1997 constitution[93], they started to merge with the broad and heterogeneous anti-Thaksin coalition formed in 2005 calling on civil rights to protect the old bond between monarchy and people. It was on this basis that rights were introduced in the post-coup constitution of 2007 even smoother than in the "people's constitution" of 1997. The prominent position of rights in Thai constitutionalism is at least partly explainable with the above mentioned thesis that rights and elements of direct democracy are perceived as potentially contributing to the disciplining and limiting mechanisms in view of the distrusted elements of electoral democracy, a notion which is underlying both constitutions but which became more accentuated after 2006.[94] A good example how much the traditional and the modern rights concept meanwhile flow in each other is the following statement in the wider context of the making of the 2007 constitution: "Concerning debate and public participation: Western citizens are considered [as] equal and expected to speak up, with peace resulting only

91 See Bagehot, *The English Constitution*, 1867, pp. 61 ff.

92 See Vitit Muntarbhorn, *"Human Rights in the era of 'Thailand Inc.'*," 2006, pp. 320, 324.

93 See for the 1997 constitution Klein, "The Evolution of Thailand's National Human Rights Commission," 2001, pp. 25, 32 f.

94 This helps to explain also the fact, that there is still no law on assembly in Thailand, leaving a grade of freedom *in practice* which is hardly enjoyed in any Western country, which also explains on the other side the harsh crackdown of those demonstrations which were supposed to turn against the substance core of the constitution in 2010.

when they are heard; Eastern citizens exist in hierarchies and are expected to keep their opinions to themselves, with peace resulting only when the ruler manages correctly."[95] This statement presents a somehow paradoxical sounding combination of a traditional view of the citizen committed to hierarchies and self-restraint with the almost menacing claim that he might resist actively any governance he perceives as incorrect. It is in fact, reflecting exactly the scenario of the demonstrations of the anti-Thaksin camp claiming to protect the monarchy and to enforce moral governance against the dictatorship of the populist based dictatorship of the majority serving corrupted politics. The high level of rights protection beyond the basic structure of the constitution is thus an expression of the overarching tendency to shift from a predominantly moral and value-based governance to a more legally defined one while, however, still serving an autochthon Thai constitutionalism. The latter is currently challenged by the forces of the Thaksin-camp and those who claim to be in support of a more universalistic constitutionalism including a universalistic rights concept. Both cases, Thailand and Malaysia, show that domestic concepts of rights are often deeper routed, more sincerely supported and normatively differentiated than it is often perceived from Western perspectives, and that they are often representing not an escape from but the formulation of an alternative version of good governance which is rather a national than a regional or global one and which is, however, increasingly contested by emerging alternative concepts.

III. Courts

Probably the most visible expression of the increasing impact of constitutionalism as a predominantly legal project is the role of constitutional courts addressed here by *Dressel*, *Hassavut* and *Weng*. While *Weng* draws an impressively encompassing picture of the not less impressive efforts of the Constitutional Court of Taiwan in differentiating constitutional law and de-

95 Pamela Hongsakul, "Democracy & Thailand," 2007, p. 90; see on the same page: „In Thailand, a country like no other country, a coup like no other, freed the citizenry from the yoke of thought and discussion. It restored a semblance of quietude. Thais gave food and flowers to the soldiers, not because they believed in military action, but because they were freed from debate. They appreciated the return to the non-story […]."

veloping constitutional doctrine by its interpretations[96], do *Hassavut* and *Dressel* focus on a specific aspect of judicial review, the court's role in the entrenchment of constitutional law in the realm of high politics, often labeled as the judicialization of politics. While *Weng* demonstrates from a purely doctrinal perspective how the Taiwanese constitutional court provided a steady and increasing stimulus for the entrenchment of democracy and the rule of law after its take off period during the 1990 s, do *Hassavut* and *Dressel* focus on the critical junctures between law and politics, constitutional review and good governance with *Dressel* in his comparative analysis providing a typology of court behavior referring to four diverging stories of court activity between restraint and activism, judicial muteness and politicization[97] where it comes to 'mega-politics'. This attempt to locate and explain judicial influence in a given political setting contributes in a wider sense to the classical debate about the appropriate power allocation in favor of courts with respect to the principle of (people's) sovereignty – an issue resonated also in *Hassavut's* contribution.[98]

However, *Dressel's* perspective is not normative but aims at providing tools to analyze the structures and processes leading to a certain judicial role in relation to politics. It is based on the assumption that "courts cannot but be deeply embedded within the political realm, which sets the general parameters in which courts can operate and also critically determines whether

96 See for Weng's personal role in this process as the president of the Taiwanese Council of Grand Justices Lee, "The Advocate and Practitioner of the Idea of Guardian of the Constitution," 2011.

97 See for another typology distinguishing between *submissive, friendly* and *assertive* courts Vanberg, "Legislative-Judicial Relations," 2001, pp. 346, 348.

98 The issue is in some respect generally related to classical problems like the above mentioned discussion of a "political constitutionalism", the dispute about the 'counter-majoritarian difficulty' or the long tradition of banning any judicial interpretation of laws to preserve the purity of the sovereign's decision from *Justinian* to the grand codifications of the era of rationalism and the early modernity and set forth in current China with the authoritative claim that any interpretation of the constitution is the sole province of the law's creator, the National People's Congress and its Standing Committee, as expressed by article 62 and 67 of the Chinese Constitution, a view which had been conformed in the official handling of the widely noticed *Qi Yuling* case in which a judicial account on constitutional rights had been attempted for the first time prompting immediately harsh reactions by the political leadership which was quickly taking complete control to ensure the further prevention of any such emancipating tendencies of constitutionalization by the courts. While this perspective is focusing on normative limits of judicial review, the perspective on judicialization is interested in the forms and reasons of transgressions of limits.

they will be propelled into the political fray". Doing so, he refers to an established literature on judicalization which is focused on politically particular active courts, while asking *in both directions*, analyzing active as well as more passive, louder and more muted courts, judicalization and judicial restraint. Even if he is stuck for an encompassing answer about the decisive mechanism or the criterion to explain judicial roles with respect to the complex interplays "between institutional, cultural, and structural factors in shaping judicial behavior", *Dressel´s* comparative perspective goes beyond the boundaries of those accounts which are solely focused either on one constitutional system or the "active" courts. This is opening up perspectives serving a more differentiated analysis of court performances within the given power structures. Remarkable as a counterpoint in this context is the older account on the phenomenon of an increasing judicial role in the political process, observing it mainly positively connoted as being anchored in macro processes of Western-prone constitutionalism and modernization. Put in relation to this view, *Dressel's* perspective reflects the departure from this merely uniform methodological account on constitutionalism towards an acknowledgment of multiple constitutionalizations as heuristic focal point. However, it seems to be promising to concretize the "institutional, cultural, and structural factors" shaping the behavior of judges and courts by taking the *link between judicial function and performance* in consideration with the given empirical power structure on the one hand and the normative mandate of the constitutional court on the other defining the function of the court, its institutional mandate.[99] The latter is of crucial importance where constitutional courts are particularly mandated with the protection of the constitutional basic structure.[100] This creates a heuristic frame with strong normative impact and relates judicial performance to a normative level where law and politics are heavily intersecting. Thus, the more constitutionalism is shaped as a legal project and the more courts are also in charge of the protection of the normative fundaments of this project, the more they are prone to perform in ways which require a maximum of methodological integrity.

99 Generally, constitutional courts might be mandated in a more limited or larger scale to act in quite different roles in varying power structures as *final interpreters* or *guardians* of the constitution, as *authoritative arbiters*, *disciplining instances* or *censors* of the constitutional powers and actors or simply to provide a citizen-initiated *feedback* about bureaucratic performance in the interest of enduring regime legitimacy and stability.

100 This is the case for the Thai court; see for instance art 68 Thai const.

Works cited

Abdul Hamid, Ahmad Fauzi, *Islam and Violence in Malaysia*, S. Rajaratnam School of International Studies Working Paper No. 123/07, Singapore: Nanyang Technological University, 2007.

Abou El Fadl, Khaled, "The Centrality of Shari'ah to Government and Constitutionalism in Islam," in *Constitutionalism in Islamic Countries: Between Upheaval and Continuity*, ed. Rainer Grote and Tilmann J. Röder, New York: Oxford University Press, 2012, pp. 35-61.

Albert, Richard, "The Cult of Constitutionalism," *Florida State University Law Review* 39 (2012): pp. 373-416.

Alexander, Larry, "Constitutionalism and Democracy: Understanding the Relation," in *The Supreme Court and the Idea of Constitutionalism*, eds. St. Kautz, A. Melzer, J. Weinberger and M.R. Zinman, Philadelphia: University of Pennsylvania Press, 2011, pp. 161-170.

Allen, William B., and Gordon Lloyd, ed., *The Essential Antifederalist*, Lanham MD/ Plymouth: Rowman & Littlefield, 2002.

Aristotle, *Politics*, Books III and IV, Translation with Introduction and Comments by Richard Robinson, with a Supplementary Essay by David Keyt, Clarendon Aristotle Series, Oxford: Clarendon Press, 1995.

Aspinall, Edward and Greg Fealy, eds., *Local Power and Politics in Indonesia: Decentralization and Democratization*, Singapore: ISEAS, 2003.

Asshiddiqie, Jimly, "Conflict of Interest between different Basic Rights from an Indonesian Pers-pective," in: *Constitutional Jurisdiction between State, Culture and Religion – Striking the Right Balance*, Singapore: Konrad-Adenauer-Stiftung, 2006, pp. 19-22.

Avril, Pierre, "Le juge et le représentant," *Le Débat* no. 74 (1993): 138-141.

Avril, Pierre, *Les Conventions de la Constitution*, Paris: PUF, 1997.

Badura, Peter, "Verfassungsänderung, -wandel, -gewohnheitsrecht," in *Handbuch des Staatsrechts*, eds. Josef Isensee and Paul Kirchhof, Vol. VII, Heidelberg: C.F. Müller, 1992, § 160.

Bagehot, Walter, *The English Constitution*, London: Chapman and Hall, 1867, reprint Ithaca NY: Cornell University Press, 1966.

Baker, Chris, and Pasuk Phongpaichit, *A History of Thailand*, Cambridge: Cambridge University Press, 2009.

Behr, Hartmut, "Moderne Theorien der Demokratie und Konzeptionen politischer Partizipation," in *Im Schatten demokratischer Legitimität*, eds. Hans-Joachim Lauth and Ulrike Liebert, Opladen/Wiesbaden: Westdeutscher Verlag, 1999, pp. 39-60.

Bellamy, Richard, *Political Constitutionalism: A Republican Defence of the Constitutionality of Democracy*, Cambridge: Cambridge University Press, 2007, reprinted 2010.

Bloch, Ernst, *Vorlesungen zur Philosophie der Renaissance*, Frankfurt a.M.: Suhrkamp, 1972.

Blumenberg, Hans, *Die Legitimität der Neuzeit*, Frankfurt a.M.: Suhrkamp, 1966, reprinted 1996.

Bogdanor, Vernon, *The New British Constitution*, Oxford/Portland OR: Hart Publishing, 2009.

Chaloemtiarana, Thak, *Thailand: The Politics of Despotic Paternalism*, Ithaca NY: Cornell SEAP Publications, 2007.

Chio, Vanessa, *Malaysia and the Development Process*, London/New York, Routledge, 2005.

Choudhry, Sujit, "Globalization in Search of Justification: Toward a Theory of Comparative Constitutional Interpretation," *Indiana Law Journal* 74 (1999): 819-892.

Choudhry, Sujit, "Bridging comparative politics and comparative constitutional law," in *Constitutional Design for Divided Societies: Integration or Accommodation*, ed. Sujit Choudhry, Oxford: Oxford University Press, 2008, reprinted 2010, pp. 3-40.

Colón-Ríos, Joel I., *Weak Constitutionalism: Democratic Legitimacy and the Question of Constituent Power*, Oxford/New York: Routledge, 2012.

Dunleavy, Patrick, "New Worlds in Political Science," *Political Studies* 58 (2010): 239-265.

Eisenstadt, Shmuel N., "Die institutionellen Ordnungen der Moderne: Die Vielfalt der Moderne aus einer weberianischen Perspektive," in *Das Weber-Paradigma*, eds. Gert Albert et al., Tübingen: Mohr Siebeck, 2005, pp. 328-351.

Forsthoff, Ernst, "Zur heutigen Situation der Verfassungslehre," in: *Epirrhosis: Festgabe für Carl Schmitt*, eds. Hans Barion et al., Berlin: Duncker & Humblot, 1968, pp. 185-213.

Frankenberg, Günter, *Die Verfassung der Republik: Autorität und Solidarität in der Zivilgesellschaft*, Frankfurt a.M.: Suhrkamp, 1997.

Frankenberg, Günter, *Staatstechnik: Perspektiven auf Rechtsstaat und Ausnahmezustand*, Frankfurt/Berlin: Suhrkamp, 2010.

Friedman, Edward, "Since There Is No East and There Is No West, How Could Either Be the Best?," in *Human Rights and Asian Values*, eds. Michael Jacobsen and Ole Bruun, Oxford: RoutledgeCurzon, 2000, pp. 21-42.

Gerhardt, Michael, "Verfassungsgerichtliche Kontrolle der Verwaltungsgerichtsbarkeit als Parameter der Konstitutionalisierung des Verwaltungsrechts," in *Allgemeines Verwaltungsrecht – zur Tragfähigkeit eines Konzepts*, eds. H.-H. Trute et al., Tübingen: Mohr Siebeck, 2008, pp. 735-748.

Guenaire, Michel, "La Constitution ou la fin du politique," *Le Débat* 64 (1991): 146-153.

Harding, Andrew, "Comparative law and legal transplantation in South East Asia," in *Adapting Legal Cultures*, eds. David Nelken and Johannes Feest, Oxford: Hart Publishing, 2001, pp. 199-223.

Harding, Andrew, "New Asian Constitutionalism: Myth or Reality?," in *Constitution Reform: Comparative Perspectives*, eds. Andrew Harding and Thawilwadee Bureekul, Bangkok: King Prajadhipok's Institute, 2008, pp. 25-51.

Harding, Andrew, and Peter Leyland, *The Constitutional System of Thailand*, Oxford: Hart Publishing, 2011.

Harris, William F. II, "Constitution of Failure: The Architectonics of a Well-Founded Constitu-tional Order," in *The Limits of Constitutional Democracy*, eds. Jeffrey Tullis and Stephen Macedo, Princeton: Princeton University Press, 2010, pp. 66-88.

Hirschl, Ran, "Constitutionalism in a Theocratic World," in *The Limits of Constitutional Democracy*, eds. Jeffrey Tullis and Stephen Macedo, Princeton: Princeton University Press, 2010, pp. 264-280.

Hongsakul, Pamela, "Democracy & Thailand: Does the Shoe fit?," in: *Law Magazine* 1 (2007): 88-90.

Isensee, Josef, "Gemeinwohl im Verfassungsstaat," in *Handbuch des Staatsrechts*, eds. Josef Isensee and Paul Kirchhof, Band IV, 3. ed., Heidelberg: C.F. Müller, 2006, § 71.

Isensee, Josef, "Verfassungsrecht als 'politisches Recht'," in *Handbuch des Staatsrechts*, eds. Josef Isensee and Paul Kirchhof, Vol. VII, Heidelberg: C.F. Müller, 1992, § 162.

Jacobsen, Michael, and Ole Bruun, "Introduction," in *Human Rights and Asian Values*, eds. Michael Jacobsen and Ole Brunn, Oxford: RoutledgeCurzon, 2000, pp. 1-20.

Jellinek, Georg, *Verfassungsänderung und Verfassungswandlung*, Berlin: O. Häring, 1906.

Jullien, Francois, *Das Universelle, das Einförmige, das Gemeinsame und der Dialog zwischen den Kulturen*, Berlin: Merve, 2009.

Kaiwar, Vasant, and Sucheta Mazumdar, "The Coordinates of Orientalism: Reflections on the Universal and the Particular," in *Asia, Europe and the Lineages of Difference*, eds. Mazum-dar, Kaiwar, Labica, London/New York: Routledge, 2009, pp. 19-42.

Kant, Immanuel, "Die Religion innerhalb der Grenzen der bloßen Vernunft," (1793) in *Immanuel Kant: Werkausgabe*, Frankfurt a.M.: Suhrkamp, 1977, Band 8, pp. 645-879.

Kautz, Steven, Arthur Melzer, Jerry Weinberger, and M. Robert Zinman, "Introduction: The Idea of Constitutionalism," in *The Supreme Court and the Idea of Constitutionalism*, eds. St. Kautz, A. Melzer, J. Weinberger and M.R. Zinman, Philadelphia: University of Pennsylvania Press, 2011, pp. 1-10.

Keane, John, "Monitory democracy?", in *The Future of Representative Democracy*, eds. Sonia Alonso, John Keane and Wolfgang Merkel, Cambridge: Cambridge University Press, 2011, pp. 212-235.

Klein, James, "The Evolution of Thailand's National Human Rights Commission 1992–2001," in *Thailand's New Politics*, KPI Yearbook, ed. M.H. Nelson, Bangkok: King Prajadhipok's Institute, 2001, pp. 25-65.

Kriele, Martin, "Freiheit und Gleichheit," in *Handbuch des Verfassungsrechts der Bundesrepublik Deutschland*, eds. Ernst Benda et al., 1st ed., Berlin: de Gruyter, 1983, pp. 129-168.

Kymlicka, Will, "The Good, the Bad, and the Intolerable: Minority Group Rights," in *Human Rights: An Anthropological Reader*, ed. Mark Goodale, Chichester: Wiley-Blackwell, 2009, pp. 58-68.

Laband, Paul, *Das Staatsrecht des Deutschen Reiches*, Vol. II, Tübingen: H. Laupp, 1878.

Lazar, Nomi Claire, *States of Emergencies in Liberal Democracies*, New York: Cambridge University Press, 2009.

Lee, Chien-Liang, "The Advocate and Practioner of the Idea of Guardian of the Constitution ('HÜTER DER VERFASSUNG'): Prof. Yueh-Sheng Weng's Contribution to the Development of Democratic Constitutionalism in Taiwan," *European-Asian Journal of Law and Governance* 1 (2011): 165-173.

Legrand, Pierre, "What 'legal transplants'?", in *Adapting Legal Cultures*, eds. David Nelken and Johannes Feest, Oxford: Hart Publishing, 2001, pp. 50-70.

Leyland, Peter, "Thailand's Constitutional Watchdogs: Dobermans, Bloodhounds or Lapdogs," Journal of Comparative Law 2 (2007): 151-177.

Lijphart, Arend, *Democracy in Plural Societies: A Comparative Exploration*, New Haven CT: Yale University Press, 1977.

Liow, Joseph Chinyong, *Piety and Politics: Islamism in Contemporary Malaysia*, New York: Oxford University Press, 2009.

Locke, John, *Second Treatise of Government* (1689), re-edition Indianapolis IN: Hackett, 1980

Loomba, Ania, *Colonialism/Postcolonialism*, London/New York: Routledge, 1998.

Lorenz, Astrid, "How to Measure Constitutional Rigidity – Four Concepts and Two Alternatives," *Journal of Theoretical Politics* 17 (2005): 339–361.

Luhmann, Niklas, "Geschichte als Prozess und die Theorie sozio-kultureller Evolution," in *Soziologische Aufklärung 3*, Opladen: Westdeutscher Verlag, 1981, pp. 178-197.

Macpherson, Crawford B., *The Political Theory of Possessive Individualism: Hobbes to Locke*, Oxford: Clarendon Press, 1962, republished Oxford University Press, 2010.

Mayer, Thomas, *Was ist Demokratie? Eine diskursive Einführung*, Wiesbaden: VS Verlag, 2009.

McIlwain, Charles Howard, *Constitutionalism: Ancient and Modern*, rev. ed., 1947, reprint Clark NJ: The Lawbook Exchange Ltd., 2005.

Means, Gordon P., *Political Islam in Southeast Asia*, Boulder CO: Lynne Rienner, 2009.

Moore, Barrington, *Soziale Ursprünge von Diktatur und Demokratie*, Frankfurt a.M.: Suhrkamp, 1968.

Muntarbhorn, Vitit, "Human Rights in the era of 'Thailand Inc.'," in *Human Rights in Asia: A Comparative Legal Study of Twelve Asian Jurisdictions, France and USA*, eds. Randall Peerenboom, Carol J. Petersen, Albert H.Y. Chen, New York/London: Routledge, 2006, pp. 320-345.

Nelson, Michael H., "Thailand: Problems with Decentralization?," in *Thailand's New Politics*, KPI Yearbook, Bangkok: King Prajadhipok's Institute, 2001, pp. 219-281.

Philpott, Daniel, "The Catholic Wave," in *World Religions and Democracy*, ed. Larry Diamond et al., Baltimore: John Hopkins University Press, 2005, pp. 102-117.

Pramoj, Seni, "Stone Inscriptions of Father King Ram Khamhaeng: First Constitution of Thailand," in *Development, Modernization, and Tradition in Southeast Asia: Lessons from Thailand*, eds. Pinit Ratanakul and U. Kyaw Than, Bangkok: Mahidol University Press, 1990, pp. 17-48.

Prokati, Kittisak, "Remarks on Ruling of the Thai Constitutional Court No. 12-13/2551, 'Cookery Show'," *European–Asian Journal of Law and Governance* 1 (2011): 123-132.

Putnam, Hilary, "Werte und Normen," in *Die Öffentlichkeit der Vernunft und die Vernunft der Öffentlichkeit: Festschrift für Jürgen Habermas*, eds. Lutz Wingert and Klaus Günther, Frankfurt a.M.: Suhrkamp, 2001, pp. 280-314.

Reuter, Thomas, "Indonesia's political and cultural transformation," in *The return of constitutional democracy in Indonesia*, ed. Thomas Reuter, Victoria: Monash University Press, 2010, pp. 1-8.

Rosanvallon, Pierre, *Counter-Democracy: Politics in an Age of Distrust*, Cambridge: Cambridge University Press, 2008.

Rosenn, Keith S., "The Success of Constitutionalism in the United States and Its Failure in Latin America," *University of Miami Inter-American Law Review* 22 (1990): 1-39.

Rousseau, Dominique, "Constitution ou la politique autrement," *Le Débat* 64 (1991): 176-185.

Rousseau, Dominique, "Questions de Constitution," *Politique et Sociétés* 19, no. 2-3 (2000): 9-30.

Sadeghi, Hossein Mir Mohammad, "The Position and Function of Judges in Islamic Law," in *Position und Aufgaben des Richters nach westlichem und nach islamischem Recht*, eds. Heinrich Scholler and Silvia Tellenbach, Tübingen: Mohr Siebeck, 2007, pp. 46-55.

Sadurski, Wojciech, "Constitutional Justice, East and West: Introduction", in *Constitutional Justice, East and West*, ed. Wojciech Sadurski, The Hague: Kluwer Law International, 2002, pp. 1-18.

Scheppele, Kim Lane, "The migration of anti-constitutional ideas: the post-9/11 globalization of public law and the international state of emergency," *The Migration of Constitutional Ideas*, ed. Sujit Choudhry, Cambridge: Cambridge University Press, 2006, pp. 347-373.

Scheuner, Ulrich, "Die Funktion der Verfassung für den Bestand politischer Ordnung," in *Regierbarkeit: Studien zu ihrer Problematisierung*, eds. W. Hennis, P. Graf Kielmansegg and U. Matz, vol. 2, Stuttgart: Klett-Cotta, 1979, pp. 102-138.

Schmit, Leo, "Decentralization and legal reform in Indonesia: The pendulum effect," in *Indonesia: Law and Society*, ed. Tim Lindsey, 2nd ed., Sydney: Federation Press, 2008, pp. 146-190.

Schmitt, Carl, "Die Formung des französischen Geistes durch den Legisten" (1942), in *Staat, Großraum, Nomos: Arbeiten aus den Jahren 1916–1969*, Berlin: Ducker & Humblot, 1995, pp. 184–218.

Sedara, Kim, and Joakim Öjendal, "Decentralization as a strategy for State Reconstruction in Cambodia," in *Beyond Democracy in Cambodia: Political Reconstruction in a Post-Conflict Society*, eds. Joakim Öjendal and Mona Lilja, Copenhagen: NIAS Press, 2009, pp. 101-135.

Shapiro, Martin, "Some Conditions for the Success of Constitutional Courts: Lessons from the U.S. Experience," in *Constitutional Justice, East and West*, ed. Wojciech Sadurski, The Hague: Kluwer Law International, 2002, pp. 37-59.

Shapiro, Martin, "Judicial Review in Developed Democracies," in *Democratization and the Judiciary*, eds. Siri Gloppen, Roberto Gargarella and Elkin Skaar, London: Frank Cass, 2004, pp. 7-26.

Shapiro, Martin, and Alec Stone Sweet, *On Law, Politics and Judicalization*, Oxford: Oxford University Press, 2002, reprinted 2011.

Simson, Werner von, "Zur Theorie der Legitimität," in *Festschrift für Karl Loewenstein*, Tübingen: Mohr, 1971, pp. 459-473.

Starck, Christian, "Grundrechtliche und demokratische Freiheitsidee," in *Handbuch des Staatsrechts,* eds. Josef Isensee and Paul Kirchhof, Vol. III, 3rd ed., Heidelberg: C.F. Müller, 2005, § 33.

Stone Sweet, Alec, *The Birth of Judicial Review in France: The Constitutional Council in Comparative Perspective*, New York/Oxford: Oxford University Press, 1992.

Tamada, Yoshifumi, *Myth and Realities: The Democratization of Thai Politics*, Melbourne: Trans Pacific Press, 2009.

Tamanaha, Brian Z., *On the Rule of Law*, Cambridge: Cambridge University Press, 2004.

Tarcov, Nathan, "Ideas of Constitutionalism Ancient and Modern," in: *The Supreme Court and the Idea of Constitutionalism*, eds. St. Kautz, A. Melzer, J. Weinberger and M.R. Zinman, Philadelphia: University of Pennsylvania Press, 2011, pp. 11-29.

Tetzlaff, Rainer, "Das Demokratieverständnis in Afrika und Asien – Alternativen zur westlichen Norm? Überlegungen zur Universalisierung von Demokratie und Menschenrechten," in *Die Demokratie überdenken: Festschrift für Wilfried Röhrich*, ed. Carsten Schlüter-Knauer, Berlin: Duncker & Humblot, 1997, pp. 345-370.

Tierney, Brian, *Religion, law, and the growth of constitutional thought, 1150-1650*, Cambridge: Cambridge University Press, 1982.

Tongyai, Tongnoi, "The Role of the Monarchy in Modern Thailand," in *Development, Modernization, and Tradition in Southeast Asia: Lessons from Thailand*, eds. Pinit Ratanakul and U. Kyaw Than, Bangkok: Mahidol University Press, 1990, pp. 153-161.

Trouillot, Michel-Rolph, "Undenkbare Geschichte: Zur Bagatellisierung der haitischen Revolu-tion," in *Jenseits des Eurozentrismus: Postkoloniale Perspektiven in den Geschichts- und Kulturwissenschaften*, eds. Sebastian Conrad and Shalini Randeria, Frankfurt a. M./New York: Campus, 2002, pp. 84-115.

Tully, James, *Strange Multiplicity: Constitutionalism in an Age of Diversity*, Cambridge: Cambridge University Press, 1995.

Tushnet, Mark, *Weak Courts, Strong Rights: Judicial Review and Social Welfare Rights in Comparative Constitutional Law*, Princeton/Oxford: Princeton University Press, 2008.

Tushnet, Mark, "The political constitution of emergency powers: Some conceptual issues," in *Emergencies and the Limed*, ed. Victor Ramraj, Cambridge: Cambridge University Press, 2008, pp. 145-156.

Vanberg, Georg, "Legislative-Judicial Relations: A Game-Theoretic Approach to Constitutional Review," *American Journal of Political Science* 45 (2001): 346–361.

Van Klinken, Geert Arend, and Joshua Barker, "Introduction: State in Society," in *State of Authority: The State in Society in Indonesia*, eds. Geert Arend van Klinken and Joshua Barker, Ithaca NY: Cornell Southeast Asia, 2009, pp. 1-16.

Vile, M.J.C., *Constitutionalism and the Separation of Powers* (1967), reprint Indianapolis: Liberty Fund, 1998.

Wachsmann, Patrick, "Die Europäische Menschenrechtskonvention und innerstaatliches Recht: Eine französische Perspektive," in *Terrorismusbekämpfung, Menschenrechtsschutz und Föderation*, eds. Johannes Masing and Olivier Jouanjan, Tübingen: Mohr Siebeck, 2008, pp. 79-107.

Wahl, Rainer, "In Defense of 'Constitution'," in *The Twilight of Constitutionalism?*, ed. Petra Dobner and Martin Loughlin, Oxford: Oxford University Press, 2010, pp. 220-242.

Wiederin, Ewald, "Österreich," in *Handbuch Ius Publicum Europaeum*, eds. A. v. Bogdandy, S. Cassese and P.M. Huber, Vol. III, Heidelberg: C.F. Müller, 2010, § 7.

Western Constitutionalism in Southeast Asia: Some Historical and Comparative Observations

Albert H.Y. Chen

Southeast Asia is a part of the world characterized by great ethnic, linguistic, religious and cultural diversity among its population. Although the peoples of Southeast Asia, with the exception of Thailand, all experienced Western colonial rule in modern times, the post-independence trajectories of the new Southeast Asian states born after the Second World War have been very different. Today, we find in Southeast Asia different kinds of political systems in which Western ideas of constitutionalism are practiced to different extents. In this paper, we seek to describe and understand such varying practices of constitutionalism from a historical and comparative perspective. Part A of the paper introduces basic concepts which supply the overall theoretical framework for the study of constitutionalism in Southeast Asia. Part B describes the practices of constitutionalism in Southeast Asia by systematically organizing and classifying the relevant historical experience of the countries concerned. Part C provides some concluding observations from a macro-historical and comparative perspective.

A.

In his famous book on *The Morality of Law*,[1] the American legal philosopher Lon Fuller describes the morality of law as a kind of "morality of aspiration".[2] Such a morality is concerned with the striving to achieve a particular good that can be realized in different degrees. The higher the degree to which the good is achieved, the more successful and excellent is the moral project concerned. The project of law, as Fuller understands it, is the project of subjecting human conduct to the governance of legal rules. Fuller develops

1 Fuller, *The Morality of Law*, 1969.
2 Fuller, *The Morality of Law*, 1969, p. 4.

eight principles, which he calls the principles of the internal morality of law, as criteria for evaluating the success of this project.

In my view, Fuller's concept of the morality of law as a morality of aspiration may be usefully applied to understand the project of constitutionalism. Whereas Fuller conceives of the project of the rule of law as one to regulate human behaviour by legal norms, the project of constitutionalism seeks to subject rulers or government to the governance of constitutional and legal rules, and to regulate the exercise of political power by means of such rules. As in the case of the rule of law, constitutionalism may also be achieved to varying extents.

Constitutionalism is not only about the making of constitutions but also about their implementation and enforcement. Political scientist Karl Loewenstein draws a conceptual distinction between "semantic", "nominal" and "normative" constitutions.[3] Semantic constitutions do not correspond to the reality of the political system at all and are no more than words. Nominal constitutions do tell us something about what the political system is and how it operates, but play no significant role in controlling the behaviour of political actors. Normative constitutions determine who become power holders, and really regulate the exercise of power and the relationship between power holders; their normative force is internalised by political actors who really take the rules stipulated in the constitution seriously, respect them and abide by them.

Constitutionalism as a theory and practice of government and law is a product of modern Western civilisation. Like science, it has been proved to have universal appeal to humanity and has in the last two centuries been transplanted to all corners of the earth. The possession of a constitution has come to be a hallmark of the modern sovereign state. Countries of different political persuasions, whether capitalist or communist, have unanimously pronounced that their constitutions are the authoritative and supreme law of their land. Like science, democracy and human rights, constitutionalism has come to be regarded as a sign of modernity and modernisation.

Despite the popularity of states enacting constitutions and seeking to derive legitimacy from them or using them as symbols to express their national identities and the collective aspirations of their peoples, different species or forms of constitutionalism may be identified in the contemporary world. These different species have been shaped by different historical and ideo-

3 See Loewenstein, *Political Power and the Government Process*, 1957, pp. 147-153.

logical contexts and traditions, and may be regarded as adaptations of the original ideas of constitutionalism to different societies and cultures and their circumstances and needs. At least three major species of constitutionalism may be identified in the contemporary world:[4]

a) Constitutionalism in its classical liberal sense (hereafter referred to as "LC" or "*liberal constitutionalism*") or constitutionalism properly so called, which is the original form of constitutionalism as it first emerged in modern Western history.[5] This includes elements such as (1) the Rule of Law, (2) the separation of powers, (3) political checks and balances, (4) civil liberties and human rights, (5) a written constitution which operates as a normative constitution (as mentioned above), (6) judicial review of the constitutionality of governmental and legislative acts, and (7) peaceful transfer of political power in accordance with constitutional norms. In the contemporary world, this kind of constitutionalism is basically co-extensive with liberal democracy, although the first constitutional states in Western history were not yet fully democratic.
b) Communist/socialist (Marxist-Leninist-Stalinist) constitutionalism, which is a form of authoritarian rule by a communist Party-State as legitimized by a written constitution defining the structure of the state and declaring the rights of citizens (hereafter referred to as "MC" or "*Marxist-Leninist constitutionalism*"). The constitution in this kind of constitutionalism is often a nominal or semantic constitution (as defined above).[6]
c) *Hybrid constitutionalism* (hereafter referred to as "HC"),[7] which is practised in states in which both elements of liberal constitutionalism and authoritarian elements that subvert or are inconsistent with such constitutionalism exist. The authoritarian elements may be derived from traditional or indigenous notions, norms, institutions and practices of politics, or a result of deliberate attempts by rulers or ruling elites (such as a one-man dictatorship, one-party hegemony, or military regime) to practise authoritarian rule behind a façade of liberal-democratic consti-

---

4 See also Chen, "Pathways of Western Liberal Constitutional Development in Asia," 2010.

5 See generally Nino, *The Constitution of Deliberative Democracy*, 1996.

6 See, e.g., the case of the People's Republic of China, discussed in Chen, *An Introduction to the Legal System of the People's Republic of China*, 2011, chapters 4-5.

7 The concept of "hybrid constitutionalism" is analogous to that of "hybrid regimes": see Diamond, "Thinking About Hybrid Regimes," 2002, p. 21.

tutional forms by, for example, manipulating or rigging electoral and other constitutional processes, determining who may participate in elections, violating human rights guaranteed by the constitution, or otherwise denying opposition forces fair opportunities to compete for political power on a level playing ground in accordance with the constitution. However, unlike communist regimes that practice MC, authoritarian, semi-democratic or pseudo-democratic regimes that practice such hybrid constitutionalism do not control all major social and economic domains, and a certain degree of social and political pluralism exists side by side with authoritarian rule in such regimes. The constitution in a state practicing hybrid constitutionalism is often a mixture of the semantic constitution and the normative constitution.

The following chart shows the relationship between the three species of constitutionalism identified here and the three kinds of constitution mentioned above:

Kinds of constitution / Constitutionalism	Nominal const.	Semantic const.	Normative const.
LC (liberal)			√
MC (Marxist)	√ OR	√	
HC (hybrid)		√ AND	√

B.

Different parts of Southeast Asia had different levels of political organization at the advent of Western imperialism and colonialism. The more highly developed forms of political organization included the Confucian kingdom in Vietnam and the Buddhist kingdoms in Thailand, Burma, Laos and Cambodia. What is today Indonesia and Malaysia had seen the civilizations of the Srivijaya and Majapahit empires, although they had declined by the time the Europeans arrived. Since the Westerners' arrival in the region in the

16th century, the colonial enterprise – first in maritime Southeast Asia and then in its mainland – resulted in the whole of Southeast Asia being partitioned by the British (Malaya, Burma), French (Indo-China), Dutch (East Indies or Indonesia) and Americans (the Philippines, originally colonized by the Spanish) by the early 20th century. Nationalist struggles against colonial rule began in parts of Southeast Asia earlier than in other parts. Rising up against the Spanish, the Filipinos first declared independence in 1898, though the republic they established was short-lived and ended with the establishment of American rule in 1901. Nationalist movements of significant size, some of which communist-inspired, also existed in Vietnam, Burma and Indonesia before the Second World War.[8]

During the Pacific War, the whole of colonial Southeast Asia came under Japanese occupation. Towards the end of the War, the Japanese encouraged some indigenous leaders to declare the establishment of independent national governments. Although the Europeans returned after Japan's defeat to take control of their former colonies, they were not able to resist the tide of decolonization for long. To preserve their empires, the French fought against the Vietnamese, and the Dutch against the Indonesians, but both were defeated by the nationalists. In 1949, the Hague Conference recognized the independence of Indonesia. In 1954, the Geneva Agreement recognized Vietnamese independence and partitioned it between North and South Vietnam. Unlike the French and the Dutch, the British were successful in engineering a smooth and peaceful transition to independent statehood in Burma (in 1948) and Malaya (in 1957), though it had to suppress the communist insurgency in Malaya that began in 1948. The USA, which had already committed itself before the War to granting independence to the Filipinos, granted independence to the Philippines in 1946.[9]

The new states of Southeast Asia were all constitutional states at the time of independence in the sense that they all had written constitutions which set out the organization of their political and legal systems, declare the rights of their citizens, and serve as a symbol of the new nation-state and its unity and identity. In the following, we will identify the different types of post-independence constitutional trajectory of the Southeast Asian states, as well as that of Thailand which was not colonized but maintained its independence.

8 See generally Osborne, *Southeast Asia*, 2000; SarDesai, *Southeast Asia*, 2003.

9 See generally Christie, *A Modern History of Southeast Asia*, 1996.

It is submitted that the following five kinds of constitutional trajectory may be distinguished:

Category	Description	Cases
A	the trajectory of Marxist-Leninist constitutionalism (MC)	Vietnam; Laos
B	a stable constitutional trajectory with features of liberal constitutionalism (LC) and hybrid constitutionalism (HC)	Malaysia; Singapore
C	checkered history with both attempts in practicing liberal or hybrid constitutionalism and authoritarian rule, leading to liberal constitutionalism (LC) at present though not completely consolidated, stable or embedded	Philippines; Thailand; Indonesia
D	international intervention in building liberal constitutionalism (LC) with some degree of success	Cambodia; East Timor
E	failure (or very low degree) of constitutionalism and the existence of authoritarian rule hardly constrained by any constitution	Myanmar (though changes have been taking place in 2010); Brunei

Each of the five categories of constitutional experience may be briefly described as follows.[10]

Category A: War-torn Vietnam was divided at the 17th parallel between the North and South until its reunification by the communist North in 1975. The first constitution of the Democratic Republic of Vietnam (in the North) promulgated in 1946 reflected the values of democracy and the rule of law

10 The following account draws on the following works: Church, *A Short History of South-east Asia*, 2009; Hill and Menzel, *Constitutionalism in Southeast Asia*, vol. 2, 2008; Tan, "The Making and Remaking of Constitutions in Southeast Asia," 2002; Owen, *The Emergence of Modern Southeast Asia*, 2005; Hassall, "Constitutional Trends in Asia," 1997; Kingsbury, *South-east Asia*, 2005; Case, *Politics in Southeast Asia*, 2002; Funston, *Government and Politics in Southeast Asia*, 2001; Beer, *Constitutional Systems in Late Twentieth Century Asia*, 1992; Beer, *Constitutionalism in Asia*, 1979; Spann, *Constitutionalism in Asia*, 1963; Hooker, *A Concise Legal History of South-east Asia*, 1978.

and contained no reference to socialism or single party rule. But the subsequent 1959 Constitution was clearly socialist-communist, so was the 1980 Constitution (of the Socialist Republic of Vietnam as the state was renamed in 1976 after unification), which was modeled on the USSR's Constitution. In South Vietnam, the 1956 and 1967 Constitutions were liberal-democratic in orientation, but were swept away as the communists overran the South. In 1986, the Communist Party of Vietnam decided to embark upon *doi moi* (renovation) and market-oriented economic reform. The 1992 Constitution is a symbol of the reform era. It affirms both human rights and property rights. Its 2001 amendment goes one step further to declare that Vietnam is a "law-governed socialist state". In recent years, there has been a lively discussion, encouraged by the government itself, on the possibility of the establishment of a constitutional court to supervise the implementation of the Constitution.

Laos, Vietnam's neighbour, also experienced the trauma of ideological division and war for almost three decades since the end of the Second World War. The French prepared Laos for independence by introducing elections and drafting a constitution (enacted in 1947). Between 1954 and 1975, Laos became part of the battleground for the Second Indochinese War (Vietnam War). The communists (Pathet Lao) intermittently fought and cooperated with the Royal Lao Government, but in 1975, they took over the country completely. For 16 years thereafter, they practiced single party rule by decree without even bothering to enact a new constitution. Finally, in 1991, a Constitution was introduced, apparently with the aim of re-centralizing power that had been acquired by regional authorities. Sources of influence on the content of this Constitution for one-party communist rule include the constitutions (prevailing at the time) of the Soviet Union, Vietnam and Cambodia.

Category B: In Malaysia and Singapore, the British legal, constitutional and political traditions played an important role in the formation of the post-colonial states, and many members of their political and legal elite had received a British education. The common foundation of the Constitutions of Malaysia and Singapore was the Malayan Constitution of 1957, which was shaped by the British constitutional tradition (though Islam was made the official religion for Malaya). Both Malaysia and Singapore have parliamentary systems of government by the majority parliamentary party, although the former is a constitutional monarchy practicing federalism and the latter a republican city-state. In each of the two countries, the same political party (the People's Action Party originally led by Lee Kuan Yew in Singapore) or political coalition (an alliance in Malaysia led by UMNO, or the United Malays National Organisation) has been continuously in power since the first crucial election in preparation for independence (in 1955 in Malaya and in 1959 in Singapore) and in the course of every national election thereafter. Although opposition political forces have been allowed to exist, civil liberties have fallen short of Western liberal standards (though it should be noted that before the race riots of 1969, Malaysia had enjoyed a period of remarkable openness and freedom in the 1960 s). Indeed, these countries have argued that Asian values are different from Western values and hence Western human rights norms are not completely appropriate to their societies which are multi-ethnic and therefore prone to conflict, which have a communitarian rather than individualistic ethos, and which need to prioritize economic development in order to catch up with the industrialized nations. Both countries have Internal Security Acts which authorize preventive detention without trial. Civil liberties, as well as the power of the courts in defending such liberties against government encroachment, have been restricted by constitutional and statutory amendments and, in the case of Malaysia, by invoking constitutional emergency powers on various occasions, particularly after the riots in 1969. In Singapore, the courts share the government's ideology of prioritizing public order and communitarian interests over individual rights. In Malaysia, the independence of the judiciary was perceived to be under attack in 1988 when the Mahathir administration removed the Lord President and two other judges of the Supreme Court. In both Malaysia and Singapore, the government has adhered to the rule of law (at least in the formal sense) by exercising power in accordance with constitutional and statutory provisions. Because of the control of Parliament by the ruling party or coalition, the government has been able to amend the Constitution almost at will. Thus as of 2008, the Malaysian Constitution has been amended 50 times, and the Singaporean Constitution 38 times.

Category C: The cases of the Philippines, Thailand and Indonesia may be considered under the same category because while they all have a checkered history in the practice of constitutionalism and have experienced ups and downs, including revolutions (in the Philippines and Indonesia) or many cycles of constitution-making, elected government and coup (in Thailand), they all currently have constitutions (the 1987 Constitution of the Philippines, the 2007 Constitution of Thailand (which has largely followed the 1997 Constitution, probably the most progressive constitution in Southeast Asia at the time of its enactment), and the Indonesian Constitution that has emerged from the constitutional amendments of 1999-2002) that are progressive, liberal-democratic and human rights-friendly in spirit and content. The establishment of constitutional courts in Thailand and Indonesia in 1998 and 2003 respectively and the work they have done are also significant indicators of the level of constitutionalism in these countries. In the Philippines, the Supreme Court has served the function of a constitutional court and has established a fair reputation for independent adjudication of difficult and politicized constitutional issues.

The Philippines has a robust constitutional tradition transplanted from the USA. Many of its political and legal elite have been much influenced by American legal culture. During its colonial rule of the Philippines, the USA consciously pursued the "democratic mission" of preparing the Filipinos for independence as a liberal-democratic constitutional state. The 1935 Constitution enacted for the Philippines Commonwealth (enjoying autonomy under American sovereignty) was modeled on the US Constitution. This Constitution continued to be used after the Philippines acquired independence in 1946, until it was replaced by the 1973 Constitution during the Marcos era. In 1946-72, liberal constitutional democracy was practiced in the Philippines, although politics was largely a matter of intra-elite struggles, the landed gentry held a disproportionate share of power and the state was weak. In 1972, Marcos declared martial law and ended the Philippines' experiment in American-style democracy. However, shortly after the national election of 1986 in which Cory Aquino ran against Marcos, the "People Power" rebellion toppled the Marcos dictatorship, and the Philippines became one of the first countries to be engulfed by the world's "Third Wave" of democracy. The progressive 1987 Constitution was both a reaction to the human rights violations of the Marcos era and a reaffirmation of the Filipino tradition of liberal democracy. Post-1987 political developments in the Philippines have stayed within the framework of the 1987 Constitution.

Like the Philippines, Indonesia also experienced authoritarian strongman rule preceded and followed by the practice of liberal constitutional democracy, except that the period of strongman rule in Indonesia was much longer and lasted for more than four decades. The independence constitution of 1945 was rather original. It expressed Sukarno's ideology of Pancasila, and was based on Soepomo's concept of the integralist or organic state rather than individualism and liberalism. However, the 1950 Constitution established a parliamentary system, and the first general election was held in 1955 in which 16 political parties secured seats in Parliament. Sukarno declared martial law in 1957, restored the 1945 Constitution, and sought to establish a new "Guided Democracy". Sukarno's strongman rule was succeeded in

1965 (following a coup during which more than half a million people, particularly communists, were massacred) by General Suharto's strongman rule with guaranteed participation of the military in the political system ("dwifungsi"). Suharto's "New Order" regime was finally overthrown in 1998 in the midst of the Asian financial crisis. Civil liberties were restored, and in 1999 the first free multi-party election since 1955 was held in which 48 political parties participated. The newly elected People's Consultative Assembly (MPR) enacted a series of constitutional amendments in 1999-2002 which turned Indonesia into a liberal constitutional democracy. Since then, several elections have been held, peaceful transfers of power have taken place, and the Constitutional Court has started to function. The political elite and the people of Indonesia seem to have succeeded in engineering a smooth transition from authoritarianism and hybrid constitutionalism to liberal constitutionalism.

Thailand is the only nation in Southeast Asia that has not undergone Western colonization, and its constitutionalism has therefore been an entirely indigenous enterprise. Thailand has a constitutional history dominated by what some observers call "vicious cycles" of constitution-making, election, conflict and military coup. It has seen 18 constitutions since the monarchy was constitutionalised in 1932. Among the 18 constitutions, 7 were interim and 11 were intended to be permanent; among the permanent constitutions (excluding the current one), only 5 survived for more than 3 years. In the 76-year period of 1932-2008, a total of 57 governments have come and gone in Thailand. The military, the King, civilian politicians and, in recent decades, ordinary people have all played significant roles in Thai constitutional politics. Pivotal moments of mass participation in politics include the "Students' Revolution" of 1973 (which was significant in East and Southeast Asia in that it preceded the "Third Wave" of democracy in the 1980 s), the popular protests in 1992 (ending in bloodshed and the King's intervention) which ushered in an era of democratic institution building culminating in the 1997 Constitution, and various assemblies and protests since 2006 before and after the military coup that toppled Thaksin Shinawatra. The 1997 Constitution was intended to consolidate liberal democracy in Thailand and to put an end to the vicious cycles of coups. Unfortunately, its hopes were dashed by the military coup of 2006 and the continuing unrest thereafter. Political stability was apparently restored after the 2011 election by which Yingluck Shinawatra came to power. Whether Thailand will finally grow out of its own brand of constitutionalism in which constitutional continuity is prone to be broken by coups remains to be seen.

Category D: Cambodia was the home of the great ancient civilization of Angkor, while East Timor is one of the youngest nation-states in the contemporary world. They share the same fate of suffering from massive violations of human rights and loss of life, followed by the United Nations' intervention leading to the establishment of a state that aspires towards liberal constitutional democracy.

Cambodia became a French protectorate in 1863 but its monarchy was preserved. Norodom Sihanouk, a king chosen by the French, ascended the throne in 1941 and played a pivotal role in Cambodian politics since then. After the end of the War, the French organized an election for a Constituent Assembly in 1946, which was the first democratic election in Cambodia. A Constitution was enacted in 1947. It established a constitutional monarchy, and contained liberal democratic features based on the Constitution of the French Fourth Republic. In 1953, Sihanouk declared martial law and dissolved the National Assembly. In the same year, the French granted Cambodia full independence. The period of 1953-1970 was one of strongman rule under Sihanouk. A series of 9 constitutional amendments were made. Authoritarian rule was practiced; opposition was suppressed. In 1970, Sihanouk was ousted by a coup. The government of the new Khmer Republic made a new constitution in 1972, but soon the Khmer Rouge took power in 1975, inaugurating a reign of terror and lawlessness (though the regime enacted a crude 21-article Constitution) in which more than one million people lost their lives. Vietnamese invasion led to the establishment of the People's Republic of Kampuchea in 1979, another one-party state which enacted a socialist/communist constitution modeled on the constitutions of the USSR and Vietnam. Hun Sen emerged as the strongman. This government was perceived by many to be Vietnam's puppet, and a civil war waged between the government and a coalition of resistance forces including the Khmer Rouge and the Royalists (supporting Sihanouk). In 1989, the constitution was reformed with references to socialism dropped and the state renamed the State of Cambodia. In 1991, in an internationally coordinated effort to settle the problems of internal conflict and external interference in Cambodia, the Paris Agreement was reached with 18 other states as parties. The United Nations Transitional Authority in Cambodia (UNTAC) was established which oversaw the election of a new National Assembly in 1993. A new constitution – the Constitution of the Kingdom of Cambodia – was drafted in accordance with liberal-democratic guidelines laid down by the Paris Agreement and enacted in 1993. Since then, regular elections have been held, opposition political parties have been allowed to exist, though

Hun Sen has remained the strongman even today. A series of constitutional amendments (including the 1999 amendment creating a Senate in the Parliament) has been introduced in response to the changing political situation as determined by electoral outcomes. A Constitutional Council has been established in 1998, which has decided a number of cases as a constitutional court.

East Timor, a Portugese colony since 1642, was annexed by Indonesia in 1975 when Portugal decided to give up the colony. Indonesian rule had been opposed by guerillas led by a political group known as Fretilin. After Suharto's fall, the new Indonesian government under Habibie agreed to let the people of East Timor exercise the right of self-determination. A UN-supervised referendum was held in 1999 in which the majority of voters expressed the preference not to be subject to Indonesian rule. This was followed by violence in which atrocities were committed by pro-Indonesian militias. A UN multinational peacekeeping force restored order in late 1999. In 2001, a Constituent Assembly was elected to draft a constitution, which was enacted in 2002 as East Timor became an independent nation-state. This constitution is a detailed and liberal-democratic constitution based on a draft prepared in 1998 by Fretilin when it was in exile, drawing on the constitutions of Portugal and Mozambique. Since independence, East Timor has suffered from episodes of civil unrest and political assassinations. An anti-government riot broke out in 2002. The army mutiny in 2006 resulted in anarchy, and order was only restored by an UN peacekeeping force. The first election since 2001 was held in 2007. 2008 saw an assassination attempt on the top political leaders.

Category E: We finally come to the "problematic" cases of Myanmar (Burma) and Brunei, which seem to have departed from the dominant trends in Southeast Asian constitutional developments as outlined above.

The Burmese kingdom was one of the strongest states in mainland Southeast Asia at the end of the 18th century, but in the course of the 19th century became weaker than the Thai and Vietnamese kingdoms. In 1886 Burma was annexed by the British and its king exiled. Burma became part of British India until it was constituted a separate colony in 1937. A nationalist movement already existed in Burma before the Second World War. The political reforms in India were extended to Burma. A new constitution was enacted in 1935 allowing the Burmese to practise self-government. The first election was held in 1936, and Burma enjoyed parliamentary government by the time the Japanese invaded it in 1942. After the War, Aung San, leader of the Anti-Fascist People's Freedom League formed during the War, negotiated with the British with a view to Burmese independence. In 1947, a constituent assembly was elected in which the League won the majority of seats, but Aung San was assassinated thereafter. The 1947 Constitution was adopted, providing for a parliamentary system and a federal state, and Burma became independent in 1948. In 1948-60, British-style liberal democracy was practised, with the League being in power. British-style rule of law was also practiced, with the Supreme Court developing Burma's constitutional jurisprudence. In 1958, the military took power, but civilian rule was restored after the 1960 election. Then came the turning point of 1962, when a military coup put a conclusive end to Burma's experiment in liberal constitutional democracy. The 1947 Constitution was set aside. For 12 years the military ruled by decree, until the new Constitution of the Socialist Republic of the Union of Burma was enacted in 1974. The Constitution sought to legitimize one-party rule by the Burma Socialist Programme Party of the regime; the courts' power to interpret the constitution was abolished. In 1988, popular protests erupted led by students and monks. While they were suppressed by the army, a military coup occurred. The State Law and Order Restoration Council (SLORC, renamed the State Peace and Development Council (SPDC) in 1997) assumed power and set aside the 1974 Constitution. An election was held in 1990 in which 92 political parties participated and the National League for Democracy (NLD) led by Aung San Suu Kyi won a landslide victory. However, the military government refused to hand over power and maintained authoritarian rule without a constitution for two decades. Suu Kyi was put under house arrest. Popular protests occurred in 2007 but were suppressed. In 2008, a new Constitution of the Republic of the Union of Myanmar was adopted after a referendum. It was perceived as an attempt to constitutionalize and perpetuate military rule. A parliamentary election was held on 7 November 2010. It was boycotted by the NLD but a total of 37 political parties, including some opposition candidates, did participate in the election. In November 2010, Aung San Suu Kyi was released from house arrest. In the national by-elections of 2012, Suu Kyi and her NLD colleagues secured seats in parliament.

Like Myanmar, Brunei – the least populous state in Southeast Asia with a population of 400,000 but rich in natural resources – has experienced absolute rule by decree with few constitutional niceties. In this case, the authoritarian ruler is a monarch who legitimizes his rule by the concept of the Malay Islamic Monarchy. Brunei became a British protectorate in 1888. In 1956, the People's Party of Brunei (PPB) was founded and demanded free elections and independence. In 1959, the British Government concluded a treaty with the Sultan granting self-government to Brunei, and its first constitution was promulgated. The Constitution affirms the Sultan's personal sovereignty and prerogative powers and contains no provisions on human rights. It established a partially elected Legislative Council. An election was held in 1962 in which the PPB won most of the votes but was still outnumbered in the Legislative Council which was only partially elected. A revolt broke out in 1962 in response to which a state of emergency was proclaimed; the emergency has since been renewed indefinitely. Since 1962 the Sultan has largely ruled by decree with the Legislative Council reduced to a rubber-stamp. In 1970 elected seats in the Legislative Council were abolished altogether. In 1983 Brunei acquired full independence. In 1983 the constitutional provisions regarding the Legislative Council were suspended. In 2004, a new Legislative Council was appointed which introduced a series of constitutional amendments that further entrench absolute monarchical rule. The Sultan's power is now total and unfettered; judicial review of government action as the last surviving means of check and balance within the system is expressly abolished by the constitutional amendment.

C.

In Part A of this paper, it has been pointed out that the project of constitutionalism, like that of the rule of law, is governed by a morality of aspirations. The project may succeed in different degrees in different circumstances; constitutionalism may be realized to varying extents depending on the situation. A state with a normative constitution may be regarded as having realized constitutionalism to a greater extent than a state with a semantic constitution; and one with a semantic constitution may be regarded as having realized constitutionalism to a greater extent than one with a nominal constitution. Liberal constitutionalism may be regarded as a fuller form of constitutionalism than Marxist-Leninist constitutionalism insofar as the power of the communist party that exercises a monopoly on power is usually not completely subordinated to or fully regulated by constitutional and legal norms. Hybrid constitutionalism is also a form of constitutionalism that fails to deliver fully on the promises made by the text of the constitution.

Ideas and practices of constitutionalism first developed in modern Western history. As Part B of this paper has demonstrated, all of the Southeast Asian states that emerged from colonial rule either had written constitutions made for them by the former colonial master or chose to adopt written constitutions at the time of their independence. Thailand, which was not colonized, embarked upon the path of constitutional monarchy on its own initiative. For many Southeast Asian states, the new constitution was a symbol of the newly born nation-state. Constitution-making was thus part of the project of state-building.

In many parts of Southeast Asia, state-building has not been an easy task. In some cases, wars of independence were fought against the colonial masters. Many societies also faced the problems of internal conflicts, civil unrest, civil war, guerilla warfare, or military intervention by foreign powers, particularly in the context of the Cold War. Until and unless such obstacles to state-building have been overcome, the project of constitutionalism could hardly begin.

In the states that emerged from French Indo-China, violence and military conflicts continued for decades which exacted a heavy toll on the constitutional project. Vietnam suffered from two Indo-Chinese Wars and achieved unification only in 1975. Laos was torn by war and internal conflicts until the communists took over in 1975. Cambodia was drawn into the Vietnam War and then suffered from the Khmer Rouge's reign of terror in 1975-1979. It was beset by civil war after the Vietnamese takeover in 1979 until the Paris Agreement of 1991 under which UN intervention paved the way for a construction of a new constitutional state.

Indo-China is the only part of Southeast Asia where the communist movement succeeded in taking state power. Vietnam and Laos became the foothold of Marxist-Leninist constitutionalism in Southeast Asia. Elsewhere in Southeast Asia, particularly in Malaya and Indonesia, communists had also been active but they were ruthlessly suppressed by the ruling authorities. In Cambodia, communist rule failed to consolidate itself and international intervention in 1991 led to the creation of a constitutional monarchy with a constitution that aspires towards liberal constitutionalism.

In the original ASEAN states of Malaysia, Singapore, Thailand, the Philippines, and Indonesia, what this paper has termed hybrid constitutionalism seems to have been the dominant form of constitutionalism for significant periods, but there is apparently a trend in favour of liberal constitutionalism in more recent decades. Part B of this paper has drawn a distinction between the cases of Malaysia and Singapore on the one hand, and those of the Philippines, Thailand and Indonesia on the other hand. Malaysia and Singapore have trodden a stable and steady constitutional path since independence. Their form of constitutionalism may be regarded as a half-way house between liberal constitutionalism and hybrid constitutionalism. Regular elections have been held, opposition parties have been allowed to exist, but there are significant legal restrictions on civil liberties. The rule of law has been largely adhered to, although the power of the courts to protect civil liberties has been circumscribed by constitutional and statutory rules.

Whereas the foundation for constitutionalism in Malaysia and Singapore was laid by the British, that in the Philippines was well laid by the Americans. The Philippines has largely practiced liberal constitutionalism since its independence, with the Marcos dictatorship in 1972-1986 being a departure from or an exception to the general pattern. Indonesia also experimented with liberal constitutionalism in the 1950 s, but the experiment ended with the authoritarian strongman rule of Sukarno followed by that of Suharto. Both attempted to practise a kind of hybrid constitutionalism involving authoritarianism and "managed" democracy. However, the fall of Suharto in 1998 has inaugurated a new era of liberal constitutionalism in Indonesia. As Indonesia is the most populous state and the largest economy in Southeast Asia and a major Islamic society in the contemporary world, its recent movement towards liberal constitutionalism may have significant regional and global implications.

Like the case of Indonesia, the case of Thailand may also inspire optimism about the prospects of liberal constitutionalism in Southeast Asia, provided that Thailand heals its internal division in recent years and puts its 2007 Constitution into practice. As mentioned in Part B of this paper, Thailand's 1997 Constitution, made in the hope of ending the endemic cycles of military coups and to entrench democracy, was a very progressive and liberal-democratic one; despite its origins in the 2006 coup, the 2007 Constitution has not been regressive and has largely preserved the gains made by its predecessor. Thus it is entirely possible that Thailand, Indonesia and the Philippines become the engines and exemplars of liberal constitutionalism in Southeast Asia in the foreseeable future. As regards Malaysia and Singapore, which already practise liberal constitutionalism to some extent, a further deepening of liberal constitutionalism at some future point is also conceivable.

It remains for us to consider the cases of East Timor, Brunei and Myanmar. East Timor is a very young nation and its future is still uncertain. There is however hope that liberal constitutionalism will work out. Brunei's absolute monarchy has been further entrenched by the constitutional amendments of 2004-06; it is likely to remain an anachronism in the region. As for Myanmar, despite a record of liberal constitutionalism from independence until 1958, continuing military rule since 1962 has also made it a political anachronism in the region. The enactment of the 2008 Constitution and the election of

November 2010 may be regarded as positive steps forward, however tiny they were, but Myanmar will have a long way to go before it can catch up with its neighbours in the practice of constitutional government.

Since the end of the Second World War and the birth of most of the Southeast Asian states that exist today, the political, constitutional, social and economic landscapes of Southeast Asia have changed beyond recognition. The age of wars and civil strife seems to be over. Most Southeast Asian states have now experienced decades of continuous peace and stability. Some have achieved rapid economic growth. Some have seen an expanding middle class and a vibrant civil society. Overall speaking, in the 68-year period following the end of the War in 1945, the project of constitutionalism has made significant progress in Southeast Asia as a whole. Constitutionalism may be called Western constitutionalism because of its origins in Western modernity. But today it has found homes in all corners of the earth. As this paper has sought to demonstrate, the Southeast Asian region is no exception to this global and universal trend.

Works cited

Beer, Lawrence W., ed., *Constitutionalism in Asia: Asian Views of the American Influence*, Berkeley: University of California Press, 1979.

Beer, Lawrence W., ed., *Constitutional Systems in Late Twentieth Century Asia*, Seattle: University of Washington Press, 1992.

Case, William, *Politics in Southeast Asia: Democracy or Less*, Richmond: Curzon, 2002.

Chen, Albert H.Y., *An Introduction to the Legal System of the People's Republic of China*, 4th ed., Hong Kong: LexisNexis, 2011.

Chen, Albert H.Y., "Pathways of Western Liberal Constitutional Development in Asia: A Comparative Study of Five Major Nations," *International Journal of Constitutional Law* 8 (2010):

849-884.

Christie, Clive J., *A Modern History of Southeast Asia: Decolonization, Nationalism and Separatism*, London: I.B. Tauris, 1996.

Church, Peter, ed., *A Short History of South-east Asia*, 5th ed., Singapore: John Wiley & Sons, 2009.

Diamond, Larry, "Thinking about Hybrid Regimes," *Journal of Democracy* 13, no. 2 (2002): 21-35.

Fuller, Lon L., *The Morality of Law*, rev. ed., New Haven: Yale University Press, 1969.

Funston, John, ed., *Government and Politics in Southeast Asia*, Singapore: Institute of Southeast Asian Studies, 2001.

Hassall, Graham, "Constitutional Trends in Asia," in *Asian Laws Through Australian Eyes*, ed. Veronica Taylor, Sydney: LBC, 1997, pp. 113-132.

Hill, Clauspeter, and Jörg Menzel, eds., *Constitutionalism in Southeast Asia*, vol. 2, Singapore: Konrad-Adenauer-Stiftung, 2008.

Hooker, M.B., *A Concise Legal History of South-east Asia*, Oxford: Clarendon Press, 1978.

Kingsbury, Damien, *South-east Asia: A Political Profile*, 2nd ed., Melbourne: Oxford University Press, 2005.

Loewenstein, Karl, *Political Power and the Government Process*, Chicago: The University of Chicago Press, 1957.

Nino, Carlos Santiago, *The Constitution of Deliberative Democracy*, New Haven: Yale University Press, 1996.

Osborne, Milton, *Southeast Asia: An Introductory History*, 8th ed., St Leonards NSW: Allen & Unwin, 2000.

Owen, Norman G., *The Emergence of Modern Southeast Asia: A New History*, Singapore: Singapore University Press, 2005.

SarDesai, D.R., *Southeast Asia: Past and Present*, 5th ed., Boulder CO: Westview Press, 2003.

Spann, Richard Neville, ed., *Constitutionalism in Asia*, London: Asia Publishing House, 1963.

Tan, Kevin Y.L., "The Making and Remaking of Constitutions in Southeast Asia: An Overview," *Singapore Journal of International & Comparative Law* 6 (2002): 1-41.

Constitutionalism as Development

Jörg Menzel

A. Introduction

This short article asks the question, if and how constitution-making, constitutional design and constitutionalism contribute to the "development" of nations. Whereas "Law and Development" has been an issue for half a century, the more specific question concerning "Constitutional Law and Development" has rarely been explored.[1] In order to discuss this issue, I will first briefly discuss the main terms, constitutionalism and development (B.). I will then address the potential contributions of constitutionalism to the development of a nation (C.), the process of constitution-building (D.) and finally the implications of globalization and increased internationality in this field (E.), before drawing some conclusions (E.). Regionally, examples used here will mostly be taken from Asia and more specifically, Southeast Asia, a region of mostly developing countries with dynamic constitutional developments over recent decades.[2]

B. Basic Concepts

I. Constitutionalism

There is no generally accepted definition of the term constitutionalism.[3] In Germany the word *"Konstitutionalismus"* sounds like a precise translation of the term, but actually stands for the period of *pre-democratic* constitutions of the 19th century. The term for the modern democratic version would be "Verfassungsstaat", literally meaning "constitutional state" but avoiding the

---

1 However, see Bryde, "Constitutional Law in 'old' and 'new' Law and Development," 2010.

2 See generally, Hill and Menzel, *Constitutionalism in Southeast Asia*, 2008/2010.

3 See Sajó, *Limiting Government*, 1999; Alexander, *Constitutionalism*, 1998; Sartori, "Constitutionalism," 1962.

Latin terminology. "Verfassungsstaatlichkeit" therefore is the German translation for "constitutionalism." Furthermore, a political and legal system based on a constitution might be called constitutionalist. The German "Konstitutionalismus" was a step on that path, as it limited the monarchies of the time through concepts of rule of law, protected (weak) human rights concepts and allowed for pre- or semi-democratic[4] participation of elected representative assemblies.[5] Historically, most systems called constitutionalist were not democratic, but aristocratic.[6] Today, formal special privileges for any kind of nobility are nearly taboo for any system that wants to be labeled as constitutionalist, though notable exceptions still exist.[7] Nowadays, limited government, defined by democracy, human rights and rule of law, are often mentioned as conditions for "real" constitutionalism.[8] But constitutionalism is not only about "having a constitution" or even the textual substance of a "good" constitution embracing those principles. Properly defined, constitutionalism is not (only) about law in the book, but law in life. It is about the actual *practice* of "limited government."

Modern constitutionalism has been on the rise in recent decades,[9] yet there remains no global standard for what this encompasses. Written constitutions have become the norm, but interestingly the very few states who traditionally do not have written constitutions as a matter of principle (Great Britain, New Zealand) are mostly labeled as "constitutionalist" despite this because they rely on unwritten constitutional conventions which are based on those principles of democracy, basic rights and rule of law. Within the many states that have written constitutions, there are a few formally established systems which quite openly are not based on those concepts (e.g. Brunei with its absolute monarchy), but much more often the text of the constitution will

4 The electoral system in Prussia between 1849 and 1918 not only excluded women but often also formalized the inequality of men's votes depending on their tax-payments or other classifications (see e.g. the Prussian three-class franchise system).

5 Good analysis by Heun, "Constitutionalism in Germany," 2010; short summary also in Heun, *The Constitutional System of Germany*, 2011, pp. 13-21.

6 For an historical account see Gordon, *Controlling the State*, 1999.

7 See e.g. Samoa, where the right of Samoans to be elected to parliament is still limited to chiefs ("matai").

8 The Venice Commission has repeatedly labeled constitutionalism "the key to democracy, human rights and the rule of law".

9 See the famous dictum of Ackermann, "The Rise of World Constitutionalism," 1997; for overviews on all constitutions see Robbers, *Encyclopedia of World Constitutions*, 2007.

not reveal the problem immediately, at least not to the "naive" reader. Constitutions have often been (to the full extent or in parts) rhetoric or programmatic at best, cold blooded lies at worst.[10] In daily life, some constitutions are completely ignored or only followed in some parts. Obviously one can have a formal separation of power with an executive, legislative and judicial branch, but have a practice in which all the branches are in fact effectively controlled by one person or one political group and in which, for example, rule of law and basic rights will only be used to protect the "honor" of the political leaders, but not the freedom of expression of those criticizing them. Democracy, rule of law, and even basic rights are all concepts which are open for misinterpretation or even systemic abuse.

Constitutionalism, as it is understood here, does not necessarily require full judicial review (particularly the review of democratically adopted statutes). This should be stressed, as the debate about constitutionalism in the USA is obviously much about this question. Internationally the "if and how" of judicial review of legislation is open for debate and is only one of the choices that a constitutionalist state can make. In Europe, the Netherlands will typically be qualified as a constitutional state, for example, despite the fact that its constitution explicitly prohibits judicial review of statutes by the courts. It has to be acknowledged, however, that judicial review has gained significant ground in recent decades, be it in the common law version of review by the ordinary courts or in the German-Austrian version of review by constitutional courts.[11] Such specialized courts are clearly on the rise, not only in Europe but around the globe and even many "Constitutional Councils" rooted in the French tradition now often have significant judicial roles.

II. Development

Development is as difficult a term to define as is constitutionalism. It has often been linked mostly to economic development. The German ministry

---

10 Among the numerous attempts to classify constitutions with respect to their legal relevance the best known one is probably Loewenstein's distinction of normative, nominalistic and semantic constitutions.

11 For a good recent book see Harding and Leyland, *Constitutional Courts*, 2009; on developments in Asia see also Harding and Nicholson, *New Courts in Asia*, 2010; on judicialization in Asia see also the contributions in Ginsburg and Chen, *Administrative Law and Governance in Asia*, 2009.

in charge of developmental cooperation was established as the "Federal Ministry of Economic Cooperation." Internationally, gross national product (GNP) per capita has often been seen as a main indicator for development levels.[12] Today it is widely acknowledged that development is a more complex term. The United Nations Development Program uses the term "Human Development" in which economic growth is only a means to an end.[13] More than two decades ago UNDP started their "Human Development Reports" by adding life expectancy, literacy to the criteria; acknowledging that this extension was not broad enough. Most notably Nobel Laureate Amartya Sen famously wrote about "Development as Freedom", arguing that freedom is the ultimate raison d'être of development, substantially changing the global discourse on development.[14]

It needs to be emphasized again however, that even economical development cannot be measured simply in terms of GDP or GNP. Historically, "economies" have often been quite successful for some time on the basis of fundamental inequality and exploitation. Ancient Egypt, Greece and Rome all were slaveholder societies, as were many centuries later the Khmer Empire in Cambodia and the early United States. European dominance in the colonial era was also based on severe exploitation of cheap labor in the colonies. Apartheid-South Africa did not formally know "slavery" during the 20th century, yet its society was based on the discrimination and exploitation of the native African population. All those systems were quite successful in their economic wealth, but obviously at the immediate cost of many in their own spheres of power. Economic development, properly defined, needs to take into account the distribution of wealth. Development has to be a shared success, not a pleasure for a few at the extreme expense of the most. The Universal Declaration of Human Rights and other global documents on fundamental rights therefore connect human dignity to economic and social conditions for a dignified living, as do most modern constitutions. Many decades after such promises were first made, they are still unfulfilled for billions of human beings. As the example of slavery shows clearly as well, freedom as an essential part of human dignity is also more than (economic) prosperity. Substantial freedom might depend to some extent on

12 See Hirsch, "Developing Countries," 2012.

13 For a comprehensive discussion see Alkire, "Human Development," 2010.

14 Sen, *Development as Freedom*, 2000; on Sen's approach see e.g. Chimni, "The Sen Conception of Development," 2008.

some economic and social preconditions,[15] but one is not free or happy just because one has enough to eat. Freedom means having choices and being respected on the basis of equality of all human beings. South Africa's apartheid system was often defended by its apologetics with the argument that the black population in South Africa was economically better off than Africans in most of the rest of Sub Sahara Africa. This argument did not convince black South Africans and it did not convince the global community (at least in the later part of the 20th century).[16] But a somewhat similar argument is still around, defending different versions of authoritarian government and claiming that (economic) "development" should come first undisturbed by too much influence of "Western" concepts like democracy or individual freedoms and rights. However, such tradeoffs are not only questionable within their inner logic, but also seem to be too narrow in defining development. Freedom should not be seen as some luxury good for the rich, but as a basic value for all humankind.

C. Constitutional Promises for Development

I. Nation and State Building

There is a lot of "building" literature published these days in the academic world of political science, international relations and law. Books promise to explain how to escape the mess of failed communities by building nations and states. Some seem to be outright manuals, given their titles,[17] and there is even a "Beginner's Guide to Nation Building"[18] which seems to be the ideal present for any aspiring leader of a coup d'état in a failed polity. Other book titles are more careful, indicating the difficulties.[19]

---

15 The importance of a guaranteed subsistence minimum for the guarantee of human dignity has just recently (9 Feb 2010) been emphasized by the German Constitutional Court (BVerfGE 125, 175, also available at www.bverfg.de); see Egidy, "Casenote," 2010.

16 On the international condemnation of apartheid see Gebhard, "Apartheid," 2012.

17 See Ghani and Lockhart, *Fixing Failed States*, 2008; Chesterman et al., *Making States Work*, 2005; Call and Wyeth, *Building States to Build Peace*, 2008; Fukuyama, *Nation Building*, 2006.

18 Dobbins et al., *The Beginner's Guide to Nation Building*, 2007.

19 See Paris and Sisk, *The Dilemmas of Statebuilding*, 2009; Bull, *No Entry without Strategy*, 2008; Stromseth et al., *Can Might Make Rights?*, 2006.

On the most fundamental level, making constitutions and establishing constitutionalism can be part of nation and state building endeavors.[20] The adoption of a constitution can be a founding moment or a milestone in nation or state building.[21] The constitutions of the United States, Australia and the German constitution of 1871 are classical examples of constitutions that effectively created new states. The South African constitution of 1997 might be seen as exercises in nation building, as the "state" was pre-existent, but a "nation" had to be rebuilt. Constitutions can even become symbols of the nation or statehood. Many countries try to utilize such potential by celebrating a "constitution day" as a national holiday. In Germany, there is not such a public holiday, but "constitutional patriotism" has become a (controversial) concept, according to which identification with the state is mainly based on the common belief in the values and structures laid down in the constitution.[22]

Nowadays it seems standard procedure that whenever a Nation or State needs to be (re-)built after a period of crisis, failure, or dictatorship, the drafting of a new constitution is one of the most immediate tasks. This is considered to be crucial in the process of reconstruction. Prominent examples of much discussed constitution making can be found in the successor states of the former Yugoslavia, in Afghanistan and Iraq, as well as currently in Nepal. As those examples illustrate, constitution making regularly is an integral and early part of state and nation building.

II. Controlled and Limited Government, Democracy

A constitution's foremost role is to provide rules for the political process. Its promise therefore is an orderly, limited and (now mostly accepted) democratic government. A constitution is a pre-commitment on rules for the political process. Some would argue that this is actually all a constitution has

20 See v. Bogdandy, "State-building, Nation-building and Constitutional Politics," 2005.

21 To be clear, not every adoption of a new constitution qualifies as what one might label a "constitutional moment" (Ackermann). On the other hand, constitutional amendments – normally not seen as fundamental in this sense – occasionally are such moments, as exemplified in the Indonesian constitutional amendments between 1999 and 2002.

22 The term was invented by political scientist Dolf Sternberger but became internationally influential because of its endorsement by philosopher Jürgen Habermas.

to do. Even such a limited definition of the role of constitutions is developmental in its core: Political stability and accountability might be seen as everything needed for internal peace and security to be guaranteed as well as the economy to prosper. Older constitutions are often based on this concept. Australia's Constitution is such a basic "organizational code", as was the German Constitution of 1871 and even the original Constitution of the United States of America, which was largely organizational until the adoption of the first ten amendments.

As mentioned above, European constitutionalism was not necessarily democratic in the 19th century and even today some constitutions are still substantially monarchic or otherwise non-democratic by concept, particularly in the Arab world. Some of them might claim to be constitutionalist, as they embrace some (more or less serious) separation of powers and limitation of government and mostly provide for some kind of elected or semi-elected body as a legislative body. In that sense they can be to a certain extent compared to the typical German "constitutionalist" constitutions of the 19th century. As mentioned before, it is clear, however, that since the end of the Cold War the standard model of constitutionalism has become that of a substantial democracy.

There have been debates if the "Western" concept of democracy actually facilitates (economic) development. Research seems to support the assumption that democratic governance indeed has competitive advantages,[23] although there are obviously examples of economically progressing non-democratic countries as well as examples of poorly-performing democracies. Most discussed is the comparison of development in China and India. At least democracy seems to prevent the worst forms of failure, if Amartya Sen's argument is still correct that there have been no major famines in democracies.[24]

III. Fundamental Rights

Modern constitutions typically guarantee individual rights. The Twentieth Century Constitution[25] has overcome the concept of the organizational

23 See Sorensen, *Democracy and Democratization*, 2008; Przeworski et al., *Democracy and Development*, 2000.

24 See Sen, *Development as Freedom*, 2000.

25 Quint, "What is a Twentieth-Century Constitution?," 2008.

statute. Not only traditional "negative" rights, but also social and economic rights are a standard content of modern constitutions. They promise development in the sense that they promise freedom and perspectives for *individual* development. The idea seems so compelling that even the most dictatorial regimes typically provide them as lip service.

As with democracy and the rule of law there have been discussions concerning whether the constitutional guarantee of rights facilitates development. This question is in fact too broad to be answered in this paper. With the end of the Cold War, economic reform was on the agenda in many countries, the global financial organizations such as the World Bank and IMF and others focused much on contract law, property rights and effective judicial structures (Washington Consensus).[26] Interestingly however, fairly unsecure property rights have not prevented the amazing economic growth and investment activities in some countries like China. Furthermore, basic rights have sometimes been interpreted in ways fundamentally in contrast to developmental needs or even human dignity in its core.[27] Constitutional property rights are not a passe-partout to good developmental policies, as the ideology of the Washington Consensus suggested, they can also block development by hindering reasonable allocation of land rights and land development,[28] as well as fair labor law protections for workers and so on. Basic rights protecting employers and basic rights protecting employees or their unions can be disruptive for economic progress alike, if drafted and interpreted in the wrong way.

With respect to basic political rights the situation is equivalent to the question of democracy in general. Evidence seems to suggest that in general more freedom will have a positive effect on the long run, although "well organized" or otherwise lucky authoritarian regimes (sitting on vast natural resources or having mighty friends for geo-strategic reasons) might be successful for some time and seem to be the exception to the rule. Over time demand for basic rights and democracy will increase with development any-

---

26 On these issues see e.g. Dam, *The Law-Growth Nexus*, 2006, pp. 91-133.

27 See e.g. the infamous US Supreme Court case of Dred Scott v. Sandford, 60 U.S. 393 (1857), where slaves were considered just as any "merchandise". See Fehrenbacher, *Slavery, Law, and Politics*, 1981. Today the decision is widely considered the worst ever delivered by the United States Supreme Court.

28 This is the reason why Singapore abolished constitutional property rights in the early phase of its remarkable development; see Thio, "The passage of a generation," 2009, pp. 19-20.

way, as stable development relies on an educated people and education typically brings with it the demand for freedom and democracy. In Asia, states like Japan, Taiwan and South Korea have proven this assumption to be true.

IV. Rule of Law

Constitutionalism embodies and demands the rule of law. This is another link to development, as the rule of law is widely considered to be among the key requirements for sustainable development.[29] "Law and Development" is therefore a field with history, although it has had its fair share of crisis.[30] The linkage between constitutionalism and the rule of law is obvious[31] and thus so is the connection between constitutionalism and development.

In Germany, constitutionalism is said to be the crowning of rule of law *(Verfassungsstaat als Krönung des Rechtsstaats)*. This might sound somewhat over the top, but at least one can say that if a constitution is in place and respected, this surely is a strong indication of the rule of law, as the supreme law of the land is not only supreme on paper but in reality. But it should be stressed that in today's world of developing countries there is no typical sequencing in the sense that first a more or less perfect legal system is established and afterwards, as a topping, a good constitution is added. In fact it is often to the opposite: Facing the legacy of a desolate legal system, a new constitution is made first, promising everything from efficient and non-corrupt administrations to independent and competent courts. In other words: The constitution is not the lofty rooftop of the legal system, but its foundation. Constitutions promise (and have to deliver on) the rule of law; they are not based on it. Under such circumstances the relevance of constitutional provisions in this field obviously cannot be measured on the basis of their immediate fulfillment, but only on the seriousness with which a system tries to work towards it after adoption.

Constitutions will often invoke the "rule of law" explicitly. Such general clauses can be the basis of comprehensive doctrine, but lack precision at the

---

29 See Trebilcock and Daniels, *Rule of Law Reform and Development*, 2008; Carothers, *Promoting the Rule of Law Abroad*, 2006; Dam, *The Law-Growth Nexus*, 2006.

30 See Trubek and Santos, *The New Law and Economic Development*, 2006; Tamanaha, "The Primacy of Society and Failures of Law and Development," 2010.

31 See Rosenfeld, "The Rule of Law," 2001.

outset, as the rule of law is one of those principles on which everybody agrees because everybody can have his own interpretation of it.[32] There are formal and substantive theories varying in degree of depth. The relevance of general rule of law clauses will very much depend on the question of whether or not they are filled with life through interpretation (for example by a constitutional court). The development of an appropriate doctrine of the rule of law will often be facilitated by the fact that certain aspects are addressed specifically in basic rights provisions, general provisions on the legal system and chapters on the judiciary. If taken seriously, most modern constitutions adopted in developing countries do provide more or less comprehensive work plans for legal and judicial reform.

V. Development, Welfare and Prosperity

After all, the establishment of a constitutionalist system based on democracy, the rule of law and fundamental human rights ideally should provide a basis for the development of a prosperous economy. However, in order to support such an effect, modern constitutions often address the subject of development, welfare and prosperity directly. They formulate policies regarding these issues or even individual social and economic rights like the right to health, to minimum living standards, to education, to work etc. Constitutional experts from some developed countries which do not have such rights in their constitutions will sometimes be critical about such rights. Even in Germany you will often find skepticism, although the modesty of the German constitution in this regard has its reason in the very specific post war situation of 1949.[33] The critics basically believe that such provisions, particularly if formulated as "rights", either will give government too much power ("big government") or curtail it too much (limiting policy choices of democratically elected governments), or that they are in risk of being ineffective due to budgetary constraints (which might lead to a decline of respect

32 For the range of definitions see e.g. Trebilcock and Daniels, *Rule of Law Reform and Development*, 2008.

33 Social and economic rights were part of the Weimar Constitution of 1919 and currently they are also part of many of the constitutions of the German states (Bavaria, Rhineland-Palatinate, Hesse, Brandenburg etc.). On the federal level the German Constitutional Court has found significant social rights within the principles of human dignity in combination with the principle of the social state (Art. 1 and 20 of the German Constitution).

for the whole constitution). Obviously one can find plenty of constitutions in which social rights seem not to be matched by reality (not least the constitutions in the socialist tradition), whereas some "wealthy" states provide welfare without constitutionally guaranteeing it. When asked about the lack of social rights in her state's constitution, a Singaporean constitutional law scholar simply replied: "Do you want a right to a house or do you want a house?" However, despite such skepticism, some interesting examples illustrate that provisions on social rights can have very meaningful consequences, without being dangerous, both within developed and developing countries.[34]

VI. International Openness

One big pillar of modern constitutionalism is international openness. Just by adopting the concepts of democracy, basic rights and rule of law in a constitution a state will make a significant step to being considered an appropriate member in the society of states. Commitment to constitutionalism opens doors with regard to foreign assistance, as most bilateral and multilateral donors insist on constitutionalist policies. Commitment to international openness itself is a regular topic at least in European constitutions nowadays, with provisions on international law, European integration etc. constitutions in developing countries are often somewhat quiet on this topic,[35] which might be a result of more recently achieved sovereignty in many cases. Sometimes constitutions indicate even some opposition to international openness, e.g. with restrictive provisions on franchise for naturalized citizens and residence requirements or with restrictions on landownership for foreigners.[36] Regarding the latter, it's obviously a matter of circumstance and standpoint, if such provisions are obstacles or guarantees of proper development. Generally speaking it is obvious that the modern state in the 21st century needs to address questions of regional and international open-

34 See e.g. Davis, "Socio-economic rights," 2011, reporting case studies from South Africa, India and Brasil; see also Sunstein, *Designing Democracy*, 2001, pp. 221-238, referring to South Africa as an example for possible positive effects of social and economic rights.

35 With respect to Southeast Asia see Menzel, "Constitutionalism in Southeast Asia," 2009, pp. 27-29.

36 Foreign landownership is constitutionally forbidden in Thailand and Cambodia, for example.

ness to allow proper development. It seems appropriate to formulate at least some principles regarding this challenge in a modern constitution.

D. Building Constitutions and Constitutionalism

As mentioned, "Constitution Building" is a fairly new term. However, in recent years, a few organizations and authors have presented themselves as promoters of the concept. Constitution making is now an area of intensive comparative research and advice.[37]

I. Extraordinary Times and Places

Times of constitution making are regularly extraordinary times in the history of a state. When reviewing the literature on constitution building, the impression of exceptionality is further strengthened by the fact that it focuses mostly on particularly difficult situations. Most of the current literature on state, nation, and constitution building is about countries with very special circumstances, in other words about "extraordinary places"[38] or "battlegrounds places."[39] Constitution making is not always as troublesome as in these places, but obviously most of the attention goes where most of the problems are. The problems themselves are quite diverse. In recent years questions of constitution making in the context of foreign occupation or international administration have been under discussion.[40] The debate is often around "post conflict settings"[41], although in many of the cases the termi-

---

37 See International IDEA publications (Stockholm) including e.g. Böckenförde, Hedling and Wahiu, *A Practical Guide to Constitution Making*, 2011; Ghai and Galli, *Constitution Building*, 2006; Samuels, *Constitution Building Processes and Democratization*, 2006; for a recent collection of good insightful case studies see also Miller, *Framing the State in Times of Transition*, 2010.

38 Örücu, "Comparatists and Extraordinary Places," 2003.

39 Soltan, "Constitution Making at the Edges of Constitutional Order," 2008, p. 1409.

40 See Elkin, Ginsburg and Melton, "Baghdad, Tokyo, Kabul," 2008; Al-Ali, "Constitutional drafting and external influence," 2011.

41 Widner, "Constitution Writing in Post-Conflict Settings," 2008; Samuels, "Post-Conflict Peace-Building and Constitution-Making," 2006; Brandt, *Constitutional Assistance in Post-Conflict Countries*, 2005; International IDEA, *Constitution building after conflict*, 2011.

nology seems questionable, as the conflicts are regularly far from being resolved. Specific questions also arise in some countries with inhomogeneous populations which are divided along cultural, ethnic, linguistic or religious lines.[42] Furthermore, problems obviously arise in countries which have experienced times of harsh dictatorship, general lawlessness or even failed statehood as well as in countries with traditions of military coups.[43]

II. Constitution Making Process

Within the past several decades of massive change around the world, many nations have attempted to re-establish a new national identity, making a complete break with the past, and setting a course to a new future. The constitution making process in South Africa after the end of apartheid probably was the most inspiring of these endeavors. Here was a nation that transformed itself from a disgraceful, oppressive system to a modern democracy. The process was well thought through and produced first an interim constitution and afterwards a final constitution. With Nelson Mandela, there was a man who after decades of incarceration became the first President of the new South Africa, being modest and peaceful and not sticking to power after his original term was finished.

Looking at case studies, there seems not that much evidence that (apart from the model case of South Africa) a long, participatory and transparent process necessarily leads to more successful results. It should be remembered that one of the most successful democratic constitutions in Asia, the Japanese constitution of 1946, actually is the antipode of adequate constitutional process.[44] Kenya is sometimes mentioned as an example for strong and inclusive process but seems not to be such a strong case since the post electoral violence in 2008. Thailand's constitution of 1997 was the result of a long and comparatively transparent process, but its history ended in accordance with the country's very specific tradition with another military coup in 2006. Despite such reasons for caution, recent literature generally

---

42 See Choudhry, *Constitutional Design for Divided Societies*, 2008.

43 Two examples for coup traditions in Asia-Pacific are Thailand and Fiji. The general problem is particularly obvious in Africa. For a somewhat apologetic assessment of coup-traditions in Africa see Collier, *Wars, Guns and Votes*, 2009.

44 For a short summary on the constitutional oktroi by the USA and the question of legitimacy of the constitution see Matsui, *The Constitution of Japan*, 2011, pp.7-21.

suggests that inclusiveness and participation are crucial. A significant part of the expert community of constitution builders strongly emphasizes this point, maybe not surprisingly, as there is a job-market for constitution-building-consultants to create and defend. On a more serious level, there is obviously an argument to be made, that under the presumption of a democracy and the people's sovereignty in the participatory process, good discourse has an advantage in giving legitimacy, and there might be a hope that such a process increases the acceptability of results for those involved. The right to participate in constitutional process also is in line with the general tendency to a right to democracy in international law.[45] There is a risk, however, that long and exhaustive processes may cause the loss of momentum, which might have been there in the initial phase of political transition which is behind the constitution making process. In other words: There is a risk that discussion does not lead to agreement, but to heavier disagreement. There are also two possible outcomes of extensive process when it comes to the substantial quality of a constitution: Discussion might lead to improvement due to elimination of weak points, but it might also lead to additional inconsistencies, vagueness (provisions which only veil disagreement) or over-regulation (as consequence of mutual distrust). It is evident anyway that good substance needs a logical, systematic and well informed approach. The political process and public participation typically create a certain amount of chaos and compromises that might not be very well thought through. You simply cannot draft a good law or a good constitution in an assembly of hundreds of people, being under the pressure of even more external groups, demonstrations, media, etc. You need a draft (or several drafts) first and for that you need a small group and within that a very small group of knowledgeable people who provide a first basis for discussion. Maybe ninety percent of a constitutional text will often be undisputed; if a wisely selected small team prepares a first draft. The framers must concentrate on the "hot" issues. It is not so much about "Proposals vs. Processes,"[46] it is about combining both.

45 See Franck and Thiruvengadam, "Norms of International Law," 2010; Hart, "Constitution Making," 2010.

46 Horowitz, *Constitutional Design*, 1999; Horowitz, "*Conciliatory* Institutions and Constitutional Processes," 2008.

III. Constitutional Design

What should a constitution look like in order to have a positive effect on development? Should it be short or long, easy or difficult to amend, contain rights or not (and which), be monarchic or republican, presidential or parliamentarian, majoritarian or consensual, unicameral or bicameral, federal or not, establishing judicial review or even have a constitutional court?

Constitution writing involves a huge number of choices and there is plenty of literature concerning this issue.[47] A lot of cases have been made in favor of one or another model. The most important rule seems to be that each and every country needs some tailor made solution. Constitutions cannot be "xeroxed" and there is no worldwide "model constitution" available as a free download for local use.[48] There are however, components available for use and this finds its expression in what has been labeled the "IKEA-theory" of constitution making.[49] Any implication that something is wrong with this should be rejected. Why should not constitution builders around the world try to assemble best parts from around the world to construct their own constitution? The assumption that constitutional concepts are about culture and therefore unsuitable for transposition is misleading. To the knowledge of this author, no state has ever claimed intellectual property rights with respect to constitutional provisions. Furthermore, the migration of concepts and the "import" of new thoughts should not be generally rejected as being anti-traditional. New constitutions will often be based on the idea that some traditions and aspects of legal or political culture need change. E.g. women's rights are guaranteed because they are not yet respected or anti-corruption bodies are established because of the existent of a culture of corruption. It is true that borrowing from other systems should be done under careful consideration of all circumstances, but that's the same as at IKEA: Intelligent

---

47 For a few recent publications see Lutz, *Principles of Constitutional Design*, 2006; Schneier, *Crafting Constitutional Democracies*, 2006; Murphy, *Constitutional Democracy*, 2007; Sartori, *Comparative Constitutional Engineering*, 1997.

48 "Model constitutions" have been developed within certain federal states etc. A "model state constitution", promoted by the National Municipal League, exists since 1921 in the United States, see Tarr, *Understanding State Constitutions*, 1998, p.152. Much more consequently, the States within the former Soviet Union were mostly provided with standardized constitutions.

49 See Frankenberg, "Constitutional Transfer," 2010, p. 563. "IKEA" is the largest furniture store chain in the world, mainly selling furniture to "take away" and assemble it by "do it yourself" at home.

people will buy bookshelves if they fit into their imagination for the interior design of their homes, not just because they look good in a furniture shop.

IV. From Constitution to Constitutionalism

A constitution must be implemented before a nation truly adopts constitutionalism. From the day a constitution becomes law, it has to prove that it works. This often proves difficult. Even the oldest of all written constitutions, the Constitution of the United States of America, has had its fare share of crises. In Germany, the initial attempts to establish constitutionalism failed altogether, the first 1848/9 within short a very short time, the second after Second World War within little more than a decade. With decolonization many countries got democratic constitutions in the first place, just to experience authoritarianism subsequently. Constitutions were changed or abused to accommodate the need of dictators, or they were simply ignored. Southeast Asia's history in the second half of the 20th century has some examples for constitutions without constitutionalism, from the abusive formalism in the Philippines of General Marcos to the meaningless constitution of Indonesia under Suharto to the absurdity of the Cambodian constitution under the Khmer Rouge. Here and elsewhere the early generations of post colonialism constitutions was not very successful.[50] But since the late 1980 s things have changed. New constitutions have been adopted and the old ones have been amended. In some cases, basic rights have been added. Constitutional courts have been established and have started operating (with varying success). Although things are still far from perfect, it is clear that the relevance of constitutions and constitutional discourses has increased in many places. And the more constitutions are taken seriously as commitments, the more they might contribute to development. Constitutional texts alone are without relevance, only when taken seriously do they matter. If taken seriously, they can not only be legal texts, but also function like policy papers, directing governments to pursue proper development and providing help to civil society in the often difficult public discourse with state authorities. It is clear, however, that constitutions do not fulfill any of such roles by themselves. They need implementation in political and legal life, which

50 See Bryde, "Constitutional Law in 'old' and 'new' Law and Development," 2010.

regularly is the more demanding and more time consuming process, compared to drafting and adoption.

V. International Cooperation for Constitutionalism

Constitutions are constructed based on experiences from home and abroad. One only needs to read the Federalist Papers to realize to what extent the U.S. Constitution is based on experiences from throughout history and many other nations. The first democratic national constitution drafted in Germany (1848) as well was much influenced by experiences of the United States, France, Belgium, and elsewhere. Obviously, the "migration of constitutional ideas"[51] is nothing new. It has always been helped by traveling experts, but whereas a hundred years ago it was quite an effort to embark on a ship for overseas travel, today a delegation from a Southeast Asian country planning to establish a constitutional court might be able to visit four or five such courts in Europe on a two week "study trip" sponsored by an international agency.

International Standards for Constitutionalism, "The Rise of World Constitutionalism", as described by Bruce Ackermann,[52] is undeniable. Even where the rise of democracy has no firm ground yet, talk about the constitution is typically abundant. To have a constitution and to give it some appearance of legitimacy seems to be the litmus test of modern statehood. Regarding process, there might be no strict international law provisions on how to organize constitution making, but there are certain standards evolving which define legitimacy from an international perspective.[53] Furthermore, the contents of constitutions increasingly have strong similarities.[54] There may still be exceptions to this trend (Myanmar 2010), but more and more constitutions follow the pattern of democracy, basic rights and the rule of law, separated powers of the legislature, executive and judiciary, as well as provide for some vertical structure in state organization (federalism, decentralization, local government etc.). However, despite a convergence based on such general concepts there is still much variety and nothing prevents local constitution builders from looking for local solutions. As with human

51 Choudhry, *The Migration of Constitutional Ideas*, 2006.
52 Ackermann, "The Rise of World Constitutionalism," 1997.
53 See Franck and Thiruvengadam, "Norms of International Law," 2010.
54 See Saunders, "Towards a Global Constitutional Gene Pool," 2009.

beings, the common gene pool does not and should not prevent differences in many details.

VI. Internationalized Constitution Building

From the very early times the theory of the constitution maker being independent form outside influences (autochthonous) was often just that: a theory. Napoleon Bonaparte, who had installed his brother Jérome as a king of Westphalia in the early 19th century, sent him a letter saying: "Mon Frère, vous trouverez ci-joint la Constitution de votre royaume“ (My brother, please find attached the Constitution for your kingdom). Ever since there have been cases of fairly evident imposition of constitutions from outside. Some famous cases are the Japanese Constitution of 1946 and again the Constitution of Bosnia-Herzegovina of 1992.[55] The drafts for the Japanese and the Bosnian Constitution were both made in English and even submitted to the local bodies in English. Recently, constitution making has been an internationalized enterprise on a few occasions. Philipp Dann and Zaid Al-Ali[56], who have taken East Timor, Iraq and Sudan as case studies, speak of an "internationalized pouvoir constituant." Elkin, Ginsburg and Melton[57] have chosen Iraq, Japan and Afghanistan to discuss the more specific question of constitution making in occupied states. Obviously the topic of sovereignty and acceptance are at the core of the problems arising in such circumstances.

International or foreign influence is not always as "forceful" as discussed above and the situation is typically quite different where no foreign occupation, previous military intervention or international administration is part of the setting. But even where "sovereignty" of the state is not in doubt, international "help" in the constitutionalization process might be abundant. A current showcase is Nepal, where numerous international and non-governmental organizations have been trying for years to assist a difficult process of drafting a new constitution. Local constitution makers here and everywhere will have to decide, which concepts are helpful and suitable under

55 For a balanced account on the latter see O'Brien, "The Dayton Constitution of Bosnia and Herzegovina," 2010.

56 See Dann and Al-Ali, "The Internationalized Pouvoir Constituant," 2006

57 See Elkin, Ginsburg and Melton, "Baghdad, Tokyo, Kabul," 2008.

local circumstances. To ignore them, just because they are "from outside", would be as wrong as just copying them without further thought.

E. Conclusion

Constitutionalism is a concept of limited and controlled government, ideally based on the principles of democracy, human rights and the rule of law. To achieve a system roughly based on these concepts or even seriously aiming for it, is a major development success as the fulfillment of each of these concepts is not only an enhancement of human freedom in itself, but will by most accounts typically create a better environment for a socially balanced economic and human development on the long run as well. As mentioned before, nearly all states with "first world" wealth are constitutionalist today, if one does not take into account the few states with wealth based on oil. In Asia, Singapore is often mentioned as an exception, but it should be noted that although Singapore probably cannot be called fully constitutionalist with regard to standards of democracy and political liberties, it has a constitution which is quite strictly followed (although often amended) and it has a good reputation for its high rule of law standards.[58] The idea, that what has been possible in the small city state of Singapore can also be possible in China, is likely to be unrealistic anyway. In Asia, which is often seen as the region most fundamentally opposed to some of the values of Western constitutionalism, there is plenty of evidence that increased development will finally reinforce just those ideas and concepts. Taiwan and South Korea are striking examples,[59] Singapore might follow sooner than often assumed.

The development of constitutionalism (properly defined) is a direct contribution to the development of a modern national society. To ask only about constitutionalism's contribution to economic development is misleading. Constitutionalism (like more generally the rule of law) is an end in itself, as its main achievement is the enhancement of freedom in the framework of the modern state. Constitutionalism is an evolutionary achievement.[60] The difficult question is how to develop constitutionalism, particularly under the conditions of a developing state. The obvious three steps are the constitution

58 For excellent accounts and analysis of Singapore's constitutional development see Thio and Tan, *Evolution of a Revolution*, 2009.

59 See Yeh and Chang, "The Emergence of East Asian Constitutionalism," 2011.

60 Luhmann, "Die Verfassung als evolutionäre Errungenschaft," 1990.

making process, constitutional design and (most challenging) the constitutionalization of the legal and political system. Solutions in each step of the process can be different depending on circumstances, and weaknesses in the first two steps can turn out to be less dramatic if step number three works well. Recently, in Myanmar a very flawed process has produced a flawed constitution by any international standards. However, since its adoption a promising process seems to have gained momentum and even this flawed constitution might end up as a strange evolutionary link between military dictatorship and constitutional governance. Undoubtedly Myanmar will have to replace or fundamentally reform this constitution in the future. In retrospective, its initial version will then probably be seen as the failed attempt of a regime to cement its power despite the forces of history, which turned out to facilitate necessary transition.

Even more than law in general,[61] constitutions are bridges in many ways. They are bridges between politics and law and between the past and future. They are often deeply rooted in a country's legal, political and societal traditions, but their job is to make the countries fit for the future. A good constitution will combine realism with vision. It will build on good traditions and it will (try to) break with bad ones. But as real bridges sometimes collapse under the burden of everyday traffic or remain empty, constitutions are often in danger of not being up to the needs of the people. Constitutional promises are not self-fulfilling; they need people and institutions filling their promises with life. If those do not exist or emerge, they will be bridges to nowhere.

Works cited

Ackerman, Bruce, "The Rise of World Constitutionalism," *Virginia Law Review* 83 (1997): 771-797.

Al-Ali, Zaid, "Constitutional drafting and external influence," in *Comparative Constitutional Law*, eds. Tom Ginsburg and Rosalind Dixon, Cheltenham: Edward Elgar, 2001, pp. 77-95.

Alexander, Larry, ed., *Constitutionalism: Philosophical Foundations*, Cambridge: Cambridge University Press, 1998.

Alkire, Sabine, "Human Development: Definitions, Critiques, and Related Concepts," *UNDP Human Development Research Papers,* No. 2010/01.

61 Bodenheimer, "Law as a Bridge between Is and Ought," 1988.

Böckenförde, Markus, Nora Hedling, and Winluck Wahiu, *A Practical Guide to Constitution Making*, Stockholm: International IDEA, 2011.

Bodenheimer, Edgar, "Law as a Bridge between Is and Ought," *Ratio Juris* 1 (1988): 137-153.

Bogdandy, Armin von, "State-building, Nation-building and Constitutional Politics in Post-conflict Situations: Conceptual Clarifications and an Appraisal of Different Approaches," *Max Planck Yearbook of United Nations Law* 9 (2005): 579-613.

Brandt, Michele, *Constitutional Assistance in Post-Conflict Countries – The UN Experience: Cambodia, East Timor & Afghanistan*, United Nations Development Programme, 2005.

Bryde, Brun-Otto, "Constitutional Law in 'old' and 'new' Law and Development," *Verfassung und Recht in Übersee* 10 (2010): 10-15.

Bull, Carolyn, *No Entry without Strategy: Building the Rule of Law Abroad*, Washington DC: United Nations University Press, 2008.

Call, Charles T., and Vanessa Wyeth, eds., *Building States to Build Peace*, Boulder CO: Lynne Rienner, 2008.

Carothers, Thomas, *Promoting the Rule of Law Abroad: In Search of Knowledge*, Washington DC: Carnegie Endowment for International Peace, 2006.

Chesterman, Simon, Michael Ignatieff, and Ramesh Chandra Thakur, eds., *Making States Work: State Failure and the Crisis of Governance*, Tokyo: United Nations University Press, 2005.

Chimni, Bhupinder, "The Sen Conception of Development and Contemporary International Law Discourse: Some Parallels," *The Law and Development Review* 1 (2008): 2-22.

Choudhry, Sujit, ed., *The Migration of Constitutional Ideas*, Cambridge: Cambridge University Press, 2006.

Choudhry, Sujit, ed., *Constitutional Design for Divided Societies: Integration or Accomodation?*, Oxford: Oxford University Press, 2008.

Collier, Paul, *Wars, Guns, and Votes: Democracy in Dangerous Places*, New York: Harper Perennial, 2009.

Dam, Kenneth W., *The Law-Growth Nexus: The Rule of Law and Economic Development*, Washington DC: Brookings Institution Press, 2006.

Dann, Philipp, and Zaid Al-Ali, "The Internationalized Pouvoir Constituant – Constitution Making Under External Influence in Iraq, Sudan and East Timor," *Max Planck Yearbook of United Nations Law* 10 (2006): 423-463.

Davis, Dennis M., "Socio-economic rights: has the promise of eradicating the divide between first and second generation rights been fulfilled?," in *Comparative Constitutional Law*, eds. Tom Ginsburg and Rosalind Dixon, Cheltenham: Edward Elgar, 2011, pp. 519-531.

Dobbins, James, Seth G. Jones, Keith Crane, and Beth Cole DeGrasse, *The Beginner's Guide to Nation Building*, Santa Monica CA: Rand Corporation, 2007.

Egidy, Stefanie, "Casenote – The Fundamental Right to Guarantee of Subsistence Minimum in the Hartz IV Decision of the German Constitutional Court," *German Law Journal* 11 (2010): 1961-1982.

Elkin, Zachary, Tom Ginsburg, and James Melton, "Baghdad, Tokyo, Kabul ...: Constitution Making in Occupied States," *William and Mary Law Review* 49 (2008): 1139-1178.

Fehrenbacher, Don Edward, *Slavery, Law and Politics: The Dred Scott Case in Historical Perspective*, New York: Oxford University Press, 1981.

Franck, Thomas M., and Arun K. Thiruvengadam, "Norms of International Law Relating to the Constitution-Making Process," in *Framing the State in Times of Transition*, ed. L.E. Miller, Washington DC: United States Institute of Peace, 2010, pp. 3-19.

Frankenberg, Günter, "Constitutional Transfer: The IKEA Theory Revisited," *International Journal of Constitutional Law* 8 (2010): 563-579.

Fukuyama, Francis, ed., *Nation Building: Beyond Afghanistan and Iraq*, Baltimore: John Hopkins University Press, 2006.

Gebhard, Julia, "Apartheid," in *The Max Planck Encyclopedia of Public International Law*, ed. Rüdiger Wolfrum, Oxford: Oxford University Press, 2012, Vol. I, pp. 461-468.

Ghai, Yash, and Guido Galli, *Constitution Building: Processes and Democratization*, Stockholm: International IDEA, 2006.

Ghani, Ashraf, and Claire Lockhart, *Fixing Failed States: A Framework for Rebuilding a Fractured World*, Oxford: Oxford University Press, 2008.

Ginsburg, Tom and Albert H.Y. Chen, eds., *Administrative Law and Governance in Asia: Comparative Perspectives*, Abingdon: Routledge, 2009.

Gordon, Scott, *Controlling the State: Constitutionalism from ancient Athens to Today*, Cambridge MA: Harvard University Press, 1999.

Harding, Andrew, and Penelope Nicholson, eds., *New Courts in Asia*, Abingdon: Routledge, 2010.

Harding, Andrew, and Peter Leyland, eds., *Constitutional Courts: A Comparative Study*, London: Wildy, Simmonds & Hill, 2009.

Hart, Vivien, "Constitution Making and the Right to Take Part in a Public Affair," in *Framing the State in Times of Transition*, ed. L.E. Miller, Washington DC: United States Institute of Peace, 2010, pp. 20-54.

Heun, Werner, "Constitutionalism in Germany," *East Asian Law Journal* 1 (2010): 91-104.

Heun, Werner, *The Constitutional System of Germany: A Contextual Analysis*, Portland OR: Hart Publishing, 2011.

Hill, Clauspeter and Jörg Menzel, *Constitutionalism in Southeast Asia*, 3 volumes, Singapore: Konrad-Adenauer-Stiftung, 2008/2010.

Hirsch, Moshe, "Developing Countries," in *The Max Planck Encyclopedia of Public International Law*, ed. Rüdiger Wolfrum, Oxford: Oxford University Press, 2012, Vol. III, pp. 70-71.

Horowitz, Donald L., *Constitutional Design: Proposals versus Processes*, 1999 (available at www.ssrn.com).

Horowitz, Donald L., "Conciliatory Institutions and Constitutional Processes in Post-Conflict States," *Mary and William Law Review* 49 (2008): 1213-1248.

International IDEA, *Constitution building after conflict: External support to a sovereign process*, Stockholm, 2011.

Luhmann, Niklas, "Die Verfassung als evolutionäre Errungenschaft," *Rechtshistorisches Journal* 9 (1990): 176–220.

Lutz, Donald S., *Principles of Constitutional Design*, Cambridge: Cambridge University Press, 2006.

Matsui, Shigenori, *The Constitution of Japan: A Contextual Analysis*, Oxford: Hart Publishing, 2011.

Menzel, Jörg, "Constitutionalism in Southeast Asia: Some Comparative Perspectives," in *Constitutionalism in Southeast Asia*, eds. Clauspeter Hill and Jörg Menzel, Vol. III, Singapore: Konrad-Adenauer-Stiftung, 2009, pp. 9-31.

Miller, Laurel, *Framing the State in Times of Transition: Case Studies in Constitution Making*, Washington: United States Institute of Peace, 2010.

Murphy, Walter F., *Constitutional Democracy: Creating and Maintaining a Just Political Order*, Baltimore: John Hopkins University Press, 2007.

O'Brien, James C., "The Dayton Constitution of Bosnia and Herzegovina," in *Framing the State in Times of Transition: Case Studies in Constitution Making*, ed. L.E. Miller, Washington DC: United States Institute of Peace, 2010, pp. 332-349.

Örücu, Esin, "Comparatists and Extraordinary Places" *in Comparative Legal Studies: Traditions and Transitions*, eds. Pierre Legrand and Roderick Munday, Cambridge: Cambridge University Press, 2003, pp. 467-489.

Paris, Roland, and Timothy D. Sisk, eds., *The Dilemmas of Statebuilding: Confronting the Contradictions of Postwar Peace Operations*, New York: Routledge, 2009.

Przeworski, Adam, Michel E. Alvarez, José Antonio Chaibub, Fernando Limongi, *Democracy and Development: Political Institutions and Well-Being in the World, 1950-1990*, Cambridge: Cambridge University Press, 2000.

Quint, Peter, "What is a Twentieth-Century Constitution?" *University of Maryland School of Law, Legal Studies Research Paper*, No. 2008-7 (available at www.ssrn.com).

Robbers, Gerhard, ed., *Encyclopedia of World Constitutions*, 3 volumes, New York: Facts on File, 2007.

Rosenfeld, Michael, "The Rule of Law, and the Legitimacy of Constitutional Democracy," *Cardozo Law School, Public Law Research Paper,* No. 36 (2001).

Sajó, András, *Limiting Government: An Introduction to Constitutionalism*, Budapest: Central European Press, 1999.

Samuels, Kirsti, "Post-Conflict Peace-Building and Constitution Making," *Chicago Journal of International Law* 6 (2006): 1-20.

Samuels, Kirsti, *Constitution Building Processes and Democratization: A Discussion of Twelve Case Studies*, Stockholm: International IDEA, 2006.

Sartori, Giovanni, "Constitutionalism: A Preliminary Discussion," *American Political Science Review* 56 (1962): 853-864.

Sartori, Giovanni, *Comparative Constitutional Engineering: An Enquiry into Structures, Incentives and Outcomes*, 2nd ed., New York: New York University Press, 1997.

Saunders, Cheryl, "Towards a Global Constitutional Gene Pool," *National Taiwan University Law Review* 4, no.3 (2009): 1-38.

Schneier, Edward, *Crafting Constitutional Democracies: The Politics of Institutional Design*, Lanham MD and Oxford: Rowman & Littlefield, 2006.

Sen, Amartya, *Development as Freedom*, New York: Anchor Books, 2000.

Soltan, Karol Edward, "Constitution Making at the Edges of Constitutional Order," *Mary and William Law Review* 48 (2008): 1409-1442.

Sorensen, Georg, *Democracy and Democratization: Processes and Prospects in a Changing World*, 3rd ed., Boulder CO: Westview Press, 2008.

Stromseth, Jane, David Wippman, and Rosa Brooks, *Can Might Make Rights? Building the Rule of Law after Military Interventions*, Cambridge: Cambridge University Press, 2006.

Sunstein, Cass, *Designing Democracy: What Constitutions do*, Oxford: Oxford University Press, 2001.

Tamanaha, Brian Z., "The Primacy of Society and Failures of Law and Development: Decades of Stubborn Refusal to Learn," *Washington University in St. Louis Research Paper* No. 10-03-02 (2010), (available at www.ssrn.com).

Tarr, Alan G., *Understanding State Constitutions*, Princeton: Princeton University Press, 1998.

Thio, Li-ann, "The passage of a generation: Revisiting the report of the 1966 Constitutional Commission," in *Evolution of a Revolution: Forty Years of the Singapore Constitution*, eds. Li-ann Thio and Kevin YL Tan, Abingdon: Routledge, 2009.

Thio, Li-ann and Kevin YL Tan, eds., *Evolution of a Revolution: Forty Years of the Singapore Constitution*, Abingdon: Routledge, 2009.

Trebilcock, Michael J., and Ronald J. Daniels, *Rule of Law Reform and Development: Charting the Fragile Path of Progress*, Cheltenham: Edward Elgar, 2008.

Trubek, David M., and Alvaro Santos, *The New Law and Economic Development: A Critical Appraisal*, Cambridge: Cambridge University Press, 2006.

Widner, Jennifer, "Constitution Writing in Post-Conflict Settings: An Overview," *William and Mary Law Review* 49 (2008): 1513-1541.

Yeh, Jiunn-Rong, and Wen-Chen Chang, "The Emergence of East Asian Constitutionalism: Features in Comparison," *American Journal of Comparative Law* 59 (2011): 805-839.

Part II:

Principles and Structures

The Notion of the "Rule of Law" and its Development in German Constitutional History

Bodo Pieroth

A. Introduction

"Rule of law" like "democracy", is a term capable of many interpretations. In fact, I have just proved the point by using it to translate the German term "Rechtsstaat". Although "rule of law" in the Anglo-American legal world is not identical to "Rechtsstaat" the terms do display similarities insofar as both form part of the overarching evolution of liberal thought and political systems in Europe and North America.[1] For this reason, there is no better translation.

German legal development is a topic of great interest outside Germany for two reasons. The first is that some important elements of the modern rule of law have been developed in Germany. Take for example, the "principle of proportionality", which represents the most important benchmark in the jurisprudence of the German Federal Constitutional Court and which has also been adopted by the European Court of Justice. This principle was developed at the end of the 19th century by the Supreme Administrative Court of Prussia in the field of police law.[2] Or take the notion of "constitutional jurisdiction", regarded by many as the high-water mark in the rule of law's development. This was incorporated into the Austrian constitution in 1920 thanks to the huge influence of the Austrian Hans Kelsen, who is regarded as a great jurist in the German-speaking world.[3] The German Federal Constitutional Court, which was established by the Basic Law in 1949, exerts such influence over the political process and enjoys such standing in the eyes of the people that it has the distinction of being a leading exporter of legal

1 See MacCormick, "Der Rechtsstaat und die rule of law," 1984.
2 See Pieroth, Schlink, and Kniesel, *Polizei- und Ordnungsrecht*, 2010, § 1 paras. 12 f.
3 Art. 137 ff.; reprinted in Gosewinkel and Masing, *Die Verfassungen in Europa*, 2006, pp. 1550 ff.

ideas.[4] In particular, it has provided a model for many states in Central and Eastern Europe following the collapse of the Soviet Union.[5]

The second reason why the development of the rule of law in Germany is of such interest to the world at large lies in its very chequered history – especially considering the way it was perverted under National Socialism.[6] This example teaches us that the rule of law has undergone many transformations during its development and therefore cannot be set in stone for all time. Indeed, "A proper understanding of this term is only possible if one is aware of its historical development."[7] I am convinced that, on the whole (*i.e.* leaving aside the break in development just mentioned), the rule of law has progressed to ever greater levels of refinement and realization. This raises the question of whether it is possible to transfer the rule of law from one country to another. Here, German constitutional history demonstrates "that the rule of law is not an hermetically-sealed concept that can only be adopted in its entirety or not at all, but a graduated principle that was only brought to fruition in Germany step-by-step".[8]

B. The Rule of Law as a Concept

It is no coincidence that the term "rule of law" was coined in Germany around the year 1800.[9] Although individual elements are certainly older, those that reflect the modern understanding of this concept stem from the enlightenment and great revolutions in North America and France.[10] In this respect, we can trace the rule of law back to two basic notions: the subjugation of the

4 See Limbach, "Das Bundesverfassungsgericht und der Grundrechtsschutz in Europa," 2001, p. 2919; with regard to the principle of proportionality also Lepsius, "Sicherheit und Freiheit," 2010, p. 32.

5 See Pieroth, "Deutscher Verfassungsexport," 2010.

6 More recent overviews: See Boldt, *Deutsche Verfassungsgeschichte*, 1993; Brandt, *Der lange Weg in die demokratische Moderne*, 1998; Frotscher and Pieroth, *Verfassungsgeschichte,* 2010; Grimm, *Deutsche Verfassungsgeschichte*, 1988; Kotulla, *Deutsche Verfassungsgeschichte*, 2008; Stern, *Das Staatsrecht,* Vol. V, 2000; Willoweit, *Deutsche Verfassungsgeschichte*, 2009.

7 Böckenförde, "Entstehung und Wandel des Rechtsstaatsbegriffs," 1969, p. 54.

8 Grimm, "Stufen der Rechtsstaatlichkeit," 2009, p. 596.

9 See Stolleis, "Rechtsstaat," 1990, col. 369.

10 See Hofmann, "Geschichtlichkeit und Universalitätsanspruch des Rechtsstaats," 1995, p. 12; Scheuner, "Die neuere Entwicklung des Rechtsstaats," 1978, p. 201.

state to the authority of law and the autonomy of the individual. I will deal with each in turn.

I. The Subjugation of the State to the Law

A state subjugated to the authority of law is one that is ruled according to law rather than the will of the ruler. This notion is most powerfully expressed in the Constitution of Massachusetts of 1780 which refers to a "government of laws and not of men".[11] In this sense, the law displays the following characteristics: it is both general and abstract in character (in other words, it does not seek to regulate individual, specific cases but rather a wide range of cases that could arise in the future); the law cannot be changed while it is being enforced and, finally, it must be applied equally. As a result, the governance of a state subjugated to the law "represents the opposite of arbitrary rule"[12].

Furthermore, this law exhibits a *binding character* – in other words, sanctions are imposed in cases of non-compliance as well as infringement. One refers to the primacy of law.[13] There are of course areas, even in a state subject to the rule of law, which are partly or even wholly unregulated. However, the point is that where the law does apply, it enjoys precedence over all other norms – be they economic, moral, ethical, religious or political. There is no doubt that some attribute greater significance to these non-legal norms but in a state subject to the rule of law they can only bind the state to the degree permitted by law (*e.g.* through the legal right to practice one's religion or adhere to one's conscience). It is the law that determines the extent of these freedoms.

This leads us to the important observation that the binding character of the law does not only apply to the citizens of a state but also to the state itself, its organs, officials and civil servants: "Under the rule of law, the state does not have the right to position itself above the law."[14] The state must also

11 Part. the first, Art. XXX; reproduced in Dippel, *Verfassungen der Welt*, 2007, Vol. 1, Part IV, pp. 19 ff.

12 Grimm, "Stufen der Rechtsstaatlichkeit," 2009, p. 596; cf. also Schmidt-Aßmann, "Der Rechtsstaat," 2004, paras. 21ff.

13 See Hesse, *Grundzüge des Verfassungsrechts*, 1995, paras. 195 ff.

14 Grimm, "Stufen der Rechtsstaatlichkeit," 2009, p. 596; Hesse, *Grundzüge des Verfassungsrechts*, 1995, para. 195.

comply with the law despite the fact that it would be difficult or even undesirable to do so (*e.g.* where assets of great importance are involved or necessity dictates otherwise). This is because it is only possible to guarantee the rule of law if one accepts that it will apply no matter how unfavourable the circumstances may be.

Last but not least, law also consists of *form*. In a state subject to the rule of law, formalities, responsibilities and procedures play an especially important role. They constitute the framework that enable the separation of powers to be realized.[15] This latter concept is a product of the enlightenment and demands a constitution. At this point, we arive at the second basic notion underlying the rule of law.

II. The Autonomy of the Individual

The autonomy of the individual represents the essence of human rights, which have formed an integral component of the rule of law ever since the revolutions in North America and France. "The rule of law enshrines the protection of the citizen's personal and political freedom."[16] Here too, we can attribute this result to long-standing traditions and lines of development. An important contribution was made by the rationalist natural law or law of reason from the 17th and 18th centuries. It adhered to the following principles: first, the law applies to all people regardless of location and time (universality); it is not founded on religious belief, unlike the natural law of the middle ages (secularity) and, thirdly, it is based on a mathematical logic (rationality).[17] It was the law of reason that promoted human rights as a generally applicable foundation of law.

Human rights also revealed the state's *raison d'être* in a completely different light, as the American Declaration of Independence of 4 July 1776 emphatically states: "We hold these truths to be self-evident: that all men are created equal; that they are endowed by their Creator with certain unalienable Rights; that among these are Life, Liberty, and the pursuit of Happiness. That to secure these rights, Governments are instituted among Men,

---

15 Comprehensively and most recently, see Möllers, *Gewaltengliederung*, 2005; summarizing: Maurer, *Staatsrecht I*, 2010, pp. 359 ff.

16 Scheuner, "Die neuere Entwicklung des Rechtsstaats," 1978, p. 207.

17 See Senn, *Rechtsgeschichte*, 2007, pp. 244 f.

deriving their just powers from the consent of the governed."[18] This declaration repeatedly drives home the revolutionary idea that human rights represent the foundation and purpose of the state, that the state is dependent from its citizens and only exists at all for their sake. The need for a constitution and the imposition of constraints on the power of the state as the means of guaranteeing freedom and equality date from the same period[19] and have formed part of the rule of law ever since.

C. Historical Epochs and Variants of the Rule of Law

I. Early Elements and Conditions

1. The Middle Ages

A legal system which displays the aforementioned constitutional attributes is the legacy of a European cultural heritage which stretches far into the past. It originated during the 11th and 12th centuries and is the result of a dispute between the Emperor and the Pope, the creation of a legal science based on Roman law and the cultural awakening of the municipalities. Law came to be regarded as independent from the spheres of politics and religion; this led to the idea that law – in the sense of a basic, constitutional law – could also bind the ruler (subject to its formal amendment).[20] The fact that feudal society was based on contractual – and therefore legal relationships – makes one realize that, in the intellectual circles of medieval European society, law was nothing less than an essential ingredient of human consciousness.[21]

Law, however, needs judges: its effectiveness depends on there being a neutral body that settles legal disputes. Broadening the scope of legal protection proved a highly significant development in this respect: indeed, it has been described as a "cornerstone of the rule of law".[22] Important progress

---

18 Reproduced in Rotunda, Nowak and Young, *Treatise on Constitutional Law*, 1986, Appendix A, pp. 524 ff.

19 See Hofmann, "Geschichtlichkeit und Universalitätsanspruch des Rechtsstaats," 1995, pp. 15 ff.; Stolleis, "Rechtsstaat," 1990, col. 369.

20 See Hofmann, "Geschichtlichkeit und Universalitätsanspruch des Rechtsstaats," 1995, pp. 7 f.; Scheuner, "Die neuere Entwicklung des Rechtsstaats," 1978, pp. 191 ff.

21 See Gurjewitsch, *Das Weltbild des mittelalterlichen Menschen*, 1989, p. 208.

22 Schmidt-Aßmann, "Der Rechtsstaat," 2004, para. 70 citing R. Herzog.

was made in this field during the late middle ages in Germany. In response to the wide-spread experience of injustice caused by wars, feuds and various eruptions of violence, the Imperial Diet of Worms in 1495 passed the "Eternal Peace between States" (*der Ewige Landfriede*) and established the Imperial Court (*Reichskammergericht*). This was a quasi-judicial dispute settlement body which, for the first time, recognized rudimentary procedural rights.[23] The civil jurisdiction of the Imperial Court was largely taken up with actions against the imperial tax authorities and dominions directly linked to the Empire as well as property disputes between them. The court also exercised criminal jurisdiction over serious offences such as public disorder. Even if the court did suffer from many weaknesses (e.g. jurisdictional limitations regarding individual classes as well as cumbersome and protracted procedures) – it nevertheless represented an important first step.

2. Absolutism

In the 17th and 18th century, the larger territories in Germany turned into absolutist dominions, despite the fact that they were still held in fief from the Empire.[24] The term "absolutism" refers to a form of state and government in which the whole power of the state is undivided and invested in the monarch or state ruler whose sovereignty is undiluted by any participation of the various classes; the absolutist state and the ruler are considered one and the same: "L'Etat c'est moi" *(Louis XIV)*. It is a peculiarity of German constitutional history that the shift towards absolutism took place regionally (*i.e.* in the individual states) rather than centrally. Jean Bodin has characterized this epoch as follows: "Sovereignty is absolute power held by the state for all eternity."[25] Thereby, absolutism is the precise opposite of the rule of law.

I have chosen to explain absolutism at this point in recognition of the fact that it created important conditions for developments in the rule of law from

23 See Diestelkamp, *Das Reichskammergericht*, 1990; Oestmann, "Menschenrechte und ihre Durchsetzung im Alten Reich," 2006; Sailer, *Untertanenprozesse vor dem Reichskammergericht*, 1999; Schildt, "Reichskammergericht," 2006; Sellert, *Reichshofrat und Reichskammergericht*, 1999.

24 Overviews: Hubatsch, *Absolutismus*, 1988; Reinalter and Klueting, *Der aufgeklärte Absolutismus*, 2002.

25 Bodin, *Les six livres de la République*, 1576, I. Book, 8th Chap. (German transl., 1981, p. 205).

the end of the 18th century onwards. The Bill of Rights in North America, for the first time, comprehensively enforced basic rights as part of the constitution (the first being Virginian Bill of Rights of 1776). It was proclaimed, with some justification, as "the great antithesis to the legal and social relationships of the old world."[26] The National Constituent Assembly of France passed the *Declaration of the Rights of Man and of the Citizen* and the *Decree Abolishing the Feudal System and all the Privileges of the Nobility* in the same month (August 1789). Many articles in the Declaration of Rights suggest that the revolution was largely a response to actual abuses of absolutist rule: examples include the remedy of *habeas corpus*, the principle of *nullum crimen sine lege* and the presumption of innocence.[27] The great demands of the North American and French Revolution for freedom and equality (and thereby the second basic notion of the rule of law), are levelled against all the privileges and dependencies which defined absolutism.

II. The Modern Understanding of the Rule of Law

1. Early Constitutional Development: the Liberal Rule of Law

The notions underlying the North American and, in particular, the French Revolutions resounded throughout Europe – including Germany. They led to the founding of the liberal movement, which flourished in Germany in the aftermath of the Napoleonic Wars between 1814 and 1824 and produced the first constitutions in many German states. The liberalism of this age did not seek to overthrow the authoritarian rule of the princes and outdated social order through revolution; instead, it aimed at reform and not a return to feudalism.[28]

Liberal activists demanded the reform of basic rights and civil freedoms, thereby emphasizing the need for freedom of speech and press freedom, constitutions that provided for representative government, the separation of powers, legal certainty by ensuring the predictability of state action, the

---

26 Hattenhauer, *Die geistesgeschichtlichen Grundlagen des deutschen Rechts*, 1996, para. 70.

27 See Art. 7-9; reproduced in Willoweit and Seif, *Europäische Verfassungsgeschichte*, 2003, pp. 250 ff.

28 Overviews: Ruppert, *Bürgertum und staatliche Macht*, 1997; Schulze, *Frühkonstitutionalismus in Deutschland*, 2002.

subjugation of the executive and judicature to the law (especially in relation to criminal matters), the subjugation of the legislature to the constitution and the restriction of state tasks to ensuring security and order instead of pursuing comprehensive welfare.[29] Calls for the rule of law were composed of such demands.[30]

The constitutions produced during the period of early constitutional development were only partially successful in realizing the liberal agenda. They were still restrictive in relation to representative government, the guarantee of human rights and binding effect of the constitution. In addition, the monarch played a crucial role: a constitution could only be established by his authority alone or with his consent. However, the large states of Austria and Prussia were even more backward and rejected calls for a constitution outright. The statement, "German constitutional thought in the 19th century centres on the monarch"[31], applied to all.

2. Late Constitutional Development: the Formal Rule of Law

As is well known, Germany was fated to tread "a long path to the west"[32]: early constitutionalism was suffocated by the restoration, the revolution of 1848/49 was defeated by the princes and the unification of Germany under the leadership of Prussia saw liberalism overtaken by nationalism. The imperial constitution of 1871 was based, as before, on the monarchical principle according to which the emperor was the holder of state power and therefore enjoyed wide-ranging powers. Nevertheless, there was also a general assembly (the Imperial Parliament) and general elections so one can argue that there was a "limited monarchy".[33]

In terms of the rule of law's development, this epoch can be designated the "formal rule of law": many achievements of the liberal rule of law during early constitutional development were retained but without the substantive

---

29 See Hofmann, "Geschichtlichkeit und Universalitätsanspruch des Rechtsstaats," 1995, pp. 4 f.; Stolleis, *Geschichte des öffentlichen Rechts,* Vol. II, 1992, pp. 156 ff.; Wahl, "Die Entwicklung des deutschen Verfassungsstaates," 2003, paras. 23 ff.; Würtenberger, "Der Konstitutionalismus des Vormärz," 1998.

30 See Stolleis, "Rechtsstaat," 1990, col. 369, referring to *Rotteck* and *Welcker*.

31 Stolleis, *Geschichte des öffentlichen Rechts,* Vol. II, 1992, p. 100.

32 Winkler, *Der lange Weg nach Westen,* 2000.

33 See Frotscher and Pieroth, *Verfassungsgeschichte,* 2010, para. 448.

elements – basic and human rights, in particular.[34] This concept of the rule of law was concisely expressed by the conservative philosopher Friedrich Julius Stahl[35]: "[The rule of law] certainly does not determine the aim and contents of the state but only the manner and character of realizing the same." In legal terms, therefore, the state was merely to be "the institution facilitating the external organization and promotion of social life".

This view is representative of leading opinion during the latter half of the 19th century. It was reflected in the imperial constitution of 1871 inasmuch as it did not contain any catalogue of basic rights. Unlike the constitutions produced during early constitutional development it did not provide for a constitutional court either: disputes relating to constitutional matters were to be dealt with by a political organ which performed a mediating role.[36] However, this should not imply that the empire was devoid of basic rights. Acts were gradually passed which met liberal demands for the greater predictability of state action (particularly in the administration of justice) and expansion of freedoms; it was just that they were not constitutionally anchored. Accordingly, imperial statutes regulated the freedom of trade, association and movement as well as religious, personal and press freedoms.[37] The Imperial Justice Acts (*Reichsjustizgesetze*) of 1877 vigorously promoted the expansion of legal protection, particularly the independence of the courts and the right to a legally competent judge.[38]

Under the banner of the formal rule of law, the struggle against state power was manifested in attempts to improve legal protection against incursions by the state. There were two opposing arguments: first, it was argued that legal protection against state power should be reinforced by the ordinary courts.[39] However, this was superseded by an argument which advocated the creation of an independent administrative jurisdiction[40] (probably because many believed this alternative was more likely to preserve the executive's influence[41] – which fortunately did not turn out to be the case). As a result,

34 See Böckenförde, "Entstehung und Wandel des Rechtsstaatsbegriffs," 1969, pp. 59ff.; Scheuner, "Die neuere Entwicklung des Rechtsstaats," 1978, pp. 201 ff.

35 Stahl, *Die Philosophie des Rechts*, 1846, 2. Vol., 2nd sect., pp. 105 f.

36 See Björner, *Die Verfassungsgerichtsbarkeit im Norddeutschen Bund und Deutschen Reich*, 2000, pp. 33 ff.

37 See Huber, "Grundrechte im Bismarckschen Reichssystem," 1975.

38 See Huber, *Deutsche Verfassungsgeschichte*, 1988, Vol. III, pp. 973 ff.

39 See Bähr, *Der Rechtsstaat*, 1864, pp. 71 ff.

40 See v. Gneist, *Der Rechtsstaat und die Verwaltungsgerichte in Deutschland*, 1879.

41 See Stolleis, "Rechtsstaat," 1990, col. 372.

administrative courts were set up in the *Länder* from 1863 onwards – including the Supreme Administrative Court of Prussia which I mentioned at the outset.[42]

3. The Constitution of Weimar: the Social Rule of Law

The revolution of 1918 heralded the end of the monarchy and birth of the republic. The Weimar Constitution of 1919 was predominantly influenced by social democracy and left-wing liberals who developed the rule of law further to incorporate the concept of social justice.[43] In particular, a social dimension of basic rights that reflected actual living and economic conditions served to expand the protection of individual rights and freedoms. Accordingly, various clauses added a new social and economic layer to the basic rights – particularly those whose object was to prevent abuses of land utilization, guarantee minimum living conditions, provide social security in the event of old age, sickness, invalidity and unemployment and to provide employees with voting rights[44]. The state was to be the architect of civil society and ensure that the working class could partake in social progress and enjoy the freedoms available; in this way the Weimar Constitution attempted to "bridge class divisions".[45]

The social rule of law realized that freedoms could only be enjoyed if factual preconditions were fulfilled. During the Industrial Revolution in Germany, many workers could not aspire to a dignified standard of living purely through their own efforts. In this respect, the social rule of law forms the counter-movement to classical liberalism, as Anatole France famously described: "The law, in its majestic equality forbids the rich as well as the poor to sleep under bridges, beg on the streets and steal bread". The social rule of law ensures that freedom can be enjoyed equally and as widely as possible through planning, steering, the provision of services and distribu-

---

42 See Stump, *Preußische Verwaltungsgerichtsbarkeit*, 1980; Sydow, *Die Verwaltungsgerichtsbarkeit des ausgehenden 19. Jahrhunderts*, 2000; v. Unruh, *Verwaltungsgerichtsbarkeit im Verfassungsstaat*, 1984.

43 See generally: Gusy, *Die Weimarer Reichsverfassung*, 1997.

44 See Pieroth and Schlink, *Grundrechte*, 2010, para. 37.

45 See Anschütz, *Drei Leitgedanken der Weimarer Reichsverfassung*, 1923, p. 26.

tion.[46] It was the Weimar Constitution that laid down the necessary foundations for such tasks. However, conservative opposition to this endeavour and the constitution's brief duration suggest that the social rule of law was only fully realized by the Basic Law. It should also be noted that this variant of the rule of law entails an additional dimension of state influence but does not dispense with its liberal and formal elements.

4. The Basic Law: the Substantive Rule of Law

The Basic Law further develops all three lines of traditions – or layers – of the rule of law referred to: first, it reflects the liberal outlook, being rooted in the western tradition of basic rights and constitutional thought; secondly, it reflects the formal understanding of the rule of law as shown by the many examples of it attaching significance to forms, competencies, procedures and guarantees. Indeed, so sophisticated is its system of legal protection that critics complain of a litigation state. Thirdly, the Basic Law clearly develops the social concept of the rule of law to a greater degree than the Weimar Constitution did. Though the social dimension of basic rights was not likewise upheld, the principle of the social state was incorporated in the cornerstone article 20 GG on the same level as the principles of democracy, rule of law and federalism. By amplifying the rule of law's substance in this way, the Federal Republic of Germany may be described as a state subject to the substantive rule of law.[47] I will present the main features of this substantive rule of law.

a) The Separation of Powers and Primacy of Law

The Basic Law not only regulates the rule of law itself but also provides a whole range of individual guarantees which further define this principle in

---

46 See Hesse, *Grundzüge des Verfassungsrechts*, 1995, paras. 209ff.; Kingreen, *Das Sozialstaatsprinzip im europäischen Verfassungsverbund*, 2003; Zacher, "Das soziale Staatsziel," 2004, paras. 32 ff.

47 See monographs: Kunig, *Das Rechtsstaatsprinzip*, 1986; Sarcevic, *Der Rechtsstaat*, 1996; Sobota, *Das Prinzip Rechtsstaat*, 1997.

practice. Central features of the rule of law are found in Art. 20 GG[48] which regulates the separation of powers and primacy of the constitution over all other state acts. This entails the subjugation of the executive and judiciary to the law and constitution. Its comprehensive and sophisticated catalogue of basic rights, crowned by the right to human dignity, leaves one in no doubt that the Basic Law is absolutely guided by the classical philosophy that the state exists for the benefit of the people and not *vice versa*.

However, the primacy of law would be ineffective if the state were able to circumvent this principle. Since the law‘s binding force depends on normative standards, the absence of law-making would give the state, in effect, unfettered freedom. This is the danger which the constitutional requirement of a specific enactment (*Gesetzesvorbehalt*) seeks to prevent. This is widely regarded as an unwritten but essential addendum to the primacy of law principle and, as such, represents a component of the rule of law (it is also regarded as expressing the principle of democracy). Accordingly, the requirement of a specific enactment obliges the state to enact statutes in certain areas. Traditionally, – and this reflects the legacy of early constitutionalism – it has only been possible to interfere in freedoms and property rights directly, by enacting enabling legislation, or indirectly, by citing legislation in support of such action (i.e. specific enactment on basic rights). In addition, a specific legal enactment is also required for organizational matters of fundamental importance (i.e. specific institutional enactment).

b) Legal protection

Besides Art. 20 GG, the most important guarantee related to the rule of law is the right to legal protection. The Basic Law grants people the right to appeal to the courts whenever the state infringes their basic rights. With the exception of the judiciary, this right extends to all acts of the state whatever form they may take. Under the Basic Law, there are no longer any sovereign acts that cannot be challenged before the courts; the only partial exception to this rule being acts of clemency, which are not subject to full judicial review.

---

48 See commentaries: G. Frankenberg, in Denninger et al (ed.), *Alternativkommentar*, 2002, Art. 20 (1) – (3) IV; B. Grzeszick, in Maunz/Dürig, *Grundgesetz*, 2010, Art. 20 VI and VII; S. Huster/J. Rux, in Epping/Hillgruber (ed.), *Grundgesetz*, 2009, Art. 20 paras. 125ff.; H. D. Jarass, in Jarass/Pieroth, *Grundgesetz*, 2010, Art. 20

Admittedly, the right to legal protection is restricted insofar as it only expressly relates to state authority and therefore impliedly excludes civil and criminal jurisdiction. However, the latter areas are covered by a number of individual provisions in the Basic Law relating to basic rights and organizational aspects. As far as the former are concerned, everyone has the right to a legally competent judge (*i.e.* in the sense that all judges have to be determined in advance by statute being of abstract and general application) and the right to a legal hearing (*i.e.* that each party to a trial must be comprehensively informed and heard; furthermore, that the court takes into account the party's arguments and justifies its decision). In addition to the civil and criminal courts, the Basic Law also provides for specialized courts covering diverse fields of law. These include administrative and fiscal courts, social security and industrial tribunals, professional and disciplinary tribunals as well as courts martial. It is also guaranteed in all courts that judges will be personally independent and objective (the main purpose of this principle is to prevent the executive issuing instructions). The upshot of all this is that the right to legal protection under the rule of law is not limited to actions of the state but also extends to civil and criminal law. The Federal Constitutional Court has contributed to the development of this concept by requiring that it must not only be available but also effective.

Courts exercising specialist jurisdiction are augmented with constitutional courts at both federal and regional level (all 16 federal states have their own constitutional courts). The constitutional courts in German provinces are distinguished by (1) institutional autonomy (i.e. they exist alongside and above specialist courts) and (2) comprehensive powers, which cover federal disputes, disputes between organs, judicial review and constitutional complaints.[49] The Federal Constitutional Court has attained the status of a citizens' court by virtue of the individual constitutional complaint which allows people to appeal to the court if their basic rights have been infringed by public authorities.[50] Public authorities in this context also refer to specialist courts which usually have to hear the case themselves before the complaint can proceed to the Federal Constitutional Court. Each year, approximately 6,000 constitutional complaints are submitted to the Federal Constitutional Court, of which approximately two to three percent are successful. This number, although it may sound small, is in fact relatively significant because it proves

49 See Schlaich and Korioth, *Das Bundesverfassungsgericht*, 2010.

50 See Häberle, "Die Verfassungsbeschwerde," 1997; Pieroth and Silberkuhl, *Die Verfassungsbeschwerde*, 2008; Zuck, *Das Recht der Verfassungsbeschwerde*, 2006.

the state infringes the constitution – and thereby acts unlawfully – about 150 times a year!

On the whole, "it is clear that the continuous work of the courts has had a fundamentally positive effect on the development of the rule of law. This includes their disciplining of public authorities, stabilizing the political process, organizing the law and, most importantly, engendering an awareness of 'legal compliance'."[51]

c) Clarity and Definiteness, Legal Certainty and Protection for bona fide acts

Aside from the regulation of the rule of law in Art. 20 GG, a second group of individual standards deal with the clarity and definiteness of legal rules. These are qualities that the Basic Law expressly stipulates for all criminal statutes, limitations on freedoms and statutory authorizations for executive legislation. On this basis, the Federal Constitutional Court imposes the following general requirements related to the rule of law: "The principle of clarity and definiteness requires that the contents, purpose and scope of any legal authorization permitting the executive to enforce administrative acts be sufficiently defined and limited so that citizens are able to quantify and, to a certain extent, predict and calculate actions of the administration."[52] Moreover, the rule of law requires the legal order to be free of contradictions[53] and legal personnel to adopt a rational methodology.[54]

In this context belong the requirements of legal certainty and protection for *bona fide* acts. Legal certainty means, objectively, that the law must be reliable whereas protection for *bona fide* acts means, subjectively, that the citizens have the right to expect this. In its case law (amounting to approximately 300 decisions), the Federal Constitutional Court has broadened the scope of the prohibition *ex post facto* laws to encompass the law as a whole, despite the fact that the Basic Law expressly restricts its application to criminal law. It mainly serves to prohibit laws which seek to increase tax debts retrospectively (*i.e.* after the state has calculated the tax debt according to the applicable law): such legislation is not possible under the rule of law.

---

51 See Schmidt-Aßmann, "Der Rechtsstaat," 2004, para. 71.

52 BVerfGE 56, 1/12; 108, 52/75; 110, 33/53 f.

53 BVerfGE 25, 216/227; 98, 83/97; 98, 265/301.

54 See Müller and Christensen, *Juristische Methodik*, Vol. I, 2004, para. 295.

d) Liability

A third group of individual standards of the rule of law deals with the liability of the state for its actions. This includes the Basic Law's doctrines of public liability, according to which the state must generally compensate victims for loss caused by the unlawful actions of its officials, and liability for expropriated property, which obliges the state to pay adequate compensation before it can expropriate property. Despite the absence of a corresponding rule in the Basic Law, these principles have also been recognized for over 200 years in relation to personal injury caused by the state (*i.e.* the *Aufopferungsanpruch* or "disturbance claim"). Apart from the rule of law principle, the basic rights also play a role here by granting citizens the right to apply for stop notices in cases of unlawful interference and sue for abatement, restoration or compensation where the state infringes their rights.[55]

e) Principle of Proportionality

The close connection that exists between the rule of law and basic rights is revealed by the principle of proportionality.[56] In fact, the Basic Law refers to both as forming the basis of this principle. Since its origins in police law, the principle of proportionality has developed into the most potent benchmark in the jurisprudence of the Federal Constitutional Court. Indeed, it has provided the crucial legal argument for almost all cases involving the basic rights. In its classical form, this principle allows state actions to be reviewed for their suitability and necessity. The test of suitability enquires whether the action taken by the state (*i.e.* administrative act or legal measure) does in fact promote its avowed aim. The purpose of the necessity test, on the other hand, is to ascertain whether the state could achieve its aim by adopting measures which are just as effective but less onerous than those in dispute.

---

55 See Ossenbühl, *Staatshaftungsrecht*, 1998, pp. 285 ff.; Röder, *Die Haftungsfunktion der Grundrechte*, 2002, pp. 199 ff.

56 See following monographs: Dechsling, *Das Verhältnismäßigkeitsgebot*, 1989; Hanau, *Der Grundsatz der Verhältnismäßigkeit als Schranke privater Gestaltungsrechte*, 2004; Heusch, *Der Grundsatz der Verhältnismäßigkeit im Staatsorganisationsrecht*, 2003; Hirschberg, *Der Grundsatz der Verhältnismäßigkeit*, 1981; Lerche, *Übermaß und Verfassungsrecht*, 1999; Schlink, *Abwägung im Verfassungsrecht*, 1976.

The additional test of whether the state's action is reasonable subjects state actions to a far greater degree of scrutiny by means of weights and balances. On the one hand, this enables the basic rights of the weak to be enforced against the state and cases are often decided on their own merits. On the other hand, the process of weighing up and balancing interests dispenses with rational and binding benchmarks, thereby providing a decision-making process in which the political will of the constitutional judge is the crucial factor.[57] Although this presents a democratic problem, especially with regard to the judicial review of parliamentary acts, it has not yet become acute owing to the sensible restraint exercised by the Federal Constitutional Court.

D. Conclusion

Despite the fact that the rule of law is over several hundred years old, it has only reached maturity in the constitutional state of the modern era. Various interruptions notwithstanding, Germany has continued to refine the modern rule of law and thereby revealed a number of different variants. The Basic Law unites the liberal, formal and social elements of prior constitutions to form a substantive rule of law which is deeply rooted in the legal consciousness of modern Germany. The way the Federal Constitutional Court has steadily developed and refined the rule of law together with its application has met with almost universal approval. In the process, it maybe can impart its concepts to other constitutional orders which are worthy of adoption.

Works cited

Anschütz, Gerhard, *Drei Leitgedanken der Weimarer Reichsverfassung*, Tübingen: Mohr, 1923.

Bähr, Otto, *Der Rechtsstaat*, Kassel: G.H. Wigand, 1864, 2nd reprint Aalen: Scientia Verlag, 1969.

Björner, Ulf, *Die Verfassungsgerichtsbarkeit im Norddeutschen Bund und Deutschen Reich (1867-1918)*, Frankfurt a. M.: Peter Lang, 2000.

57 See Pieroth and Schlink, *Grundrechte*, 2010, paras. 303 f.

Böckenförde, Ernst-Wolfgang, "Entstehung und Wandel des Rechtsstaatsbegriffs," in *Festschrift für Adolf Arndt zum 65. Geburtstag*, eds. H. Ehmke and W. Abendroth, Frankfurt a.M.: Europäische Verlagsanstalt, 1969, pp. 53-76.

Jean Bodin, *Les six livres de la République*, 1576 (German translation, *Sechs Bücher über den Staat*, Munich: C.H. Beck, 1981).

Boldt, Hans, *Deutsche Verfassungsgeschichte*, 2nd ed., Munich: dtv, 1993, Vol. 2.

Brandt, Hartwig, *Der lange Weg in die demokratische Moderne*, Darmstadt: Wissenschaftliche Buchgesellschaft, 1998.

Dechsling, Rainer, *Das Verhältnismäßigkeitsgebot*, Munich: Vahlen, 1989.

Denninger, Erhard, Wolfgang Hoffmann-Riem, Hans-Peter Schneider, and Ekkehard Stein, eds., *Kommentar zum Grundgesetz für die Bundesrepublik Deutschland (Alternativkommentar)*, 3rd ed., Neuwied: Luchterhand, August 2002.

Diestelkamp, Bernhard, ed., *Das Reichskammergericht in der deutschen Geschichte: Stand der Forschung, Forschungsperspektiven*, Cologne/Vienna: Böhlau Verlag, 1990.

Dippel, Horst, ed., *Verfassungen der Welt vom späten 18. Jahrhundert bis Mitte des 19. Jahrhunderts*, Munich: K.G. Saur, 2007.

Dolzer, Rudolf, Wolfgang Kahl, and Christian Waldhoff, eds., *Bonner Kommentar zum Grundgesetz*, Heidelberg: C.F. Müller, July 2010.

Dreier, Horst, ed., *Grundgesetz: Kommentar*, Vol. II, 2nd ed., Tübingen: Mohr Siebeck, 2006.

Epping, Volker, and Christian Hillgruber, eds., *Grundgesetz: Kommentar*, Munich: C.H. Beck, 2009.

Frotscher, Werner, and Bodo Pieroth, *Verfassungsgeschichte*, 9th ed., Munich: C.H. Beck, 2010.

Gneist, Rudolf von, *Der Rechtsstaat und die Verwaltungsgerichte in Deutschland*, 2nd ed., Berlin: Julius Springer, 1879.

Gosewinkel, Dieter, and Johannes Masing, eds., *Die Verfassungen in Europa 1789-1949*, Munich: C.H. Beck, 2006.

Grimm, Dieter, *Deutsche Verfassungsgeschichte 1776-1866*, Frankfurt a.M.: Suhrkamp, 1988.

Grimm, Dieter, "Stufen der Rechtsstaatlichkeit," *Juristenzeitung* (2009): pp. 596-600.

Gurjewitsch, Aaron J., *Das Weltbild des mittelalterlichen Menschen*, 4th ed., Munich: C.H. Beck, 1989.

Gusy, Christoph, *Die Weimarer Reichsverfassung*, Tübingen: Mohr Siebeck, 1997.

Häberle, Peter, "Die Verfassungsbeschwerde im System der bundesdeutschen Verfassungsgerichtsbarkeit," *Jahrbuch des öffentlichen Rechts* (1997): 89-135.

Hanau, Hans, *Der Grundsatz der Verhältnismäßigkeit als Schranke privater Gestaltungsrechte*, Tübingen: Mohr, 2004.

Hattenhauer, Hans, *Die geistesgeschichtlichen Grundlagen des deutschen Rechts*, 4th ed., Heidelberg: C.F. Müller, 1996, para. 70.

Hesse, Konrad, *Grundzüge des Verfassungsrechts der Bundesrepublik Deutschland*, 20th ed., Heidelberg: C.F. Müller, 1995.

Heusch, Andreas, *Der Grundsatz der Verhältnismäßigkeit im Staatsorganisationsrecht*, Berlin: Duncker & Humblot, 2003.

Hirschberg, Lothar, *Der Grundsatz der Verhältnismäßigkeit*, Göttingen: Schwartz, 1981.

Hofmann, Hasso, "Geschichtlichkeit und Universalitätsanspruch des Rechtsstaats," *Der Staat* (1995): 1-32.

Hubatsch, Walther, ed., *Absolutismus*, 2nd ed., Darmstadt: Wissenschaftliche Buchgesellschaft, 1988.

Huber, Ernst Rudolf, "Grundrechte im Bismarckschen Reichssystem," in Ernst Rudolf Huber, *Bewahrung und Wandlung: Studien zur deutschen Staatstheorie und Verfassungsgeschichte*, Berlin: Duncker & Humblot, 1975, pp. 132-151.

Huber, Ernst Rudolf, *Deutsche Verfassungsgeschichte seit 1789*, 3rd ed., Stuttgart: Kohlhammer, 1988.

Jarass, Hans D., and Bodo Pieroth, *Grundgesetz für die Bundesrepublik Deutschland: Kommentar*, 11. ed., Munich: C.H. Beck, 2010.

Kingreen, Thorsten, *Das Sozialstaatsprinzip im europäischen Verfassungsverbund*, Tübingen: Mohr Siebeck, 2003.

Kotulla, Michael, *Deutsche Verfassungsgeschichte vom Alten Reich bis Weimar (1495-1934)*, Berlin: Springer, 2008.

Kunig, Philip, *Das Rechtsstaatsprinzip*, Tübingen: Mohr, 1986.

Lepsius, Oliver, „Sicherheit und Freiheit – ein zunehmend asymmetrisches Verhältnis, " in *Der Rechtsstaat unter Bewährungsdruck*, eds. G. F. Schuppert et al., Baden-Baden: Nomos 2010, pp. 23-54.

Lerche, Peter, Übermaß und Verfassungsrecht, 2nd ed., Goldbach: Keip, 1999.

Limbach, Jutta, "Das Bundesverfassungsgericht und der Grundrechtsschutz in Europa" *Neue Juristische Wochenschrift* (2001): 2913-2918.

McCormick, Neil, "Der Rechtsstaat und die rule of law" *Juristenzeitung* (1984): 65-70.

Mangoldt, Hermann von, Friedrich Klein, and Christian Starck, eds., *Kommentar zum Grundgesetz*, 5th ed., Munich: Vahlen, 2005.

Maunz, Theodor, and Günter Dürig, eds., *Grundgesetz: Kommentar*, Munich: C.H. Beck, January 2010.

Maurer, Hartmut, *Staatsrecht I: Grundlagen, Verfassungsorgane, Staatsfunktionen*, 6th ed., Munich: C.H. Beck, 2010.

Möllers, Christoph, *Gewaltengliederung: Legimitation und Dogmatik im nationalen und internationalen Rechtsvergleich*, Tübingen: Mohr Siebeck, 2005.

Müller, Friedrich, and Ralph Christensen, *Juristische Methodik*, Vol. I, 9th ed., Berlin: Duncker & Humblot, 2004.

Münch, Ingo von, and Philip Kunig, eds., *Grundgesetz-Kommentar*, Vol. 2, 5th ed., Munich: C.H. Beck, 2001.

Oestmann, Peter, "Menschenrechte und ihre Durchsetzung im Alten Reich," in *Altes Reich und neues Recht: Von den Anfängen der bürgerlichen Freiheit*, eds. G. Schmidt-von Rhein and A. Cordes, Wetzlar: Gesellschaft für Reichskammergerichtsforschung, 2006, pp. 57-74.

Ossenbühl, Fritz, *Staatshaftungsrecht*, 5th ed., Munich: C.H. Beck, 1998.

Pieroth, Bodo, "Deutscher Verfassungsexport: das Bundesverfassungsgericht," *Anwaltsblatt* (2010): 8-12.

Pieroth, Bodo, and Bernhard Schlink, *Grundrechte: Staatsrecht II*, 26th ed., Heidelberg: C.F. Müller, 2010.

Pieroth, Bodo, Bernhard Schlink, and Michael Kniesel, *Polizei- und Ordnungsrecht*, 6th ed., Munich: C.H. Beck, 2010.

Pieroth, Bodo, and Peter Silberkuhl, eds., *Die Verfassungsbeschwerde: Einführung – Verfahren – Grundrechte*, Münster: ZAP, 2008.

Reinalter, Helmut, and Harm Klueting, eds., *Der aufgeklärte Absolutismus im europäischen Vergleich*, Vienna: Böhlau Verlag, 2002.

Röder, Daniel, *Die Haftungsfunktion der Grundrechte*, Berlin: Duncker & Humblot, 2002.

Rotunda, Ronald D., John E. Nowak, and J. Nelson Young, *Treatise on Constitutional Law*, St. Paul MN: West Publishing Co., 1986.

Ruppert, Karsten, *Bürgertum und staatliche Macht in Deutschland zwischen Französischer und deutscher Revolution*, Berlin: Duncker & Humblot, 1997.

Sachs, Michael, *Grundgesetz: Kommentar*, 5th ed., Munich: C.H. Beck, 2009.

Sailer, Rita, *Untertanenprozesse vor dem Reichskammergericht: Rechtsschutz gegen die Obrigkeit in der zweiten Hälfte des 18. Jahrhunderts*, Cologne: Böhlau Verlag, 1999.

Sarcevic, Edin, *Der Rechtsstaat*, Leipzig: Leipziger Universitätsverlag, 1996.

Scheuner, Ulrich, "Die neuere Entwicklung des Rechtsstaats in Deutschland," in Ulrich Scheuner, *Staatstheorie und Staatsrecht: Gesammelte Schriften*, Berlin: Duncker & Humblot, 1978, 185ff.

Schildt, Bernd, "Reichskammergericht – Geschichte, Verfassung und Überlieferung," *Jura* (2006): 493ff.

Schlaich, Klaus, and Stefan Korioth, *Das Bundesverfassungsgericht: Stellung, Verfahren, Entscheidungen*, 8th ed., Munich: C.H. Beck, 2010.

Schlink, Bernhard, *Abwägung im Verfassungsrecht*, Berlin: Duncker & Humblot, 1976.

Schmidt-Aßmann, Eberhard, "Der Rechtsstaat," in *Handbuch des Staatsrechts*, eds. Josef Isensee and Paul Kirchhof, Vol. II, 3rd ed., Heidelberg: C.F. Müller, 2004, § 26.

Schulze, Carola, *Frühkonstitutionalismus in Deutschland*, Baden-Baden: Nomos Verlag, 2002.

Sellert, Wolfgang, ed., *Reichshofrat und Reichskammergericht: Ein Konkurrenzverhältnis*, Cologne: Böhlau Verlag, 1999.

Senn, Marcel, *Rechtsgeschichte – ein kulturhistorischer Grundriss*, 4th ed., Zurich: Schulthess Juristische Medien, 2007.

Sobota, Katharina, *Das Prinzip Rechtsstaat*, Tübingen: Mohr Siebeck, 1997.

Stahl, Friedrich Julius, *Die Philosophie des Rechts*, 2nd ed., Heidelberg: Mohr, 1846.

Stern, Klaus, *Das Staatsrecht der Bundesrepublik Deutschland*, Vol. V, Munich: C.H. Beck, 2000.

Stolleis, Michael, "Rechtsstaat," in *Handwörterbuch zur deutschen Rechtsgeschichte*, eds. Adalbert Erler and Ekkehard Kaufmann, Vol. IV, Berlin: Erich Schmidt, 1990, Sp. 367-375.

Stolleis, Michael, *Geschichte des öffentlichen Rechts in Deutschland*, Vol. II, Munich: C.H. Beck, 1992.

Stump, Ulrich, *Preußische Verwaltungsgerichtsbarkeit 1875-1914*, Berlin: Duncker & Humblot, 1980.

Sydow, Gernot, *Die Verwaltungsgerichtsbarkeit des ausgehenden 19. Jahrhunderts*, Heidelberg: C. F. Müller, 2000.

Umbach, Dieter C., and Thomas Clemens, eds., *Grundgesetz*, Heidelberg: C.F. Müller, 2002.

Unruh, Georg Christian von, *Verwaltungsgerichtsbarkeit im Verfassungsstaat: Probleme und Entwicklung*, Herford: Maximilian-Verlag, 1984.

Wahl, Rainer, "Die Entwicklung des deutschen Verfassungsstaates bis 1866," in *Handbuch des Staatsrechts*, eds. Josef Isensee and Pauf Kirchhof, Vol. I, 3rd ed., Heidelberg: C.F. Müller, 2003, § 2.

Willoweit, Dietmar, *Deutsche Verfassungsgeschichte*, 6th ed., Munich: C.H. Beck, 2009.

Willoweit, Dietmar, and Ulrike Seif, *Europäische Verfassungsgeschichte*, Munich: C.H. Beck, 2003.

Winkler, Heinrich August, *Der lange Weg nach Westen*, Bonn: Bundeszentrale für politische Bildung, 2000.

Würtenberger, Thomas, "Der Konstitutionalismus des Vormärz als Verfassungsbewegung" *Der Staat* (1998): 165-188.

Zacher, Hans F., "Das soziale Staatsziel," in *Handbuch des Staatsrechts*, eds. Josef Isensee and Pauf Kirchhof, Vol. II, 3rd ed., Heidelberg: C.F. Müller, 2004, § 28.

Zuck, Rüdiger, *Das Recht der Verfassungsbeschwerde*, 3rd ed., Munich: C.H. Beck, 2006.

An Introduction to the Historical Constitutionalism of the English Common Law

J. W. F. Allison

A. Introduction

At the outset, I would like to emphasise that, in view of my relatively recent acquaintance with, and limited knowledge of, Thai constitutionalism, I will simply be presenting an English legal and historical understanding of the British constitution, and will not be making any express comparison with constitutional developments in Thailand. On the basis, however, of what I have read to date about those developments, I have selected for attention certain English constitutional legal propositions and related issues that I hope will be of interest and relevance.

In the absence of a comprehensive constitutional enactment – for want of any text called "The British Constitution" – to which I can refer you by way of introduction, I will introduce the constitutionalism of the English common law by explaining, qualifying and assessing three common propositions about the British constitution. The first proposition is that the constitution is unwritten. The second is that it is a legal constitution. The third proposition is that, when compared with most other constitutions, it is peculiar or distinctive. Although common, these propositions, I will show, vary in the degree to which they are accepted and in the degree to which they require qualification and reformulation.

B. First Proposition: The constitution is unwritten; it is an unwritten constitution.

By this proposition is not meant that written constitutional legal sources are lacking. Clearly, there are numerous statutes by which written rules of constitutional legal significance are enacted. Rather, what is meant is that there is no single all-embracing document that regulates the organs of government, their interrelations, their duties towards citizens, the rights of those citizens etc. The absence of such a document was a point of nationalist pride to, amongst many others, Albert Venn Dicey, who, more than anyone else, helped found modern English constitutional law. In his enormously influential book *Law of the Constitution*, first published in 1885, he portrayed "an absence of those declarations or definitions of rights so dear to foreign constitutionalists" as intrinsic to the English rule of law.[1] For Dicey, the rules and principles of the constitution were the outcome of the ordinary law of the land, in other words, of ordinary statutes and of ordinary decisions of judges in dealing with particular cases or in granting particular remedies.[2]

Proud claims, however, to the absence of a written constitution or declaration of rights must now be qualified. The constitutional legal culture averse to written constitutions, at times, for example, likened by Dicey and others to "paper constitutions" not much better than paper money compared to real gold,[3] as in the case of culture more generally, was not uniform or homogeneous. In the later stages of British imperial rule and the creation of a Commonwealth of Nations, the British Colonial Office (later to be merged into the Foreign and Commonwealth Office) played a crucial role in the drafting of constitutions for numerous new Commonwealth nations. Already in 1951, a British lawyer had some reason to claim that there "are in all something like seventy separate constitutions in the Commonwealth and most of them were made in Britain".[4] Furthermore, although domestically Britain lacked an all-encompassing constitutional document, it did celebrate in the thirteenth-century feudal compact of Magna Carta – the Great Charter of the Liberties of England – and in the grand statutes – the Bill of Rights 1689 and the Act of Settlement 1701 – by which the outcome of the seventeenth-century constitutional struggles was consolidated.

In recent decades, further grand statutes have been enacted by parliament and have, arguably, acquired or are acquiring special constitutional status[5] because they are, or would seem, immune from being repealed by implication through the enactment of a later statute inconsistent with them. These statutes are the European Communities Act 1972 (implementing Britain's

1 Dicey, *Law of the Constitution*, 1959, p. 197.

2 Dicey, *Law of the Constitution*, 1959, pp. 195 ff.

3 *The Oxford Edition of Dicey*, Volume II: Comparative Constitutionalism, 2013, p. 187. The analogy has been explained by Linda Colley, "When did the British Constitution Become Un-written?", The Mark Pigott Lecture, 21 October 2010, Cambridge.

4 Colley, "When did the British Constitution Become Un-written?"

5 See *Thoburn* v. *Sunderland City Council* [2003] QB 151 at [60]-[64]; [2002] 1 CMLR 50.

entry into the then European Communities), the Human Rights Act 1998 (an incorporation of the European Convention on Human Rights and Fundamental Freedoms 1950) and the Constitutional Reform Act 2005 (creating, *inter alia*, the new Supreme Court to fulfil the judicial function of the former House of Lords). Vernon Bogdanor, the former Professor of Government at the University of Oxford, has some reason to claim that Britain is half way to a written constitution by "piecemeal means"[6] and to entitle his recent book "The New British Constitution".[7]

In the last few years, there seems to have been more talk than ever before of actually introducing a written constitution and completing the piecemeal process. While still Chancellor of the Exchequer, Gordon Brown vaguely suggested the possibility,[8] but he did not make anything of that possibility after he became Prime Minister. In their recent election manifestos, whereas the Liberal Democrat Party undertook to introduce "a written constitution" as well as "a Freedom Bill",[9] the Conservative Party only undertook to replace the Human Rights Act 1998 with "a UK Bill of Rights".[10] No doubt, because of the difference of undertaking or commitment, the Conservative and Liberal coalition partners did not include the introduction of a written constitution in the formal agreement that governs are current coalition government. They only included the introduction of "a Freedom Bill" and the establishment of "a Commission to investigate the creation of a British Bill of Rights that incorporates and builds on all our obligations under the European Convention on Human Rights".[11] But the introduction of a written constitution in the coming years cannot be ruled out, particularly if some serious constitutional crisis in future is attributed to the absence of a written constitution.

As regards my assessment of what may be, or what may become, a drift towards a written constitution, I am not in opposition. The process of introducing a written constitution would encourage clarification through deliberation and debate, and the eventual product would probably have considerable clarity, unifying symbolic value and educative utility in being some-

6 Bogdanor, "Conclusion," 2003, especially at p. 719. See also Bogdanor, "Our New Constitution," 2004, especially at pp. 246, 259.

7 Bogdanor, *The New British Constitution*, 2009.

8 See speech to the Labour Party Conference, Manchester, 25 September 2006.

9 *Liberal Democrat Manifesto 2010*, pp. 87-88, 93.

10 *The Conservative Manifesto 2010*, pp. 79.

11 HM Government, *The Coalition: Our Programme for Government*, 2010, p. 11.

thing that could readily be taught and learnt at school. My basic sense, however, is one of the insufficiency of such a written constitution, indeed of any written constitution. If a written constitution were to be introduced, numerous pressing questions would still require answers. Two questions would stand out. First, what role should be played in the interpretation of the written constitution by principles or institutions that would be left out or would be given little treatment? And what is of great constitutional significance might well be left out for one of two contrasting reasons: either that it would be too contentious for agreement on incorporation, or that it would be too much assumed or taken for granted for incorporation in the constitutional text to seem necessary. Secondly, there would be the following question: If that constitution were amended or replaced with a further constitution or constitutions, what principles would govern its amendment or the relationship between one constitution and the next, which one would expect, at least as an economy of drafting or institution-making, to resemble its predecessor?

In my recent book, which recognises the insufficiency of any written constitution,[12] I have sought to elaborate on the British constitution as a historical constitution from an English legal perspective. The constitution was commonly conceived as a historical constitution until early in the twentieth century, when talk of the unwritten British constitution became much more common. The phrase "unwritten constitution", although often assumed to be synonymous with the phrase "historical constitution" is an unfortunate corruption – a mere negative (what is not written) making a superficial, purely comparative, reference to what is lacking in comparison with the constitutions of most other countries. My purpose in writing the book was to bring to the fore a constitution more fundamental than the necessarily limited provisions of any constitutional text or texts. It was thus to elaborate on a historical constitution that would survive the introduction of a written constitution if one were to be introduced. In discussing the second and third propositions about the constitution, I hope to suggest the advantages of understanding the constitution historically, thus to show the value in conceiving of the British constitution as a historical constitution and not merely as an unwritten constitution.

12 See Allison, *The English Historical Constitution*, 2007, especially at pp. 41-45, 237-244.

C. Second Proposition: The constitution is a legal constitution.

That this proposition even needs to be made, let alone explained, might seem strange to those from countries with a written constitution, which enjoys legal primacy, which is the basic law, a source of rules that are at least legal. In the English legal context, that proposition is principally the outcome of Dicey's pioneering textbook *Law of the Constitution* and the enormous influence it had upon successive generations of English lawyers and statesmen. In that textbook, Dicey delineated "the true nature of constitutional law" by expressly adopting a legal view of the constitution, dealing with legal rules and principles, which he expressly distinguished from the political view of the constitution – that of "political theorists" – which "deals solely with conventions of [the] constitution".[13] Those conventions, such as a minister's responsibility to explain to parliament departmental conduct and to redress grievances when necessary, he placed in a set of rules consisting "of conventions, understandings, habits, or practices which, though they may regulate the conduct of the several members of the sovereign power, of the Ministry, or of other officials, are not in reality laws at all since they are not enforced by the courts".[14] In Dicey's largely unpublished comparative constitutional lectures, which I am currently editing,[15] he went so far as to say that the very spirit[16] of the English constitution was legal, viewed from the point of view of lawyers, people with "a legal turn of mind" in their love for forms, fictions and precedents, which they "import into their political arrangements".[17]

That the English constitution was legal, not political, in the way described by Dicey has long been subject to significant criticism and qualification, indeed direct contestation. Critics have questioned Dicey's distinction be-

13 Dicey, *Law of the Constitution*, 1959, pp. 1 ff, especially at p. 19.

14 Dicey, *Law of the Constitution*, 1959, p. 24.

15 See *The Oxford Edition of Dicey*, Volume II: Comparative Constitutionalism, 2013, p. 70.

16 An adaptation of Montesquieu's notion of *l'ésprit des loix*, which Dicey used to refer to the "subjective side of [the] working" of a nation's institutions, lecture entitled "English Constitutionalism under George III", *ibid.*

17 Lecture entitled "Historical Constitutions and Non-historical Constitutions," *ibid*, pp. 181 f. That legal spirit of the English constitution, Dicey contrasted with the military spirit of late nineteenth-century Prussian constitutionalism and the civil administrative character of French constitutionalism, lectures entitled "Prussian Constitutionalism" and "French Constitutionalism", *ibid,* pp. 107 ff., 90 ff.

tween law and political convention. The more recent criticism is that of constitutional theorists who emphasise the importance of principles of legal and political morality in the interpretation of constitutional law, and see those principles as underlying, or as implicit or reflected in, both law and convention, and both thus relevant to interpretation by courts.[18] They would, for example, readily see a constitutional legal principle of political accountability implicit in the convention of ministerial responsibility to parliament.

Prominent critics, however, have gone further than simply questioning the positivist Diceyan distinction between law and political convention. They have refuted the very proposition that the constitution is legal, and their counter-proposition is that Britain has a political constitution.[19] These political constitutionalists oppose the legal view of Dicey and of legal theorists who emphasise the role of liberal principles of legal and political morality in the interpretation of law. Their concern is to minimise the role played by the courts in the judicial resolution of public law disputes and to maximise the role played by democratic political institutions in the resolution of problems through politics or democratic political activity. Here again, constitutional legal culture has been far from uniform, homogeneous or constant. On the contrary, it has been marked by contestation and has moved simultaneously in different directions away from Dicey's simple legal view of the constitution.

When viewed and assessed from a historical perspective on English constitutional developments, the strange dichotomy of a legal constitution and a political constitution is transcended.[20] The English historical constitution is both political and legal, and has provided a wide berth, I will suggest, both for politics and for judicious judicial intervention.

Consider, first, the berth for politics. Despite all Dicey's legalism – his exposition of a legal constitution from a legal point of view – one of his greatest contributions was to bring political conventions to the forefront of constitutional thought and practice. They are to restrict but not unduly constrain politics. In considering whether a rule has been established as a binding

18 See, *e.g.*, Allan, *Law, Liberty, and Justice*, 1993, ch. 3. See Allison, *English Historical Constitution*, pp. 93 f.

19 See, *e.g.*, Griffith, "The Political Constitution," 1979; Loughlin, *The Idea of Public Law*, 2003; Tomkins, *Our Republican Constitution*, 2005; Bellamy, *Political Constitutionalism*, 2007. See generally Allison, *English Historical Constitution*, 2007, pp. 33 ff.

20 See Allison, *English Historical Constitution*, 2007, especially at pp. 39 f.

convention, political actors are required to determine the following: first, whether precedents or examples of past practice were in accordance with the rule; secondly, whether political actors followed the rule because they believed they were bound by the rule to do so; and, thirdly, whether there is a good reason for the rule.[21] If there is not a good reason for the rule, then the absence of a good reason can be used to justify not-compliance and to avert or curtail the consequent political censure or fall-out, which is the sanction for breach of convention. And, through deliberate and justified non-compliance, the convention may change or develop. Although conventions may well express principles relevant to the judicial interpretation of law, they are first and foremost devices to facilitate the working of politics. To the political actor, on the one hand, conventions are both useful guides to political reaction in the event of non-compliance as well as demanding standards of self-restraint. Political actors are required to comply with them and may only depart from them if they truly believe they have a good reason by which they will truly be able to justify their non-compliance. To the citizen, on the other hand, conventions are all standards of accountability by which political actors may be held to account, and key conventions, such as individual and collective ministerial responsibility, also have as their very content political accountability to parliament and thus to the electorate.

Consider, then, the berth for the courts in the English historical constitution. Viewed from a historical perspective, the significant role of the courts has been unmistakeable for centuries and is fully recognised as such. A significant constitutional legal role has been possible for at least two basic reasons. First, although not dictated by a constitutional enactment of the separation of powers as such,[22] the English courts have long assumed and shown a degree of judicial independence – as the centrepiece of the rough English separation of powers – that has promoted the general legitimacy of their decisions.[23] Secondly, the English courts have historically been able to play a significant constitutional role by not doing, and not appearing to do, too much. What I have called the economy of the English common law has, I have argued,[24] been crucial to its development.

21 This test for whether a rule has been established as a binding convention is broadly that of Jennings, *The Law and the Constitution*, 1959, ch. 3, especially at p. 136.

22 Until the recent enactment of the "guarantee of continued judicial independence", Constitutional Reform Act 2005, section 3.

23 See Allison, *English Historical Constitution*, 2007, pp. 87 ff.

24 See Allison, *English Historical Constitution*, 2007, ch. 5.

Various forms of the common law's economy have been the means by which the English courts have avoided encroaching unduly upon the spheres of the legislature and administration. One general form of economy has been judicial minimalism – minimal revision or piecemeal development of the law by choosing a narrow ground for decision and thus establishing a limited judicial precedent. A second form, in the judicial review of administrative action, has been the formalistic coupling of a judicial decision to the intention of parliament. The court has simply carried out or appeared to carry out parliament's intention by merely ensuring that an authority has not acted *ultra vires*, that is, beyond its powers as laid down by, or read into, a particular statute, which parliament is free to amend. A third form of economy, also in the judicial review of administrative action, has been a longstanding judicial preference for procedural controls, leaving the administrative authority free to decide on the substance of administrative policy. A fourth form has been the continuing judicial endeavour to elaborate doctrines to restrict judicial intervention where appropriate. In the past, courts invoked the blunt doctrine of non-justiciability to justify not intervening to overturn administrative decisions – whether on national security or on the allocation of scarce resources – that they regarded as beyond their procedural and institutional judicial competence because of their high policy element. Blanket invocations of non-justiciability are, however, now seen to compromise the right to a fair trial in article 6 of the European Convention on Human Rights and Fundamental Freedoms 1950. So, taking the place of non-justiciability since the Human Rights Act 1998 came into force, a doctrine of judicial deference has been developed by the courts to avoid their encroaching unduly upon the administrative and legislative spheres of government.

Other occasional and mainly historic forms of the common law's economy have been highly pragmatic and much more problematic than those already listed. One form of economy has been the historic use of legal fiction, by which, in previous centuries, the English courts avoided the controversy and unpredictability of openly changing the law. By legal fiction, a legal or factual requirement of a rule or institution has, on occasion, been deemed to have been met *ad hoc*, for a particular limited purpose.[25] Another form of

25 See, *e.g.*, the sixteenth-century use of the Bill of Middlesex to give the court of the King's Bench direct jurisdiction, Baker, *An Introduction to English Legal History*, 2002, pp. 41-42. For constitutional examples of the use of fiction, see the fiction, below, that King Charles II had immediately succeeded King Charles I; and see generally Allison, *English Historical Constitution*, 2007, pp. 56 f.

economy has been general obfuscation or vagueness in the reasoning used to justify a judicial decision. The court has tried to avoid its decision appearing contentious by failing to explain or acknowledge all the issues at stake and thus not clearly or specifically to address them. These last forms of economy have been peculiarly problematic because they have contradicted the value of legal certainty required by the English rule of law as well as that of judicial accountability, which English courts have sought to uphold precisely so as to promote and not undermine the legitimacy of their decisions through the giving of reasons in doing justice in particular cases. Not succumbing to basic contradiction is the arduous task of courts at times of constitutional crisis, in which they are understandably concerned to keep their heads below the parapet but must also remain true to the longstanding values by which their role is sustained.

The English common law's historical constitution has thus evolved as both a political and a legal constitution. At an abstract ideological level, it can be seen as the outcome of contestation between legal and political constitutionalists, between those who emphasise the political, and those who emphasise the legal, controls of government.

D. Third Proposition: The constitution is peculiar or distinctive when compared with most other constitutions.

Central to consideration of this common proposition are the grounds for the constitution's peculiarity or distinctiveness. The usual grounds put forward to show or explain its peculiarity are that it has enjoyed for centuries a high degree of continuity in its evolution (being largely uninterrupted by revolution or invasion) and that the constitution is unwritten or historical. Other grounds – substantive grounds – for peculiarity include the traditional lack of a strict separation of powers enactment[26] and neglect of the state in the English rule of law[27] in contrast with, for example, the *Rechtsstaat* centred on the state in German constitutional theory.

As in the case of each of the first two propositions, this third proposition is also in need of qualification. Continuity – the first ground of the constitution's peculiarity – was substantial and has been widely recognised as such

26 See Allison, *English Historical Constitution*, 2007, ch. 4.

27 See Allison, *Continental Distinction in the Common Law*, 2000, ch. 5, especially at pp. 78 ff.

but was in fact broken from 1649 to 1660, the period between the reign of King Charles I and that of King Charles II, by the Commonwealth of England and then The Protectorate. Continuity, however, was, arguably, maintained to a considerable extent in form and substance: In form, *de iure* through a legal fiction of continuity – that Charles II had immediately succeeded Charles I – and, in substance, through the reversal of most of the legal reforms of the Commonwealth of England in the Restoration of the monarchy (with a few notable exceptions).

A further challenge to the claim to continuity is made by Professor Vernon Bogdanor in his recent book *The New British Constitution.*[28] In the devolution of governing powers to Scotland and Wales towards the end of the last century and in the separation of powers that was secured near the beginning of this century through the creation of a new Supreme Court by the Constitutional Reform Act 2005, he identifies a break in continuity sufficient to justify his claim to the existence of a new British constitution. From my historical perspective on a historical constitution,[29] however, I recognise many changes of varying significance as well as much continuity.

The second ground of the constitution's peculiarity or distinctiveness – that it is unwritten – has lost validity to the extent that the constitution has, through the various grand statutes of recent decades – the European Communities Act 1972, the Human Rights Act 1998 and the Constitutional Reform Act 2005 – come half way to a written constitution "by piecemeal means", as argued by Professor Bogdanor.[30] If, as I have argued, however, the unwritten constitution should be reconceived as a historical constitution, which would survive, at a deeper or more fundamental level, the introduction of a written British constitution, and if something comparable is conceived to exist in other jurisdictions,[31] which do have written constitutions, the historical constitution in the English legal context would not be alone or particularly distinctive.

Consider now the substantive grounds for the constitution's peculiarity. From a historical perspective, the substantive grounds in the constitution's rough separation of powers, principally to secure judicial independence, and its rule of law do have some validity but are also striking illustrations of interaction and cross-fertilisation between English constitutionalism and the

---

28 Bogdanor, *The New British Constitution*, 2009.

29 See generally Allison, *English Historical Constitution*, 2007.

30 See Bogdanor, "Conclusion," 2003, especially at p. 719.

31 See, *e.g.*, Ginsburg, "Constitutional Afterlife," 2009.

constitutionalism developing in other European jurisdictions. Montesquieu's theory of separate powers – legislative, executive and judicial – in France is well known to have been domesticated by William Blackstone in his *Commentaries on the Laws of England*,[32] where Blackstone transforms it into a requirement of judicial independence fitting English legal preoccupations. Montesquieu for his part misunderstood the rough English separation of powers but is well known to have developed his own theory in view of the English constitution.[33] Such were a few of the interactions in the development of the English separation of powers.

Interactions occurred in the development of the English rule of law and the Germanic notion of the *Rechtsstaat* comparable to those in the development of the separation of powers.[34] In recent decades, prominent and influential legal or constitutional theorists in England[35] have drawn on Friedrich von Hayek's concept of the *Rechtsstaat* or rule of law[36] in developing a more sophisticated conception of the English rule of law. Now, the formative influences upon Hayek's concept of the *Rechtsstaat* are various. According to Hayek himself, one influence came from the "early nineteenth-century discussions in Germany about the nature of the *Rechtsstaat*", to which he accredited the most fully elaborated concept of the rule of law.[37] Hayek also, however, identified another influence – an English influence. He described what he regarded as the origins of the rule of law in England of the seventeenth and early-eighteenth centuries.[38] In particular, he attributed lasting effects to John Locke, from whom he derived what Hayek regarded as the crucial insight that "there can be no liberty without law".[39] Despite traditional English legal claims to the peculiarity of the constitution, from a his-

---

32 Blackstone, *Commentaries on the Laws of England*, 1765-1769, Vol. I, pp. 257-260, especially at p. 259.

33 Montesquieu, *The Spirit of the Laws*, Bk. 11, ch. 6. See Shackleton, *Montesquieu*, 1961, pp. 298-301; Vile, *Constitutionalism and the Separation of Powers*, 1998, pp. 91-93; Allison, *Continental Distinction in the Common Law*, 2000, pp. 16-18.

34 See Allison, *English Historical Constitution*, 2007, pp. 199-205.

35 See, *e.g.*, Raz, "The Rule of Law and its Virtue," 1977; Allan, "Legislative Supremacy and the Rule of Law," 1985.

36 See Hayek, *The Road to Serfdom*, 1944, especially ch. 6.

37 See Hayek, *The Road to Serfdom*, 1944, p. 54, n. 1.

38 See Hayek, *The Constitution of Liberty*, 1960, ch. 11.

39 Hayek, *The Road to Serfdom*, 1944, p. 62, n. 1. A passage from Locke that expresses this insight is the epigraph to Hayek's chapter on the origins of the rule of law, *Constitution of Liberty*, 1960, ch. 11, p. 162.

torical perspective, constitutional interaction through borrowing and adaptation, in short much cross-fertilisation, has been as evident as constitutional peculiarity or distinctiveness.

In conclusion, I would emphasise two related features of English constitutional development. Firstly, if one understands the development of the English common law's constitutionalism as an evolution within constitutional legal culture, that legal culture has been interactive, not insular, despite traditional English legal pretensions to the contrary. That legal culture has certainly not been uniform, homogeneous or monolithic. Secondly, the evolution of the English common law's historical constitutionalism has been characterised by considerable contestation. Indeed, the English common law's historical constitution is itself, to a significant extent, the outcome of arguments of principle and about practice, for instance, as between advocates and opponents of a written constitution, as between legal and political constitutionalists and as between those proud of domestic peculiarity and others inclined to look elsewhere for inspiration.

Works cited

Allan, T.R.S., "Legislative Supremacy and the Rule of Law: Democracy and Constitutionalism," *Cambridge Law Journal* 44 (1985): 111-143.

Allan, T.R.S., *Law, Liberty, and Justice: The Legal Foundations of British Constitutionalism*, Oxford: Oxford University Press, 1993.

Allison, J.W.F., *A Continental Distinction in the Common Law: A Historical and Comparative Perspective on English Public Law*, rev. edn., Oxford: Oxford University Press, 2000.

Allison, J.W.F., *The English Historical Constitution: Continuity, Change and European Effects*, Cambridge: Cambridge University Press, 2007.

Baker, J. H., *An Introduction to English Legal History*, 4th edn., London: Butterworths, 2002.

Bellamy, Richard, *Political Constitutionalism: A Republican Defence of the Constitutionality of Democracy*, Cambridge: Cambridge University Press, 2007.

Blackstone, William, *Commentaries on the Laws of England*, 4 vols., Facsimile of 1st edn. of 1765-1769, Chicago: University of Chicago Press, 1979.

Bogdanor, Vernon, "Conclusion," in *The British Constitution in the Twentieth Century*, ed. Vernon Bogdanor, Oxford: Oxford University Press, 2003, pp. 689-720.

Bogdanor, Vernon, "Our New Constitution," *Law Quarterly Review* 120 (2004): 242-262.

Bogdanor, Vernon, *The New British Constitution*, Oxford: Hart, 2009.

Dicey, Albert Venn, *An Introduction to the Study of the Law of the Constitution*, 10th edn., London: Macmillan, 1959.

Dicey, Albert Venn, *The Oxford Edition of Dicey*, ed. J.W.F. Allison, 2 vols., Oxford: Oxford University Press, 2013.

Ginsburg, Tom, "Constitutional Afterlife: The Continuing Impact of Thailand's Postpolitical Constitution," *International Journal of Constitutional Law* 7 (2009): 83-105.

Griffith, J.A.G., "The Political Constitution" *Modern Law Review* 42 (1979): 1-21.

Hayek, Friedrich A., *The Constitution of Liberty*, London: Routledge & Kegan Paul, 1960.

Hayek, Friedrich A., *The Road to Serfdom*, London: Routledge, 1944.

Jennings, W. Ivor, *The Law and the Constitution*, 5th edn., London: University of London Press, 1959.

Loughlin, Martin, *The Idea of Public Law*, Oxford: Oxford University Press, 2003.

Montesquieu, Charles de, *The Spirit of the Laws*, ed. and tr. A. M. Cohler, B. C. Miller and H. S. Stone, Cambridge: Cambridge University Press, 1989.

Raz, Joseph, "The Rule of Law and its Virtue," *Law Quarterly Review* 93 (1977): 195-211.

Shackleton, Robert, *Montesquieu: A Critical Biography*, Oxford: Oxford University Press, 1961.

Tomkins, Adam, *Our Republican Constitution*, Oxford: Hart, 2005.

Vile, M.J.C., *Constitutionalism and the Separation of Powers*, 2nd edn., Indianapolis: Liberty Fund, 1998.

Levels of the Rule of Law – On the Possibility of Exporting a Western Achievement*

Dieter Grimm

A. Introduction

The question of whether a state is governed by the rule of law plays an ever-increasing role for the cooperation between states and the work of international organisations. International financial assistance for states is conditioned upon whether the recipient state is governed by the rule of law. States develop a growing interest in the rule of law of other countries. Dialogues between constitutional states are aimed to promote the spread of the rule of law across the globe. These dialogues, however, often lack a sufficient awareness of the demanding nature of the rule of law. Additionally, there is a lack of understanding that rule of law is not a closed concept that can only be adopted in full or not at all. Rather, the idea of the rule of law is a continuum, which also in Germany has only been realised gradually. In the context of its rule of law initiative the State Department recently organised a conference on the topic "The rule of law – a cure-all for the entire world"? The text below is a revised version of the opening lecture held at that conference.

B. Adherence of Governmental Action to the Law

At the core of the idea of the rule of law is the requirement that the state exercises its power in the form of law.[1] This means that the state governs

---

* Reprint from *European-Asian Journal of Law and Governance* (EAJLG), Vol. 1, No. 1, Summer 2011.

1 The literature on the rule of law is vast. See Sobota, *Das Prinzip Rechtsstaat*, 1997; *Šarčević, Der Rechtsstaat*, 1996; Luhmann, *Das Recht der Gesellschaft*, 1993, pp. 422 et seq; Kunig, *Das Rechtsstaatsprinzip*, 1986; Böckenförde, "Entstehung und Wandel des Rechtsstaatsbegriffs," 1969; Hesse, "Der Rechtsstaat," 1962; Scheuner, *Die neuere Entwicklung des Rechtsstaats in Deutschland*, 1960.

according to, and confined by legal rules. Governing according to legal rules means that the state not only prescribes rules for its people but also submits to rules itself. Governing by legal rules means that what the state demands from the people is articulated through, and based in, law. It is in the nature of legal rules that they are not designed to address a particular case but rather that they apply to a wide range of future cases; that law will not be changed as a particular case is being decided; that the law treats everyone equally; and that it decides like cases alike. Governing under the rule of law is the antithesis of arbitrary rule.

The exercise of public power in the form of law prevents the state from converting power into orders or measures too easily. In a rule of law regime, the use of power is divided among many jurisdictions and procedures. Only the compliance to them establishes the binding character of acts of power. A traffic guard may not divorce a couple; a registrar cannot control vehicles. In parliamentary proceedings, no one can be punished; in criminal proceedings the parliament cannot be dissolved. When the state lacks jurisdiction or violates its procedural requirements, the state is in the wrong if it still commands – not the citizen who refuses to comply. In sum, the core of the rule of law is that governmental action is bound by law. The state does not have the right to flout the law in a state governed by the rule of law.

The state is, however, the source of the law. The vast majority of the law owes its validity to an act of government. That means that the state can revoke or amend the law anytime. Yet, the right to amend does not include the power to ignore the law. It must be followed even if its compliance is inconvenient to the rulers or has implications that they find detrimental. Not only lower authorities have to comply with the law. Also the highest branches of government must comply with the law – that is the essence of the rule of law. To put it more concretely, the primary concern is that the executive power complies with the laws the legislature enacted. In this context, lawyers speak of the concept of legality of the administration.[2]

The regularity of government action, which is designed to reduce arbitrariness, is a value in itself – independent of the content of the law that comes into force. It is a value in itself because it makes government action predictable for those who are affected by it. To mention just two examples, the stability of laws allows citizens to organise their behaviour in such a way that they do not come into conflict with the law and it allows corporations

2 See Jesch, *Gesetz und Verwaltung*, 1968.

to act rationally. Hence, an important part of any rule of law regime is the prohibition against retroactive laws[3] because retroactivity means that private behaviour entails legal consequences that were not part of the law at the time of the action so that it was impossible to foresee them and to organise one's behaviour accordingly. The benefits of the rule of law are absent in a system with retroactive laws.

C. Legal Certainty as an Intrinsic Value

As plausible as the postulate of the law abidingness of the state may be, achieving it is just as precarious. Compliance to the law can hinder politicians from pursuing certain goals or taking certain actions which are important to them. Compliance with legal norms by the authorities may have undesirable consequences. Criminal suspects may be set free because the evidence against them is not sufficient. Other times evidence may not be used because it was obtained illegally. In these kinds of situations, obedience to the law can appear to be empty formalism which thwarts the achievement of substantive justice. A state, which then overrides these legal requirements, frequently has public opinion on its side. But it would not be a rule of law state if it did not have the willingness to comply with the law, even when it is unpopular, inconvenient, or annoying.

If the state wants to remedy an unsatisfactory arrangement, it has to change the law for the future, but it cannot disregard it now. Once it becomes accepted that there may be reasons to ignore the law under exceptional circumstances, it is only a small step away from disregarding the law for all kinds of illegitimate purposes: because it does not correspond to one's subjective sense of justice; because the outcome in this particular case does not appear desirable; because there are benefits in disregarding the law; to avoid trouble with those in power; because political opponents or rivals may be harmed by doing so, etc. If a rule of law state wants to succeed, it needs to appreciate legal certainty as an intrinsic value regardless of whether one believes that the outcome of legal protection is good, bad, useful or harmful.[4]

3 See Pieroth, *Rückwirkung und Übergangsrecht*, 1981.

4 See v. Arnauld, *Rechtssicherheit*, 2006.

The requirements for this are not equally favourable everywhere. The reason lies in a fundamental difference whose importance will come up more than once. There are states that see themselves in the service of a predetermined absolute truth. This might be a religious or secular truth. In this case, political authority derives its legitimacy from that truth. It is legitimate insofar as it helps to enforce the truth. But there are also states that do not identify themselves with a particular truth but acknowledge a plurality of truth claims. They do not derive their legitimacy to rule from one sole truth that is binding for all, but from the consensus of its citizens as to the conditions of peaceful coexistence despite disagreement about the good and just.

For the rule of law state this difference is significant, because states that see themselves in the service of an absolute truth have greater difficulties adhering to rule of law principles than pluralistic ones. They do not view the law as autonomous and develop a purely instrumental relationship to positive law. When truth claims conflict with legal duties, they usually give preference to the truth without much second thought. Pluralistic societies, with competing ideas of the common good and justice, are more prone to accept the rule of law because the law is the product of a political decision that followed established rules and can be changed at any time.

D. Reservation and Binding Force of Laws

Making the law obligatory on state power as a core value of the rule of law assumes another aspect. The binding character, which the rule of law demands, is derived from legislation. Consequently it extends only as far as legislation exists. Where there is no law there can also be no legal constraints. Since the state is also the legislator, it therefore has the extent of the binding character of its law in its own hands. Insofar as the state refrains from establishing laws, it is not submitted to rules. Under these circumstances, the rule of law shows gaps. The state can exploit these legal gaps for all kinds of purposes. Therefore, rule of law is only achieved if the state can pursue certain goals only on the basis of a statutory authorisation to do so, the so-called reservation of the law.[5]

5 See Jesch, *Gesetz und Verwaltung*, 1968, pp. 30 et seq; Hoffman-Riem, "Gesetz und Gesetzesvorbehalt im Umbruch," 2005, p. 5.

Traditionally, the area, in which the state may not act without statutory authorisation, is demarcated by fundamental rights. The state may not infringe upon one's fundamental rights without statutory authorisation. Obviously, these statutory authorisations must also have a regulatory content capable of binding state authorities in order to function effectively. This is particularly important in areas where the individual is intensely affected by state actions, such as in criminal or police law. Blank checks to government power cannot result in binding force. Neither do laws consisting of vague and open-ended phrases produce sufficient binding effects. It should not be inferred from this, however, that the binding force of the law increases, the more detailed a law gets. The more casuistically a legislature tries to regulate an issue, the more loopholes it will leave behind.

Yet, the degree to which a law is binding is not only dependent on the willingness of the politicians to formulate binding norms. It is also influenced by the subject matter the law seeks to regulate. As long as the task of the state was largely confined to maintaining an existing social order that was regarded as just, an effective regulation of government activity was rather easy. Maintaining order is a retroactive, narrowly defined and predictable activity. It can be captured in legal norms that follow the "if-then" pattern, clearly define what counts as a violation of the order, and indicate what legal consequences the relevant authorities may take to prevent disorder or to restore order.

By contrast, the tasks of the modern regulatory and welfare state are prospective, comprehensive, and less predictable. The norm type tailored towards maintaining a given order does not apply here. Therefore, in these areas a norm type prevails, which, in contrast to the traditional conditional programs, is identified as a purposive programme. The legislature in the modern regulatory and welfare state can only set certain policy goals and name a number of viewpoints, which have to be considered in the pursuit of the goals by the administration. But *how* agencies achieve these goals in practice is largely left up to them in the process of implementing these norms. I described this situation several years ago in my book "Wachsende Staatsaufgaben – sinkende Steuerungsfähigkeit des Rechts".[6] This is a problem of the rule of law in developed countries with a commitment to rule of law principles.

6 See Grimm, *Wachsende Staatsaufgaben – sinkende Steuerungsfähigkeit des Rechts*, 1990; Grimm, "Der Wandel der Staatsaufgaben," 2002; Rossen, *Vollzug und Verhandlung*, 1999.

E. Material Rule of Law Through Binding Fundamental Rights

When it was said in a previous statement that the submission of the state to law is a value in itself it must be added now, that it is only a limited value. A rule of law state that would exhaust itself in submitting the executive to laws remains purely formal. The binding character would only extend to the form of the law, while the content of the law would be unimportant. Rule of law in a purely formal sense is compatible with oppressive, exploitative and discriminatory legislation. Such a formal view of the rule of law developed in Germany in the second half of the 19th century.[7] Yet, at that time the underlying foundation of a liberal legal culture was always tacitly assumed. The consequences of this narrowed conception of the rule of law only came to light through the decay of the legal culture during the Nazi regime. Experiencing first hand that the law can also become a tool for injustice led to a return to the original, material understanding of the rule of law.

A state devoted to the rule of law in a substantive sense is therefore not only one, in which the state is submitted to the law, whatever its content may be, but one, in which law reflects certain notions of justice. Obviously everything then depends on the question of what notions of justice are decisive in the legislative process. If it is about a notion of justice based in an absolute truth, from which no one can be exempt, then the rule of law will have a hard time being achieved. As mentioned earlier, when truth claims and legal duties conflict, the latter generally yields to the former. The rule of law state, in contrast, rests on ideas of justice which recognise the intrinsic value, the freedom, and equality of every individual.

The attempt to achieve the justice of a social order through a structure of fundamental rights is not without its demands. Fundamental rights are primarily designed to limit government power in the interest of individual self-determination. As the experience of the 19th century shows, this goal can only be attained if the state is not blind to the actual conditions for the enjoyment of freedom. Otherwise, freedom is either useless for those without the necessary means or coercive, because it drives people into conditions of dependence. It is because of this experience that the rule of law state gradually evolved into a welfare state, in which the government is committed to provide for the basic needs of the citizens, to care for the sick, the unemployed and elderly, and to eliminate the exploitation of its weakest members.

---

7 See Jouanjan, *Figures de l'Etat de droit,* 2001.

Furthermore, the rule of law state as understood in a substantive sense would also be incomplete if it did not address the dangers for fundamental rights that emanate, not from the government, but from third parties and other social forces. These dangers have increased considerably with the unparalleled progress in science and technology and the commercial use of its results. It is true that the state possesses means to mitigate these risks. But as they grow out of activities that are themselves protected by fundamental rights, laws are needed to address the risks. If the legislature were permitted to remain passive in this conflict of constitutional rights, the most assertive interests would tend to prevail over the interests of those in need of protection. It therefore is an essential element of a substantive rule of law concept today that fundamental rights not merely serve as checks on government power, but also incorporate a duty to protect its citizens against the dangers that result from the constitutionally protected activities of third parties.[8]

F. Legal Protection Against State Actions and Judicial Review

After all these remarks, it is not to be expected that the idea of the rule of law is one that will sell itself. This holds true not only for autocratic or theocratic regimes, but also for pluralistic societies and democratic states. Therefore, it is of paramount importance to ask what threatens a state, when it chooses to ignore its submission to the law. If individuals act illegally the state may intervene with its police powers. But if the state itself breaks the law, there is no higher authority to enforce the law. The rule of law state is therefore dependent on the existence of devices within its own structure, which monitor the lawfulness of state action. In common law countries, these devices have always existed. The executive could be sued in court. In countries with an absolutist past, the state was able to evade this kind of judicial scrutiny.

Generally speaking, it took enormous efforts until the judiciary regained the power to review the legality of governmental acts. In Germany, the legal protection against the state became the most important demand after the attempt to democratise it had failed in 1849. The result of these efforts was the establishment of special administrative courts, not the competence ex-

8 See Grimm, "Rückkehr zum liberalen Grundrechtsverständnis?," 2002.

pansion of ordinary courts as in the common law model.[9] There are, however, still countless countries, in which citizens cannot hold public authorities accountable – neither on the highest nor on the lowest level. In states, which derive their legitimacy from an absolute truth rather than from consensus, the lack of judicial review tends to be the rule. As all experience teaches us, the rule of law is on shaky ground without judicial review.

If the rule of law is not only defined in formal but material terms, then it does not exhaust itself in the legality of the administration. The legislature is also submitted to the legal constraints that are laid down in the constitution. However, the adherence of the legislature to the constitution cannot be determined by administrative courts. If the legislature should not be allowed to ignore the constitution with impunity, then its actions must also be subject to judicial review. This is the conclusion to which the United States was already drawn at the time when its constitution was adopted. In the rest of the world, this insight has only found gradual acceptance after bitter experiences with blatantly unjust regimes. The second half of the twentieth century saw the triumph of constitutional adjudication, with judicial review of legislation at its core.[10] Today, judicial review is widely regarded as an integral component of the rule of law.

The existence of judicial review alone means very little, however, if courts are not independent, but remain bound by the political chain of command. It is an essential part of the rule of law that laws, once they are enacted, are shielded from political control and obtain an autonomous status, i.e.: that they will be interpreted and applied according to legal, not political criteria. This is the only way to guarantee that the political branches are bound by law. The guarantee for this is the separation of powers.[11] This is why the rule of law is not only weak where there is no judicial review but also where there is no separation of powers. Separation of powers is more than the exercise of public functions by various departments. It adds to this division the independence of powers within its functional areas. Again, that is difficult to accept for countries that are committed to an absolute truth. Absolute truths demand hierarchy; separation of powers prevents hierarchy.

---

9 See Ogorek, "Individueller Rechtsschutz gegenüber der Staatsgewalt," 1988.

10 See Tate and Vallinder, *The Global Expansion of Judicial Power*, 1995.

11 See Möllers, *Gewaltengliederung*, 2005; Möllers, *Die drei Gewalten*, 2008. For judicial independence see Bettermann, *Die Unabhängigkeit des Richters*, 1969; Eichenberger, *Die richterliche Unabhängigkeit als staatsrechtliches Problem*, 1960; Grimm, "Politik und Recht," 2001.

G. Conditions of the Rule of Law

In sum, the rule of law proves to be full of conditions. This also answers the question of whether it is a cure-all for the entire world. It is not because the conditions for its realisation are lacking in many parts of the world. They also cannot be brought about that easily. Only at first glance does the rule of law seem to be a merely technical legal device, which could be established anywhere if only the political will was there. In truth, it is a cultural achievement, which does not necessarily take roots in other cultural contexts. In the Western world it helped to bridge the tension between political power and individual self-development by imposing legal boundaries on governance in the interest of individual liberties. The rule of law does not find favourable ground in cultures, in which self-development has no worth and law is not associated with the protection of freedom.

However, this does not mean that the spread of the rule of law outside of the cultural context, from which the concept emerged, presents an insurmountable obstacle. In order to export the idea of the rule of law, it is rather of crucial importance to realise that there are different levels of the rule of law. Rule of law is not a matter of all or nothing, but of more or less. In fact, rule of law is not a process, as it is often claimed; it is a state of affairs. However, the realization of the rule of law can take the form of a process, level by level. Even in the Western world, not all levels were achieved at the outset. Many were only won after bitter setbacks and hard struggles. Still today these levels differ from country to country.

Each new step means a step forward compared to the previous level. Even the minimum concept of making the law binding on the administration – irrespective of the content of the law – is progress compared to arbitrary rule. The more elementary the level embarked upon, the greater the demand for it. This demand to be subjected to a rule-based rather than arbitrary government can be expected to meet universal approval. For the fulfilment of such a demand, one can easily mobilize popular support. Other levels of the rule of law may be in the interest of the political leaders themselves – albeit the interest will often be a pragmatic, not necessarily a principled, interest in the rule of law. For example, a state that relies on economic growth will accept that rule of law elements, which are conducive to economic growth.

However, the realization of the rule of law becomes more demanding with each additional level. This not only affects the prospects of success but even the mere willingness to try it out. Not every progress in the realization of the rule of law can count on popular support. Anyone who is convinced of the existence of a God-given order, over which human beings are not allowed to dispose, will have a hard time seeing the benefits that religious freedom and freedom of expression bring. Without acceptance of freedom as a human right, there can be no rule of law in the substantive sense described above. Where all public power is in the service of an absolute truth, it would appear contradictory if the supreme power could be prevented from enforcement of such truth by an independent body of judicial review.

H. Rule of Law and Democracy

That brings us finally to the relationship between the rule of law and democracy. Does one only go with the other? This question is obviously of great significance for the global spread of the rule of law. From a historical perspective, the question can be answered in the negative. Before it became a democracy, Germany had been a rule of law state for more than one hundred years. As early as in the enlightened absolutism of the 18th century, the rule of law became increasingly accepted. This was the time when the great codifications began. The rulers gave up using their prerogative to repeal court judgments and replace them with mere authoritative decisions. In the constitutional monarchy of the 19th century, princes bound themselves in the exercise of public power by constitutions, which granted fundamental rights to its citizens and allowed elected representatives to participate in the legislative process.

However, these pre-democratic states did not reach all the levels, which we would associate with the rule of law idea today. Even if the enlightened monarchs were willing to treat their subjects in accordance with the laws, which they had unilaterally enacted, they were not prepared to subordinate their power to the law. They were bound by the law only to the extent that they were willing to comply with it. They could depart from it at any time. The subjects lacked the means to enforce the law against the ruler. The constitutional monarchs did not derive their power from the constitution. They had granted the constitutions voluntarily by way of self-binding, but were no longer free to unilaterally take them back. The binding force of the constitution did not extend further than as granted by the monarch, and judicial review was considered incompatible with monarchical principles. Only administrative courts were permitted later.

Thus, by today's standards the rule of law is not fully realised in non-democratic states. On the other hand, it is not the case that democracies are always accompanied by a fully developed rule of law regime. Just as there are many different political regimes that could be called "non-democratic", so too are there countless forms of governance that could be called "democratic". Where democracy is identified with majority rule and protection of minorities and a guarantee for free political competition and communication is lacking, democracy can easily turn into a tyranny of the majority. This notion of a dictatorship of the majority alone should suffice to demonstrate that a democracy without rule of law appears contradictory and develops a tendency toward self-destruction.

Just as a democracy without rule of law is not immune to the disfranchisement of minorities, so is the rule of law without democracy not immune to particularism too. When those who are affected by a law cannot participate in the law's making, it is unlikely that a reasonable balance of interests between all sectors of the population will be achieved. Those who are not involved in the formation of the state's will can easily, and without consequences, be neglected in the political decision-making process. They will become mere objects of governmental power, no matter how well-meaning this power may be. For these reasons, left on its own, both the rule of law and democracy are in danger of failing the common good. Only in conjunction do they constitute the achievement that ultimately secures the common interest.[12]

Works cited

Arnauld, Andreas von, *Rechtssicherheit*, Tübingen: Mohr Siebeck, 2006.

Bettermann, Karl August, *Die Unabhängigkeit des Richters*, Cologne: Freiherr-vom-Stein-Gesellschaft, 1969.

Böckenförde, Ernst-Wolfgang, "Entstehung und Wandel des Rechtsstaatsbegriffs," (1969), in Ernst-Wolfgang Böckenförde, *Recht, Staat, Freiheit*, Frankfurt a.M.: Suhrkamp, 1991, pp. 143-169.

Eichenberger, Kurt, *Die richterliche Unabhängigkeit als staatsrechtliches Problem*, Bern: Stämpfli, 1960.

Grimm, Dieter, *Wachsende Staatsaufgaben – sinkende Steuerungsfähigkeit des Rechts*, Baden-Baden: Nomos, 1990.

---

12 See Jürgen Habermas, *Faktizität und Geltung*, 1992, esp. pp. 166 ff.; Habermas, "Inklusion," 1996; Habermas, "Über den internen Zusammenhang von Rechtsstaat und Demokratie," 1996.

Grimm, Dieter, "Politik und Recht," in Dieter Grimm, *Die Verfassung und die Politik*, Munich: C.H. Beck, 2001, pp. 13-32.

Grimm, Dieter, "Der Wandel der Staatsaufgaben und die Krise des Rechtsstaats," in Dieter Grimm, *Die Zukunft der Verfassung*, 3rd ed., Frankfurt a.M.: Suhrkamp, 2002, pp. 159-175.

Grimm, Dieter, "Rückkehr zum liberalen Grundrechtsverständnis?," in Dieter Grimm, *Die Zukunft der Verfassung*, 3rd ed., Frankfurt a.M.: Suhrkamp, 2002, pp. 221-240.

Habermas, Jürgen, *Faktizität und Geltung*, Frankfurt a.M.: Suhrkamp, 1992.

Habermas, Jürgen, "Inklusion – Einbeziehen oder Einschließen? Zum Verhältnis von Nation, Rechtsstaat und Demokratie," in Jürgen Habermas, *Die Einbeziehung des Anderen*, Frankfurt a.M.: Suhrkamp, 1996, pp. 154-184.

Habermas, Jürgen, "Über den internen Zusammenhang von Rechtsstaat und Demokratie," in Jürgen Habermas, *Die Einbeziehung des Anderen*, Frankfurt a.M.: Suhrkamp, 1996, pp. 293-305.

Hesse, Konrad, "Der Rechtsstaat im Verfassungssystem des Grundgesetzes," (1962), in *Rechtsstaatlichkeit und Sozialstaatlichkeit*, ed. Ernst Forsthoff, Darmstadt: Wissenschaftliche Verlagsgesellschaft, 1968, pp. 557-588.

Hoffman-Riem, Wolfgang, "Gesetz und Gesetzesvorbehalt im Umbruch" *Archiv des öffentlichen Rechts* 130 (2005): 5-70.

Jesch, Dietrich, *Gesetz und Verwaltung*, 2nd ed., Tübingen: Mohr, 1968.

Jouanjan, Olivier, *Figures de l'Etat de droit. Le "Rechtsstaat" dans l'histoire intellectuelle et constitutionnelle de l'Allemagne*, Strasbourg: Presses universitaires de Strasbourg, 2001.

Kunig, Philip, *Das Rechtsstaatsprinzip*, Tübingen: Mohr, 1986.

Luhmann, Niklas, *Das Recht der Gesellschaft*, Frankfurt a.M.: Suhrkamp, 1993.

Möllers, Christoph, *Gewaltengliederung*, Tübingen: Mohr Siebeck, 2005.

Möllers, Christoph, *Die drei Gewalten*, Weilerswist: Velbrück Wissenschaft, 2008.

Ogorek, Regina, "Individueller Rechtsschutz gegenüber der Staatsgewalt: Zur Entwicklung der Verwaltungsgerichtsbarkeit im 19. Jahrhundert," in *Bürgertum im 19. Jahrhundert*, ed. Jürgen Kocka, Munich: dtv, 1988, Vol. 1, pp. 372-405.

Pieroth, Bodo, *Rückwirkung und Übergangsrecht*, Berlin: Duncker & Humblot, 1981.

Rossen, Helge, *Vollzug und Verhandlung*, Tübingen: Mohr Siebeck, 1999.

Šarčević, Edin, *Der Rechtsstaat*, Leipzig: Leipziger Universitätsverlag, 1996.

Scheuner, Ulrich, *Die neuere Entwicklung des Rechtsstaats in Deutschland*, Karlsruhe: Müller, 1960, as well as in *Rechtsstaatlichkeit und Sozialstaatlichkeit*, ed. Ernst Fasthoff, Darmstadt: Wissenschaftliche Verlagsgesellschaft, 1968, pp. 461-508.

Sobota, Katharina, *Das Prinzip Rechtsstaat*, Tübingen: Mohr Siebeck, 1997.

Tate, C. Neal, and Torbjörn Vallinder, *The Global Expansion of Judicial Power*, New York: New York University Press, 1995.

Election Law and the Constitutional Order in Germany*

Rudolf Mellinghoff

In today's community of states, there is hardly any phenomenon which is as widespread as that of voting. Therefore it is a particularly important project to speak about election law and constitutional requirements under the rule of law.

The citizens' right to freely and equally determine the representatives and the contents of public authority through elections and voting is the basic element of democractic government. Since the end of the 18th century, the idea of freedom that is based on human rights and the idea of freedom that is based on democracy have developed as the foundations of legitimation of the state in large parts of Europe.

A. Elections and the Electoral System

Because in a representative democracy the people exercise state authority through state bodies, the transfer of sovereign power to these state bodies is of fundamental importance. On principle, the transfer of sovereign power takes place through elections. The parliamentary election is the act in which the people bindingly expresses their will concerning the composition of the representative body of the people. The election is often the only action in which the people can decide in a legally binding manner.

Thus, elections are the foundation of every democracy under the rule of law. Through elections, the people determine the persons of which the state bodies are composed, and they determine who will exercise power in the state.

The organisation of the electoral procedure, and hence the respective electoral system, have a considerable influence on the voters' opportunities to express their opinions and to make decisions, and on the chances of parties

---

* Keynote speech, delivered at the first annual conference "Constitutionalism and Good Governance" of the German-Southeast Asian Center of Excellence for Public Policy and Good Governance, 15-17 November 2010, Bangkok, Thailand.

and candidates in the competition. In modern democracies, in which the party-political composition of parliament is the predominant factor of the decision on who is in power, electoral procedures are of interest as a means of influencing the composition through the manner in which votes translate into seats in parliament. Electoral procedures are used in a targeted manner in order to achieve a governing majority and to promote majorities in Parliament, or to create such majorities in the first place.

The electoral systems which are most commonly known are the two basic types of proportional representation and of majority voting. This, however, is only a very rough typology. Election researchers try to further differentiate these types. They distinguish, for example, relative and absolute majority voting in single-seat constituencies. In this type of voting, members of parliament are elected, as for example in England, in single-seat constituencies by a simple or an absolute majority. In majority voting with minority representation, the decision is taken according to the majority that has been reached, while a representation of minorities is ensured through a restriction on the number of votes. To achieve this, the election must take place in multiple-seat constituencies.

Apart from relative majority voting in single-seat constituencies, proportional representation in medium-sized and large constituencies is the most widespread electoral system. Unlike majority voting in single-seat constituencies, proportional representation in medium-sized and large constituencies has a large range of variations.

Apart from the majority voting systems and proportional representation with its broad range of variations, there are other electoral systems which constitute a mixture of the two basic types. In Germany, for example, personalised proportional representation exists, which combines elements of majority voting and proportional representation. Both systems are also combined in the case of compensatory proportional representation. In this system, direct seats and list seats are not set off against each other; compensation is achieved instead by assigning a larger number of seats determined according to proportional representation. Majority voting and proportional representation are also combined in segmented electoral systems like the so-called ditch system; in this system, part of the members of parliament are elected according to majority voting, the other part according to proportional representation, without a compensation between the two groups taking place.

This classification of electoral systems is a very rough typology which does not yet take the different elements of the electoral procedure into account. The size of the constituency has an influence on the electoral decision, as has the respective electoral formula. What must also be taken into account is the number of persons to be elected, and thus the ratio between voters and members of parliament, as well as possible barrier clauses. Finally, the types of candidature and the types of lists which are possible determine the form in which the possibilities for election are presented to the voters and which possibilities of choice the voters have. Also rules on decision, such as for instance, relative majority voting, absolute majority voting or the possibility of preference votes, have an influence on who will ultimately be elected. Elements concerning the technicalities of an election can be combined almost at will. This results in the existence of a very large number of different election procedures.

Electoral systems have a considerable influence on the distribution of political power. It is therefore not surprising that bitter struggles among the political actors take place when it comes to agreeing on electoral systems.

However, it must also be said that the importance of the electoral systems also depends on the democratic quality of the respective political system. If no fair elections are guaranteed, or if election results may be rigged, the electoral system plays only an insignificant role. Its relevance is all the more limited where powerful groups in society ultimately determine who will win the election or where capital and corruption steer the political conduct of the people's representatives.

B. Electoral Principles

If, on the one hand, elections are the foundation of the democratic state under the rule of law but on the other hand, it is acknowledged that a large number of different electoral systems and types of elections exist, the question arises of whether there are general guidelines and standards that have to be observed in all elections. First of all, there are the classical electoral principles which are recognised in almost all democratic states. These classical electoral principles have in recent times been complemented by other substantive guidelines. Finally, elections can only be referred to as democratic if certain framework conditions are complied with.

I. The Classical Electoral Principles

Certain conditions must be complied with so that an election may be called democratic. Elections must be general, direct, free, equal and secret.

1. The General Nature of Elections

According to its historical development, the principle of the general nature of elections prohibits a restriction of the right to vote due to specific characteristics which are related to the individual, such as a person's social position, gender, financial circumstances, profession, occupation or religion. This principle prohibits the legislature from excluding certain groups of the population from exercising their right to vote for religious, political, economic or social reasons, and it demands that, in principle, everyone should be able to exercise his or her right to vote in as equal a manner as possible. The principle of general suffrage underlines the citizens' equality and thus ensures that foundation of the democratic legitimation of state power is as broad as possible.

However, restrictions of the general nature of elections are possible if there is a commendably important reason for them. Under this perspective, the following restrictions of the principle of the general nature of elections are discussed: a minimum age for the exercise of the right to vote and of the right to stand for election, citizenship as a necessary condition of the right to vote, domicile or permanent residence in the electoral territory, exclusion from the right to vote for mental defects for lack of legal capacity, and exclusion from the right to vote by virtue of a court ruling.

2. The Direct Nature of Elections

The principle of the direct nature of elections requires that the members of the people's representation are elected directly without the participation of electoral delegates. It excludes any election procedure in which after the act of voting, there is an instance between voter and candidate which selects the representative on its own discretion, thereby depriving the individual voters of the possibility to autonomously designate the future members of the people's representation by their act of voting.

3. The Free Nature of Elections

Among other things, the free nature of elections consists of every voter being able to exercise his or her right to vote without compulsion or other external influence. The voter is to be able to reach his or her judgment in a free and open process of opinion-formation.

The principle of the free nature of elections has two aspects. On the one hand, it is to enable the free formation of the voter's will. On the other hand, the voter is to be able to freely express his or her will; this also includes the fight against electoral fraud. The free realisation of the voter's will in the act of voting can be ensured by a great variety of organisational precautions, especially in the polling station. In contrast, it is considerably more difficult to realise the protection of the free formation of the voter's will.

Strict neutrality must be demanded of the state, which is competent for the preparation and organisation of elections. Neutrality also relates to the media, to canvassing, to the right to demonstrate publicly and to the financing of the parties and of the candidates. In Germany, the Federal Constitutional Court has dealt in particular with the government's official public-relations activities in times of election campaigns. During election campaigns, the government may not influence the election through state funds.

It is particularly difficult to find criteria for the impermissibility of unofficial influencing of an election. Private actors, such as business enterprises, trade unions or other interest groups may not threaten to impose sanctions on a certain electoral conduct. It is also difficult to draw a dividing line between permissible canvassing through small campaign gifts and impermissible bribery of voters or vote-buying. Where, for example, gifts like ballpoint pens, key ring pendants or shopping bags that bear the logo or a slogan of a candidate are distributed, this does not pose any problems. If, however, candidates bribe voters by giving them money and thereby influence the election, this does infringe the free nature of elections.

4. The Equal Nature of Elections

Just like the principle of the general nature of elections, the principle of the equal nature of elections ensures the equality of the citizens, which is presupposed by the principle of democracy. In a free and democratic fundamental order, the equal treatment of all citizens with regard to the exercise of their right to vote is one of the essential foundations of state order. The distinguishing feature of equal suffrage is its formal character: Everyone should be able to exercise his or her right to vote or to stand for election in a way that is as equal as possible from a formal perspective. Every citizen is entitled to the right to vote irrespective of his or her gender, origin, language, education, ideology or religion.

According to the Federal Constitutional Court's case-law, every vote must have the same influence on the election result, that is, it must have the same counting value and the same legal chance to contribute to success. In a majority voting system, this has different consequences than in a system with proportional representation. In majority voting systems, the equal nature of elections only requires, apart from the equality of the counting value, that all voters must be able to participate in the creation of a political body on the basis of constituencies whose size is as similar as possible so that the weight of their votes is approximately equal. Systems with proportional representation also guarantee an equal contribution of each vote towards success, that is, an equal influence of each vote on the composition of the elected body. In this context, the legislature only has narrow latitude for differentiations. To be justified, differentiations require an objective which is legitimised by the constitution, and which carries a weight "that is similar to equal suffrage."

Particular problems arise when a party's entry to parliament depends on its obtaining a certain number of votes. What is particularly discussed in Germany are barrier clauses, which only take a party into account in the distribution of seats if it has obtained a certain percentage of votes cast. At present, only parties which have obtained at least five per cent of votes cast or at least three direct mandates may enter to the German *Bundestag*. The Federal Constitutional Court only permits such restrictions if they are necessary to ensure the parliament's ability to act.

5. The Secrecy of Voting

The principle of secret suffrage guarantees that only the voter has knowledge of his or her electoral decision. The secrecy of voting is the most important institutional protection of the freedom of voting. It obliges the legislature to take the measures required for the protection of the secrecy the ballot (for example covered voting papers, voting booths which cannot be seen into). Any investigation of persons entitled to vote about how they intend to vote, are voting or have voted is prohibited.

Exceptions from secret suffrage are only permissible in favour of the right to vote itself, in other words, if the principle of general and equal suffrage requires a voting procedure in which absolute secrecy of the ballot cannot be ensured in every case. In Germany, for example, voters who are disabled or seriously ill can make use of the help of a person of their confidence. What is especially problematic in this context is postal vote because the secrecy of the ballot during the very act of voting cannot be secured by state agencies. Therefore the Federal Constitutional Court has permitted postal vote only under very narrow preconditions.

II. Other Electoral Principles

Other preconditions of democratic elections, apart from these conventional electoral principles, are that they comply with the principle of the public nature of an election and that they take place regularly.

1. The Public Nature of Elections

In its decision on voting computers, the Federal Constitutional Court has developed, apart from these classical electoral principles, the constitutional principle of the public nature of elections.

The public nature of elections is the fundamental precondition of a democratic formation of the political will. It ensures the correctness and the retraceability of the election events and thus creates an essential precondition of the citizens' well-founded trust in the correctness of the election.

In a representative democracy, the election of the people's representation constitutes the fundamental act of legitimation. The casting of votes in the elections to the German *Bundestag* is the essential element of the process of the formation of the political will from the people to the state bodies and thus it is at the same time the foundation of political integration. Compliance with the electoral principles which apply in this context, and confidence in such compliance, are therefore preconditions of a democracy that is able to function. Only the possibility to examine whether the election complies with the electoral principles under constitutional law can ensure that there is no deficiency in the delegation of state authority to the representatives of the people. Only if the voters themselves can reliably verify the correctness of the act of delegation, in other words, only if the election takes place "under the eyes of the public" can the confidence of the people, as the sovereign, in the composition of Parliament corresponding to the will of the voters be guaranteed.

The principle of the public nature of elections requires that all essential steps in the elections are subject to public examination unless other constitutional interests justify an exception. Particular significance attaches here to the monitoring of the election act and to the ascertainment of the election result.

Accordingly, voting machines which record the votes in electronic form and ascertain the result of the election electronically only meet the constitutional requirements if the essential steps in the act of voting and in the ascertainment of the results can be checked by the citizen reliably and without special expert knowledge. The voters themselves must be able to verify even without a more detailed knowledge of computers whether their vote is recorded truthfully as a basis for counting or at least as a basis for a subsequent re-count. The major scope of the effect of possible errors in the voting machines or targeted election falsifications requires special precautions to be taken in order to comply with the principle of the public nature of an election. While manipulations or election-rigging are, under the conditions of the valid provisions, only possible with considerable effort and with a very high risk of discovery, which has a preventive effect, programming errors in the software or targeted election-rigging through manipulation of the software of electronic voting devices are far more difficult to recognise.

According to the German Constitutional Court, electronic voting devices can indeed be used in elections. It must, however, be ensured that a reliable correctness check is possible. In its decision, the Federal Constitutional Court left open what technical possibilities exist which comply with the principle of the public nature of elections by making it possible for the electorate to trust in the correctness of the procedure in which the election result is ascertained because the procedure is retraceable. The Federal Constitutional Court merely indicated possible solutions which are discussed by experts or which are already being used in other countries, for example voting devices which, in addition to recording the vote in electronic form, print out a paper record of the vote cast that is visible to the respective voter (a so-called VVPAT = Voter Verified Paper Audit Trail); the VVPAT can be checked before the definite casting of the vote and is subsequently collected to make verification possible.

From my point of view, numerous incidents from recent times confirm that modern technologies may be used in parliamentary elections only under strict reservations. In October 2008, for example, evidence became known for electronically controlled voting machines, which are deployed in 34 states of the USA, having suppressed votes during the counting of votes. This had been noticed in primaries in Ohio. Meanwhile, the manufacturer of the voting devices has admitted that this was due to a fault in the software which had already been in the system for ten years. In February 2009, a CIA official declared in a hearing before the U.S. Election Assistance Commission in Florida: "(...) wherever the vote becomes an electron and touches a computer, that's an opportunity for a malicious actor potentially to (...) make bad things happen." He stated that the CIA had registered irregularities during elections in Venezuela, Macedonia and Ukraine. After a referendum on President Chavez's removal from office in 2004, which had been held as the result of a plebiscite, in which 19,000 voting machines had been used, and which Chavez had won with a support of almost 60 per cent, local researchers had doubted the correctness of the voting result. They had mentioned technical manipulations of the voting devices because Chavez had obtained good results especially in regions where he actually did not have many supporters. In the presidential elections in Ukraine in 2004, the supporters of candidate Viktor Yanukovych had secretly placed a "non-authorised computer" in the headquarters of the returning officer. This had been discovered by means of intercepted phone calls, with the result that the election had later on been declared invalid by the Supreme Court in Kyiv and was ordered to be repeated. Yanukovych then lost the repeated election to his competitor Viktor Yushchenko. From Macedonia, the CIA reported a so-called "voters' genocide" in which members of the Albanian minority had been deleted from the digital voters' lists by means of a simple "Delete" command. Hackers in the nation of Georgia proceeded the other way round: They added to the voters' lists names of persons some of who had died in the 18th century.

2. Regularity of Elections

Another, unwritten, characteristic of democratic elections is that they take place at regular intervals. Democracy is the "struggle for political power" which is waged to win the majority and which is regulated as regards its procedure. It is a constitutive element of the democratic organisation of state authority that the majority "can always change", that a multi-party system exists and that there is a right "to organised political opposition".

Accordingly, the International Covenant on Civil and Political Rights and the Protocol to the European Convention on Human Rights provide for the recurrent character of elections.

C. Final Remarks

An election is the largest mass procedure provided for by law. Elections are the foundation of the democratic state under the rule of law. They have to comply with certain constitutional requirements. However, elections can only be called democratic if further conditions like for example the guarantee of the liberty rights, legality and clarity of statutes and the procedural securing of the principles of electoral law are ensured.

In the time at my disposal, it was only possible for me to deal with part of the various problems that are connected with guaranteeing democratic elections. I have refrained in particular from addressing the relationship between electoral law and the party system. Whoever speaks about elections as the foundation of the democratic state under the rule of law should actually also have a look at the organisations that play a decisive part in the organisation of the people's will. The connection between the electoral system and the party system is a focus of discussion in political science. It would, however, go beyond the scope of this paper to address the complex issues that arise in this context.

Therefore, I would only like to point out that electoral law and the party system have a major influence on the political development of a country. This became apparent in the year 2000 when the Inter-American Development Bank (IADB) while discussing the connection of political institutions and governability, expanded its mandate by starting an initiative to examine the relations between electoral systems, electoral reforms and governability in Latin America. In recent times, international organisations have increasingly observed electoral law and electoral systems. The United Nations Development Program (UNDP) and other international initiatives for the promotion of democracy will, apart from the respective national efforts for reform, keep the subject of the reform of electoral systems as part of institutional reform to increase governability on the political agenda.

Democracy and Majority Rule

Ingwer Ebsen

A. Some Reflections on the Elements and Requirements of Democratic Majority Rule

I. Majority Rule as the Core of the Principle of Democracy and its Legitimization From the Mutual Recognition as Equals

Political rule requires legitimization. That is not just a normative statement but also a question of effectiveness. Political rule is instable without a minimum amount of acceptance on the part of those subjected to rule. This applies now more than ever given the complex conditions of modern societies and economies. And the conditions of modern societies also mean that the justification of legitimate rule based on tradition or religion or other absolute truths is not sufficient. A justification is instead only sustainable based on a combination of three positions, which in conjunction result in the principle of democracy: of the mutual recognition as equals, from their consent in principle to participation in the society constituted as political union and from the insight that instead of a general consensus that is not achievable in practice the decisions of the political majority are also binding for those who do not concur with them.

Due to the fact that there are no convincing reasons to give any one person as such more political power than others, i.e. irrespective of an office that is transferred in a proper procedure, the legitimizing consent for a political order cannot be expected without the mutual recognition of equality.[1] The existence of a political order with the applicable laws of a state that protects and also provides infrastructure and services is now more than ever a prerequisite for human existence. Due to the fact that because of the different viewpoints and interests of the people the formation of a political union is not possible without terminating discussion through decisions there is also

1 See Kelsen, *Vom Wesen und Wert der Demokratie,* 1929, pp. 4 ff.; similar already Locke, *Two treatises on Government*, 1689, Vol. II, sect. 95; Rousseau, *The Social Contract*, 1762, Book I, chapter 6.

a need for rule in a society of equals.[2] The only form of rule which does not contradict the recognition in principle of equality is majority rule and indeed – as it is inferred from the equality in principle in terms of political power – based on the same suffrage. It is perhaps a bit of an exaggeration, as the early theoreticians of utilitarianism claimed, to assume that the principle of such a system of majority rule gives rise "to the greatest happiness of the greatest number of people".[3] You can formulate this argument in less enthusiastic terms and for instance, state as the Austrian constitutional theorist Hans Kelsen did that majority rule leads to a situation "that if not all of them – at least as many people as possible should be free, i.e. as few people as possible should be at odds with the general will of the social order".[4]

But majority rule can also be jusitifed in a much more pragmatic way. As we know that conflicts of group interests and power competition are inevitable in human societies, and as we have to accept that the rightness of decisions cannot be intersubjectively proven, and due to the fact that decisions nevertheless must be taken, the majority principle is most likely to be accepted by the minority. If it is accepted that decisions have to be taken, a minority has no argument why the majority should follow them. So, the pragmatic reason to justify majority rule is that nobody has found any acceptable alternative.

II. Limits and Requirements of the Principle of Majority Rule

The pragmatic character of majority rule in itself provides us with reasons to not consider this as an absolute imperative. However, the democratic principle of majority rule also has inherent limits in principle, i.e. with regard to its legitimization.

If this decision rule is ultimately based on the mutual recognition of one another as free and equal citizens who accept their integration within the society constituted to be a state it can be assumed that this kind of integration is not unconditional. Majorities can be misled and they can pass decisions

2 See Locke, *Two treatises on Government*, 1689, sect. 98.

3 Jeremy Bentham; refer to Burns, "Happiness and Utility," 2005, pp. 46-61, concerning the use of this phrase in Bentham's work; see also Mill, *Utilitarianism*, 1863, Chapter 1; more critical about the legitimacy of majority rule in matters of individual preferences Mill, *On Liberty*, 1859, passim.

4 Kelsen, *Vom Wesen und Wert der Demokratie,* 1929, p. 5.

that are unjust, cruel and restrict freedom unnecessarily. Even in antique political theory there was agreement that not only could a monarchy be deformed into a tyranny and an aristocracy into an oligarchy, but also that democracy could deform into an oclocracy (mob rule).[5] There are thus generally precautions built into the constitutions for democratic political orders to prevent the perversion of the principle of majority rule through its restriction. The most important ones are:

- the binding constitution itself, which can only be amended by a qualified majority, and in the constitution:
- material and procedural standards which set limits for simple legislation,
- division of powers which provides the judiciary in particular with independence vis-à-vis the political organs,
- additional "checks and balances" such as federal structures with deviations from the majority rule principle.

Interestingly most of the limiting mechanisms were put into effect for the first time in the constitution of the United States of America. Thus this constitution still bears witness to the practical wisdom of those people who drafted it. And the Federalist Papers which accompanied the constitutional process of that time in the form of the articles by Alexander Hamilton, John Jay und James Madison bear impressive testimony to this wisdom.[6]

The constitution[7] that is binding for the simple legislative majority, i.e. it can only be amended with a qualified majority and typically in a certain procedure, restricts the freedom of the majority by providing a sufficiently large minority with a veto position and thus so to speak – albeit only to prevent changes – provides an element of minority rule. Consequently, the institutions themselves that are regulated in the constitution also participate in the limitation of majority rule through the requirement of a qualified majority such as the freedoms and individual legal positions guaranteed under constitutional law. In addition, this applies to the procedural rules for elections and legislation, the independence of the judiciary including constitutional jurisdiction which can also inspect the observation of the constitution by the legislator and legal positions of institutions which act as "checks and

---

5 See Demandt, *Antike Staatsformen*, 1995, p. 40; Polybius, *Histories*, Book 6, Chapter 4.

6 See Brugger, "Freiheit, Repräsentation, Integration," 2001.

7 Refer to Bryce, *The American Commonwealth*, 1888, Vol. 1, Chapters 23, 31 and 33 concerning the key significance of this tool and its protection by a working judiciary.

balances" such as the requirement of cooperation with second legislative chamber in particular which is formed according to criteria other than the pure majority principle, and ultimately the rights of the states in a federal system. All these and additional rules that restrict the political majority protect the citizens' freedom and make majority rule and the power necessarily linked with it for the partisan enforcement of specific interests bearable. Finally, those rules which secure a fair political struggle and thus the option of a change in majorities rank among the rules which make majority rule bearable. They are, in a sense, game rules of the political struggle for power. By way of a summary and putting it simply we can say that it represents a paradox of the democratic majority rule system that it is only bearable when limited and only in this way can it be secured in the long run.

III. Conditions for a Successful Government by the Majority

In addition to the standard conditions of legitimate democratic majority rule which are typically to be formulated in a written constitution there are also factual preconditions that need to be considered. These cannot be simply produced through the drafting of a constitution but have to be present and frequently also cultivated as real social facts of life so that a political system that is based on the principle of majority rule works. This also includes the fact that the legal positions that are guaranteed in the constitution and that can thus not be removed by simple majorities also do actually cover the essential interests or values of essential groups. In the respective societies and at the respective historical times these can be very different items – e.g. of social stratification or classes[8], of religious[9] or ethnic/cultural[10] nature – which are experienced by large numbers of the members of the society as essential and therefore as a key criterion for the emergence of social groups. The compatibility and mutual recognition of such essential interests and values as a requirement for the acceptance of majority rule in a body politic

8 These contradicitons made an essential contribution towards the failure of the first German democracy estabished in 1919.

9 A modern example for decades was also the formation of groups along denominational lines in Northern Ireland.

10 The Belgian state could fall apart due to the differences between the national groups of the French-speaking Walloons and the Flemish. In the Balkans several states disintegrated due to such differences.

can be termed as the necessary minimum level of social homogeneity. And this also involves a situation in which the formation into groups is not so markedly and so clearly and so permanently fixed between majorities and minorities that changes in the political majority are illusory. This is because in such a case the inferiority of the minority would have been structural and the precondition of the factual legitimization of majority rule would have ceased to apply.

The practical "solutions" in such a case can be very different – civil war, peaceful division into different political systems or also the suppression of a group by the other – at any rate the model of democratic majority rule has (for the time being) failed in all these cases.

B. Constitutional Law Elements of the German Model of Democratic Majority Rule

Following the rather general and therefore very abstract comments on the theory of the democratic constitutional state I would like to become a bit more specific, based on the example of one model, i.e. the German model. This shall be performed in several steps. To begin, a few of the central provisions for the German system of democratic majority rule shall be represented. Then I want to draw attention to some problems using the example of a few debates based on constitutional law and at the same time demonstrate what part the Federal Constitutional Court plays in German government practice. And ultimately the specific nature of the forming of the democratic will shall be demonstrated once more by looking at the decision making process of the European Union through the eyes of the Federal Constitutional Court.

I. The Fundamental Decision for Democracy in a Federal State

The German Basic Law contains a few provisions which are set apart from the others to the extent that they cannot be legally repealed under any circumstances. This is stipulated by article 79 section 3 of the Basic Law:

> Amendments to this Basic Law affecting the division of the Federation into *Länder*, their participation on principle in the legislative process, or the principles laid down in Articles 1 and 20 shall be inadmissible.

In addition to the commitment towards the inviolability of human dignity and the recognition of directly applicable human rights, to the federal order of the state, and to the principles of the rule of law and of the social state, the principle of democracy as it is formulated in Article 20 Section 2 of the Basic Law is included too:

> All state authority is derived from the people. It shall be exercised by the people through elections and other votes and through specific legislative, executive and judicial bodies.

This is in particular the principle of democratic legitimisation as it formulated in the first sentence: There shall be no state authority – whether in the form of the legislature, executive or judiciary, which cannot legitimize itself through a (majority) decision of the citizens of the state by way of an uninterrupted chain of elections, nominations or powers to direct. An important aspect but not one which is emphasised by article 79 section 3 of the Basic Law is the principle of representative democracy recognised by the second sentence: It is democratically acceptable that the people themselves are mainly restricted to elections and that for the rest the state power is exercised by special organs.

Democratic legitimisation is not only conveyed by means of elections at the level of the overall state, but – this is part of the federal state principle combined with the guarantee of communal self-government – also by means of elections and parliaments at the level of the federal states and communal authorities. This is stipulated by article 28 section 1 of the Basic Law:

> The constitutional order in the *Länder* must conform to the principles of a republican, democratic and social state governed by the rule of law, within the meaning of this Basic Law. In each *Land*, county and municipality the people shall be represented by a body chosen in general, direct, free, equal and secret elections.

Due to the fact that the democratic process in modern large states cannot be organised without political parties the Basic Law recognises the function of political parties but simultaneously demands that they have a democratic structure and that they have transparent funds, as formulated in article 21 section 1 of the Basic Law:

> Political parties shall participate in the formation of the political will of the people. They may be freely established. Their internal organisation must conform to democratic principles. They must publicly account for their assets and for the sources and use of their funds.

Due to the fact that all forms of democratic legitimization of state actions have to begin with elections by the people, the principles for these elections and their observation constitute the most fundamental precondition for democratic rule. These principles are laid down by the Basic Law in article 38 section 1 of the Basic Law for elections to the *Bundestag*, the federal parliament, and are determined once again for the *Länder* and the local level in article 28 section 1 of the Basic Law. Article 38 Section 1 first sentence states:

> Members of the German *Bundestag* shall be elected in general, direct, free, equal and secret elections.

Each of these five election principles is linked with certain preconditions that are drafted in the legislation and the legal literature which in conjunction shall guarantee a fair election and thus ensure that the results of the election, i.e. the composition of the parliament, actually express the political preferences of the people on election day. In the next section I will concern myself in a bit more detail with the principle of election equality that is evidently particularly important for the majority rule principle. What you might call a "technical" implementation of the principle of majority rule to be achieved through equality of votes can be found for the *Bundestag* in Article 42 of the Basic Law:

> Decisions of the *Bundestag* shall require a majority of the votes cast unless this Basic Law otherwise provides.

This means that generally, if nothing else is laid down, the so-called simple or relative majority that is attained by the position which is awarded the highest number of votes is sufficient. Another ruling, namely the requirement of an absolute majority, i.e. of the majority of the members of the *Bundestag,* is demanded, for instance, by article 63 section of the Basic Law for the election of the German federal chancellor.

II. Restrictions and Qualifications of the Principle of Majority Rule

The most marked qualification of the principle of democratic majority rule results from the provisions of the Basic Law which – for the implementation of the principles of a federal state – regulates the participation of the *Länder* in the political decisions at a federal level The provisions concerning the composition and the tasks of the *Bundesrat* are most important in this respect. The *Bundesrat* is primarily the second legislative chamber of the federal German state. It is composed – and this distinguishes it from the second chambers of the states which follow the senate model of the United States – of the executive governments of the *Länder*. These governments have different numbers of votes in the *Bundesrat* depending on their populations as laid down by Article 51 Section 2 of the Basic Law:

> Each *Land* shall have at least three votes; *Länder* with more than two million inhabitants shall have four, *Länder* with more than six million inhabitants five, and *Länder* with more than seven million inhabitants six votes.

This ruling demonstrates that the size of a *Land* is not irrelevant, but that *Länder* with a smaller population are favoured over those with a large population. In accordance with the current distribution of the population between the *Länder* it emerges from this ruling that in the *Land* of Bremen with a population of some 660,000 inhabitants there is one vote for every 220,000 inhabitants in the *Bundesrat*, whilst there is only one vote for every 3 million inhabitants in North Rhine Westphalia which has a population of some 17.8 million inhabitants. This means that the influence of the Bremen voter upon the *Bundesrat* via the election of his/her *Land* Government is approximately 13 times greater than the influence of a voter in North Rhine Westphalia.

This difference leads to a differing level of influence *upon* the legislation on the federal level as the *Bundesrat* participates – for various laws in different ways – in the federal legislation. Normally the *Bundesrat* can object to a bill which only means that the *Bundestag* must pass a vote on a law once more to *reject the objection* (article 77 section 3 Basic Law). However, if the *Bundesrat* lodges an objection with an absolute majority of its current 69 votes, i.e. with 35 votes, the *Bundestag* can now also only reject this objection by means of an absolute majority. And in the event of an objection with two thirds of the votes submitted in the *Bundesrat* the same quorum even applies for the *Bundestag*:

> If the objection is adopted by the majority of the votes of the *Bundesrat*, it may be rejected by a decision of the majority of the Members of the *Bundestag*. If the *Bundesrat* adopted the objection by a majority of at least two thirds of its votes, its rejection by the *Bundestag* shall require a two thirds majority, including at least a majority of the Members of the *Bundestag*.

In some cases, also including an amendment of the Basic Law itself, the consent of the *Bundesrat* is required for a bill to become a law.

The deviation from the majority principle and thus from the equality of the political weight of the citizens that is essential for a democracy is justified due to the last key reason for the federal state structure: The citizens of the smaller *Länder*, represented by their governments, shall be protected from being outvoted too easily by other *Länder* and by the citizens of the nation state. This qualification of the democratic principle makes it easier for regional minorities represented by the *Länder* to accept this principle and thus ultimately serve to provide for its stability. At the same time making legislative decisions with a narrow majority more difficult leads to a situation whereby more consensus has to be organised in the political process for a parliamentary bill which usually also has a stabilising effect. This is an example of "checks and balances" in the democratic process.[11]

III. Constitutional Jurisdiction

The constitutional jurisdiction would of course be worth a lecture in its own right. However, it cannot also remain unmentioned in the context of the democratic process and majority rule. Its role in this context is implied from the provisions of the powers of the Federal Constitutional Court and the election of its judges. If we slightly simplify things we arrive by means of the constitutional provision concerning the powers of the court (article 93 Basic Law; concerning the scrutiny of the election of the *Bundestag* refers also to article 41 section 2 Basic Law) at the three main functions, which in some cases overlap, i.e.:

- the resolution of disputes between the supreme constitutional bodies and also in the federal system of *Bund (*federal government) and *Länder,*
- the protection of basic rights and the democratic rights of participation of the citizens and the rights of self-administration of the communities and
- the clarification of the validity of legal provisions if these are called into question.

11 In the famous No. 51 of Federalist Papers its author Autor Madison had the following to say about this: "In republican government, the legislative authority necessarily predominates. The remedy for this inconveniency is to divide the legislature into different branches; and to render them, by different modes of election and different principles of action, as little connected with each other as the nature of their common functions and their common dependence on the society will admit. It may even be necessary to guard against dangerous encroachments by still further precautions." (Hamilton, Jay and Madison, *The Federalist Papers*, 1787/88, p. 290).

As a result recourse can be made to the Federal Constitutional Court concerning all issues which concern the Basic Law, and it can pass decisions on this with the highest level of authority in the state. It is thus also the highest guardian of the constitutional norms which regulate the democratic process. The meaning of the provisions of the Basic Law in their respective constellations ultimately emerges from its decisions. Consequently, what a politician and later Chief Justice of Supreme Court once said about the US judiciary also applies to the Federal Constitutional Court: "We are under a Constitution, but the Constitution is what the judges say it is...."[12]

The Federal Constitutional Court consists of 2 senates of 8 judges respectively, half of whom are elected by the *Bundestag* (or more precisely by a committee of the *Bundestag*) and half are elected by the *Bundesrat*. Article 94 Basic Law stipulates the following concerning this:

(1) The Federal Constitutional Court shall consist of federal judges and other members. Half the members of the Federal Constitutional Court shall be elected by the *Bundestag* and half by the *Bundesrat*. They may not be members of the *Bundestag*, of the *Bundesrat*, of the Federal Government, or of any of the corresponding bodies of a *Land*.

(2) The organisation and procedure of the Federal Constitutional Court shall be regulated by a federal law, which shall specify in which instances its decisions shall have the force of law.

It is an interesting paradox that one of the most important provisions concerning the election of the constitutional judges which is key concerning the role and the position of the court and simultaneously constitutes an additional restriction to the principle of majority rule, i.e. that principle of the electoral quorum, is not to be found in the constitution but only in the Federal Constitutional Court Act. Article 6, section 2 and 5, and article 7 of this law stipulate the constitutional court judges shall be elected with a two thirds majority:

Article 6

...

(2) The *Bundestag* shall, by proportional representation, elect a twelve persons electoral committee for the Federal Constitutional Court judges....

...

12 Hughes, *Addresses and Papers*, 1908, p. 139; similarly the German scholar Rudolf Smend, "Das Bundesverfassungsgericht," 1962/1968, p. 582: "Nowadays, the Basic Law is valid as it is interpreted by the Federal Constitutional Court,...".

(5) To be elected, a judge shall require at least eight votes.

Article 7

The judges to be elected by the *Bundesrat* shall be elected with two thirds of the votes of the *Bundesrat*.

In practice to date this has led to a situation whereby a constitutional court judge could never be elected without the joint consent of the forces supporting the government and the opposition. If an attempt was ever made to abolish this quorum the real German constitution would be changed more markedly than would have been the case in a lot of the provisions of the Basic Law. This was clearly illustrated when a parliamentary bill was discussed in 1956 in the *Bundestag* in accordance with which a simple majority of the members was deemed to suffice in the second ballot once the first ballot had failed.[13] A lot of things seem to suggest that the qualified majority for the election of the constitutional judges – and indeed the same quorum as would apply for the amendment of the constitution itself – is comparable to the conventions in accordance with the unwritten British constitution: It can only be done away with in theory.

C. Three Examples of Constitutional Law Discussions About Democratic Majority Rule

I. The Principle of Equal Suffrage in the Constitutional Jurisdiction

The constitutional principle of equal suffrage is a necessary condition of democracy and majority rule. A distinction is made between two aspects of this principle in the constitutional law debate: In principle, equal suffrage only applies if firstly the votes of all the votes are counted in the same manner to determine the election results (counting value) and secondly also ultimately contribute towards the composition of the parliament with the same weighting (success value). Whilst the counting value is rarely a problem – it is simply forbidden to assign the votes submitted different counting val-

13 See Laufer, *Verfassungsgerichtsbarkeit und politischer Prozeß*, 1968, pp. 185 et seqq., who addresses this in detail; in a debate in the *Bundestag* attention was – tellingly by an MP of a small party – drawn to the role of the Federal Constitutional Court as the "guardian of the rights of the minority".

ues[14] – the problems and discussions concerning the success value are much more complex.

This can be illustrated looking at the potential electoral systems. Germany has an electoral system of „personalized proportional representation“ in which on the one hand individual candidates face each other in constituencies and on the other hand by means of candidate lists at the *Länder* level. It is ensured that the composition of the parliament ultimately corresponds to the ratio of votes of the parties that compete with one another. As in the case of all pure types of proportional representation this system essentially leads to the same success value of the votes.[15]

The classic system of majority election (first past the post) as for instance applies for the election to the British House of Commons is different. In this system, on the one hand only the votes which are given to the respective winner in the constituency have a success value. And on the other hand both the different number of voters per constituency and also the different distribution of political preferences in the constituency can once again lead to considerable differences in the success value. Electorates of different sizes evidently lead to a different weighting of the votes in them. But what is of more practical importance in the political process, which always also represents social interests, are tangible differences in the electorate. If the constituencies are formed in such a way that one political faction wins regularly but by a tight margin whilst the opposing faction regularly wins constituencies by a large majority but only a few of them, the minority of voters can attain a structural majority of parliamentary seats.

The Federal Constitutional Court has not yet had to pass a decision on this matter, but has expressed the view several times in obiter dicta that the different success value is necessarily laid down in the first past the post system, but that this does not affect the freedom of the legislator to also select this electoral system at its own discretion.[16] We can reflect on whether this is not a very loose form of interaction with the demand for the equality of

14 It has nevertheless been suggested that parents of minors should receive additional votes for their children; see Westle, "Wahlrecht von Geburt an," 2006.

15 Minor differences which can be ignored can result here from different mathematical procedures for allocation of the last seat to remain votes.

16 As the Federal Constitutional Court once ruled in a decision dated 5 April 1952, File No. 2 BvH 1/52, Court Decisions Vol. 1, pp. 208-261) and several times subsequently (most recently decision of 30 June 2009, File No. 2 BvE 2/08 and other, Court Decisions Vol. 123, pp. 267-437).

suffrage.[17] At any rate in a first past the post system one must inspect more closely than in the case of proportional representation whether the layouts of the constituencies bring about structural advantages or disadvantages for political factions. This is also recognized in principle by the Federal Constitutional Court based on the theory that in the case of a first past the post system the same success value cannot be demanded but nevertheless the same opportunity of success can be.[18]

Within proportional representation systems the constitutional jurisdiction is stricter towards deviations from the equality of the success value. This can be demonstrated by the example of election thresholds which should prevent the formation of splinter groups in parliament. Based on the viewpoint that a large number of small parliamentary groups would unreasonably impair the parliament's ability to function, i.e. the formation of a stable government majority and the ability to act and take decisions of the parliament, there are electoral provisions in Germany which demand a minimum share of the vote so a party can have members in parliament in the first place. Such barring clauses were the objects of constitutional jurisdiction several times. They do not affect the counting value, but evidently the success value of the votes submitted as the votes which do not attain the necessary quorum in total do not have any success value. In the constitutional judicature a barring clause of 7 % was considered unconstitutional as it went beyond the legitimate target.[19]

5% clauses for parliaments on the other hand were consistently deemed constitutional by the Federal Constitutional Court because the observation of the parliament's ability to work has the same constitutional ranking as the equality of the success value.[20] This argument was even recognized with

17 Very decidedly Meyer, *Der Überhang*, 1994, pp. 347 et seqq.

18 For the first time in detail by the Federal Constitutional Court dated 10 April 1997, File No. 2 BvF 1/95, Court Decisions Vol. 95, p. 335 (in its decision concerning the boundary problem of proportional represent the competent 2nd senate of the Federal Constitutional Court was divided 4:4); most recently decision of 30 June 2009 (footnote 16); refer also to Pauly, "Das Wahlrecht," 1998, pp. 247 et seqq. concerning this.

19 Federal Constitutional Court dated 5 April 1952, 2 BvH 1/52.

20 Federal Constitutional Court dated 5 April 1952, 2 BvH 1/52; dated 23 January 1957, File No. 2 BvE 2/56, Court Decisions Vol. 6, p. 84; dated 29 January 1990, File No. 2 BvE 1/90 among others; Court Decisions Vol. 82, p. 322.

much less conviction for the German elections to the European Parliament.[21] Set against this, 5 % clauses of the communal parliaments were viewed as unconstitutional in the recent past because the arguments relating to the functionality would not carry the same weight as they would at the level of state parliaments.[22] At any rate this debate demonstrates the relatively large amount of attention paid to the jeopardisation of the equality of suffrage and thus also of the democratic principle of majority rule.

II. "Government Propaganda" as a Problem for a Fair and Open Political Struggle for Majorities

This attention can also be discovered in the case of a theme which is not connected with an individual constitutional provision but with the "spirit" of the constitution in terms of the legitimacy of democratic majority rule. In just the same way, that the political minority is having a real opportunity of becoming a majority by means of democratic elections and thus of achieving governmental power is a necessary precondition to ensure the legitimacy of the government system (see above chapter I), fair conditions of political struggle are an important precondition to provide this opportunity. In this context the Federal Constitutional Court has imposed limits upon government propaganda in relation to several aspects. Also in a political system in which the freedom of political communication is as comprehensively secured by means of fundamental rights (freedom of opinion, press freedom and freedom of broadcasting, the freedom to found parties and other organizations) as it is in Germany, the state apparatus that is controlled by the government can gain an illegitimate advantage with propaganda using state funds.

For the first time the Federal Constitutional Court had addressed this issue when the federal government made the attempt in 1960 to install a government television broadcaster by founding a company under private law. What is probably more important than the statement of reasons for the clarification

---

21 Federal Constitutional Court dated 22 May 1979, File No. 2 BvR 193/79 and 197/79, Court Decisions Vol. 51, p. 222.

22 Constitutional court of North Rhine Westphalia dated 6 July 1999, File No. 14/98 and 15/98, *Deutsches Verwaltungsblatt* (1999): 1271; Federal Constitutional Court dated 13 Feb 2008, File No. 2 BvK 1/07, Court Decisions Vol. 120, p. 82; refer also to Ehlers, "Sperrklauseln im Wahlrecht," 1999.

of the powers between the *Federal government* and the *Länder* in the broadcasting field was the statement of reasons of Federal Constitutional Court[23] in the first "television trial" for a constitutional requirement of a separation of the state – more precisely a separation of politics – from the public service broadcasters[24].

Government propaganda can also take place through the general public relations work of the state bodies, and this is something that cannot be completely forbidden due to the legitimate information tasks of the government. Here the Federal Constitutional Court has attempted to delineate the legitimate information task from the illegitimate propaganda whereby the proximity to the respective parliamentary elections in particular plays an important part.[25] The basis of this is the ban on partisan intervention on the part of state organs, that is derived from the principle of democracy and the demand for equal opportunities of political parties, upon the election for the representative bodies of the people and the canvassing of the government in itself for its reelection. Neither state money nor the authority of state bodies is to be used in the political power struggle.

In overall terms one can state that the conditions of fair competition for political power are well looked after by the Federal Constitutional Court as the arbitrator in this power struggle. There are no indications that this could change.

III. The German Federal Constitutional Court and Democracy in the European Union

The reflections on democracy and majority rule shall be finally rounded off with the jurisdiction of the Federal Constitutional Court concerning the European Union and its organization. The European Union is very complex in constitutional law terms and is a new structure in just the same way that the federal state was in the 18th Century upon the creation of the United

23 Federal Constitutional Court dated 28 February 1961, File No. 2 BvG 1/60 and 2/60, Court Decisions Vol. 12, p. 205.

24 Every realist knows that this can only ever be enforced approximately, but it is also nevertheless an important target.

25 Federal Constitutional Court dated 2 March 1973, File No. 2 BvE 1/76, Court Decisions Vol. 44, p. 125; concerning this and additional aspects of equality of opportunity in political struggle: See Pauly, "Das Wahlrecht," 1998, pp. 271-274.

States. On the one hand the EU is a contract based organization under international law and on the other hand, due to the transfer of elements of state sovereignty and to the primacy of its law over the laws of the member states, it is quite different to other organizations under international law. Its description as "supranational" expresses this status between a contractual organization and a state very well.

The transfer of sovereignty to the EU is a problem, if viewed in relation to the requirement of democratic legitimization for all state decisions: On the one hand the parliaments and governments of the member states are thus not completely accountable to their voters in democratic terms. However, on the other hand there is not (yet) a European nation which the organs of the EU can be accountable to, and there is also a lack both in organizational terms and also in terms of the real political process of the essential preconditions for sufficient democratic accountability at an EU level.

The Federal Constitutional Court addressed these issues especially when contractual changes were made which strengthened European integration and thus the national surrendering of sovereignty respectively. In its judgement concerning the Maastricht treaty establishing the European Union dated 7 February 1992 and the corresponding ratification act of *Bundestag*, which also changed the basic law, even the minimum requirements of the democratic principle that are protected against constitutional changes by article 79 section 3 Basic Law were in the courts concern.[26]

The court viewed a constitutional complaint that was based on article 38 section 1 of the Basic Law (election principles) as admissible. This decision is thus a "strategic" one in that it was now clear for the future that the Federal Constitutional Court can inspect additional surrendering of sovereignty when a constitutional complaint is received by a person entitled to vote by applying the standards of the Basic Law. In the words of the Federal Constitutional Court: "The Germans entitled to vote are guaranteed the subjective right to participate in the election of the German *Bundestag* and thus to contribute to the legitimization of the power of the state by the people at a federal level and to influence the way it is exercised." In this way the court had opened up a substantive inspection standard for itself: The subjective right of each elector "from article 38 of the Basic Law can be violated accordingly if the observation of the powers of the German *Bundestag* are

---

26 Federal Constitutional Court dated 12 October 1993, File No. 2 BvR 2134/92 and 2159/92, Court Decisions Vol. 89, p. 155.

transferred to such an extent to an organ of the European Union or the European Communities formed by the governments that the minimal requirements of democratic legitimization of the public authority that are indispensable according to article 20 section 1 und 2 in conjunction with article 79 section 3 Basic Law can no longer be fulfilled." Although a violation of these principles was denied, the Federal Constitutional Court still reserved itself the inspection power of also measuring the EU's future practice based on these standards.

The second major decision in this context concerning the ratification act of the Treaty of Lisbon amending the Treaty on European Union and the Treaty establishing the European Community dated 13 December 2007 and the renewed amendments of the Basic Law[27] that go with it confirms this approach and makes it even more clear than before that, and indeed how, the core elements of the constitution that coin its identity and are specially protected by article 79 section 3 of the Basic Law can be enforced by the Federal Constitutional Court by means of a constitutional complaint of any citizen of the state. Whilst advancing this jurisdiction the Federal Constitutional Court then stresses the connection between the option of surrenders of sovereignty and the degree of the realization of democratic principles in the EU: "An enhancement of integration can be unconstitutional if the level of democratic legitimization does not keep pace with the scope and the weight of the supranational ruling power." The level of democratic legitimization of the restructured new EU is then inspected. According to the court, the EU cannot be viewed as an autonomous democratic system because the allocation of parliamentary seats to the member states at variance with their population does not observe the principle of the equality of suffrage. This would lead to a situation whereby "the weighting of the votes of a citizen from a member state with a low population can be twelve times greater than the weighting of a vote from a citizen of a member state with a large population." This is only held acceptable in an upper chamber but not in the representative body of the people itself. Due to the decisive influence of the EU-Council which is an organ of the governments of the member states and is not accountable to any joint representative body of the people the EU is "excessively federalised measured in terms of the principle of representative democracy."

---

27 Federal Constitutional Court dated 30 June 2009. File No. 2 BvE 2/09 and others, Court Decisions Vol. 123, p. 276.

In these judgements concerning the limitations of Germany with respect to the transfer of sovereign rights to the EU the Federal Constitutional Court has not only set standards for Germany's participation in the process of European integration but also precisely laid down the basic elements that make up the principle of democracy and that are declared unalterable by article 79 section 3 of the Basic Law.

Works cited

Brugger, Winfried: "Freiheit, Repräsentation, Integration: Zur Konzeption politischer Einheitsbildung in den 'Federalist Papers'," in *Verfassung – Philosophie – Kirche: Festschrift für Alexander Hollerbach zum 70. Geburtstag*, eds. Joachim Bohnert et al., Berlin 2001, pp. 515-532.

Bryce, James, *The American Commonwealth*, 1888, ie-edition Indianapolis: Liberty Fund, 1995 (http://oll.libertyfund.org/index.php?option=com_staticxt&staticfile=show.php%3Ftitle=809&layout=html).

Burns, J.H., "Happiness and Utility: Jeremy Bentham's Equation," *Utilitas*, 17 (2005): 46-61.

Demandt, Alexander, *Antike Staatsformen: Eine vergleichende Verfassungsgeschichte der Alten Welt*, Berlin: Akademie Verlag, 1995.

Ehlers, Dirk, "Sperrklauseln im Wahlrecht," *JURA* (1999): 660-666.

Hamilton, Alexander, John Jay, and James Madison, *The Federalist Papers*, 1787/88, edited by C. R. Kesler, C. Rossiter, New York: Mentor Books, 1999. (Project Gutenberg version: http://thomas.loc.gov/home/histdox/fedpapers.html).

Hughes, Charles Evans, *Addresses and Papers of Charles Evans Hughes, Governor of New York, 1906 – 1908*, New York/ London: G. P. Putnam's sons, 1908. (http://openlibrary.org/works/OL2542736W/).

Kelsen, Hans, *Vom Wesen und Wert der Demokratie*, 2nd ed. Tübingen: Mohr, 1929.

Laufer, Heinz, *Verfassungsgerichtsbarkeit und politischer Prozeß*, Tübingen: Mohr, 1968.

Locke, John, *Two treatises on Government*, 1689, 6th reprint, London: A. Millar et al., 1764.

(http://openlibrary.org/books/OL23695759M/).

Meyer, Hans, "Der Überhang und anderes Unterhaltsame aus Anlaß der Bundestagswahl 1994," *Kritische Vierteljahresschrift für Gesetzgebung und Rechtswissenschaft* (1994): 312-362.

Mill, John St., *On Liberty*, 1859, 3rd ed., London: Longman et al., 1864. (http://openlibrary.org/books/OL24140399M/).

Mill, John St., *Utilitarianism*, London: Parker, Son and Bourn, 1863. (http://openlibrary.org/books/OL7196800M/).

Pauly, Walter, "Das Wahlrecht in der neueren Rechtsprechung des Bundesverfassungsgerichts," *Archiv des öffentlichen Rechts* 123 (1998): 232-285.

Polybius, *The Histories*, Vol. VI, ed. William R. Paton, Cambridge MA: Harvard University Press, 1927 (http://penelope.uchicago.edu/Thayer/E/Roman/Texts/Polybius/).

Rousseau, Jean Jaques, *The Social Contract*, 1762, translated into English by Maurice Cranston, Harmondsworth: Penguin, 1968 (http://www.constitution.org/jjr/socon.htm).

Smend, Rudolf, "Das Bundesverfassungsgericht," in Rudolf Smend, *Staatsrechtliche Abhandlungen und andere Aufsätze*, 1962, 2. ed., Berlin: Duncker & Humblot, 1968, pp. 581-593.

Westle, Bettina, "'Wahlrecht von Geburt an' – Rettung der Demokratie oder Irrweg?" *Zeitschrift für Parlamentsfragen* (2006): 96-114.

Federalism and Decentralization

Dirk Ehlers

A. Introduction

Social systems tend to react to complexity with differentiation. The same may also be said for the political community and consequently for countries. However, the full particulars of a state's constitutive nature depend on multiple circumstances. What is beneficial for one country is not necessarily adequate for another. The main focus of my lecture will be the situation in Germany. There, and in almost every other state in Europe – with the possible exemption of France – we made the experience that a firmly centralized political system creates problems. This is due to the fact that various new problems frequently surface which may not be surveyed and solved appropriately from a centralist perspective. Just as important for a democracy and a separation of powers in the sense of checks and balances[1] is the division of the federal state into autonomously acting subsystems.

Until the 19th century there was only a relatively loose confederation of states – *i.e.* not a federal state as it is today – in Germany: the Holy Roman Empire of the German Nation.[2] Sovereignty was only enjoyed by the numerous German states. It was not before 1871 that the first federal state was created. As far as a centralized state developed – which happened under different circumstances in the time of National Socialism and in the German Democratic Republic – it was coupled with the occurrence of abuse of power as well as offences against the rule of law.[3] A division of the federal state into smaller, autonomous and democratic entities increases both democratic

---

1 See for this the fundamental work of Montesquieu, *L'Esprit des Lois*, 1748; for the American understanding of the relation between central and each states' power Mc-Culluc v. Marylan, 17 U.S. (4 wheat.) 316 (1819).

2 To impact and characteristics: see Frotscher and Pieroth, *Verfassungsgeschichte*, 2010, § 4.

3 See for the national socialist injustice: Bracher, *Die deutsche Diktatur*, 1997; Broszat, *Der Staat Hitlers*, 2000, Grawert, *Staatsvolk und Staatsangehörigkeit*, 2003. For the German Democratic Republic: see Lüderssen, *Der Staat geht unter, das Unrecht bleibt?*, 1992, Laufs, *Recht und Unrecht der DDR*, 1998.

participation and self-government of the citizens. Moreover, it facilitates the exertion of political influence for regional minorities. Additionally, it enables the integration of the opposition into the democratic system.[4] Thus, the opposition is not only limited to criticism if it has the majority in smaller entities. It rather has the opportunity to take on responsibility and point out alternatives. Even the Law of the European Union has acknowledged that the members of the European Union are not monolithic blocks. As a result, the European Union, according to the principle of subsidiarity for the areas not entirely encompassed by its competence, may only act insofar as the objectives of potential actions cannot be achieved sufficiently by central, regional or local levels of government.[5] The decision if and to what degree the Member State is divided, however, is left to the Member States.

The organisation of the Federal Republic of Germany is characterized by the two guiding principles of federalism and decentralisation. That is to say the co-operation of states and the division into different legal entities. As indicated by its name, the Federal Republic of Germany is a federal state which means it consists of a state at federal level – the "Bund" – and its 16 constituent states – the "Länder" (from Schleswig-Holstein in the North to Bavaria in the South). The "Länder" are endowed with strong sovereign powers, restricted to certain matters, which are approved by but not derived from the "Bund".[6] Simultaneously, the Constitution, named Grundgesetz or Basic Law of the Federal Republic of Germany, acknowledges multiple self-administrating entities at various levels below the federal one. Of special importance in this context are the local/municipal self-administrations as they are territorial entities with extensive self-dependent responsibilities.[7] Therefore the system is occasionally characterized as a tripartite system: the Bund, the Länder and the local/municipal entities.[8] This is legally incorrect because the municipalities are in fact subdivisions of the Länder. However, this characterisation points out the importance which is allocated to the municipalities in Germany.

4 See Hesse, *Grundzüge des Verfassungsrechts,* 1995, para 226.
5 Art. 5 III TFEU (=Treaty of the Functioning of the European Union).
6 BVerfGE 1, 14 (34).
7 See Art. 28 II Grundgesetz (GG).
8 See Thieme, *Die Gliederung der deutschen Verwaltung*, paras 44 ff.

B. The German Features of a Federal State

Let us begin with a look at the federal state. Although Thailand, as opposed to Indonesia, is organized in a centralistic way, it is worthwhile to familiarise us with the advantages and disadvantages of a different conception. I will not delve into the subject and restrict myself to the delineation of some general principles.

I. Vertical Separation of Powers

In the German variety of a federal state the legislative, administrative and judiciary competencies as well as the fiscal sovereignty are shared. The Länder exercise the governmental power and perform the governmental responsibilities as long as the Basic Constitutional Law does not state or allow otherwise.[9] Thus, the Länder generally also have the legislative power.[10] However, to a large degree exclusive legislative powers were assigned to the Bund.[11] In the area of competing competencies[12] the Länder generally only have the legislative authority as long as the Bund has not made use of it so far. Nonetheless, the Länder may adopt rules which differ from federal laws in particular cases. In sum, the brunt of the legislation lies with the "Bund" even if the "Länder" have the legislative power to regulate for example matters concerning the police, schools or universities. On the other hand, the administration is primarily a task of the "Länder", even if they are not concerned with their own but federal law.[13] Apart from the Federal Constitutional Court and the constitutional courts of the states, the judiciary is split into different levels of jurisdiction. The courts generally are district courts with the exception of the Supreme Courts being federal courts.[14] Of utmost importance to the federal system is the allocation of revenue sources. Only financial self-sufficiency ensures independence. As the most important taxes in Germany are raised federally and the tax revenue of the Länder[15]

---

9 Art. 30 GG.

10 Art. 70 I GG.

11 Art. 73 GG.

12 Art. 74 GG.

13 Art. 83 ff. GG.

14 Art. 95 I GG.

15 Art. 105 II a, 106 II GG.

does not suffice for an appropriate funding, the tax revenue is divided between Bund and Länder according to a special key.[16]

II. Homogeneity of Bund and Länder

In spite of the vertical separation of powers, Bund and Länder are parts of a common system that have to co-operate in many ways. To this end a certain degree of homogeneity is required. It is secured that the constitutional order of the Länder has to be consistent with the principles of a state which is republican, democratic and welfare orientated in the sense of the Basic Constitutional Law.[17] In case of a collision between federal law and state law the former supplants the latter if the Basic Constitutional Law is being obeyed.[18] Furthermore, constitutional jurisprudence has developed the principle of federal allegiance which is deduced from the Basic Constitutional Law.[19] It obliges Bund and Länder to be considerate of each other while using their powers. This leads to special requirements with regard to procedures as well as to the political style. Be that as it may, the accessory nature of the federal allegiance principle does not single-handedly create a set of rights and obligations.

III. Possibilities for Exertion of Influence: Länder on Bund and Vice Versa

"Bund" and "Länder" do not just exist separately but also do work together. For this purpose the Länder act through a federal entity – the Federal Council or "Bundesrat"[20] – which represents their interests in the federal legislative process as well as to some extent in the federal administration. This is of enormous practical importance. The members of the Federal Council are members of the state governments. Their number varies according to the size of their particular state.[21] If the Federal Council does not agree with federal

16 See particularly Art. 106 III GG.
17 Art. 28 I 1 GG.
18 Art. 31 GG.
19 BVerfGE 12, 205 (254 f.); 81, 310 (337 f.); 92, 203 (230 ff.).
20 Art. 50 GG.
21 Art. 51 II GG.

laws it may take the law to the mediation committee[22] which is composed of members of the German Parliament – the Bundestag – and members of the Federal Council. If the Council disagrees with the result it may appeal[23] against the mediation committee – and the Parliament is only able to rebut the appeal with the same majority.[24] If the consent of the Federal Council is necessary – which is often the case – the law does not come into existence without explicit approval by the Federal Council.[25]

On the other hand, the Bund has the power of supervision[26] and regulation[27] with regard to the application of federal laws by the Länder. Should all other methods prove insufficient, the Bund may even exercise its federal authority over the Länder which could be termed as "federal coercion".[28] In practice, however, this power has never been exercised so far.

Disputes are usually resolved by the Federal Constitutional Court, the "Bundesverfassungsgericht".[29]

IV. Competing or Cooperating Federalism

A federalist system is either primarily oriented towards competition or towards cooperation.[30] Diversity is supposed to create competition on the marketplace of ideas. Actually for a long period of time the unitaristic currents were popular in Germany.[31] For example Bund and Länder co-operate in different common institutions[32] despite the prohibition of a mixed administration.[33] The same is the case for the Länder. They coordinate their legislature to a large extent even though it is not required. For instance all the Länder have very similar police or administrative laws. The same applies

---

22 Art. 77 II GG.
23 Art. 77 III GG.
24 Art. 77 IV GG.
25 Art. 78 GG.
26 Art. 84 III, 85 IV GG.
27 Art. 84 V, 85 III GG.
28 Art. 37, 91 II GG.
29 Art. 93 I Nr. 2-4 GG.
30 See on the one hand Würtenberger, "Neugliederung," 2008, paras 9 et seq, on the other Rudolf, "Kooperation im Bundesstaat," 2008.
31 See Hesse, *Der unitarische Bundesstaat*, 1962.
32 Art. 91 a ff. GG.
33 BVerfGE 63, 1 (38 ff.); 108, 169 (182); 119, 331 (365).

to education, which is one of the core legislative powers of the Länder and streamlined through the Standing Conference of the Ministers of Education and Cultural Affairs of the Länder. Strong unitarist effects emanate from the Basic Constitutional Law and its basic rights which bind all authorities. If the constitution mentions the establishment of comparable living conditions[34] it does however not mean a leveling of living conditions. It is rather supposed to prevent the living conditions diverging too much. To achieve this, a vertical revenue equalisation between "Bund" and "Länder" is installed,[35] financial assistance of the "Bund" for important investments of the Länder is provided[36] and the Länder additionally have a horizontal revenue equalisation amongst them.[37] Their aim is to support the poorer "Länder" according to the idea of solidarity. Although there are occasional conflicts between richer and poorer states the fundamental idea is not disputed.

C. New Developments

Within the last years two efforts were made to modernise the federal system using reforms of federalism under constitutional law. The main idea of the first federalist reform in 2006 was to transfer legislative powers from the "Bund" to the "Länder" on the one hand and to reduce approval requirements of the Federal Council on the other hand in order to reduce the risk of stalemates between the two houses in the legislative process.[38] It is highly contentious whether those changes were successful. The second federalist reform which was passed in 2009[39] dealt with the reorganisation of the financial relations between the Bund and the Länder and intended to bolster the independence of territorial authorities as well as the financial endowment for their duties. Effectively only a debt limit was inserted into the Basic Constitutional Law. The Bund in 2016, respectively the Länder in 2020, is obligated to present a balanced budget without using any revenues from credits to achieve this goal.[40] Although the prohibition of new indebtedness

34 Art. 72 II GG in contrary to Art. 91 a I GG (improvement of living conditions), 106 a, 106 b.

35 Art. 106, 107 I, II 3 GG.

36 Art. 104 b GG.

37 Art. 107 II GG.

38 52nd Amendment of the Grundgesetz, 28 August 2006, BGBl I p 2034.

39 57th Amendment of the GG, 29 July 2009, BGBl I p. 2248.

40 Art. 109 III, 115 II, 143 d GG.

is an important topic, it has only a partial link to the Bund-Länder financial relations.

If we finally compare the German federalism concept for example with the one of Switzerland and the United States, it reveals major differences. Still, the commitment to federalism is not questioned in any of the afore mentioned states.

D. Local Self-Administration

I. Basic Elements of Local Self-Administration

Usually, the citizens and residents of a state tend to be more involved with their local community in which they live than with the federal state. It is the municipality which is responsible for the administration and the operation of facilities which are necessary for the economic, social and cultural support of its residents: *e.g.* through the provision of schools, kindergartens, streets, hospitals, nursing homes, cemeteries, town halls, sports facilities, theatres, museums, supply of electricity, gas, water and local public transit or garbage and sewage disposal services. This happens by means of self-administration by the citizens. According to the words of the German Federal Constitutional Court, the main goal of the local self-administration is the "activation" of citizens for their own affairs "uniting the popular forces" of the local community for the "autonomous performance of public function". The aim is to "further the people's welfare and preserve historical and local characteristics".[41] Responsible for local self-administration are the municipalities and the associations of local authorities (especially the counties) which may work together based on partnership. In the following I will only focus on the local municipalities: that means villages, towns and cities.

II. Local Self-Administration

The right of local self-administration is guaranteed to the municipalities not only by the law but by constitution.[42] Although the municipalities are integrated into the federal system as indirect federal administration agencies,

41 BVerfGE 11, 266 (275 f.).

42 Art. 28 II 1 GG and the corresponding provisions in the constitutions of the Länder.

they have the right to regulate all matters relating to the local community within the lawful scope on their own responsibility. The rationale behind local self-administration is a triple one.[43] First, it prevents an abolition of the municipalities. Second, it functions as a guarantee to administer all local matters in a self-dependent way and by civic participation. A special legal delegation is not necessary. In this context "self-dependent" means that the municipalities are able to decide independently about the entire extent of their administrative activities. There is no utility control as only a legal control persists at the state level. Also, the municipalities have the capability to enforce their rights within the judicial system. They may take action against laws through a communal constitutional complaint.[44] Third, the administration has to be organized in a civic way which means that it must be possible to directly or indirectly trace every administrative decision back to the local citizens. Thus, the municipalities are small democracies with their own population and representation.[45] Although the local self-administration is allowed only within the lawful scope, the constitutional guarantee would be meaningless if the legislator would have the power to arbitrarily reduce the right of local self-administration. Consequently, there are limits to the legislator, namely an inviolable core of local self-administration[46] and the requirement to apply the principle of proportionality.[47]

III. Communal Representation of the People

As illustrated in the explanation above, the municipalities must have a representation of the people which is elected in public, direct, free, equal and secret elections.[48] Although the representation is not a parliament it has a comparable legal structure. Generally the representation has to decide all important matters. All the strict principles which Mr. Mellinghoff has described have to apply to the election of the representatives. The residents of

43 See Ehlers, "Die verfassungsrechtliche Garantie der kommunalen Selbstverwaltung," 2000.

44 Art. 93 I Nr. 4 b GG and the corresponding provisions in the constitutions of the Länder.

45 Art. 28 I 2 GG.

46 BVerfGE 1, 167 (175); 22, 180 (205); 79, 127 (155).

47 See Ehlers, "Die verfassungsrechtliche Garantie der kommunalen Selbstverwaltung," 2000.

48 See for this explicitly Art. 28 I 2 GG.

the municipalities of a certain age, including the EU-citizens,[49] but no other foreigners, are eligible to vote. The electorate usually has several votes with the right to split or cumulate their votes – meaning he or she can give the votes to candidates of different lists or all the votes to one candidate.[50] As opposed to the federal level there is no barring clause to hold back small parties.[51] The elected representatives exercise an honorary mandate which entitles them to an allowance and to recover loss of earnings. The principle of the free mandate protecting each representative against disadvantages of any kind, applies like in parliamentary law.

IV. Plebiscitary Participation of Citizens and Residents

The right of the citizens to participate in the communal affairs is not limited to the election of representatives every few years. In fact there are many other rights of participation today. Examples are the "Einwohnerantrag" (a proposition of the citizens that the public representation has to decide), the "Ratsbürgerbescheid" (a decision of the counsel that a citizens' decision will take place) and the "Bürgerbegehren" (a petition for a referendum where the citizens decide).[52] In these cases a certain quorum has to be reached. Furthermore some topics are not allowed to be the subject of a referendum (e.g. those who have illegal aims or which are directly concerned with the budget).[53] There is an increasing exercise of the public's rights of participations. However, plebiscitary participations also lead to delays and expenses.

V. Administrative Personnel of the Municipalities

The performance of communal obligations rests with its employees. The directly elected mayor is the head of the communal administration and usually at the same time chairman of the people's representation. A deselection

49 Art. 22 TFEU; 28 I 3 GG.
50 See Ehlers, "Die Gemeindevertretung," 2007, para 8.
51 See for the unconstitutionality (in the case of Schleswig-Holstein) BVerfGE 120, 82.
52 See the summary of Schmidt-Aßmann and Röhl, "Kommunalrecht," 2008, paras 89 et seqq.
53 In North Rhine-Westphalia it is graded from 10 % of the citizens in smaller villages to 3 % in towns with more than 500.000 inhabitants (§ 26 IV GO NRW (municipal code of NRW).

is also possible under certain circumstances.[54] Nowadays, the communal administration often uses private companies to carry out their obligations instead of doing it on its own. This co-operation may take place in various forms. The municipalities retain the responsibility for a proper provision of the services. It has to set the framework and to act on its own if it is necessary.

VI. Communal Finance

The self-administration is only able to work if its financial foundation is secured. The Basic Constitutional Law contains a corresponding guarantee.[55] The municipalities, for instance, must have own sources of revenue. Additionally, the "Länder" (states) support the municipalities by annual allocation of funds as well as the revenue equalisation which especially benefits the needy municipalities. Nevertheless, a lot of the municipalities are over-indebted. The Association of German Cities and Towns expects a deficit of 15 billion Euros for the fiscal year 2010 which is due to multiple reasons. Most importantly the municipalities don´t have sufficient tax revenue for themselves (mainly with the exception of business tax and real estate tax). Another reason are the multiple obligations of the municipalities. However some of the problems are self-inflicted as the municipalities have not always acted economically in the past.

To react to these problems, the federal government established a commission for communal finance.[56] Naturally, the municipalities will profit in the case of economic improvement and growth, which presently takes place. However, this does not solve the structural problems of communal finances. At any rate the new constitutional provisions which only permit the states to transfer new duties to the municipalities if they take over the costs for performing these duties do constitute a progress.[57]

54 See for instance § 66 GO NRW.

55 Art. 28 II 3 GG.

56 „Kommission zur Erarbeitung von Vorschlägen zur Neuordnung der Gemeindefinanzierung" that has been established in 2010.

57 To the so-called „connexity principle": see Schoch, *Finanzierungsverantwortung*, 1995: Henneke, *Die Kommunen in der Finanzverfassung*, 2008.

E. Conclusion

In summary, every country has its strengths and weaknesses. In my opinion, the principles of federalism and local self-administration, despite all their shortcomings, are among the strengths of the German legal system. I believe that the local self-administration of the citizens in Germany is in fact one of our biggest legal export hits.

Works cited

Bracher, Karl-Dietrich, *Die deutsche Diktatur*, Berlin: Ullstein, 1997.

Broszat, Martin, *Der Staat Hitlers*, 15th ed., Munich: dtv, 2000.

Ehlers, Dirk, "Die verfassungsrechtliche Garantie der kommunalen Selbstverwaltung," *Deutsches Verwaltungsblatt* (2000): 1301 et seqq.

Ehlers, Dirk, "Die Gemeindevertretung," in *Handbuch der Kommunalen Wissenschaft und Praxis*, eds. Thomas Mann and Günter Püttner, Vol. 1, 3rd ed., Berlin: Springer, 2007, § 21.

Frotscher, Werner, and Bodo Pieroth, *Verfassungsgeschichte*, 9th ed., Munich: C.H. Beck, 2010.

Grawert, Rolf, "Staatsvolk und Staatsangehörigkeit," in *Handbuch des Staatsrechts der Bundesrepublik Deutschland*, eds. Josef Isensee and Paul Kirchhof, Vol. I, 3rd ed., Heidelberg: C.F. Müller, 2003, pp. 235 et seqq.

Henneke, Hans-Günter, *Die Kommunen in der Finanzverfassung des Bundes und der Länder*, Wiesbaden: Kommunal- und Schulverlag, 2008.

Hesse, Konrad, *Der unitarische Bundesstaat*, Karlsruhe: Müller, 1962.

Hesse, Konrad, *Grundzüge des Verfassungsrechts der Bundesrepublik Deutschland*, 20th ed., Heidelberg: C.F. Müller, 1995.

Laufs, Adolf, *Recht und Unrecht der DDR*, Heidelberg: C. Winter, 1998.

Lüderssen, Klaus, *Der Staat geht unter, das Unrecht bleibt?*, Frankfurt a.M.: Suhrkamp, 1992.

Montesquieu, Charles de, *L'Esprit des Lois*, 1748.

Rudolf, Walter, "Kooperation im Bundesstaat," in *Handbuch des Staatsrechts der Bundesrepublik Deutschland*, eds. Josef Isensee and Paul Kirchof, Vol. VI, 3rd ed., Heidelberg: C.F. Müller, 2008, § 141.

Schmidt-Aßmann, Eberhard, and Hans-Christian Röhl, "Kommunalrecht," in *Besonderes Verwaltungsrecht*, eds. Eberhard Schmidt-Aßmann and Friedrich Schoch, 14th ed., Berlin: de Gruyter, 2008, ch.1.

Schoch, Friedrich, *Finanzierungsverantwortung für gesetzgeberisch veranlasste kommunale Aufgaben*, Baden-Baden: Nomos, 1995.

Thieme, Werner, "Die Gliederung der deutschen Verwaltung," in *Handbuch der Kommunalen Wissenschaft und Praxis*, eds. Thomas Mann and Günter Püttner, Vol. 1, 3rd ed., Berlin: Springer, 2007, § 9, pp. 147-168.

Würtenberger, Thomas, "Neugliederung," in *Handbuch des Staatsrechts der Bundesrepublik Deutschland*, ed. Isensee and Kirchof, Vol. VI, 3rd ed., Heidelberg: C.F. Müller, 2008, § 132.

Federalism and Human Rights in Nepal's Constitutional Design: Challenges for the Judiciary*

Andreas Føllesdal

A. Introduction

The Constituent Assembly has until May 28, 2011 to write a new constitution. Once the CA delivers their recommendations their main task is finished. However, they can only do their work well if they craft the constitution in light of how others will in turn interpret and apply it. The CA members must design the constitution with these future functions clearly in mind. It is therefore of particular interest to consider how the Nepal judiciary will and must use it, since such expectations should affect the substitive contents of the constitution. The lessons should also inform the educational strategies of the judiciary in Nepal.

The new constitution will challenge the Nepal judiciary in several ways, some old and some new. For instance, both federalism and the increased attention to human rights will require a stronger focus on the rule of law – and therefore measures to ensure an even more independent and competent judiciary. In addition, the federal features will change and increase the responsibilities of the judiciary . In order to discern feasible and fair ways to move forward, the CA must especially consider the complex composition, circumstances and potential for conflicts by and among the many groups and minorities that constitute the people of Nepal. How the new constitution will secure minorities' and groups' rights, their immunities and political influ-

* This article expands on some perspectives to be published in *International Journal of Minority and Group Rights*, 2011. Some of these thoughts were presented at the Alliance for Social Dialogue (ASD), at SAP Falchha, Martin Chautari, Kathmandu October 24, 2008, (in Nepali) in Bk, Man Bahadur, and Chakram Bishwakarma, *Dalits in Federalism*, Kathmandu: Dalit Welfare Organization, 2008; at a seminar at the National Judicial Academy, Nepal August 3, 2010, and at Universitat Pompeu Fabra, Barcelona October 7. I am grateful for these occasions, and for all comments from the participants and from Kåre Vollan. The research is part of the ERC project MultiRights – www.multirights.net. – and the Centre of Excellence PluriCourts – www.pluricourts.net – at the University of Oslo.

ence, is of the outmost urgency, and arguably a central touchstone of a legitimate constitution. In this sense the CA is in the position of Otto Neurath's famous seafarers, who must rebuild their ship in open sea, without being able to take it apart in a dock and build it up of its best constituents from the bottom up.

The judiciary faces similar challenges: past history and present group identities shape individuals' expectations for the future, and must affect the interpretation of the constitution and the laws.

One of the most intriguing and important tasks of the Nepal Constituent Assembly concerns *federalism*. The CA must comply with voters' demand to create a *federal* Nepal. So the question is not whether Nepal should be a federal state, but rather *what sort* of federal state Nepal should be. And at the same time, the CA must write a constitution that secures equal dignity and respect for all Nepali citizens, regardless of ethnicity and caste. The combination is difficult to secure, both in a constitution and when applying it.

The task of the CA is to translate such ideas of federalism into a constitution – the 'operating system' – of a democratic, human rights-respecting Nepal republic. The judiciary must then interpret and apply this constitution. For instance: Should the federal borders of Nepal reflect ethnicity and geography, as the Maoists urged? Or should the CA follow the CPN (UML) and Nepali Congress manifestos, and create provinces based on geography, natural resources, language, or culture? Indeed: How many provinces should there be? 11, as the Maoists called for? Should there be one united province for the Tarai, as the Madhesi Janadhikar Forum insist?

The challenge for the CA is to choose federal institutional design elements that are faithful to the best interests of the Nepal people; and the judiciary may do well to heed such interpretive principles and objectives. Both these tasks are difficult, since there are many different ways that the institutions of a state can be democratic, ensure human rights – and embody federal features. There is clearly no 'best' institutional blueprint for all states: That depends on the national histories and memories, geography, and cultures.

The following reflections by an 'outsider' seek to sketch and assess four varieties of federal elements, drawn from an interpretation of other states' experiences. Two of are territorial: Constitutional and Political. The others are non-territorial: Minority Rights, and Minority Representation. Hopefully, some of the arguments and lessons are helpful also for Nepal's challenges.[1]

Two features of the *peoples* of Nepal are especially salient for this discussion.

Recall that the national poet Bhanubhakta Acharya (1814-1868) is said to have "braided the people of Nepal into a national string." This braid metaphor, by poet Madhav Prasad Ghimire, is highly appropriate: Nepal consists of *very many different groups*: over 100 caste and ethnic nationalities, 70-90 languages, 9 religious groups – and these often overlap.[2] Secondly, these groups often *live side by side*. Few ethnic groups are the sole inhabitants of any area; instead, many castes and ethnic groups live fully dispersed among each other.

B. The Puzzle: If Federalism is the solution, what is the problem?

One way to start the assessment of federal alternatives is to ask why so many Nepali citizens and their political parties urged federalism. If this is perceived as a solution, what exactly to they perceive to be the problem? Many observers seem to agree that a main reason for calls for federalism was the wide spread perception that central Nepali authorities *dominated* many other ethnic groups and castes. Calls for federalism expressed a call that the central powers must be constrained or even removed, in order to secure a better distribution of opportunities and living conditions and end other forms of domination. Indeed, this has historically been impartant functions of human rights constraints and federal arrangements.

C. European History of Federalism

The history of federal experiments in Europe may help identify some features that the CA might draw from. Johannes Althusius (1557-1630) is regarded as the "father of federalism" in Europe. Living in Emden in Germany,

1 For this taxonomy see Follesdal, "Federalism," 2010. Central contributions to and reviews of federal thought include Riker, "Federalism," 1993; Elazar, *Federalism as Grand Design*, 1987; Watts, "Federalism," 1998; Karmis and Norman, *Theories of federalism*, 2005.

2 See M. Thapa, *Forget Kathmandu*, 2005.

he sought protection for his own minority religion within Emden, as well as protection for the city itself. His group faced two threats of domination: from the 'Local Centre' – the Lutheran provincial Lord - and from the 'Central Centre': the Catholic Emperor. These central authorities, he argued, should grant religious freedom to his and other groups who were living side by side in the realm. Only thus could the authorities avoid violent upheavals. Two lessons are particularly relevant:

1. Federal thought has long been concerned to *prevent domination* from several power sources.
2. The history of federalism teaches us several different means to combat domination, – not only territorial subdivisions. For instance, one common arrangement concerning religious diversity has been local autonomy – immunity from interference by the centre. Another example is 'consociational' arrangements, where different religious or ethnic groups within society cooperate by each having a share in the exercise of central powers.

D. Four Federal Features

Four different institutional arrangements within this European federal tradition may merit attention as means to reduce conflict and domination. They reduce the need for complete agreement, since those who disagree can instead agree to decide separately about these contested policies. These arrangements can protect from interference and thus remove domination, some times. But they do not remove all conflicts.

To the contrary, each of these arrangements require attention to two central contested issues – issues that also create disagreements within the Committee on Restructuring of the State and Distribution of Power, if we look at their draft proposals. *To resolve both of these issues the judiciary may have to play new, central roles.*

1. How determine the composition of the sub-units, be they geographical or demographic. Where and how should the borders be drawn? Who decides the criteria for group divisions, and who decides contested cases of membership? For instance, two conflicting concerns might guide such decisions: either allow those with ethnic or religious bonds to create separate units with some forms of political autonomy, or deliberately promote diversity within each unit in order to foster more cooperation and toleration across such boundaries.

2. Which powers should the sub-units have: should they have final say over school curriculum, taxation, official language or holidays, land reform, agricultural policies, cultural subsidies, water management, and/or land reform?

I. Territorial Constitutional Federalism

In this version of federalism the constitution divides the country into territorial regions, granting some powers to them, and some to the centre. This is typical of federal states, such as the USA, India, Canada or Germany. The benefit of such entrenchment of power divisions is that it may reduce or remove fears of domination by the centre. An 'ethnic federation' might thus include geographical provinces whose boundaries allow one ethnic group to express their preferred mode of life within each unit. However, this approach may not prevent domination of ethnic groups, especially those whose members live on both sides of the territorial borders. Two cases are especially relevant for Nepal. Given that groups live intermingled in Nepal, each such sub unit will include minorities who will not only continue to risk domination from the centre, but who will now also risk domination from the 'Local Centre' where decisions will reflect the interests of the local majority. One response to this conundrum might be to establish autonomous regions within each of the provinces. But such a response will at best be a very complex political structure with nested sites of political autonomy. A second weakness of such territorial constitutional federalism appears when we consider widely dispersed and disadvantaged groups. These arrangements do not alleviate the plight of such groups, for instance the Dalits in Nepal. Human rights protections will still constrain both local and central authorities, but the territorial federal arrangement will not benefit the Dalits. To the contrary, territorial federalism will leave members of such groups at new risks, of being subject to domination by their provincial authority, in addition to risking domination by central authorities in Kathmandu.

In short: Territorial Constitutional Federalism does not guarantee the end of domination of ethnic minorities, but may simply create more sites of 'local' domination in the various sub-units, especially when different ethnic groups and castes live intermingled. One important new role for the judiciary will be to be vigilant also with regard to human rights violations by these local authorities.

Such constitutional federalism may have several disadvantages. The entrenched division of powers is and must be difficult to change. However, change should not be impossible, since future challenges may require a reshuffling of borders or powers. How to design the requisite balance between stability and flexibility is a major challenge. Some also fear that this sort of arrangement may fuel calls for secession, though that risk may be alleviated by several factors. Firstly, the regional authorities also enjoy a share of the central powers, which they would lose by secession. Secondly, the attraction of full secession may be reduced by international insistence that any new state would have to protect the human rights of its own minorities – which might limit the benefits obtained for the majority group. Yet others fear that such federalism may hinder a shared 'national identity.'

Finally, note that such arrangements may hinder equalization of living conditions across regions, since richer regions will question why they should take responsibility for the poorer areas. *This risk may amount to added challenges to citizens' economic and social human rights – which the judiciary will have to protect.*

II. Territorial Political Federalism: Decentralisation

An alternative territorial arrangement is to let the central parliament grant local authorities autonomy over specific issues. Such solutios allow the local communities more control over matters important to them, while avoiding the rigidity problems of constitutional entrenchments.

However, this advantage comes at a cost, since these arrangements will not provide as strong safeguards against future domination. Central authorities may at any time withdraw the powers they have granted. With the possibility of dynamic change of borders and allocation of powers comes the risk of political manipulation for inappropriate objectives.

Moreover, the ethnic and other minorities that live within each region face similar risks of domination under this system as they face in a unified state with centralized power. The only difference is that domination is now perpetrated by a regional majority.

These disadvantages may to some extent be alleviated if the judiciary is empowered to secure due process and impose stringent rule of law standards on attempts to centralise decisions. For instance, the constitution might require that on some issue areas, central authorities may only intervene when such actions have been shown to be markedly better than the uncoordinated decisions by the regions. Such requirements, familiar from discussions about the 'Principle of Subsidiarity', may help reduce the risk of undue centralization.

Two 'non-territorial' federal features also merit consideration, since they may reduce domination of ethnic or other groups. They give various groups more protection, or more power, but without tying these privileges to the interest in controlling a specific territory. Instead, the arrangements secure a variety of other interests individuals have, such as urgent and important matters of religion, language, culture, education or even some forms of taxation – without any claims to territorial control. Some such arrangements may ensure representatives voice and votes in common decision-making bodies, but these persons do not represent specific territories.

III. Nonterritorial Minority Rights

A third institutional arrangement is what Althusius urged for his own religious group: collective rights and other human rights for groups who otherwise face risks of domination. Such rights may be freedom from interference, or more substantive autonomy. The rights may concern issues such as religious practices or language teaching in the schools. Rights to territorial control are not part of these clusters of rights, since there members of several such groups may live side by side. We find expression of some such rights in ILO Convention number 169 on Indigenous and Tribal Peoples. Other rights may concern 'reverse discrimination', to alleviate the impact of past and present injustice and oppression.

Such arrangements can benefit minorities who are geographically dispersed or who live intermingled with other groups. Yet they also have some drawbacks. In particular, the appropriate set of rights may have to be carefully tailored to the specific needs and histories of each group. An extensive system of special rights may also hinder a national sense of unity and solidarity. Some have also warned that special rights may create new risks to vulnerable persons *within* this minority. For instance, special care must be taken to protect women from harmful elements of some traditional cultures and practices. Many human rights can provide some safeguard against these sources of domination.

Other problems arise for efforts to alleviate past injustice: Many supportive measures, extra resources etc will tend to benefit the most privileged members of disadvantaged groups, rather than the worst off members. Insofar as membership criteria and benefits is a matter of political debate there is obviously also the risk of manipulation: Scarce resources may not reach those ethnic groups and castes, and especially those members thereof, whose claims are most urgent.

There are also challenges with regard to the kinds of powers and immunities that may be granted to each group while preserving sufficient opportunities for common responses to shared problems and opportunities, and to avoid unintended domination over those groups that do not enjoy such privileges.

A further challenge to attempts at implementing such solutions in Nepal is the sheer number of groups that may reasonably make claims to such autonomy and immunity rights: the contested claims of more than 100 groups must be handled responsibly. It is a major challenge to any constitutional committee to identify, coordinate and predict the benefits and risks of all these bundles of political authority and immunity both for members of each group and for other members of Nepal society.

Such group rights will require vigilant judicial review over legislation and administration at all levels, and may obligate the judiciary to make very hard and politically contested trade offs among the claims of different groups.

IV. Nonterritorial Minority Representation

The fourth form of arrangement grants various groups representation in the regional or central bodies that make common decisions – groups which need not be tied to different specific territories. One example is the consociational system mentioned above, where various social groups are represented and may even enjoy veto over common decisions.

Among these mechanisms we may count quotas or designated seats in legislatures for specified minorities. These arrangements may be especially important in 'first-past-the-post' systems, but systems with Proportional Representation (PR) also face a risk that no one represents the urgent interests of small minorities.

Other measures include deliberate over-representation of certain minorities to ensure them not only voice but also weight when decisions come to a vote. Other arrangements may regulate the composition of political party slates. For instance there may be legal requirements to secure a sufficient number of women and other specified groups within each party group in parliament.

Among the benefits of such arrangements may be that they give voice and political influence to previously subjected groups in ways that also ensure on-going recognition and concern for their situation.

Some disadvantages also merit mention. One concern is to determine which among many groups need such representation in common bodies, another is to fine-tune the extent of over-representation, if any. Yet, other challenges relate to ensuring that these measures do not entrench existing conflicts, or prevent solutions to new injustices. Thus the lists of 'deserving' groups over time must be open to revision as past injustices are corrected, and new injustices arise or are discovered. This need for a dynamic list adds to the risk of manipulation. Procedures for change must be set up in ways that prevent suspicion that powerful groups will tweak the system to their further advantage. A final concern is that some of those elected as representatives of these groups may not act in the groups' best interests, partly because they themselves may well be among the more privileged segment of the minority.

There are several important issues that one must consider when designing such non-territorial arrangements. When many groups have legitimate need for representation, it may make sense to not insist on specified quotas but rather require a minimum threshold of representatives. This may be particularly helpful when the vulnerable segments of society overlap, such as women in certain castes or ethnic groups. Another fundamental question is whether such quotas or thresholds should be applied to the principal chamber, or to a chamber of peoples with specified powers.

Note again that such mechanisms will typically require that the judiciary plays important roles to maintain trust that the procedures are not abused. This increases the need for an independent and trustworthy judiciary.

E. Conclusion

These reflections have sought to illuminate some aspects of the new roles and responsibilities of the judiciary, when it seeks to interpret and apply federal features in the new, human rights-respecting constitution.

Human rights protections combined with federal elements of Nepal's new constitution must serve to prevent future domination, especially by the centres, over the many ethnic groups and castes. There are reasons to hope that this may be the result of judicious incorporation of some of the four different federal elements culled from the European federal tradition: Constitutional and Political Territorial arrangements, Minority Rights, and systems of Minority Representation.

To select, fine-tune and combine some of these federal features into a sustainable and just constitution that is recognizably federal is one of the important obligations of the Constitutional Assembly. It must braid a constitution that will protect and promote the best interests of the braid that is the Nepali people and peoples.

It is then the task of an independent judiciary, together with the legislative powers, well trained in the particularities of federalism and human rights protections, to ensure that the constitution indeed will help create a Nepal free from domination from all centres of power, central as well as regional.

Works cited

Althusius, Johannes, *Politica Methodice Digesta*, 1603, reprint, Indianapolis: Liberty Press, 1995.

Bhatta, Diwakar, "Federalism and restructuring of the judiciary in Nepal: Whilst creating a new Constitution," *National Judicial Academy Law Journal, Nepal* 2 (2008): 69-94.

Bhattarai, Ananda Mohan, "Judicial Education in Nepal: Achievement and Challenges," *National Judicial Academy Law Journal, Nepal* 3 (2009).

Chapagain, Raju Prasad, "National application of international human rights law: A Nepali Perspective," *National Judicial Academy Law Journal, Nepal* 3 (2009).

Elazar, Daniel J., *Federalism as Grand Design: Political Philosophers and the Federal Principle*, Lanham MD: University Press of America, 1987.

Follesdal, Andreas, "Subsidiarity," *Journal of Political Philosophy* 6 (1998): 231-259.

Follesdal, Andreas, "Subsidiarity, Democracy and Human rights in the Constitutional Treaty for Europe," *Journal of Social Philosophy* (2006): 61-80.

Follesdal, Andreas, "Human Rights, Democracy and Federalism – Part of the problem or part of the solution? Securing stability in the European Union and the People's Republic of China," *Current Politics and Economics of Asia 17* (2008): 211-236.

Follesdal, Andreas, "Federalism," in *Stanford Encyclopedia of Philosophy*, 2010, at http://plato.stanford.edu/entries/federalism/ (retrieved June 21, 2010).

Ghai, Yash, "Constitutional asymmetries: communal representation, federalism, and cultural autonomy," in *Architecture of Democracy: Constitutional Design, Conflict Management, and Democracy*, ed. Andrew Reynolds, Oxford/New York: Oxford University Press, 2002.

International Labour Organization, *Convention 169 on Indigenous and Tribal Peoples*, 1989, at http://www.ilo.org/ilolex/cgi-lex/convde.pl?C169.

Karmis, Dimitrios, and Wayne Norman, *Theories of federalism: A Reader*, New York: Palgrave, 2005.

Kunwar, Tek Narayan, *Global standards of judicial independence*, *National Judicial Academy Law Journal, Nepal* 1 (2007): 73-90.

Lijphart, Arend, *Patterns of democracy: Government forms and performance in thirty-six countries*, New Haven: Yale University Press, 1999.

Neurath, Otto, *Protokollsätze*, Erkenntnis 3, 1932 (Transl. in Otto Neurath, *Philosophical Papers 1913-1946,* Dordrecht: Reidel, 1983).

Riker, William H., "Federalism," in *A Companion to Contemporary Political Philosophy*, eds. Robert E. Goodin, and Philip Pettit, Oxford: Blackwell Publishing, 1993.

Shrestha, Ram Prasad, "Role of Nepali Judiciary in Strengthening the Rule of Law," *National Judicial Academy Law Journal, Nepal* 3 (2009).

Thapa, Manjushree, *Forget Kathmandu: An Elegy for Democracy*, New Delhi: Penguin. 2005.

Thapa, Rom, "Self-determination of indigenous pepoles in Nepal: A right to autonomy?," *National Judicial Academy Law Journal, Nepal* 3 (2009).

Watts, Ronald L., "Federalism, Federal political systems, and federations," *Annual review of political science* 1 (1998): 117-137.

Cambodia and the ASEAN: Which Choice Between the Regional and Global Powers?

Son Soubert

A. Introduction

Some twenty years ago, there was a debate on the Western and Asian models of democracy, having Prime Minister Lee Kwan Yu of Singapore as advocate of an Asian model opposed to the Western one, an antagonism which President Kim Dae-Jung of South Korea rejected asserting that there are only universal values expressed by one democracy. The concept of democracy originated in Athens, as opposed to Sparta's military aristocratic system of government, and culminated in the 5th century B.C. known as the century of Pericles, before degenerating in a system of demagoguery with sycophants and denouncements. However, in all these systems leaders had to gain personal legitimacy to rule. In all ancient societies, either Asian or Western, authorities lie upon the father of the family, the Latin *Pater Familias*; in that sense Confucius had not invented anything, because it is the natural order as the point of departure of any evolution of public power.

A next step in the development of public power can be exemplified with the Holy Book of the Jewish people, where we can see the evolution of power shifting from the patriarchs to the representatives or messengers of God in the persons of Moses and Aaron. After this split of patriarchic power, in priests or prophets and judges, who may have abused of their authorities, was followed by kingship with kings as chosen by God. Gods themselves have been the Devārâja or God-Kings as they dominated the 9th century Angkor Khmer period.

Whatsoever, the choice of a certain type of leadership or system of government remains always the same since prehistoric times: It is always and inevitably the quest for security: food security, physical safety and protection. This motivated the emergence of another principle of political power, the formation of a group or several connected groups which can help each other to ensure the satisfaction of these needs. This fundamental principle is what we call alliances, ranging from the tribe to nationhood, from internal to external relations of political entities.

B. The Formation of the ASEAN vis-à-vis an Integrated Europe

The reason for the creation and emergence of the European Communities in 1957 is an immediate reaction to the devastating Second World War. Two visionary leaders, namely French President General Charles de Gaulle and the German Chancellor Konrad Adenauer initiated this development, alongside with French Prime Minister Robert Schumann as a means of regional security. The formation of the ASEAN Community was more complicated, even it nowadays considers the European concept as a reference to some extent, especially concerning its first step, the creation of a common market to be achieved with the ASEAN Economic integration not before 2015. However, it has to be remembered that the purpose of the formation of the European Communities with the Rome Treaty amidst the Cold War period was to prevent any further military conflict among the European nations.

The same is true with the formation of the ASEAN Community, based on the concepts of national security and common interest as a continuation of the principles which dominated the Cold War era. In the wake of the Vietnam War after the Americans had replaced the French colonial power in Indochina as the new hegemon, defending their interests against the Soviet Union. After communism took grip in Southeast Asia and the USSR encouraged Asian countries to join their economic block COMECON with its allies in Eastern Europe plus China as observer and North-Vietnam, SEATO (South-East Asian Treaty Organization) was formed as a military defense alliance for the Asia – Pacific region, initially with the Philippines and Thailand as only Southeast Asian members besides Australia, France, New Zealand, Pakistan, the UK and the US. Besides the military insignificance of SEATO, it contributed symbolically to the increasing divide of Southeast Asia along the global cleavages of the Cold War. As other states also Cambodia was forcefully encouraged into this overarching alliance by former Secretary of State Foster Dulles. However, Cambodia's charismatic national leader, King Sihanouk, resisted by joining the Non-Aligned Movement, under the advice of Pandit Jawaharlal Nehru whom the King considered as His Guru and who also urged Him to foster relationships with China. Among the Founding Members of the Non-Aligned Movement were Nehru of India, Gamal Nasser of Egypt, Broz Tito of Yugoslavia, Ne Win of Burma, King Sihanouk of Cambodia. Zhou Enlai from China and Pham Van Dong from North Vietnam also joined the 1955 Bandung Conference as well as other leaders from Muslim and Arab countries. The Bandung Conference stuck to the Five Principles of the Peaceful Coexistence, namely belief in God, nationalism, universal brotherhood, social justice and democracy. At the same time, it condemned imperialism under all its manifestations, as suggested Premier Zhou Enlai, and advocated the non-interference in other countries' affairs. Notwithstanding its foreign policy towards the Non-Aligned Movement Cambodia was the only country to respect the 1954 Accords of the Geneva Conference on French Indochina, especially by abiding the stipulations on General Elections under the supervision of the International Control Commission, headed by India and seconded by Poland and Canada.

However, in the frame of the Cold War division of the world and its inflammation of the region, the only sensible option for Cambodia, located next to the battlefield of Vietnam and close to the Chinese giant was neutrality. Initially we allied with the USA for our defense against the threat of communism – we remember that the Communist Block wanted Cambodia to be divided into two countries like Vietnam and Laos at the July 1954 Geneva Conference with one part of which to be communist. Nevertheless, Cambodia, given its geo-strategic location, did not discard relationships with China and North-Vietnam in order to preserve her future territorial integrity and independence. Even after severing relationships with the USA in 1963, because of the assassination attempt on the person of King Suramarit and the Queen, a coup encouraged by the CIA operating from South-Vietnam and Thailand and the large scale of corruption that has been brought in the country by the American assistance, Cambodia did maintain relationship also with many countries in the West, especially with France of General de Gaulle. It is in this context, with the unifying personality of Prince Sihanouk as Chief of State[1], that we could develop our country in the midst of the destruction of the Vietnam War. It was unfortunate that when Prince Sihanouk decided to resume relationship with the USA by 1968, as an act of balance against China – itself in the midst of the Cultural Revolution – and North Vietnam which shamelessly tried to meddle in our internal affairs by destabilizing the royal regime by the support of communist insurgents and violated its territory for the use by North Vietnamese forces and the Vietcong, dragging Cambodia deeper and deeper into the Vietnam War, the USA

1 King Sihanouk has been enthroned in 1941, declared Cambodia's full independence against the colonial claims of the French in 1953, abdicated in favor of His father in 1955 and, after the death of His father remained a kind of prince regent and became head of state until the Coup d'état of 1970, eventually followed by to the victory of the Khmer Rouge in 1975 and the Vietnamese invasion of 1979. (Editors' remark)

carelessly lent a hand to this scheme, by encouraging the coup d'état staged by General Lon Nol to overthrow the Chief of State in 1970.

During this period, there was no meaningful self-determined Southeast Asian political cooperation on the regional level. It was only on 8 August 1967 that SEATO was transformed into the Association of Southeast Asian Nations (ASEAN) with the first five members: the Philippines, Thailand, Singapore, Malaysia and Indonesia, by an agreement signed in Bangkok (Thailand). Brunei Darussalam joined the grouping under the recommendation of Singapore on January 7 1984. Vietnam joined ASEAN only after the 1991 Paris Peace Agreement on Cambodia, ending the Vietnamese occupation of Cambodia, on July 28 1995, Myanmar on July 23 1997 as well as Laos, while Cambodia was the last country to join on April 30 1999, because of internal problems. These finally 10 ASEAN member states would regularly meet with the ASEAN + 3 (China, South Korea and Japan), and also ASEAN + 6 (the previous 3 countries + India, New Zealand and Australia). In the year 2012, it is up to Cambodia to chaire the ASEAN meetings.

C. Cambodia and the ASEAN

Perhaps it was for the principle of non-interference that during the period of the most massive violations of human rights of the Cambodian people perpetrated by the Pol Pot Khmer Rouge regime not one country nor any of the usual human rights organizations did protest against that odious regime from 1975 to 1979. However, when Vietnam ignored the same principle of non-interference by invading Cambodia in the end of 1978, China, the USA, the ASEAN, and some Western European countries, including the Federal Republic of Germany, joined together in opposing this aggression, despite the fact that morally the regime of the Khmer Rouge, which had occupied *de facto* and *de jure* the seat of Cambodia at the UN since 1975, was unacceptable. Since the 1970 overthrow of Prince Sihanouk as Chief of State and his stay in Beijing, it was obvious that any solution to the Vietnam War would have to go through China. At the wake of their withdrawal from Vietnam, after the 1973 Paris Agreement on Vietnam, the USA had to ensure that the vacuum left by their departure would be filled by a regional power, namely China, which finally, after a secret visit of the Secretary of State Henry Kissinger in 1973 to Beijing, allied itself with the USA in Southeast Asian affairs. In that period of the 1970 s, the Khmer Rouge military faction was supported by most of the Western leftist intellectuals and mass media, who were ideologically also the natural allies of the China of the Cultural Revolution and the Gang of Four admired by the Khmer Rouge who tried to even trump their radicalism.

Even before the end of the 1970 s, Thailand, member country of the ASEAN, had already courted China with Prime Minister M.R. Kukrit Pramoj received by President Mao Zedong. Indonesia having had bad experiences with the Chinese during President Sukarnos time kept a more reserved attitude. However the unity of the ASEAN countries during the 1980 s has helped put forward the strategy for a peaceful resolution of the conflict in Cambodia, with the combined efforts of the USA, China and other Western and pro-western countries. They promoted a coalition government of Democratic Kampuchea with Prince Sihanouk as President and Mr. Son Sann[2] as Prime Minister, after the failure by the UN to promote an International Conference on Kampuchea (ICK). Before the 1991 Paris Peace Agreements on a Comprehensive Solution to the Cambodia Conflict, there were many other initiatives from the ASEAN, especially from Indonesia and H.E. Ali Alatas, the Foreign Minister, in Jakarta in 1987, known as JIM I (Jakarta Informal Meeting) which first took place on the Mountain resort of Bogor, followed by the JIM I Working Group in Jakarta, with all the antagonists present, then the Pataya and Bangkok Meetings and finally JIM II. Even when the two Cambodian camps, formed by FUNCINPEC and the Cambodian People´s Party, represented by the two Prime Ministers (Cambodia concurrently had to overcome the civil war), Prince Ranaridh and Hun Sen, clashed in July 1997, again the ASEAN countries stepped in, with meetings with the First Prime Minister in Bangkok and an ASEAN delegation meeting the Second Prime Minister in Phnom-Penh.

As a regional grouping, ASEAN has demonstrated its capacity to solve regional problems for the benefit of common security and economic advantages. But still, despite wise proposal from Indonesia, ASEAN could not arrive at a solution of the old territorial conflict erupting again between Cambodia and Thailand concerning the Khmer temple of Preah Vihear at the Thai-Cambodian border, after a jointly decided enlisting of the temple by UNESCO as World Heritage in 2008 eventually resulted in claims made by Thailand in the wake of changing internal politics that finally lead Cam-

2 Son Sann, the father of H.E. Son Soubert, was a confidant of King Shanouk, had also served as Prime Minister in 1967-1968 and founded the Khmer People's National Liberation Front (KPNLF) and after 1991 the Buddhist Liberal Democratic Party. He died in 2000. (Editors' remark)

bodia to resort to the International Court of Justice in the Hague which already had decided in favor of Cambodia on the issue in 1962.

D. The ASEAN Achievements and Beyond

Despite the antagonistic historical background of the formation of the ASEAN, when the 6 Western orientated ASEAN states were fighting the 3 socialist Southeast Asian countries of the former French Indochina, namely Vietnam as the 'team leader' of Laos and Cambodia during the Cold War, the inclusion of Vietnam, Laos, Cambodia and also Myanmar seems to have generated a qualitively new grouping of the ASEAN. Thus, finally it seems that ASEAN may offer a framework for a new thinking in terms of regional governance. In the case of Burma/Myanmar, it is obvious that the policy of positive engagement of the ASEAN may have brought fruit, with the participation of the other dialogue countries, since Myanmar is liberalizing now, heading its leadership of the ASEAN in 2014.

One of the main achievements of these developments is the ASEAN Charter which was signed in Singapore on November 20, 2007. The main purposes, as stipulated in the Article I of the Charter, are three folds: political cooperation for peace and security including a zone free from Nuclear and other weapons of mass destruction (points 1-2-3-4) "to strengthen democracy" and "to respond effectively [...] to all forms of threats [...]"; economic cooperation "to create a single market and production base", "to alleviate poverty and narrow the development gap within the ASEAN through mutual assistance and cooperation", and social and cultural cooperation for the development of social welfare and social stability.

For the present time the ASEAN countries face strong inequality in terms of economic, social and educational development. If we consider the average annual income of a citizen of each country, we can notice the disparity: The richest in the decreasing order are the 6 former ASEAN, with 36,520 US Dollars for Brunei, 8,617 US $ for Malaysia, 5,281 $ for Thailand, 5,071 $ for Singapore, 3,469 US $ for Indonesia and 2,255 US $ for the Philippines; while the 4 new ASEAN members have Vietnam with 1,360 US $, Cambodia with 1,200 US$, Laos with 835 US $ and Myanmar with 804 US $. This income disparity reflects also the stage of educational development in Cambodia, which cannot match the level of that of Singapore, Malaysia or Thailand. Because of delay in the development of a proper and sound education curriculum to respond to the regional development, Cambodia seems driven to develop a policy which aims only to offer labour, if not skilled labour, to other regional or international developed countries instead of building an educated and skilled citizenry to develop its own performance. Cambodia, for the time being, is a consumer country for manufactured goods. Its vocation is mostly agricultural like other ASEAN countries, with the production of raw material for rubber and other agricultural products such as cassava, cashew nuts, coffee etc. exported raw to the neighbouring countries. Farmers still depend totally on the fluctuation of the market price fixed by the buyers or the middlemen. Besides the revenues earned by tourism mainly due to the huge temple complexes of Angkor, the only factories in place are garment- and cement factories most of them foreign owned. Cambodia therefore has to choose a regional specialty which it can fit in, because it cannot compete with industrialized neighbor countries like Thailand, the biggest exporter of rice, besides all the industries existing there. Lack of skilled labour is a main hindrance to attract more foreign industrial investment for the time being. The exodus of manpower to the neighbouring and other Asian countries, for better paid job is an increasing problem, leaving the country lacking of its human resource. Because of inequalities like these the ASEAN economic integration has been postponed beyond 2015.

Therefore a more integrated legal system of the ASEAN is also a long way to go. Obstacles to overcome are manifold. One of them is legal pluralism as it is to be observed in some countries like Thailand, Indonesia, Malaysia with strong minority or majority Muslim population respectively and Shariah law to be applied aside the diverse Western originated legal systems.

Another obstacle, to be exemplified from a Cambodian perspective again, is a persisting reluctance to take justice seriously. Although we not only adhere to the UN Human Rights Charter but also experienced atrocities like those committed by the Khmer Rouge as a national trauma of immense scale, a special UN Envoy is yearly visiting the country, making recommendations to the government and the ruling power, which are hardly to be realized because of a use of judicial power to indulge legally in these violations, under the pretext of justice and the implementation of laws. Facing this parody of justice one is reminded of an alternative which is represented by the Khmer tradition of the monarchy, which provided for a venue for an audience of the King taking place once a week. During the rule of Prince Sihanouk from 1955 to 1970, this tradition was embodied in the Constitution and called the 'National People's Congress' – which was to be held every year and in which the Ministers had to be present under the chairmanship of the King or the

Chief of State respectively – to answer the questions and complaints of the people. Although this National People's Congress is stipulated in the 1993 Constitution again, an organic law has yet to be drafted and presented to the National Assembly for adoption. Failing a Regional ASEAN Court of Justice or International Court of Justice providing access to the people and not only to the governments, human rights will be violated without hindrance and abused with impunity, as in the recent case of Mr. Mam Sonando, the outspoken director and owner of the only free Beehive Radio broadcasting in Cambodia.

With a lacking system of fair justice, corruption will continue to be another plague too. The civil society, without sound justice, cannot serve the interest of common ordinary people well who are the victims of the abuse of power and corruption, since the court is also venal. To achieve an international standard of justice, the ASEAN countries need to promote the international standards and should start to care for the human rights of migrant workers such as the Cambodians and the Philippinos in Malaysia. When there are violations of the rights of these workers, which jurisdiction can they refer to, beside the local jurisdiction? There should be a mechanism of an inter-ASEAN jurisdiction for those cases as a first step.

However, decisions among the ASEAN member countries are made by consensus. Therefore there will be many problems which might not be resolved soon. As major differences prevail:

The differences in creed and religious practices: what would be the options to evolving problems so far? One would be the declaration of non-religious or lay states, with freedom of expression and practice for each religious group, as it is practiced in some European countries, especially in France. Another possible one is the rule of the majority religious group, guaranteeing tolerance and freedom for other religious groups. But what would be the rights of the minority groups, in countries claiming a religious dominance for instance for Islam or Buddhism? Clashes between the Rohingya Muslims and the Rakhine Buddhists in Myanmar recently occurred again and remind of those between Christians and Muslims in Sulawesi (Indonesia). In Cambodia, as Buddhism is tolerant, there is no problem with the Khmer-Islam, for the time being. But, how can we promote sustainable interfaith understanding? An option could be the promotion of multi-cultural religious freedom with equal rights. Yet, another one would be an atheist communist state which would control any religious group under the state laws; and finally the option of a dictate of the majority religious group which identifies the state and their identity to their religious faith, such as the state of Israel, some Muslim states like Iran, Afghanistan where the intolerance of the Taliban religious group has destroyed the big Buddha image of Bamyan, or Malaysia following the recent trend to identify Islam as the state ideology and identity for the Malay ethnic group, or like in Cambodia and Thailand where Buddhism is state religion.

The other differences are our historical relationships among the ASEAN countries, which can linger on with suspicions and can lead to negative reactions: these are the historical differences between Burma (Myanmar) and Siam (Thailand), between Siam (Thailand), Cambodia, Laos and Malaysia; between Annam (Vietnam), Cambodia and Laos; between Malaysia, Indonesia and Singapore; between the Philippines and Indonesia regarding the Mindanao part etc. How to come to terms with all these differences, except by promoting mutual understanding and by making the peoples openly and frankly discuss their understanding of their respective history? In 2002, there was an organized attack on the Thai Embassy in Phnom-Penh, due to some unfounded rumors concerning a Thai actress who would have said derogatory remarks on Angkor Vat Temple that the Prime Minister of Cambodia had reported in one of his broadcast speeches. In the 21st century of modern technology with internet and facebook, the ASEAN peoples should be able to consult each other and cooperate in writing a history book according to the facts and their understanding of these facts.

Differences in the state institutions and regimes: Among the 10 ASEAN countries, there are 6 republics among which 2 communist states (Laos and Vietnam), and 4 monarchies among which is an absolute monarchy (Brunei Darussalam), a rotating monarchy (Malaysia), a hereditary constitutional monarchy (Thailand) and an elective constitutional monarchy (Cambodia where the Crown Council composed of the Sangharājas of the two Buddhist orders, the Presidents and Vice-Presidents of the Senate and the National Assembly and the Prime Minister would elect a new King).

Differences of approaches to the regional problems: Because of the past historical background and the recent one, added to the geo-political situation, each country of the ASEAN does not have the same interest and perspective for its security. Most of the ASEAN countries were culturally influenced by India, either through religions or the concept of Kingship, except Vietnam, formerly the Đai-Viet which had eliminated the Hindu Kingdom of Champa by mid 18th century of the Christian era, and which was under the Chinese dominion until the 10th century. Despite the Theravāda Buddhism practiced by both Burma and Siam, the destruction of Ayuthyā at the end of the 18th century had created ill feelings and suspicions from the Thai people against the Burmese. Despite many similarities in cultural and religious traditions and kingship, the Khmers and the Thai have a strange relationship of pride and inferior complex, not to say suspicion. The question of the Temple of Preah Vihear exacerbated the nationalistic sentiments of these two peoples. Likewise is the situation of the relationship between Laos and Siam-Thailand. The Philippines, because of their isolation as islands did not have problems with continental countries of the ASEAN, but with Indonesia, because of the Muslim population of Mindanao. The recent question of the South China Sea did not promote any consensus on a solution to adopt as a response of the 10 ASEAN countries to the involvement of China in the South China Sea. Vietnam, because of its proximity and common border with China, had always needed a powerful security umbrella to protect itself, in the Cold War the protective umbrella was the Soviet Union, now the USA, a former arch-enemy of North Vietnam. The Philippines and Vietnam are directly confronted with this question, at the less extent Malaysia and Brunei, and have reacted quite strongly.

In conclusion, what then is left for the ASEAN to do, in terms of their common identity, facing the globalization? Do we have a ground for community? How far can we go with human rights for our citizens? How would be our common legal or judicial system? Are we ready to delegate or transfer our sovereignty for an ASEAN Union and common currency? Finally, in the context of the troubled waters over the issue of the South China Sea and the emergence of two huge economic and military powers at the boundaries of the region, namely India and China, which choices will the ASEAN have to consider in terms of foreign policy? We hope that the champions of neutrality and non-alignment, as they have been promoted by India and Indonesia once, would steer the ASEAN in the future.

Constitutionalism in Thailand: Problems and Perspectives

Boonsri Mewongukote

A. Introduction

Thailand has experienced a series of dramatic developments both in political and economic aspects. Thanks to the political reform, which started in 1994, whereby the Thais could rally through the hardship of economic crisis in 1997 without dramatic political change as already happened in other countries. However, the outcome of the political reform, i.e. the government with absolute majority, mismanagement in many constitutional organs and systematic corruption of the leading politicians, which would further on be referred to as "the old power", has led to another coup d'état, the *ultima ratio* of the Thai politics. After the promulgation of the current Constitution the ousted old power resumed to get majority in the Parliament through the election and then tried to amend the Constitution for their own favors. A group of people, known as 'the yellow shirts', protested against this attempt. Meanwhile two prime ministers of the old power were disqualified by the Constitutional Court. The coalition government was then spluttered and lost the majority. But the old power did not give up. A movement outside of the Parliament, so called "the red shirts", was formed to oppose the new government. This seems to be a confusing situation. This paper will therefore try to light up the historical background, which will help us understand the current situations in Thailand.

B. Political Reform as an Effort to Overcome the Malpractices in Politics

In 1994 a well-known activist from the incident of May 1992, Chalard Worachatra, who followed Gandhi's principle of 'satyagraha' (passive resistance) by means of his threats to fast until death, demanded that the democratic process should further be developed to fulfill the democratic spirits of the heroes and heroines who sacrificed their lives in the incident of May 1992. His concrete proposal was, as revealed later, merely that the Governor of each province should be elected directly from the people. In order to comply with his demand, the Speaker of the Parliament appointed the Commission for Democratic Development to study the best way to develop democracy in Thailand. This commission organized a team of public lawyers to do their research on 15 topics concerning crucial problems in Thai politics, such as the rights and liberties of the people, the electoral system etc. The chairman of the commission could hand in the result of the research and the proposal of the commission to the Speaker of the Parliament in the middle of 1995.

There was another demand for political reform by a well known lawyer, Prof. Dr. Amorn Chandrasomboon, formerly Secretary of the Council of State. Bearing the French model of political reform a la de Gaule in mind, he dreamed of such a personality for Thailand as well. Once there was no such a personality in Thailand, he proposed his second choice, namely the constitution should totally be renewed by amending the provision on Amendment of the Constitution. And the amendment should not be accomplished by the Parliament itself, but by an impartial commission, which consists of about 25 experts, especially in public law. To the question why the matter should not be left to the Parliament, his answer gave a hint to sociological back ground, because the politicians were not expected to do things that were against their interests, as Prof. Dr. Amorn Chandrasomboon argued. The Parliament could only in toto receive or reject the whole worked out Constitutional bill.

Early 1995 there was a total amendment to the Thai Constitution, in which every article was amended. But after that amendment all the principles remained the same. Besides a great number of changes in wording there was nothing new. This event did confirm what Prof. Dr. Amorn had beforehand predicted.

By the end of 1995 there was a general election as a result of a censure in Parliament about the practice of land reform giving reformed land to the millionaires. The Chart Thai Party, which was in the former election on the Junta's side was clever enough to put the proposals of the Commission for Democratic Development into its programme. The Thai people, once blamed of their forgetfulness, verified once more this statement by voting for the Chart Thai Party, which could form the Coalition Government.

This Government, which the renown German weekly magazine 'der Spiegel' could hardly differentiate from the mafiosi, apart from approving the subway to ease traffic in Bangkok, had done the only good thing carrying out its political reform programme just as promised in the campaign during the general election. The reform proposal was introduced into the Parliament.

But during the amendment of the Constitution in 1996, representatives from each of the 76 provinces were added to the Constitution Drafting Council. These representatives were selected in dubious ways from applicants in each province, who chose among themselves, one representative for each province. So that it is not astonishing, that under the Constitution of 1997 the interests of the local politicians were taken into more consideration than any previous Constitution.

When the amendment was finished on 27th September 1996 the reforming process could run by itself regardless whether the political climate was appropriate or not. This was the intention of the reformer because on the same day the Parliament was dissolved so as to escape the vote of the censure in the Parliament. With the hope for betterment the Thai people were rather calm in comparison to other member Countries of the ASEAN after the economic crisis of 1997.

The aims of the Constitution Drafting Council (CDC) were three-dimensional.

Firstly, to change the practicing politics of the politicians into the politics of the citizens by giving more rights and liberties to the citizens and adapting the purely representative democracy into democracy through participation of the citizen.

Secondly, to form the political and bureaucratic system which is faithful and legitimate in using powers by increasing effectively controlling power at every level to the citizen.

Thirdly, to create an effective government with the Prime Minister as political leader to be able to solve the problems of the country and an effective Parliament as well.

I. To change the practicing politics of the politicians into the politics of the citizens by giving more rights and liberties to the citizens and adapting the purely representative democracy into democracy through participation of the citizen

This aim could according to the CDC be realized by 3 measurements, namely:

- Recognizing more rights and liberties as well as equality of the people
- Making these rights and liberties practicable for the reality

- Increasing the duties of the State and the possibility for the people to participate in every level of the political and administrative process

1. Recognizing more rights and liberties as well as equality to the people

Rights and liberties recognized by the Constitution are increased from 30 to 53 articles, as followed:

a) Human Rights

- It was the first time that human dignity was recognized by the Thai Constitution (Sec. 4, 26, 28).
- Torture, brutal acts, or punishment by cruel or inhumane means was prohibited. However, the death penalty remained valid, so that the punishment by death penalty as provided by law was not deemed as the punishment by a cruel or inhumane means (Sec. 31) and, instead of shooting to death, infusion of chemicals to death was chosen to implement the capital sentence according to the penalty law. Moreover, no arrest and detention of a person could be made except that an order of the Court was obtained and the arrested person should be sent to the Court within forty-eight hours (Sec. 237).
- A person's family rights, dignity, reputation or the right of privacy were also protected (Sec. 34) and it's the duty of the State to protect children, youth and family members against violence and unfair treatment (Sec. 53). Moreover it's the fundamental state policy to develop family integrity as the most important unit of the society (Sec. 80).
- A person should enjoy according to the Constitution full liberty to profess a religion, a religious sect or creed and observe religious precepts or exercise a form of worship (Sec. 38). And it's also the fundamental state policy to protect religions and to promote mutual understanding and harmony among followers of all religions as well as encourage the application of religious principles to create virtue and develop the quality of life (Sec. 73).
- A witness and injured person in a criminal case had for the first time the right to protection, proper treatment, as well as necessary and appropriate remuneration from the State as provided by law, whereas any person, who suffered an injury to life, body or mind on account of the commission

of a criminal offence without one's own fault, had the right to receive aid from the State (Sec. 244 –5).

- The alleged offender or an accused had the right to a speedy, continuous and fair trial.

b) Rights of the Thai Citizen

- There were improvements concerning the right to expression. The closure of a pressing house or a radio or television station in deprivation of the liberty under this section should not be permitted (Sec. 39). The transmission frequencies for radio or television broadcasting and radio telecommunication were declared national resources, which should be utilized for public interests by an independent state agency (Sec. 40). Officials or employees in a private sector undertaking newspaper or radio or television broadcasting business should enjoy their liberties to present news and express their opinions only under the constitutional restrictions as well as their professional ethics (Sec. 41). Moreover it was the fundamental state policy to develop information infrastructure in the locality thoroughly and equally throughout the country (Sec. 78)
- The Thai people enjoyed academic freedom (Sec. 42) and had an equal right to obtain fundamental education free of charges for the duration of not less than 12 years (Sec. 43).
- Children and youths with no guardian should have the right to receive care and education from the State, as provided by law (Sec. 53).
- The Thai people who were over sixty years of age and had insufficient income to maintain their livings should have the right to aids from the State, as provided by law (Sec. 54).
- The disabled or handicapped should have the right to public conveniences and other aids from the State, as provided by law (Sec. 55).
- The Thai people living together in a traditional community should have the right to conserve or restore their customs, local wisdom, arts or culture of their community and of the nation and to participate in the management, maintenance, preservation and sustainable exploitation of natural resources as well as the environment, as provided by law (Sec. 46).
- The right of a Thai to participate with the State and communities in the preservation and exploitation of natural resources and biological diversity should be protected, as provided by law. Any project or activity which might seriously affect the quality of the environment should not

be permitted, unless its environmental impact assessment had been pursued and opinions of an independent organization had been taken into consideration prior to the operation of such project of activity. More over it was the right of an individual to sue a government agency to perform its above mentioned duties (Sec. 56).

- Government officials are obliged by the Constitution to perform their duties in compliance with the law in order to protect public interests and provide convenience and services to the people and shall be politically impartial. If this is not the case, the interested person shall have the right to request them or their chief to declare or request them to act in compliance with the above mentioned provisions (Sec. 70).

2. Making these rights and liberties practicable for the reality

In order to ensure that the rights and liberties recognized by the Constitution were also relevant for the real life, the CDC had given various instruments to the people for their self- protection, as followed:

a) The state organs were obliged to respect the rights and liberties and the subjective rights of the people were entitled.

- Rights and liberties recognized by this Constitution expressively, by implication or by decision of the Constitutional Court, should be protected and directly binding on the Parliament, the Cabinet, Courts and other state organs in enacting, applying and interpreting laws (Sec. 27). In exercising their powers, all State organs should have to respect human dignity, rights and liberties in accordance with the provisions of the Constitution (Sec. 26).
- The restriction of such rights and liberties as recognized by the Constitution should be valid only by virtue of provisions of law specifically enacted for the purpose determined by the Constitution and only to the extent of necessity and provided that it should not affect the essence of such rights and liberties (Sec. 29).
- A person whose rights and liberties recognized by the Constitution are violated could directly invoke the provisions of the Constitution to bring lawsuit or to defend him- or herself in the Court (Sec. 28).

- It's also the right of a person to sue a state organ which is a juristic person to be liable for an act or omission done by its officials or employees (Sec. 62).
- In the case where a person or a political party had committed an act to overthrow the democratic regime of government, the person perceiving such an act should have the right to submit a request to the Attorney-General who has to investigate to find facts and then to submit a motion to the Constitutional Court to forbid such an act (Sec. 63).
- During the procedure before the Court, a party to the case could raise an objection that the provision of law applying to the case did not conform to the Constitution. The Court should stay the proceeding and submit its opinion to the Constitutional Court for consideration and decision (Sec. 264). But without a case before the Court a person had furthermore right to submit his or her complaint to the Ombudsman (Sec. 197), arguing that the provisions of law begged a question of constitutionality, the Ombudsman should submit the case as well as their opinion to the Constitutional Court (Sec. 198).

b) Right to Information and Expression of Opinion

According to the fact that the people are able to protect themselves only under the condition that they know what is going on. The CDC had thus guaranteed following rights.

- The right to get access to public information in possession of a state organ (Sec. 58).
- The right to information prior to permission of any project or activity which might affect the quality of the environment, health and sanitary conditions, the quality of life, as well as right to express one's opinion in the process of public hearing, as provided by law (Sec. 59).

3. Increasing the duties of the state and the possibility for the people to participate in every level of the political and administrative process

The CDC had increased the number of provisions of the Constitution in chapter V concerning directive principles of fundamental state policies as well as increased the possibility for the people to participate in every level of the political and administrative process, as followed.

a) More Duties of the State

To create subjective rights for the people, it was inevitable that more duties must be imposed on the state. The Constitution imposed following duties:

- The state should promote and encourage public participation (Sec. 76).
- The state should pursue the decentralization of power to localities (Sec. 78).
- The state should encourage a free market economic system, ensure and supervise fair competition (Sec. 87).

b) Constitutional Mechanism to Enforce the State Duties

In order to ensure that the above mentioned duties were really pursued the Constitution provides furthermore following mechanism:

- In stating its policies to the Parliament, the Cabinet should have to clearly state the activities intended to be carried out to implement the directive principles of fundamental state policies and should prepare and submit to the Parliament once a year a report on the result of the implementation, including problems and obstacles encountered (Sec. 88).
- The State should establish the National Economic and Social Council to be charged with the duties to give advice and recommendations to the Cabinet on economic and social problems (Sec. 89).
- In the case that the state does not, or is not willing to enact a law to cope with the demand of the people, a number of 50,000 people should have the right to submit a petition to the Speaker of the Parliament to consider such a law as mentioned in Chapter 3 (Rights and Liberties of the Thai People) and Chapter 5 (Directive Principles of Fundamental State Policies) (Sec. 170).

II. To form a political and bureaucratic system which is faithful and legitimate for the use of powers by increasing effective controlling power at every level to the citizen

According to the CDC, this aim should be fulfilled by the following means:

- Minimizing the vote buying practice
- Preventing corruption
- Increasing of the control system

1. Minimizing the Vote Buying Practices

In order to minimize the vote buying practice, which has been long rooted in Thailand, the CDC tried to use every imaginable measure, as followed:

a) It is duty for every person to exercise his or her right to vote (Sec. 68).
b) The outgoing ministers should not exercise their power to appoint, transfer or dismiss any government official, without the approval of the Election Commission (Sec. 215).
c) The limitation of electoral expenditure; imposition of a duty on a candidate to appoint a treasurer; inspection of electoral expenditure as well as publication of the result of the inspection (Sec. 326).
d) The establishment of the Election Commission as an independent organ (Sec. 136- 48).
e) In each constituency the votes from every polling station should be counted altogether at only one single place (Sec. 104).
f) Using of a mixed electoral system (Sec. 98-104).
g) The political party could be formed easiest so far (Sec. 328).
h) The Senate should consist of two hundred members to be elected by the people (Sec. 121). But they were not allowed to be a member of or holder of other positions of a political party [Sec. 126(1)].

2. Preventing Corruption

In order to achieve that the investment of buying votes from the people should not be easily reimbursed, the corruption must be prevented:

a) The state should prepare a political development plan, moral and ethical standards for holders of political positions and government officials (Sec. 77).
b) Persons holding political positions are subject to submit an account showing assets and liabilities of themselves, their spouses and children to the National Counter Corruption Commission and these accounts should be disclosed to the public (Sec. 291).
c) Transparency in exercising power
    - The voting of each Member of Parliament should be recorded and disclosed to public (Sec. 156).
    - The procedure of the Senate for the removal of persons from office should be open (Sec. 331).
    - Every judge of the Constitutional Court who constitutes a bench should give a decision on his or her own part (Sec. 267).

3. Increasing of the Control System

The CDC separated legal and political liability as independent from each other and created new court systems: both the Constitutional Court and Administrative Court, as well as constitutional control organizations, i.e. the Election Commission, the National Counter Corruption Commission and the State Audit.

III. To create an effective government with the Prime Minister as political leader to be able to solve the problems of the country and an effective parliament as well

The use of the party lists system, in parallel to the majority system, with a 5% clause, as used in Germany, empowered the political party enormously. As a result of this electoral system, the Thai Government was for the first time in the modern Thai history able to be formed by only one party. The fear for dictatorship among the intellectuals was at that time greater than ever. The complicatedly structured Constitution seemed not to be able to curb the so powerful Government.

In order to avoid loopholes in the constitutional text the CDC had not forgotten to enact in Sec. 7 that whenever no provision under this Constitution is applicable to any case, it should be decided in accordance with the constitutional conventions in the democratic regime of constitutional Monarchy. But the CDC had forgotten, just as the drafter of all the former constitutions had done, to recognize the customary international law[1], so that it might cause problems when conflicts occurr.

C. The Roots of the Problems

According to the Constitution a Thai voter, alike the one in Germany, has the right to cast a vote for one of the lists of candidates prepared by political parties and, in an election on a constituency basis, for one candidate in that constituency. But the electoral system applied in the Thai Constitution was a mixed system, in comparison to the proportional system with constituencies' mandates as applied in Germany. In Thailand the proportional system was totally separated from the simple majority system. Moreover, instead of using the proportion of 1 to 1 as applied in Germany, the Thai system is 1 to 4 between the list-mandates and the constituency-mandates from the total seats of 500 in the House of Representatives.

As the fruit of the local politicians oriented-CDC, the senators were for the first time in the Thai Constitutional history directly elected from the people of each province. Each of the voters in the whole province could cast a vote for only one candidate, the one from the heart. In the case where a province could provide more than one senator, as the number of the senators of each province depends on the size of its population, the candidates who receive the highest number of the votes in respective order to the number of senators that the province can provide are elected. With the power to recall the Prime Minister as well as high ranking officials and the power to appoint Judges of the Constitutional Court and the Supreme Administrative Court as well as members of control organizations, i.e. the Election Commission or the National Counter Corruption Commission, the Senate was assumed to be the most powerful organ of the land.

Instead of democratizing the political parties the CDC chose to set limits upon them. In order to keep the senate impartial, the Constitution forbade the senators to have any connection to a political party, although through over 70 years of democracy, the political parties had already won their Huakhanaen (canvasser) in the most part of the country. It was thus only an

---

1 Jumphot Saisoonthorn, *Public International Law*, Vol. I, 2004, pp. 140-144 (in Thai).

illusion to propagate 'politics without political parties' for the Senate as the Constitutional Drafting Council had already done. This false premise undermined the complicated structure of the whole current Constitution, highlighted as the first one created under participation of more than one million people in public hearings during the drafting process. It was also not surprising, when there was report in the newspaper that the Government has not less than 120 Senators under control.

According to the fact that this Constitution had created new court systems, both the Constitutional and Administrative Court, as well as a number of constitutional control organizations, all of these totally new organizations needed simultaneously a lot of qualified persons to fulfill their tasks. There were further problems in the selection process. So it was on the one hand not always the case that the right man was put on the right job. All but one candidate from the academics for the position of Judges of the Supreme Administrative Court were rejected by the Senate.[2] The majority of the Senators saw on the other hand to it that government friendly personalities were appointed to these important positions. And it is also not amazing that most of the constitutional control organizations had no remarkable out-put. All members of the National Counter Corruption Commission were even charged with malfeasance in duties and then sentenced by the Supreme Court's Criminal Division for Political Office Holders and then removed. No new commissioners have been appointed. Many corruption cases came under the statute of limitation.

The judges of the Constitutional Court were also appointed by the Senate, and the above mentioned problems were also inherent in the court system. According to the Constitution the judges of the Constitutional Court could issue, but only unanimously, its own procedural order. However, the issued procedural order was rather a primitive one. So it was not surprising, when its decisions were not always well-accepted by the public. Many of them were proven incorrect and caused problems for the administration. For more than 2 years there was no functional Auditor-General to run the State Audit and this problem arose from a false decision of the Constitutional Court.

The last controversial decision of the Constitutional Court was the rejection of a petition, submitted by a group of Senators against the then Prime

2 The mentioned Senate was formed under the former constitution.

Minister[3] accusing him of having done an act prohibited by the Constitution section 209.[4] The Court gave the reasoning that the petitioners had not given sufficient evidence to the Court, although the Constitutional Court had the power according to the Constitution section 265[5] to demand documents or relevant evidences from any person. With this rejection, the Thai people lost their last resort, which was inevitably disadvantageous to the democratic development. Because democracy always comes together with transparency and control.

It was not surprising that a lot of people gave flowers to soldiers after the coup d'état on 19th September 2006, although the true reason of which was not a political one. Nevertheless the political reform of 1997 had been torn

3 The same Prime Minister was in 2001 set free by 8 out of 15 Judges of the Constitutional Court after being accused by the National Counter Corruption Commission of failing to submit the account showing assets according to Section 295: "Any person holding a political position who intentionally fails to submit the account showing assets and liabilities and the supporting documents as provided in this Constitution or intentionally submits the same with false statements or conceals the facts which should be revealed shall vacate office as from the date of the expiration of the time limit for the submission under section 292 or as from the date such act is discovered, as the case may be, and such person shall be prohibited from holding any political position for five years as from the date of the vacation of office. When the case under paragraph one occurs, the National Counter Corruption Commission shall refer the matter to the Constitutional Court for further decision, and when the decision of the Constitutional Court is given, the provisions of section 97 shall apply mutatis mutandis." The majority of the judges used the word "honest failure" to justify the acquittal, which was held up to ridicule for years.

4 Section 209: "A Minister shall not be a partner or shareholder of a partnership or a company or retain his or her being a partner or shareholder of a partnership or a company up to the limit as provided by law. In the case where any Minister intends to continue to receive benefits in such cases, such Minister shall inform the President of the National Counter Corruption Commission within thirty days as from the date of the appointment and shall transfer his or her shares in the partnership or company to a juristic person which manages assets for the benefit of other persons as provided by law. The Minister shall not do any act which, by nature, amounts to the administration or management of shares or affairs of such partnership or company."

5 Section 265: "In the performance of duties, the Constitutional Court shall have the power to demand documents or relevant evidence from any person or summon any person to give statements of fact as well as request the Courts, inquiry officials, a State agency, State enterprise or local government organisation to carry out any act for the purpose of its consideration. The Constitutional Court shall have the power to appoint a person or a group of persons to carry out duties as entrusted."

up long before this coup by the malpractices of the leading politicians.[6] The coup was believed, as usual, to be the only measure to put an end to the political chaos of 2006 following the selling of Shin-Corp shares of the Prime Minister's family to the Temasek of Singapore without paying any tax.

D. Attempts to Solve the Problems

The Constitution of 2007 has according to the Draft Commission[7] the aim to correct the weaknesses inherent in the 1997 Constitution and addresses those problems on four fronts, including:

I. Protection, promotion, and expansion of the rights and freedoms of the people;
II. Reduction of concentration of power and elimination of its abuses;
III. Making politics transparent, moral and ethical; and
IV. Strengthening and increasing the effectiveness of the scrutiny process by making the scrutiny bodies independent, stronger, and more efficient.

I. Protection, Promotion, and Expansion of the Rights and Freedoms

1. The present Constitution provides in comparison with the 1997 Constitution more rights and freedoms. The new features include:
    - Protection of the privacy of personal information (Section 35);
    - Increase of rights in the criminal justice process through reform to improve access to the justice process, making it easier, quicker, more convenient, and more widely available at reasonable costs. Children, youths, women, the old, and the disabled and handicapped will get appropriate protection in the criminal procedure (Section 40). And more significantly, for the first time the people will have the right to bring a case before the Constitutional Court directly (Section 212);

6 Years before the coup there was a book published by one of the member of the CDC, Kanin Boonsuwan, titled "The Constitution is dead."

7 "Concepts of the Constitution of Thailand (2007)", in: *The Constitution of Thailand (2007)*, 4th ed., Bangkok: King Prajadhipok Institute, 2008, pp. 273-302.

- Legislation for the first time of labour rights to safety and welfare at work and security of employment during and after employment (Section 44);
- The protection of the rights and freedoms of the press, prohibiting not only closure of mass media, but also interference in the presentation of information, directly or otherwise (Section 45 and Section 46); prohibiting ownership or share-holding in mass media by holders of political offices to prevent the use of mass media to advance their own personal benefits (Section 48);
- Twelve years of free education with special support for the needy, the disabled or handicapped, or those in financial difficulty so that they may receive education on par with others (Section 49). In addition, there will be educational courses and trainings by vocational units and the private sector. Alternative education, self-education, and learning as a life-long process will also receive support from State as appropriate (Section 49);
- Children, youths, and family members enjoy more rights for physical, mental, and intellectual development compatible with their potential and environment (Section 52);
- Homeless persons with inadequate income to have the right to receive state aids for the first time (Section 55);
- Extension of community rights to cases where individuals get together, with duration not long enough to be an original local community (Section 67 paragraph one). Further, before undertaking any project or activity which may cause serious environmental damage, the public, particularly those directly affected, will have to be consulted (Section 67 paragraph two). The community can bring a lawsuit against a government agency, state agency, state enterprise, local government, or other state agency which is a juristic person to ensure compliance with the community rights provisions (Section 67 paragraph three);
- Rights for the people to monitor and to demand scrutiny of the performance of duties of a holder of a political office for the first time (Section 62 paragraph one), including access to detailed contents of bills being considered by the National Assembly (Section 142 paragraph five) in addition to the right of access to official information (Section 56);
- Public hearings to be required before signing any international agreement with an impact on the people. After signing the agreement, the

state has to give the people access to the detailed contents of the agreement signed and promptly provide remedies for those adversely affected in a fitting and just manner (Section 190 paragraph two and paragraph four); and
- People of 50,000 or more to be able to petition to get the Constitution amended [Section 291(1)].

2. To make the exercise of rights easier through the following measures:
   - Rights and freedoms are arranged in a clear and readable form: rights and freedoms of individuals (Section 32-Section 38), rights of the criminal justice, rights of information and complaint (Section 56-Section 62), rights of community (Section 66-Section 67), rights to protect the Constitution (Section 68-Section 69), etc.;
   - Rights and freedoms provided in the Constitution may be invoked even if they have not been enacted; the people may exercise those immediately in courts (Section 28 paragraph three);
   - The state has to promote, support, and help the people to exercise rights and freedoms (Section 28 paragraph four); and the number of signatures needed to recall a holder of a political office be reduced to 20,000 from 50,000 (Section 164 and Section 270 paragraph three).
3. Making the exercise of rights and freedoms more efficient with clear safeguards:
   - Removing the phrase "as provided by law" from all sections on rights and freedoms, which means the provisions of the people's rights and freedoms take immediate effect upon the passage of the Constitution, not pending their enactment;
   - Setting a time limit on enactment of organic-law bills, so as to prevent those in authority from delaying their passage to restrict rights and freedoms (Section 303 and Section 308);
   - Giving the people the right to bring before the Constitutional Court directly cases involving violation of the rights and freedoms provided in the Constitution (Section 212);
   - Giving a community the right to bring cases involving violation of the rights and freedoms directly before the Court (Section 66 paragraph three); and
   - Allowing the National Human Rights Commission to initiate legal action in the Constitutional Court and the Supreme Administrative Court where a law, rules, or injunctions contravene the Constitution,

or human rights have been violated (Section 257(3) and to file lawsuit on behalf of the injured person [Section 257(4)].

4. Making the directive principles of the fundamental state policies explicit all round and more binding than before on the government by:
   - Clearly differentiating the Chapter on the directive principles of the fundamental state policies to cover all aspects, including security, religion, society, education and culture, law and justice, international affairs, economy, land, natural resources and environment, science, intellectual property, energy, or public participation;
   - Increasing the principles of the fundamental state policies in key areas. Inter alia, the State
   - has to develop a work system that stresses development of quality, morality and ethics of its staff (Section 78 (4));
   - has to encourage the state agencies to adopt good governance (Section 78 (4));
   - has to carry out law and criminal justice reforms (Section 81 (4));
   - has to encourage and support the philosophy of sufficiency economy (Section 83);
   - has to restructure the tax and duty system to make it more equitable (Section 84 (3));
   - has to protect the interests of farmers in production and marketing (Section 84 (8));
   - has to provide basic public utilities and to prevent them from falling into private monopoly (Section 84 (10));
   - has to regulate land uses based on sustainable developments throughout the country (Section 85 (1));
   - has to give farmers rights to participate in decision-making concerning land-use (Section 85 (1)), etc; and
   - requiring the in-coming government to declare its policy to the National Assembly ensuring that it is in line with the directive principles of the fundamental policies, stating clearly what it plans to do and the appropriate timeframes. In addition, it has to submit an annual report to the National Assembly documenting the implementation progress and results as well as problems or obstacles encountered at least once a year (Section 75).
5. Allowing public participation in the administrative activities of the local government and greater decentralization of powers to local governments so as to make them the foundations of democracy at the national level.

- The local government has the freedom to manage its own affairs in all aspects, including organization of public services with variety and diversity (Section 281 paragraph one) and determination of its own administrative structure to suit the local conditions and needs (Section 283 paragraph two).
- Personnel management of the local government will be reformed such that the personnel will have the status of civil servants like their counterparts at the national level, with their own committees independent of the central government's control, powers to transfer personnel across agencies, and their own ethic committee as well (Section 288).
- Public participation at the local level will be boosted, allowing local residents to hold referendums on local matters of importance (Section 287 paragraph one and paragraph two), reducing the number of signatures required to recall a holder of local political office and to legislate local ordinances (Section 285 and Section 286), making the local government inform the public with respect to budgeting, spending, and performance so that the latter can take part in scrutinizing and monitoring its management (Section 287 paragraph three).
- The supervisory and monitoring system of the local government will be restructured to improve its efficiency, adopting a common standard so that the administration can operate independently, giving due consideration to the suitability and difference in development levels and management efficiency of the area. The local authority is to be encouraged to determine its own modus operandi according to its needs and to set up their scrutiny mechanism (Section 273 paragraph two).

II. Reduction of Concentration of Power and Elimination of its Abuses

The 1997 Constitution wanted a strong and efficient government. However, if the strength and efficiency is concentrated in the hands of a few, it can easily lead to abuses of powers, as it obviously occurred. It is therefore necessary to reduce concentration of power and adjust the balance of power. This Constitution tries to reach these aims by the following measures:

1. Empowering the people so that they become players by virtue of the numerous Sections, for example:

- Allowing public participation in all political spheres, e.g., in administering affairs of the state (Section 56, Section 142 paragraph four, and Section 190 paragraph two), holding referendum on important issues (Section 165), and amending the Constitution (Section 291 (1));
- Giving the people and the community power to sue the state for improper use of powers (Section 208 and Section 66 paragraph three); and making it easier for the people to exercise their rights, e.g., reduction in the number of signatures required to recall a politician and to propose a law both at the national and local level (Section 164, Section 165, Section 271, and Section 285).

2. Preventing monopoly and abuse of state powers by the government as follows:
   - The Prime Minister can only serve two terms or eight years (Section 171 paragraph four);
   - In issuing a Royal Decree, the government will be subjected to scrutiny by the Constitutional Court. Such legislation is reserved only for an unavoidable emergency, not just to evade the scrutiny of the National Assembly (Section 184).
   - A chapter on money, finance, and budget is to be added for the first time in Thailand to prevent undisciplined spending and creation of a financial burden on the future government and on the country (Section 167 to Section 170). Under the present Constitution, the government is required, specifically in its budget statement, to clearly state objectives, activities, plans, and projects (Section 167 paragraph two);
   - The National Assembly, courts, and statutory independent agencies can request amendment directly to parliamentary committees so that the government can no longer use budget appropriations as a bargaining chip (Section 168 paragraph eight). Similarly, the statutory agencies can table amendment to its own regulations directly to the National Assembly (Section 142 (3));
   - The Office of Public Prosecutors will be independent from the government and can thus inspect the exercise of state powers without the government's interference, especially in proceedings against holders of political office (Section 255);
   - The scope of responsibilities of the care-taker government will be defined clearly such that it will not be able to interfere with civil servants' performance of duties, nor to use state apparatus to support

any political party or any candidate in a general election (Section 181).
- Merger of political parties with sitting members is prohibited during the term of the House to prevent excessive majority (Section 104 paragraph two).

3. Enhancing the chance of ordinary people to sit in the House of Representatives and setting free the members of the House from the undue influence of their party so that they can fully and truly represent the interests of the electorate and country, with the following provisions:
   - The electoral system of the House of Representatives has been changed. Constituencies are now larger so that candidates can compete with their affluent counterparts. The one list system as used in 1997 Constitution has been replaced by proportional representation in constituencies based on provincial groupings rather than the whole country, which will prevent excessive concentration of representatives from the central region. The 5% cutoff rule has also been repealed, which will give small parties a better chance, thus conducive to political diversity.
   - Members of the House of Representatives will be free from parties' resolutions in interpellating, debating, and even voting on a motion of no confidence (Section 162 paragraph two); and
   - A bill will be tabled by only 20 Members of the House of Representatives without his or her own party's permission (Section 142 (2)).
4. The Senate shall consist of one hundred and fifty members to be elected from each province, one member being elected from each province, and to be selected in the number equivalent to the total number hitherto stated deducted by the number of elected senators (Section 111). The Senators Selection Committee shall select suitable persons from those nominated by organizations in the academic sector, the public sector, the private sector, the professional sector and other sectors, who are of value to the performance of duties of the Senators as Senators (Section 114).
5. Members of the House of Representatives and of the Senate are prohibited from intervening and interfering with the performance of duties by civil servants to advance their own or party's interests, directly or otherwise, as well as in posting, appointment, move, transfer, promotion or salary increases (Section 266).

III. Making Politics Transparent, Moral and Ethical

Political transparency, morality and ethics were in serious deficit in the 1997 Constitution. Flouting those rules, the ruling politicians used all tricks and cunning to get round the law, breed conflict of interests, and enrich themselves on the back of hardships of the nation. For good governance, the present Constitution offers the following solutions:

1. A full chapter on morality and ethics for holders of political office and state officials:
   - The ethics for holders of political office and state officials will set a code of conduct and criteria, apparatus, and system for efficient performance of duties, complete with a penal procedure for breaches of the code (Section 269); and a serious breach will, under the present Constitution, result in removal from office (Section 270).
2. Measures to prevent political conflict of interests:
   - Members of the House of Representatives and of the Senate are not permitted to hold any position in the civil service, state agencies, state enterprises, local councils, or as an administrator or civil servant in the local government. They must not receive, infringe, and interfere in the award of concessions from the state, civil service agencies, state agencies or enterprises, or be a partner in contract with the state, civil service agencies, state agencies or enterprises construable as monopoly, collusion, or partnership or holding shares in companies that obtain concessions or be a partner in contract thereof, directly or otherwise. They are not permitted to receive any payments or benefits from civil service agencies, state agencies or enterprises beyond what the civil service agencies, state agencies and enterprises offer others in a comparable business deal. Nor are they permitted to be partners or shareholders in companies involved in mass media, or partners in contract (Section 265);
   - The Prime Minister, ministers, spouse, and minor offspring are prohibited to be a partner or a shareholder in partnership companies or companies, or to retain partnership or shares in the partnership companies or companies in amounts as specified by law. If the Prime Minister or a minister wishes to continue to receive the said benefits, he or she must inform the President of the National Counter Corruption Commission within 30 days of his or her appointment to office. He or she must transfer all the shares into a trust to be managed by

an assets management company as required by the law. And he or she must refrain from any act that bears the resemblance of management of the shares or in the activities of the company in question (Section 269).

3. Stricter rules over the declaration of assets and liabilities for the holder of political office. Apart from his or her own, his or her spouse's, and minor offspring's, the amounts declared must include assets entrusted to others as well, directly or otherwise (Section 259). Just like ministers, members of the House of Representatives and of the Senate are also required to disclose their wealth to the public (Section 261).
4. Removal of members of the House of Representatives, of the Senate, the Prime Minister, and ministers on judgment by the court
   - Upon the final judgment of imprisonment by the court, regardless whether it is a suspended sentence or not, a member of the House of Representatives or of the Senate is considered officially removed from office except in the case of negligence or minor offence (Sections 106 (11) and 119 (8)).
   - Upon delivery of a prison sentence regardless whether a final judgment or a suspended sentence, the Prime Minister or the minister is considered officially removed from office, except in the case of negligence, a minor offence, or defamation (Section 182 (3)).
5. The President and Vice-President of the House of Representatives, the Prime Minister and ministers are prohibited from engaging in anything that bears the characteristics of a conflict of interests.
   - The President and Vice-President of the House of Representatives are not permitted to concurrently hold an executive post in a political party (Section 124 paragraph five).
   - The Prime Minister and ministers are not permitted to vote on matters relating to post assignment, performance of duties, or being party to the benefits thereof (Section 177 paragraph two).

IV. Strengthening and increasing the effectiveness of the scrutiny process by making the scrutiny bodies independent, stronger, and more efficient

The scrutiny bodies and statutory independent agencies, which were the high hope of the people in the 1997 Constitution, were subjected to heavy political meddling and in the crucial event failed to discharge their duties effectively. They are now restructured.

1. The Selection Committee comprises the President of the Constitutional Court, the President of the Supreme Court, the President of the Supreme Administrative Court, the President of the House of Representatives, and the opposition leader.
2. The powers and duties and the way the scrutinizing bodies work have been improved. The Constitution proposes the following measures:
   - Under the present Constitution, the Constitutional Court is vested with the power to consider cases of rights and freedoms violation brought before it directly by the people (Section 212).
   - The Supreme Court of Justice's Criminal Division for Political Office Holders considers cases of politicians accused of not declaring their assets and liabilities or cases involving falsification of assets and liabilities declared (Section 249 paragraph two).
   - The National Counter Corruption Commission handles only cases involving high-ranking political officer holders and civil servants so as to increase its efficiency (Section 250 (3)).
   - The Ombudsman may initiate lawsuits where public damage has occurred or public interests must be protected without waiting for complaints (Section 244 paragraph two).
   - The National Human Rights Commission receives a boost in power as it will be allowed to bring cases before the Constitutional Court and the Supreme Court if any law, ordinance, decree, or act contravenes the Constitution; and to act for and on behalf of the injured party whose human rights have been violated [Section 257 (3) and (4)].
   - The National Economic and Social Advisory Council has to give comments on all related bills (Section 249).
   - The statutory independent agencies, the National Assembly, and the courts can amend their own budgets directly before the parliamentary committees (Section 168 paragraph nine).
   - Members of the House of Representatives can censure the Prime Minister easier if they can gather votes of one-fifth of the total number of the existing members of the House (Section 158 paragraph one). They can also lodge a no-confidence debate against a minister who has moved to another cabinet post to avoid sanctions (Section 159 paragraph two and paragraph three). Both the Prime Minister and ministers can now be made to answer questions in person on the House floor (Section 162).

- The Office of Attorney-General will be separated from the government so that it can work more independently in the scrutiny of the exercise of state powers (Section 255).

3. Setting up a system of scrutiny over the performance of the statutory independent agencies
   - Issues of a decision revoking the right to vote ("red card") and a decision requiring a new election ("yellow card") by the Election Commission can now be appealed to the Supreme Court. Similar problems at local government elections can be dealt with by the provincial appellate court or regional appellate court (Section 240 paragraph two).
   - If, in the commission of an act which violates the Organic Act on the Election of Members of the House of Representatives and the Acquisition of Senators or the Rule or Notification of the Election Commission by the candidate of a political party, there has appeared convincing evidence that any leader of a political party or any member of the executive committee of a political party has connived at or allowed the commission thereof or, having known of the commission thereof, failed to prevent or take remedial action in order to render the election to proceed in an honest and fair manner, it shall be deemed that such a political party has committed an act with a view to acquiring the power to rule the country by any means which is not in accordance with the modes provided in this Constitution under section 68, and in the case where the Constitutional Court has delivered an order dissolving that political party, there shall be revoked the right to vote of the leader of such political party and members of its executive committee for the period of five years as from the date of the dissolution order (Section 237 paragraph two).
   - Rules, orders, or other actions of the statutory bodies relating to the application of law or to performance of administrative duties can be scrutinized by the Administrative Court (Section 223 paragraph one).
   - The Ombudsman will have power to investigate negligence of duties or misfeasance of other statutory agencies or agencies within the justice process (Section 244(1)).

E. Getting the Problems in Perspective

The Constitution Drafting Council (CDC) of the 1997 Constitution and the CDC of the present Constitution had at least one point in common; they kept their hand off the political parties. Although the latter tried to elaborate in details to improve the weak points of the former Constitution. Nevertheless the CDC overlooked the main cause of the political problems in Thailand: the political parties. Instead of restructuring and democratizing the political parties to make them parties of the people, the CDC of the present Constitution made it easier to dissolve them.

One of the parties in the opposition now experienced her second reincarnation within a year and stays active supporting the ousted Prime Minister, whereas the coalition party is waiting for her fate in the near future. Such practices set Thailand in a journey to nowhere and caused enormous casualties.

Now it is time to 'change' and to get the problem in perspective. The political parties in Thailand need to be democratized and restructured as follows:

1. The members of the political parties must pay member fees. Up to now almost all political parties in Thailand do not demand membership fees. The membership of most political parties is used as an alibi for democratic legitimacy, but in reality the ordinary members are only onlookers in their own parties without any right to participate in the party's decisions. In order that their status gets recognition and respect, the members of the political parties must pay membership fees. A party member, with whom the party has to reckon, should be able to identify with his or her party's program and ready to support the party by paying a membership fee.
2. The party's assembly should represent all members of the party. In most of the leading political parties in Thailand the decision powers are concentrated among the party's leaders and the members of the House of Representatives according to regulations on party's assembly of each party. Such regulations give the party's leader a good chance to control the party systematically; from investment in election to harvest in allocation of the state's budgets. Breaking this systematic control will help ease both vote-buying and corruption practices.
3. The party's candidates should be selected by the party's assembly. Selection of party's candidates is the most important task of the party. But

up to now the leader of the political party or the executive committee of the political party decides who shall be candidates of the party. Such a practice resumes and supports the patron-clients relationship of the old Siam. Relocation of this power to the party's assembly will help boost the democratic conscience among the party's members as well as democratic legitimacy in the party.[8]

All of these 3 proposals must altogether be implemented at the same time. The question is: who would enforce these proposals, when the amendment of the Constitution and the law-making process are in the hands of the politicians?

Works cited

Boonsuwan, Kanin, รัฐธรรมนูญตายแล้ว ("The Constitution is dead"), Bangkok 2005.

Mewongukote, Boonsri, แนวทางการปฏิรูป ระบบการเลือกตั้งและพรรคการเมือง ("Concepts for Electoral Law and Political Parties Reform in Thailand"), Bangkok: King Prajadhipok's Institute, 2010.

Saisoonthorn, Jumphot, กฎหมายระหว่างประเทศ ("Public International Law"), Vol. I, 5th ed., Bangkok: Winyuchon, 2004.

8 Boonsri Mewongukote, *Concepts for Electoral Law and Political Parties Reform*, 2010, p. 145 (in Thai).

Part III:

Rights

Some Critical Observations on the Freedom of Assembly in Thailand

Warawit Kanithasen

The demonstrations[1] in Thailand during the past few years, including those that took place a few months ago in April/May 2010 captured world-wide attention and are a topic of on-going discussions among academicians and laymen alike. However, since most of the debates have been of political nature, often characterized by emotional feelings, the need for a more critical discussion on the legal aspects of this topic seems to be justified, even though one has to admit that a purely legal standpoint, because of its normative character, cannot provide a comprehensive empirical overview of the complexity of the problem. The observations have been termed "critical", not in the sense that they are characterized by a tendency to find errors and flaws within the Thai legal system, but rather in the sense that the critical observations are to be understood as a careful evaluation of the topic in question, whereby certain non-legal considerations had to be taken into account, whenever necessary.

Without going to any details at this stage, a glance into the Thai constitutional provisions regarding the freedom of assembly shows that it is indeed one of the basic rights guaranteed by the present constitution. The fact that the three-year old present Constitution is the 18th charter since the introduction of democracy in Thailand in 1932, is mainly a reflection of a high degree of political instability and the frequency of coups the nation faced.[2] Thailand's present Constitution, promulgated in 2007, replaced an interim constitution which came into being as the direct result of the army-led coup in 2006.

1 The words "demonstration" and "assembly" and their derivatives have been used interchangeably in the general context of this paper.

2 See Politics of Thailand, Wikipedia, last updated on 12 October 2010, http://en.wikipedia.org/wiki/Politics_of_Thailand.

Unlike the so-called People's Constitution which was promulgated 10 years earlier in 1997 and widely hailed as a landmark in democratic political reform, the current Constitution is regarded by many as one with a controversial origin. It is, however, interesting to note that provisions on the freedom of assembly according to the present Constitution had been literally transcribed from the previous Constitution, word for word.

Article 63 of the Constitution of Thailand B.E. 2550 (2007) stipulates:

> A person shall enjoy the liberty of peaceful and unarmed assembly.
> Restriction of such liberty under paragraph one is prohibited except by virtue of law specifically enacted in the context of public assembly and to secure convenience for the people using public space, or to maintain order while the country is at war or during the time the state of emergency or martial law has been declared.

Before proceeding to making further comments on the freedom of assembly in Thailand as such, at this stage, it seems to be more appropriate to provide a brief background information on the development of modern Thai law in general.

Being under pressure from the Western powers, Siam at the beginning of the 20th Century modernized her legal system through a process of codification. Though the country always had high regard for England, but because of the very nature of the English Common Law, a legal transplantation of centuries-old customs and principles into Siamese law would have been hardly possible. Siam had to turn to Continental Europe and Japan where codification of laws in the respective countries was already in existence. The drafting of the Thai Civil and Commercial Code was done in English and used mainly Japanese law as a basis, which, in turn, was more or less a direct result of the German *Bürgerliches Gesetzbuch,* the German Civil Code, also known as the *BGB*. After the translation into Thai was completed, the Thai Civil and Commercial Code was promulgated. Thus Thailand and Germany belong to the same legal family, but it would take a few decades more until the Thai law students in general would become aware of this legal relationship with Germany.[3] Fikentscher[4] rightly remarked that Thailand adopted from the West only what may be called "legislative law" and almost nothing from the two realms of law, which together with the former form the whole body of law, people's law *(Volksrecht)* and legal practitioners' law *(Juristenrecht)*. To be fair, it must not be overlooked that Germany in the 19th Century was already a highly advanced nation, if not *the* leading nation in the fields of science, humanities and culture and it was precisely during that period when the German Civil Code was drafted following a lengthy debate between various schools of thoughts. The German Civil Code was finally proclaimed in the year 1900. In the light of the above, Thailand should strengthen the people's law and the legal practitioners' law, because after all, it is the attitude towards the law that distinguishes the Westerners from the Easterners,[5] the Thais from the Germans.

How true this is can be seen from the historical events in Thailand that have influenced the attitude of her people towards law and democracy. When democracy was introduced in 1932, absolutism was abolished, but the state of mind of some of the promoters of the revolution later revealed that they were not quite prepared to serve under the new democratic régime.[6] On the whole, however, Thailand was on the way to become a modern constitutional monarchy after having experienced the first 15 years of democratic government, when the process was violently interrupted by a military coup. Ever

---

3 The influence of German public law in Thailand took place at a later stage. While the commentaries of Professor Dr. Yud Saeng-Uthai, the first Thai legal scholar who graduated from Germany, were mainly on constitutional law, it was the educational reform at the Faculty of Law of Thammasat University that began in the 1970 s by Professor Dr. Preedee Kasemsup that paved way to legal reforms which finally led to the establishment of the Constitutional Court and Administrative Court at the turn of the 21st century. However, it should be noted that the influence of French legal concept on public law in Thailand was equally strong, if not stronger, particularly in the field of administrative law. It is of interest to note, that Professor Dr. Pridi Banomyong, who was educated in France, had already begun teaching Administrative Law at a time when Siam was still under absolutism. A few years later, he founded the Thammasat University in 1934. Today, Pridi is known as the Father of Thai Democracy.

4 See Fikentscher, *Modes of Thought*, 1995, p. 329.

5 See Fikentscher, *Modes of Thought*, 1995, p. 328.

6 [During the 19th Century until the Weimar Republic] faithfulness to monarchy rather than democracy, to order rather than liberal freedom, to national legal traditions rather than universal human rights, and to national unity rather than pluralism were supposed to be typical German values. Cited from Bryde, "Fundamental Rights as Guidelines and Inspiration," 2007, p. 192.

since the coup d'état of 1947 Thailand was many years under dictatorship. Yet with each change of government whether by election or coup the number of Thai people seeking for the rule of law and democracy increased, particularly in view of the emergence of the middle class in Thailand. The many years of being taught to simply obey and to memorize since early age have left a deep visible mark, particularly in the field of education that would influence the attitude of the Thai people towards law. As part of the process towards modernization, we Thais have yet to learn to discuss and debate and, most of all, to first learn to listen to other people's views. Rote learning is still part of legal education in Thailand. In order to pass the barrister exam, Thais students, besides having to memorize the various legal codes, also have to learn the judgements of the Dika Court – the Supreme Court of Justice of Thailand – by heart.

Thus it comes to no surprise that the method of interpretation of law in Thailand is often confined to a case law or casuistic approach, whereby it is interesting to note that casuistry is the standard form of reasoning applied in Common Law.[7] Thus, Thailand finds herself in the Civil Law tradition, but with a somewhat Common Law spirit. Whether this has been the direct influence caused by the first batch of Thai legal scholars abroad who were mainly educated under the Common Law system in England at the turn of the 20th Century or whether it was the result of those trained in Continental Europe, but not long enough to have been absorbed by the dogmatic and doctrinal teachings of law that have determined the discursive character of a typical German or French judgment,[8] is at this stage irrelevant, but might be useful for future debates on policy planning for legal education. Whatever opinion one may have about casuistry, the fact remains that the case law approach has long been with the Thai legal system and will certainly continue to stay as long as it cannot be substituted by the more modern doctrinal and systematic teachings of law. What seems to be more important at this stage is the immediate need for a value-oriented society in humanities where first and foremost human dignity and human rights are to be respected.[9] This has been always the noble mission of modern Thai legal scholars, but the strong influence of legal positivism has often been an obstacle in this process. From the Western point of view, the Thai society on the whole might not have

7 [7] For more details on Casuistry, see Jeramy Townsley, Casuistry – A Summary, Website December 2003, http://www.jeramyt.org/papers/casuistry.html.

8 See Zimmermann, "Characteristic Aspects of German Legal Culture," 2005, p. 27.

9 See Fikentscher, *Modes of Thought*, 1995, pp. 328-329.

completely reached the age of enlightenment as rational, analytical and critical thinking is often still lacking. With regard to legal science, the emergence of scientific research in the various fields of law, including in Constitutional Law, even though it may still be very much in the embryonic stage, renders hope that Thailand is moving into the right direction leading to the enhancement of the rule of law and democracy.

In principle, the core of the Freedom of Assembly in Germany and in Thailand is more or less the same. In both countries, the assembly has to be peaceful and without arms and is subject to restriction by law. The freedom of assembly, being a fundamental right as in the case of the right to human dignity or the freedom of expression, just to name a few, is primarily a right of the individual to defend or to be protected against state interference and has its roots in human rights which in turn, traces back to the concept of natural law according to which law and morality cannot be separated. In Thailand, the concept of fundamental rights is even reflected as positive law in Sections 26 to 29 of the Constitution. For example, in exercising its powers state authorities shall have to take human dignity, rights and liberties into consideration. Rights and liberties recognized by the Constitution expressly, by implication, or by decisions of the Constitutional Court, shall be protected and directly binding on the various state organs in enacting, applying and interpreting laws. Unlike in Germany where there is a federal law regulating in greater details about the freedom of assembly called *Gesetz über Versammlungen und Aufzüge von 1953* which was revised several times until as recent as in 2008, Thailand does not have a corresponding enactment. Moreover, the Thai courts have not dealt much with the freedom of assembly as such, but rather with the dispersal of the assembly according to which measures are to be taken "*only when necessary in consideration of the appropriateness (of the situation), whereby procedural steps in accordance with the international practice on the dispersal of assembly are to be followed.*"[10]

The absence of a specific legislation on the restriction of the freedom of assembly, coupled with the limitations posed by the restrictive nature of the rather archaic casuistic method of legal interpretation as practiced in Thailand, the demonstrators, the police and the courts find themselves in a rather difficult situation since there are no immediate guidelines that they can cling

10 Order of the Central Administrative Court Black Case 1065/2551. Academic research in Thai language on the subject of the freedom of assembly in Thailand has so far been limited to a few dissertations and articles.

to. A closer look at the Constitution of Thailand reveals that the fundamental rights, which include the freedom of assembly, are also to be promoted by the state, which apparently reflects the importance of those rights. However, the exercise of the rights and liberties of the fundamental rights, including the freedom of assembly, can only be done to the extent that it does not violate the rights and liberties of other persons or is contrary to the provisions of this Constitution or good morals.[11]

Using the above-cited federal enactment, namely the *Gesetz über Versammlungen und Aufzüge,* the *Bayerisches Versammlungsgesetz von 2008,* revised in 2010, the decisions and judgments related to the freedom of assembly by various German courts, which includes in particular the *Brokdorf decision*[12] as a guideline, the legal aspect of the freedom of assembly according to Section 63 of the Constitution of Thailand with regard to the demonstrations that took place, especially those in and around Bangkok, could perhaps be summarized as follows: The demonstrations in Thailand do not need approval. It follows that informing the authorities about the upcoming assemblies is primarily meant as a request for traffic clearance and seeking assistance from the police for safety and security during the demonstrations, whereby information on purpose, plan and routing of demonstration would be beneficial to all sides involved, including the general public. Police are required to respond to the said request as far as necessary. Names of demonstration leaders should be given to police, but at the same time demonstrators should be ready to identify themselves if requested to do so by the police. Demonstrators are to assemble peacefully in public places and without arms. With the exception of wooden sticks used to support the posters, other kind of sticks are not to be permitted as they could be used as weapons. Objects that could harm the body or life of other persons are not permitted. Demonstrators should not be masked as not to conceal their iden-

11 See as a comparison also the Lüth case, decided by the Federal Constitutional Court of Germany (BVerfGE 7, 198) that: "*It is equally true, however, that the Basic Law has set up an objective value system. This value system centred round the human personality developing freely in the social community, and its dignity must be regarded as the basic constitutional decision for all spheres of law. Legislation, administration, and the judiciary are given guidelines and inspiration (Richtlinien und Impulse) by it. Accordingly, it also manifestly influences the civil law: no provision of civil law may be in contradiction with it; each one must be interpreted in its spirit.*" Cited from Bryde, "Fundamental Rights as Guidelines and Inspiration," 2007, p. 197.

12 Brokdorf-Beschluß, BVerfGE 69, 315.

tity. Demonstrations on certain streets, particularly during rush hours, violate the rights of others and should therefore not be permissible. Analogous to the German cases where the demonstrations on the *Autobahn*, the German super highway, are not permitted, the assembly on the Thai expressways or other motorways meant for mass communication should not be allowed. Important public places, especially those that represent democratic institutions, such as the Government buildings, the Constitutional Court and the Parliament, for example, should have a zone around them where demonstrations are prohibited.[13] The Central Administrative Court of Thailand[14] ordered that an assembly that makes people fear of their lives, bodies, liberties so much that they do not dare to enter or come out of the Parliament is an assembly that violates the rights and liberties of others and is not considered to be peaceful and hence is not protected by Section 63 of the Constitution.

Owners and operators of food stalls and other vendors, insofar they are not part of the demonstrations, do not enjoy the rights in accordance with the freedom of assembly even though they may physically be in the areas where the public assembly is being held. Experience tells us that during each public gathering, there will always be some demonstrators not behaving in compliance with the law and thereby disturbing the otherwise peaceful character of the demonstration. Police shall therefore have the right to immediately arrest them, but would not have sufficient ground to disperse the demonstration. An encirclement of the demonstrators by the police is not considered to be a dispersal of the public assembly, nor would it make a difference whether the demonstrators where moving from place to place or not. But once the gathering is dispersed, the demonstrators have the duty to move out of the demonstration area immediately. In one of the cases concerning demonstration in Thailand, the Administrative Court ruled that the dispersal shall have to be taken step by step in accordance with the international practice, as mentioned before.

---

13 In Germany this protective measure, called *Bannmeile* or *Bannkreis* has its origin during the period of the Weimar Republic and was meant to ensure that the work of the parliament was not hindered by demonstrators. See Wikepedia: Bannmeile, http://de.wikipedia.org/wiki/Bannmeile.

14 Order of the Central Administrative Court Black Case No 1065/2551, see also Order of the Songkhla Administrative Court Red Case No. 495/2546 and Decision of the Songkhla Administrative Court Red Case No. 51/2549.

Although there may be individual incidences during the demonstrations that call for immediate police action, as long as the overall picture is basically peaceful and without arms, the demonstrations shall enjoy the constitutional protection according to the relevant provisions. Otherwise the demonstrations must have their legal limits if they are in violation of the applicable provisions of the constitutional law or of the law of torts of the Thai Civil and Commercial Code.[15] Normally purely technical laws, like the Land Traffic Act B.E. 2522 (1979) on their own cannot limit the freedom of assembly, unless there has been a gross violation of the law in question, and in particular if the demonstrators have already been warned about this at least a few times. A gross violation of the Land Traffic Act mentioned above usually would also violate other laws as well and most likely not be consistent with the intention and purpose of the freedom of assembly. It should be noted that applying technical laws to limit the freedom of assembly should be done only on a case by case basis after careful evaluation.

> Demonstrators and police should co-operate with each other as much as possible. Dispersal of demonstrations shall have to be the last resort if they are inconsistent with the true spirit of the freedom of assembly. In this regard, the United Nations has made the following recommendations relating to the dispersal of unlawful, but non-violent and of violent assemblies to various governments as follows:[16] In the dispersal of assemblies that are unlawful but non-violent, law enforcement officials shall avoid the use of force or, where that is not practicable, shall restrict such force to the minimum extent necessary. In the dispersal of violent assemblies, law enforcement officials may use firearms only when less dangerous means are not practicable and only to the minimum extent necessary. Law enforcement officials [...] shall not use firearms [against persons] except in self-defense or defense of others against the imminent threat of death or serious injury, [...] to prevent the perpetration of a particularly serious crime involving grave threat to life, to arrest a person presenting such a danger and resisting their authority, or to prevent his or her escape, and only when less extreme means are insufficient to achieve these objectives. In any event, intentional lethal use of firearms may only be made when strictly unavoidable in order to protect life. [...] Law enforcement officials shall identify themselves

15 Section 420 "*A person who, willfully or negligently, unlawfully injures the life, body, health, liberty, property or any right of another person, is said to commit a wrongful act and is bound to make compensation therefore*". Note the striking similarity to Article 823 [*Unerlaubte Handlungen*] of the German Civil Code – BGB. .

16 See Office of the High Commissioner for Human Rights, Basic Principles on the Use of Force and Firearms by Law Enforcement Officials, Adopted by the Eighth United Nations Congress on the Prevention of Crime and the treatment of Offenders, Havana, 27 August to 7 September 1990.

> as such and give a clear warning of their intent to use firearms, with sufficient time for the warning to be observed, unless to do so would unduly place the law enforcement officials at risk or would create a risk of death or serious harm to other persons, or would be clearly inappropriate or pointless in the circumstances of the incident.

The general rule of the freedom of assembly according to the current Constitution of Thailand is that people shall have the right to assemble peacefully and without arms. The above liberty can be restricted by law or by virtue of law, which forms the exception to the rule in normal situations. Moreover, in distress situations, as in the case of war, or when the state of emergency or martial law has been declared, the freedom of assembly can also be restricted. Such was the case when the April-May 2010 demonstration was regarded as not in consistent with the spirit of the freedom of assembly and the Emergency Decree had been declared for Bangkok and a number of provinces. The said Decree was lifted for some of the provinces, but still remains in force for Bangkok area. Should no incidences occur in the meantime, then it is expected that the Emergency Decree be lifted by New Year 2011. Whatever the case may be, on the long run, a national legislation, devoted entirely to the freedom of assembly detailing certain procedures and measures for both demonstrators and law enforcement officers, would not only be useful, but also consistent with the very concept of excellence for public policy and good governance.

Works cited

Bryde, Brun-Otto, "Fundamental Rights as Guidelines and Inspiration: German Constitutionalism in International Perspective," *Wisconsin International Law Journal* 25 (2007): 189-208.

Fikentscher, Wolfgang, *Modes of Thought: A Study in the Anthropology of Law and Religion*, Tübingen: Mohr, 1995.

Zimmermann, Reinhard, "Characteristic Aspects of German Legal Culture," in *Introduction to German Law*, ed. Reimann, Mathias and Zekoll, Joachim, München: C.H. Beck, 2005, pp. 1-53.

Constitutional Rights in Multiethnic States – The Case of Malaysia

Claudia Derichs

A. Introductory Remarks

The constitution of a modern nation-state is one of its core institutions. It covers the fundamental normative orientations of a country and reflects the values that guide administration and society in their interaction. Institutions in comparative politics can be seen as a variable in the theoretical setting of system comparison. They serve the purpose of structuring the analytical framework, but their impact on the unfolding of certain types of political systems should not be overestimated. Accordingly, comparative politics and its extension to comparative policy analysis in particular, tend to emphasize political processes and procedures instead of focusing exclusively on institutions.[1] Yet 'institutions matter' and they provide for an important analytical approach to the analysis of polities, politics and policies. In the present paper, I will try to shed a light on the political outcomes institutions generate with respect to rights of freedom (our panel topic), and relate them to the situation in a multiethnic Southeast Asian society, namely Malaysia. I will not deal with 'classical' examples of political institutions like the bureaucracy, parliament, or political parties, but concentrate on the constitution.[2] The ethnic and hence cultural dimension of codified norms is obvious in the Constitution of Malaysia, albeit not always expressed explicitly in its respective articles. Malaysian politics has always been determined and performed along ethnic communal lines. The institutional manifestation of the administration of multiethnic relations is quite unique in its kind and merits a closer look. My overall assessment of the provisions in the Constitution and the outcomes that have been generated in Malaysia's 'everyday politics' is ambivalent. On the one hand, Malaysia's political stability over decades is remarkable and has been pointed out by many scholars and comparativists. On the other hand, communal tension and articulated worries about viola-

---

1 See, for instance, Beyme, *Die politischen Theorien der Gegenwart*, 1992.

2 I am using a "c" as first letter when I talk about the constitution as an institution in general, and "C" when I refer to the Constitution of Malaysia.

tions of the constitution have increased in recent years. They have not come about by chance, but as a result of

(a) a rather authoritarian policy implementation and
(b) the 'hijacking' of control over law and order by one segment of society.

The paper consists of four sections plus some concluding reflections. In the first section, I will introduce Malaysia as a research subject and highlight some aspects that merit attention in respect to the topic of our panel. The second section addresses the constitutional setting. It discusses the articles and clauses which refer to ethnic relations, cultural markers and privileges for the biggest ethnic group, *i.e.* the Malays. These clauses have a direct impact on the regulation of citizens' rights of freedom. The third section illustrates how the constitutional provisions have worked out in the shape of the country's New Economic Policy and how they have been received by the country's citizens. In the fourth section, I wrap up the central aspects of the preceding paragraphs and give a concrete example of an outcome of the New Economic Policy in the field of education. Another example of policy outcome refers to a civil society coalition that strives to preserve the status of the Constitution as the country's supreme law. The coalition epitomizes the communal tensions that have apparently increased during recent decades. The conclusion draws a question mark concerning the power of the constitution to guarantee citizens' rights of freedom.

B. Malaysia as a Research Subject

Malaysia may not seem to be a very spectacular case study for cross-cultural comparisons at first sight, but it becomes an increasingly interesting subject for research when we look at how it has dealt with the ethnically and culturally heterogeneous composition of its population. There have been no major upheavals and social unrests for four decades, although prophecies of doom have been articulated frequently.[3] Malaysia belongs to the predominantly Muslim-populated countries in the Southeast Asian region. It displays a fairly stable political and societal order, although we find numerous challenging situations that lead observers to doubt the peaceful surface.

Malaysia gained independence and became a sovereign state in 1957, released from the colonial status as part of the British Empire, which had only been interrupted shortly by a Japanese occupation between 1942 and 1945. It was not yet called *Malaysia* in 1957, but *Federation of Malaya*, and it had not yet achieved the final stage of territorial rearrangements. Singapore joined the Federation in 1963, together with Sabah and Sarawak on Borneo island.[4] This whole entity was called *Malaysia* then, indicating that it was not only ethnic Malays who belonged to the 'nation', but also ethnic Chinese, Indians, and several groups of indigenous people.[5] Singapore's integration into the Federation, however, lasted but a mere 23 months. In 1965 the tiny peninsula was compelled to leave the Federation; it declared its separation from the mainland to become a sovereign state. Ever since, ethnic Malays form the majority of Malaysia's population (appr. 60 to 65%). They are

---

3 The reform movement which was mobilised in the wake of the sacking of Deputy Prime Minister Anwar Ibrahim in September 1998 may be regarded as a form of social unrest, but it was cooled down by the government authorities relatively quickly and has rather turned into a peaceful-but-demanding social movement. After the general elections of March 2008, this social movement made heavy inroads into formal politics: Its followers in the opposition parties won an unexpectedly high number of votes and got to control five out of 13 States.

4 For Malaysia's international relations in those days, which directly shaped domestic policymaking, see Sopiee, *From Malayan Union to Singapore Separation*, 1974; Abdullah, *Tengku Abdul Rahman and Malaysia's Foreign Policy*, 1985.

5 Malaysia: Official Yearbook 1997 gives absolute figures, but the proportions are well detectable: The estimation of the total population for 1997 was 21,665,400. 9,802,400 count as Malays, 4,631,900 as Chinese, 1,524,100 as Indians, and the rest as aborigines (*Orang Asli*) and indigenous races. Roughly calculated then, the three major groups would show figures of 45% Malays, 21% Chinese, and 7% Indians. "Others" would thus comprise 26% of the population. Other official estimates, however, tell figures of 55% Malays, 35% Chinese, 10% Indians and other minorities. The figures differ because of different categories utilized in the census to distinguish between Malay, Chinese, and natives. Statistically it makes an difference, *e.g.*, when *bumiputera* in Sabah and Sarawak are counted as Malays or not, or when persons of mixed origin like Sino-Orang Asli or Sino-Iban are counted as Chinese. Both figure combinations are officially accepted. In determining the quota for Bumi and non-Bumi in the tertiary sector of higher education, the ethnic breakdown of 55:35:10 is taken as the relevant base.

followed by ethnic Chinese (appr. 25-30%) and ethnic Indians (appr. 7%). The remaining percentage is made up of various indigenous communities.

The ethnic constellation changed considerably through the dissociation of Singapore, which is mostly inhabited by citizens of Chinese origin. Malaysia had in fact insisted on the incorporation of Sabah and Sarawak into its territory because it sought to prevent a Chinese majority in Malaysia.[6] From the very beginning of its existence as the entity *Malaysia*, the country has had to handle the fact of ethnic rivalry, potential racial clashes, and diverse cultural nationalisms. Research thus refers to the childhood period of the young Malaysian state as a period of striking *communalism*. Like Ongkili (1985) states in the preface of his great work on nation-building in Malaysia between 1946 and 1974, communalism has been the fundamental problem of nation-building in Malaysia. Communal groups can be political parties, ethnic minorities, or communities who just strive for representation in the nation. Communalism had to be taken into account while shaping the nation; it determined the social, political and economic policy at length.[7]

The challenge for politicians in 1957 lay in the task of inventing and implementing a political system and social order that would prevent communal clashes and enhance stability. The situation today seems not much different, for we still find a vaguely balanced ethnic composition, a political party system that represents the major ethnic groups and their concerns, and a state-sponsored concept of reformist Islam which is designed to be progressive and moderate (*Islam Hadhari* or "civilizational Islam"), but has not succeeded in convincing the country's non-Muslims of its integrative capacity. Despite the government's ambitions to shape Malaysia as a knowledge-based, IT-savvy and business-oriented society, questions of equal access to education and profession, shared goods and shared meanings in a multiethnic society still occupy the political agenda. The post-colonial government has been successful in establishing formal democratic structures and some form of 'unity through diversity' with comparatively few disruptive incidents.[8] This has been achieved through a combination of at least three vividly pursued goals:

---

6 See Lau, *A Moment of Anguish*, 1998, pp. 11 f.

7 See Ongkili, *Nation-building in Malaysia*, 1985, p. V.

8 For comparative cases in the Asia-Pacific region see Brown and Ganguly, *Government Policies and Ethnic Relations in Asia and the Pacific*, 1997. Ganguly, "Ethnic Policies and Political Quiescence in Malaysia and Singapore," 1997 puts the particular case of Malaysia into perspective.

- rapid economic growth,
- cultivation of a culture of 'developmentalism' (accompanied by middle class growth),
- consolidation of a strong, one-party dominated state[9] (which resorted to coercive laws to maintain its rule).[10]

In the following paragraphs I will look at how the ethnic and cultural diversity is reflected in the constitutional arrangement of the Malaysian state. A central observation is that social, political, and economic inequalities are institutionally stipulated, but functionally levelled in that an alternative system of institutional organisation evolved from the sheer need of the 'minorities' to offset the disadvantages deriving from Malay dominance. The Malaysian Constitution will be looked at to convey an idea of how critical the issue of Malay dominance was in the vision of the 'plural society' that Malaysia's founding fathers planned to create.[11] A second area to examine will be the concept of *bumiputera* ('sons of the soil'), which applies to ethnic Malays and indigenous people or 'natives'. It will be raised as an example for the institutionalisation of difference. Both the second and the third topic are wrapped in the framework of the so-called New Economic Policy (NEP, 1971-1990), which stands out as the most elaborate affirmative action policy of post-colonial Malaysia.

C. The Constitutional Setting

The Constitution of Malaysia, as it is called since *Malaysia Day* (16 September) 1963, is an extended version of the Constitution of 1957, which is also referred to as the *Merdeka Constitution* (Independence Constitution). The *Merdeka Constitution* was ratified shortly before the independence of the Federation of Malaya was proclaimed on 31 August 1957 and is therefore still the reference.[12] The term 'Federation' was retained in the Constitution of Malaysia and is used throughout its text; Art. 1(1) states that the "Feder-

---

9 Strictly spoken, it is not one single party that dominated during Malaysia's post-colonial time, but a coalition of roundabout 14 bigger and smaller component parties. The strongest party within this coalition is the United Malays National Organisation or UMNO, which is generally considered the ruling party.

10 See Loh Kok Wah, "Managing Ethnic Conflict and Violence in Malaysia," 2006.

11 See also Shamsul, "The Making of a 'Plural' Malaysia," 1997.

12 See Andaya and Andaya, *A History of Malaysia*, 1982, p. 262.

ation shall be known, in Malay and in English, by the name Malaysia".[13] The Malaysian Federation accordingly consists of 13 States and two Federal Territories (the capital Kuala Lumpur and the island Labuan on the East coast). The States enjoy the legislative rights of local government entities in a federalist state, *i.e.* they are sovereign in every regard except for issues belonging to the 'Federal List' and the 'Concurrent List' of lawmaking. It is worth mentioning that Malaysia was for a long time the only nation state in Southeast Asia that subscribed to a federalist state organisation. (Myanmar, which would be a second example, cannot really be called federalist). Indonesia implemented a decentralization scheme since 2001, but it differs from Malaysia in that it has elevated the autonomy of the local districts (*daerah*) rather than endowing the provinces with effective powers of self-government.

The organisation of the State governments in Malaysia reveals some peculiarities which are directly related to some 'Malay legacies' of the past. With the Sultans as Heads of State[14] we find an institution that dates back to the old times of a dynastic polity. The Sultan system itself is informed by the concept of *raja*, or royalty, and connotes "communitarian assumptions that underpinned the old kerajaan [Malay kingdom; C.D.]".[15] The Head of State is also Head of the religion of Islam in that respective State, so that Islamic religious affairs can be linked to the notion of Malay-Muslim tradition, and political order can be traced to Malay royal tradition as well as to the modern federalist system. Indeed, the States themselves as administrative entities, called *negeri* in Malay language, resemble the *kerajaan* model of Sultanates in today's Peninsular Malaysia. Integrating the system of Sultans and *negeri* into a modern polity increased the credibility of the nation-state model introduced in 1957 and attended to the narrative of Malay religious and political tradition. On the national level, the Supreme Head of the Fed-

---

13 For this and other clauses of the Constitution in this paper see full text internet version of the 1957 *Constitution of Malaysia* at http://en.wikisource.org/wiki/Constitution_of_Malaysia.

14 Yang di-Pertuan Negeri refers only to the Heads of State in Malacca, Penang, Sabah and Sarawak, which are cited in the Constitution as 'States not having a Ruler' (Art. 3(2)) and which do not have a "history" as Islamic Sultanates. For these four States (and for the Federal Territories), the Supreme Head of the Federation (Yang di-Pertuan Agong; monarch) can be authorized to represent the Head of the religion of Islam when Islamic religious matters extend to the Federation as a whole (Art. 3(2)).

15 Milner, "Ideological Work in Constructing the Malay Majority," 1998, p. 161.

eration (*Yang di-Pertuan Agong*) is elected as king by the *Conference of Rulers* for five years. This form of electing the monarch is also unique to Malaysia. Although the *Conference of Rulers* includes both the dynastic Sultans and the non-Sultanic Heads of States (see note 6 below), the latter are not eligible for the status of king. The *Conference of Rulers* is exclusive to the Sultans in cases of "any proceedings related to the election or removal of the Yang di-Pertuan Agong or relating solely to the privileges, position, honours and dignities of Their Royal Highnesses [*i.e.* the Sultans; C.D.] or to religious acts, observances or ceremonies".[16]

There are more hidden messages in this small passage of the Fifth Schedule of the Constitution than apparent at first glance. The Malay bias is obvious in that the Malay Muslim Rulers of the States, hence the Sultans, are the only persons entitled to assume the position of the Supreme Head of the Federation (king). In the States not having a Sultan, a modified form of the Sultan system has been installed to create a structural similarity between all States of the Federation. The monarch's oath of office – in Malay language – contains the phrase "We shall at all time protect the Religion of Islam".[17] It clearly prescribes a full commitment to the religion of Islam. Since 'Malayness' is defined by the three keywords *bahasa* (language), *agama* (religion = Islam) and *raja* (royalty), it is clear that the sultan-monarch system underscores an important feature of Malay cultural nationalism: A Malay is a Muslim, speaking the Malay language and showing loyalty to the king. A concession to liberal democratic ideas of the separation of powers and checks and balances was made by establishing in every State an elected Legislative Assembly and an Executive Council with a Chief Minister at the top to avoid a concentration of power.

The constitution does not preclude the possibility of non-Malay rule through these legislative and executive institutions – in the States as well as on the federal level. In this regard, it displays fidelity towards the 'plural society' vision. In political reality, a non-Malay ruler is inacceptable.[18] 'Malay dominance' and the preservation of 'Malayness' are recognized and nurtured in politics and society; Malay hegemony is firmly consolidated in

---

16 Constitution of Malaysia 1957, Fifth Schedule, Item 7.

17 Constitution of Malaysia 1957, Fourth Schedule.

18 The discussion of a non-Malay prime minister gained momentum after the elections of 2008. The opposition coalition *Pakatan Rakyat*, which is composed Malay and non-Malay parties alike, agreed on a Malay prime minister in case this issue came up at some point in future (Malaysia Today, June 8, 2010).

the political world. But the commitment to a 'plural society' concept is nevertheless allowed for by the Constitution. Moreover, in terms of economic skills and performance we still find Chinese Malaysians in the forefront. The dualism of the Constitution – in the sense of its dual commitment to the features of Malay-Muslim primacy and to the plural society concept – reflects a special attention to one particular ethnic community in the multi-ethnic state, while recognizing the reality of ethnic pluralism. Following both orientations at the same time means to walk a tightrope. In the Constitution, the effort to cater to both requirements condenses in a peculiar provision of 'special rights' for Malays in exchange for a citizenship status for non-Malays – an inter-ethnic 'social contract', so to speak.

The primacy of Malays and 'natives' is expressed in Article 153 of the Constitution. The Article symbolizes the successful struggle of UMNO[19] partisans in the mid-1940 s to mobilize support for their idea of a 'Malay' nation state. It guarantees special rights for Malays – rights that automatically accompanied the Sultan system when it was (re-)installed at the time of the Federation of Malaya in 1948. After declaring these rights a part of the *Merdeka Constitution* and hence declaring them Article 153 of the current Constitution, they could be utilized in party politics to legitimize communally oriented party programs. In the case of UMNO for instance, Shamsul (1996 a) speaks of four phases of implementation of the UMNO-sponsored model of a plural society nation. The model was based on the notion of a special position Malays enjoy and ought to enjoy, while acknowledging the reality of a multiracial Federation. Emphasis on Malay interests became particularly strong from up the second phase, which began with the rule of Prime Minister Tunku Abdul Rahman. The Tunku, as people commonly called him, advocated a purely 'Malay UMNO'. This meant that he was "retaining it as a communal party and thus emphasizing the primacy of Malay ethnic interests while recognizing the interests of other ethnic groups".[20] After the 1969 racial riots, Tunku's successor Tun Abdul Razak continued to appreciate the framework of the 'plural society nation', but at the same time promoted Malay political hegemony. Abdul Razak's rule can be considered the third phase; his views became reflected in an amendment of the Constitution and "subsequently incorporated as a principle in the formulation of public policies and institutions, particularly in the form of the NEP

19 United Malays National Organisation, see note 9.
20 Shamsul, "Debating about Identity in Malaysia," 1996, p. 487.

(New Economic Policy; C.D.), popularly known as the *bumiputera* policy".[21]

Until today, Article 153 has not been repealed, although the NEP project formally ended in 1990. Through this Article, the Constitution assures Malays and natives of Sabah and Sarawak prior recognition in respect to education and training, positions in public service, and permits and licences for trade and business. The terms 'Malay' and 'natives' are separately defined in the Constitution:

> 'Malay' means a person who professes the religion of Islam, habitually speaks the Malay language, conforms to Malay custom and –
> (a) was before Merdeka Day born in the Federation or in Singapore or born of parents one of whom was born in the Federation or in Singapore, or is on that day domiciled in the Federation or in Singapore; or
> (b) is the issue of such a person.[22]

Art. 161A.(6) then explains that 'native' means

> (a) in relation to Sarawak, a person who is a citizen and either belongs to one of the races specified in Clause (7) as indigenous to the State or is of mixed blood deriving exclusively from those races; and
> (b) in relation to Sabah, a person who is a citizen, is the child or grandchild of a person of a race indigenous to Sabah, and was born (whether on or after Malaysia Day or not) either in Sabah or to a father domiciled in Sabah at the time of the birth.

Clause (7) mentions 20 different races as indigenous to Sarawak, among them Malays. The inclusion of the natives into the group of constitutionally privileged persons is important not because the smack of sole and absolute preference of Malays is diminished through it, but rather because the concept of *bumiputera* relies on the image of natives and Malays as 'sons of the soil' of Malaysia (see below).

Special provisions for Malays and natives as *bumiputeras* mean that the king is responsible for safeguarding the special position of Malays and natives, but also for safeguarding "the legitimate interests of other communities".[23] All the provisions mentioned in the Article, *e.g.* the ensurance of positions in the public service (national level), of scholarships or other educational privileges, of permits or licences for the operation of trade or business when required by federal law, can be determined "as he [= king; C.D.]

21 Shamsul, "Debating about Identity in Malaysia," 1996, p. 487.

22 Constitution of Malaysia 1957, Art. 161(2).

23 Constitution of Malaysia 1957, Art. 153(1).

may deem reasonable".[24] In political practice the reasonability is not determined by the monarch, but by government and bureaucracy. Interesting though in the context of institutions and multiethnic society is the close conjunction of special rights and king. It confirms that the royalty is considered a central element of Malayness, and that the special rights for Malays and natives are ultimately tied to the institution of the monarchy and the Sultan system. The interrelation between cultural and political elements is meant to reconcile an ethnic primacy demand with a plural society vision. If the constitutional monarchy and the federalist-turned Sultan system were abolished, the whole construction of this institutional arrangement would probably collapse. The very fact that Malaysia's federalism is based upon if not legitimized by the traditional concepts of *raja* and *negeri* reveals how manifold the background of the institutional setting is. The cultural contestations hidden behind the curtain of the plural society model and the constitutional provisions are to a certain extent reflected in the category of *bumiputera*, which will be discussed in the following paragraphs.

D. The Concept of Bumiputera and the NEP

The cognitive definition of the concept of *bumiputera* and on how it was shaped as a political category is an essential element of the politics of multiethnic Malaysia. Lacking a judicial binding, the category of *bumiputera* is principally a mere a policy instrument, although it generates law-like authority as seen in the stipulation of special rights for Malays and natives. Shamsul reasons that *bumiputera* has never been a real legal category because it was never defined directly and clearly in the Constitution.[25] Nobody (of the *bumiputera* population) could, for instance, sue the government for not being accorded a particular privilege, claiming that he or she deserves it through the provisions in the Constitution. The *bumiputera* concept could rather be deemed a kind of 'by default' or 'by implication' legal concept, while certainly being used in policy formulation. What was the *bumiputera* concept initially meant to stand for and how did it affect the plural society model of the nation? I will turn to the early years of independence again to examine these questions.

24 Constitution of Malaysia 1957, Art. 153(2).
25 Personal conversation, 23.3.1999.

Two outstanding facts have penetrated the history of independent Malaysia from the beginning until present. On the one hand, Chinese predominance in the economic and business world formed a matter of fact. On the other hand, Malay hegemony in politics had never been seriously questioned, be it because of a very 'generous' attitude of the non-Malays or because of the acceptance of a legitimate claim of the Malays to be the ethnic community or race with the longest history of inhabiting the state territory. The racial cleavage issue has to be put into perspective, though. The idea of distinguishing people along the lines of 'race' had been introduced through European colonisation.[26] Applied in the census taking of the colonial period, the categories of race and ethnicity became consolidated in the Malaysian world view. Shamsul (1998) states that the social construction of difference through the official census initiated and established a countrywide trend toward minority and majority discourse, especially at the official level. This "was particularly true after the 1921 census, when Malays came to realize that they were outnumbered by the immigrant Chinese and Indian population and hence were a minority in their own 'motherland'".[27]

One can easily imagine that the Malays' feeling of belonging to a minority and backward to other communities in terms of economic skills and proficiency was an unfavourable condition for a take-off as the leading community ('sons of the soil') of the country at the time of de-colonisation.[28] The *Merdeka Constitution* thus provided special rights for Malays. But when Singapore, Sabah and Sarawak joined the Federation in 1963 – and also after Singapore left it again in 1965 – it stood to some reason that the communities most deprived of economic well-being were longing to be accorded some channels and tools to get access to the sources of economic wealth. The factual economic gap between the poor Malay peasants, paddy farmers and petty traders in rural areas and the Chinese shopkeepers and owners of small, family-based enterprises in the urban areas also lead to a perception gap, making it difficult to imagine a dynamic money-making Malay businessman. In Sabah and Sarawak, the indigenous people had their own system of passing native land on to the members of the community (communal land-

26 See Shamsul, "Identity Construction, Nation Formation, and Islamic Revivalism," 1997, p. 209.

27 See Shamsul, "Bureaucratic Management of Identity in a Modern State," 1998, p. 137.

28 This (alleged) ‚backwardness' became most prominently spelled out in Mahathir Mohamad's book *The Malay Dilemma*, 1970.

holding), whereas in the Malay Peninsula the land was passed on to and divided between the offspring. Both mechanisms did not promote the experience of growth or develop management skills. Moreover, money was considered merely "a convenience, used as a substitute for goods in bartering".[29] Prime Minister Mahathir (1981-2003) in his retrospective of the situation of the Malays in Malaysia before the racial riots of May 1969 recalls that money as capital was not appreciated. Malay farmers rather "agreed to surrender their next harvest to the local Chinese shopkeeper or rice mill-owner, as an advance to meet their daily needs and the requirements of the next planting season".[30] Accounts, value of harvest or goods, or any proofs of the accurate calculation of the shopkeeper or mill-owner was not a big concern to them. They were just happy with the money they got for their goods. For interest they did not care as well, because as a Muslim you do not care for interest anyway.

A similar attitude towards money and accumulating capital could be described for the indigenous communities. Hence, the value of possessing land and keeping it in the hands of one's own community was regarded as more important than creating wealth with it. This cultural feature was something the Malays and the natives had in common, so that they were named *bumiputera*: "They might be poor in financial terms, but they had land, and land ownership symbolised their right to the country, their 'special' position as bumiputeras, or 'sons of the soil'".[31] The symbolic meaning of 'land' and the attitudinal, customary and behavioural dimensions underpinning it functioned on the positive account as something that generated the *right* of the *bumiputeras* to the country, and on the negative account as something that underscored the *backwardness* of the *bumiputeras* in comparison to the economic achievements of the non-*bumiputera*. Against this background, Mahathir stresses that it is culture and not ethnicity that distinguishes people.[32] One has to admit though that only certain ethnic communities have developed and cherished a truly shared culture that would make it reasonable to talk of the *bumiputeras* as one group of people that can be distinguished from others.

The term *bumiputera* contains the notion of the soil (*bumi*), and the notion of the son as the male descendant (*putra*) who inherits the land from his

29 Mahathir, *The Way Forward*, 1998, p. 113.
30 Mahathir, *The Way Forward*, 1998, p. 113.
31 Mahathir, *The Way Forward*, 1998, p. 115.
32 See Mahathir, *The Way Forward*, 1998, p. 121.

father and is therefore the legitimate inhabitant of the country (the native, the aborigine). The term *putra* in Malay carries several connotations, reaching from its original meaning in Sanskrit, which is 'prince' (*putri* then means 'princess'), to the reminiscence of Malaysia's first Prime Minister Tunku Abdul Rahman Putra. In the PM's name, 'Putra' indicated the royal lineage of the Tunku. The word is widely used in names of vehicles, buildings, public places and so on – last but not least the newly constructed government site south of Kuala Lumpur is called *Putrajaya* ('prosperous city of Putra') to honour Tunku Abdul Rahman. Shamsul dates the first official application of the concept back to 1965, when UMNO held a Malay economic congress as a result of which the Bank Bumiputera was established as a financial institution to support and encourage Malays' business efforts and to break the Chinese and foreign monopoly of the banking segment of commerce.[33] After the congress, the term *bumiputera* came into popular use.[34]

The term became internalised in the wake of a huge policy shift took that place after the racial clashes in the capital Kuala Lumpur in May 1969 (see below). A New Economic Policy (NEP) was formulated immediately after the clashes and launched in 1971. The NEP became quickly referred to as *bumiputera* policy. Why is this so and why is the concept of *bumiputera* a policy instrument rather than a legal category? The main objectives of the policy as such can be summarized as follows. The *bumiputeras*, comprising 56% of the population in those days, controlled only 2.4% of the nation's economic wealth, whereas the non-*bumiputera* controlled over 34%. Foreigners, *i.e.* non-citizens (predominantly the former colonists), controlled a share even larger than the Malaysians altogether (60%), primarily because they had still had prime access to the sources of wealth. In the framework of the NEP, a new key figure for the distribution of national wealth was agreed upon by representatives of all major ethnic groups. The proportional allocation to be reached in 20 years (1970-1990) was 30% for *bumiputeras*, 40% for Chinese and Indians, and 30% for foreigners.[35] That Chinese and Indians would be able to increase their share was beyond doubt, but the *bumiputera* community would well need special incentives, privileged access and preferential treatment. Capital, opportunities, education and

---

33 See Shamsul, "The Construction and Transformation of a Social Identity," 1996, p. 27.

34 See Shamsul, "The Construction and Transformation of a Social Identity," 1996, p. 27; Mahathir, *The Way Forward*, 1998, p. 46.

35 See Mahathir, *The Way Forward*, 1998, pp. 11, 24 f., 56, 80 f., 90.

knowhow were deemed necessary to narrow the gap between *bumiputeras* and non-*bumiputeras*.

The *bumiputeras* were encouraged to participate in the world of business through several preferential measures, like government contracts, licences, set-up of state-owned companies to exploit the timber and mineral resources, a 30% allocation of shares of every new or expanding company, and others. After 30 years since the launching of the NEP, the objectives had been met to a considerable extent; at least there is no race that were completely underrepresented in Malaysia's economic performance. The relation between race and policy formulation shall yet be looked at a little closer.

Since events overlapped in the period between 1965 and 1971, we may speak of a multi-layered functional concept of *bumiputera*. First, there was the need for UMNO to fulfil what it had promised for years: pro-Malay politics and the implementation of pro-Malay policies. When Sabah and Sarawak became part of Malaysia, it was of course necessary to somehow include the indigenous people of East Malaysia in the process of building the Malaysian nation. The cultural affinities of Malays and natives of Sabah and Sarawak facilitated the invention of the idea of a united segment of *bumiputeras* in the Malaysian nation. The fact that the *bumiputeras* in general occupied very low positions in the scaffold of the economy could have had a uniting function like it is known from the theory of class struggle, but the already heated-up atmosphere of 'race talk' (Shamsul A.B.) fuelled the particular confrontation of Malays and Chinese in the capital Kuala Lumpur. The clashes of May 1969 in the city evolved in the wake of demonstrations of a proclaimed Chinese victory in the elections (primarily on the State level) which in turn lead the Malays to demand permission of a procession, too. The parades of both groups ended up in violence and mutual aggression; people were attacked and killed. By attacking and killing Chinese, "the Malays were confident that they were destroying Chinese property".[36] The emergency situation – declared by the king – required a quick and effective strategy to resolve the tension between the races. This was the birth of the New Economic Policy.

The tension had mounted mainly between Chinese and Malays, but the subsequent analysis of the riots brought forth a more specific identification of the causes: Economic disparities were depicted as the source of tension, although nobody could ignore the element of race that was linked to it. Since

36 Mahathir, *The Way Forward*, 1998, p. 50.

racial differences were hardly to eliminate, reducing the economic disparities became the objective of policymaking. The idea of assembling the different native, indigenous, aborigine and Malay ethnicities collectively under the roof of *bumiputera* had derived from the *cultural* dimension of similarity and difference. The similarity of the *economic* position of the *bumiputeras* in Malaysian society had contributed substantially to defining the *political* concept of *bumiputera*, or, in other words, to provide the cognitive definition of collective identities under the NEP.

For the Malaysian government, or more correctly for UMNO, the concept of *bumiputera* set it free of being accused of a too strong Malay bias, because it could claim that the category favoured not only the interests of Malays but of all economically deprived communities in the country. With the distinction between *bumiputera* and non-*bumiputera*, the prominent polarisation of Malays and Chinese could be blurred a little. The non-Malay natives (*i.e.* aborigenes on the Peninsula and natives/ indigenous groups in Sabah and Sarawak) should not feel excluded from the politics of lifting up the positions of economically backward groups, and, finally, the non-*bumiputeras* (Chinese and Indians in particular) should not feel exploited for the cause of the *bumiputera* population. The NEP accordingly had two central targets, namely the eradication of poverty irrespective of race, and the elimination of the identification of race with economic function. The policy was called *bumiputera* policy though, because the setting of these goals was intended to move the *bumiputeras* into the mainstream of economic activity by discriminating them positively. According to the prime minister, there was no fitting model of a policy in history that could have been applied in Malaysia, so the NEP was quite a specific creation. Others concede that there have well been examples during the colonial period, like the enactment of the Malay Reservation Act in 1913 or the introduction of the Rural Industries Development Authority (RIDA) in 1950.[37] After 1957, the policy of affir-

37 Personal interview with A.B. Shamsul, 23.3.1999. – The Malay Reservation Act (1913) by law protected the Malays from becoming displaced in their own native land. It reserved certain areas of land for Malays only. – RIDA had been started by the British and was tasked largely with helping the rural Malays financially, *e.g.* through scholarships to study in commercial schools in Kuala Lumpur. After 1957, training institutions for Malay entrepreneurs were established. In 1965, RIDA was renamed 'Majlis Amanah Rakyat' (MARA), or 'Council of Trust for the People'; its tasks were expanded, but it did not perform very well (see Mahathir, *The Way Forward*, 1998; Shamsul, "Bureaucratic Management of Identity in a Modern State," 1998).

mative action in the United States of America served as point of orientation, but differences are easy to detect, for instance in regard of the political power of the native Americans, which is simply not existing.

Although differences cannot be denied, the similarity of US-American affirmative action and Malaysia's NEP is pointed out clearly by Mahathir Mohamad. In Mahathir's eyes, affirmative action in the US is "an attempt to counter the results of negative action, in the form of the enslavement and decades of prejudice against the blacks and, more recently, the Hispanics too".[38] The result does not always justify the means, but "to reject the means and so perpetuate an unjustice would seem to be carrying out a principle without political or common sense".[39] The NEP was a moderate form of affirmative action. The proponents of the NEP regard the policy as fair and just, whereas critics point to several imbalances the policy generated over the years. These were, however, rarely discussed in public during the decades of the 1970 s and 80 s. The late-coming discussion of the pros and cons of the policy, its background – the race riots – and its several episodes of failure have only become more openly and publicly debated since the late 1990 s. At the time of the NEP's launching it was prohibited to conduct 'race talk'. The so-called Sedition Act of 1970 "declared seditious and punishable any public discussion on Malay special rights"[40] and was a legislation especially introduced "to ensure that bumiputeras' interests be regarded as non-negotiables and [that] 'politicking' on bumiputera-related issues was deemed illegal".[41] Malay privileges were declared non-debatable. Since the critique directed against the NEP was coercively subdued, no official justification of the preferential treatment of *bumiputeras* was needed. Today, Malays and non-Malays can discuss 'sensitive issues' in public; students at universities learn about ethnic relations in a special module devoted to the ethics of multiethnic interaction. While this development may be regarded a welcome outcome of Malaysia's affirmative action policy, critics point to the fact that inter-ethnic tensions have increased through the years and that the constitution should be referred to not only with regard to Malay privileges but also with regard to the rights of freedom for all Malaysians. I will discuss this critical view in light of the *Article 11* movement. Before attending to this movement, I will summarize how the constitutional provisions of *primacy*

38 Mahathir, *The Way Forward*, 1998, p. 71.

39 Mahathir, *The Way Forward*, 1998, p. 71.

40 Shamsul, "The Construction and Transformation of a Social Identity," 1996, p. 29.

41 Shamsul, "The Construction and Transformation of a Social Identity," 1996, p. 29.

cum plurality translated into *realpolitik* and brought about the NEP as the core policy that has shaped Malaysia's political, social and economic development for several decades.

E. Politics, Institutions and Ethnic Relations

British imperial rule in Malaya and the Straits Settlements introduced the category of 'race' to the region and constituted it as an element of distinction in census taking, administration, politics and economics. Indian and Chinese labour influxes into the state territory created complex and heterogeneous race/ ethnic realities, soon mirrored in the spheres of administrative, commercial and educational performance. As a result, the Malays found themselves economically and socially disadvantaged and even backward after the British had left and Malaysia obtained independence. Disparities and unequal distribution of wealth and power were reflected in 'race talk' and culminated into ethnic violence in 1969. At the cost of discursive and political liberty, a political strategy was formulated to keep the country in peace, eradicate poverty and achieve economic growth. Colonial legacies, economic factors, demographic, geographic and cultural patterns, developmental agendas, and government policies all contributed to what we comprehend as 'multiculturalism' in today's Malaysia.

The constitutional setting contains a clear ethnic bias in that the Malays and the natives of East Malaysian Sabah and Sarawak enjoy 'special rights' which are guarded by the Supreme Head of the Federation, the king. The same Constitution then subscribes to the model of a plural society nation, hence stresses ethnic plurality and equality. The ethno-cultural and political contestations underlying the process of formulating the text of the *Merdeka Constitution* reveal that the Malays were only endowed with special provisions thanks to the struggle of the United Malays National Organisation (UMNO), which served as the single influential organisation to articulate and aggregate *Malay* interests at that time. Since independence UMNO has dominated the multi-ethnic ruling coalition *Barisan Nasional* (National Front); it is de facto *the* ruling party of the state. UMNO's partisans managed to bridge tradition and modernity as well as ethnic pluralism and Malayness. Albeit not in every State of the Federation, the (re-)installation of the Sultan system at least in the majority of the States symbolizes the peculiar combination of modern federalist principles and traditional royalty. To legitimize the rule, polity, and administration of a state, the Malaysian governments since 1957 have well succeeded in adjusting tradition to modern demands. The Heads of State may be called a traditional-modern institution, feeding the concept of Malayness and being part of the country's historical heritage.

I. Education

The politics of education reveal an area where the special rights provided for in the Constitution have been translated into a tangible policy within the framework of the NEP. Education stands for only one of the various areas touched by the NEP. As a platform for the fundamental preparation for a person's life in a competitive surrounding, the institutions of primary, secondary and tertiary education were of prime concern for every ethnic community in Malaysia. Ethnic plurality was recognized in private primary schools, where the native tongue could be taught. But all state-run schools had, from 1969 onwards, to use Malay as the language of instruction – at all levels including higher education. This regulation only became softened in the mid-1990 s.[42] In the public sector of post-secondary education, a quota system of admission to universities was installed to secure constant access to higher education for a certain percentage of Malays and natives. This seemingly harsh way of institutionalising the preferential treatment of *bumiputeras* was watered down in 1995 by allowing the non-*bumiputeras* to establish their own institutions in the private sector. Since then, such private institutions have spread rapidly and their reputation is very good.[43] Regarding the vast expansion of the private sector of higher education, we may reason that the demand must have been high and that equal access to education for all ethnic communities was not perceived as given under the NEP. The question remains, however, whether cross-cultural relations have thereby been improved or not, because the majority of private institutions in the tertiary sector are run by Chinese Malaysians.

The concept of *bumiputera* may be seen as one attempt to escape the tone of 'race talk' by dividing the Malaysian society in only two groups, namely *bumiputeras* and non-*bumiputeras*. The discussion of the development and the cultural background of the concept shows that the notion of *bumiput-*

42 See M. Lee, "Education Reforms during the Mahathir Era," 2004; M. Lee, "Public Policies on Private Education in Malaysia," 2000.

43 See M. Lee, "Education Reforms during the Mahathir Era," 2004.

era had a uniting function for all the communities suffering from educational and economic deprivation. What became institutionalised, for instance in the field of education, was something rather Malay-biased, but at the same time the connotation of race was pushed aside by simply distinguishing between only two types of citizens. 'Race talk' eventually became prohibited with the Sedition Act, and only recently it seems that more open discussions are dared despite the Act. Employing the concept of *bumiputera* for the policy of lessening racial tension was a clever gambit of the ruling coalition. The *bumiputeras* themselves could trace the concept back to the very culture of cherishing land ownership and could legitimize the right to the country and the soil – a *special* right indeed. The non-*bumiputeras* were certainly discriminated against by this form of affirmative action, but, as the proliferation of private universities demonstrates, they were still able to get their piece of the pie. On the whole, the NEP deserves respect in terms of implementing the idea of the redistribution of national wealth. Redistribution did not mean a mere transfer of a part of the existing wealth from one stratum of society to another (like in the theories of class struggle), but a more equitable share of the wealth that had to be produced jointly in the years to come. Aside from the merits of the NEP, its cultural policy elements promoted a strong sense of Malaysia as a primarily Islamic nation.[44] Islamic values became the predominant guideline of the government's ideational orientation and Islam was supposed to become the core of the Malaysian nation.[45] As the example of the *Article 11* coalition illustrates, not all citizens are happy with the repercussions of Islamization in their private and public lives.

II. Article 11 Movement

Islamic resurgence in Malaysia commenced in the 1970 s among students and the Muslim and youth was subsequently promoted by the government. The government's Islamization policy was combined with a call directed at the Malays to care for economic advancement and a business-oriented, en-

44 This development is ultimately linked to the long-term political leadership of Prime Minister Mahathir Mohamad (1981-2003). For detailed analyses of this period see Milne and Mauzy, *Malaysian Politics under Mahathir*, 1999; Hng, *CEO Malaysia*, 1998; Khoo, *The Paradoxes of Mahathirism*, 1995.

45 For an account of the political process of Islamization led by UMNO and PAS see Liow, *Piety and Politics*, 2009.

trepreneurial mindset. "In Malaysia, advancing the Islamic agenda, in effect, advances a Malay agenda, and ethnic politics has dominated Malaysian politics before and since independence."[46] Islam is a marker of an ethnic identity (as stated in the Constitution's definition of 'Malayness') as well as an area of political engagement. Islamic moral principles, ethics and virtues reach out into such mundane spheres as shopping and personal consumption.[47] In spite of Islam's superior position among Malaysia's religions, Article 11 of the Constitution reads as follows:

11. Freedom of religion.

Every person has the right to profess and practise his religion and, subject to Clause (4), to propagate it.

No person shall be compelled to pay any tax the proceeds of which are specially allocated in whole or in part for the purposes of a religion other than his own.

Every religious group has the right –

(a) to manage its own religious affairs;

(b) to establish and maintain institutions for religious or charitable purposes; and

(c) to acquire and own property and hold and administer it in accordance with law.

State law and in respect of the Federal Territories of Kuala Lumpur, Labuan and Putrajaya, federal law may control or restrict the propagation of any religious doctrine or belief among persons professing the religion of Islam.

This Article does not authorise any act contrary to any general law relating to public order, public health or morality.

Julian Lee has examined the nexus between the political face of Islam and what he calls the "failure of legal challenges to Islamically founded restrictions on freedom of religion".[48] I take the freedom of religion a case in point to show how the unwritten 'social contract' between Malaysia's ethnic communities as enshrined in the Constitution (special rights in exchange for citizenship) has become very porous. I consider this a worrying tendency which was certainly not intended by the founding fathers and mothers of the Malaysian nation-state.

In June 2004, a coalition of lawyers and civil society activists formed an advocacy group in order to raise awareness for "the erosion of constitution-

46 J. Lee, *Islamization and Activism in Malaysia*, 2010, p. 16.
47 See Fischer, *Proper Islamic Consumption*, 2008.
48 J. Lee, *Islamization and Activism in Malaysia*, 2010, p. 83.

ally enshrined liberties".[49] Their alert derived from several episodes involving non-Muslim citizens, Muslim citizens who decline to follow state sanctioned interpretations of Islam or women who suffer from Family Laws that are rooted in Islamic law. The pluralism of legal systems in Malaysia renders certain cases of jurisdiction particularly difficult. One example is the question whether a Syariah[50] court is authorized to summon a non-Muslim woman just because her husband converted to Islam without her knowing about it. Aside from the gender-related hierarchy involved here, the constitutionality of the act is at stake: Article 8(1) of the Constitution guarantees equal treatment of all persons before the law. The civil courts increasingly tend "to confer away jurisdiction on matters pertaining to Islam"[51] and declare that jurisdiction rests with the Syariah court even if the person involved is a non-Muslim. The activists of *Article 11* were thus concerned that "Islamic law is gaining greater legal weight than the Constitution".[52] A telling example is the following one, which Lee recalls from an *Article 11* forum that he attended. It is a story told by a non-Muslim person called Singh:

> He (= Singh) also explained that in some areas of Malaysia, there are restrictions on the architectural appearance of certain religious buildings. Sikh temples (*gurdwara*) around the world have domes. According to Singh, however, in some places, authorities say that temples should not have domes because Muslims may mistake them for mosques. Singh went on to note that this restriction has been enforced even though there was no law to that effect. He went on to note that before a religious building can be built, it must be proved that there are five thousand people of the given faith in a given area. Singh related that there had been no such 'catchment area' in the past. [...] The causes of these restrictions and impositions on non-Muslims were owing, according to Singh, to political pressures. The declaration that Malaysia was an Islamic state allowed civil servants and law-makers to create and enforce laws that impinged on the rights of non-Muslims.[53]

Appalled by such occasions, *Article 11* activists toured the country in 2006 and advocated the acceptance of the Constitution as Malaysia's supreme law.

---

49 J. Lee, *Islamization and Activism in Malaysia*, 2010, p. 84. The subsequent statements are primarily based on Julian Lee's chapter 'Social Activism and the Article 11 Coalition' in J. Lee, *Islamization and Activism in Malaysia*, 2010, pp. 83-97. There are other sources to refer to, but for the exemplary discussion of this issue Lee's analysis and findings serve the purpose perfectly.

50 I stick to the Malaysian way of spelling the term *shari'a*.

51 J. Lee, *Islamization and Activism in Malaysia*, 2010, p. 88.

52 J. Lee, *Islamization and Activism in Malaysia*, 2010, p. 88.

53 J. Lee, *Islamization and Activism in Malaysia*, 2010, p. 88.

However, the attempt to mobilize support for this idea was forcefully interrupted by protestors who raided the forum halls and were not stopped by the police.[54] Consequently, *Article 11* has stopped its 'physical' mobilizing efforts and resorts to digital information.[55] The message of *Article 11*'s fate is nonetheless clear: The result of the government's affirmative action policy, which was based on the agreed-upon provision of special rights for Malays and natives in the Constitution (Art. 153), has led to an erosion of constitutionally guaranteed rights *for all* Malaysians such as the right of freedom of religion. Moreover, it has led to the curtailing of civil advocacy in favour of the Constitution, thus curbing citizens' freedom in a double sense. Along with accounts by other authors of the country's politicised version of Islamization[56], the situation as described above leads to the impression that Malaysian Islam has ceased to be inclusive, progressive, and tolerant.

F. Concluding Remarks

Institutionalised cultural and ethnic hegemony of the Malays is criticised by the non-Malays or non-*bumiputeras*. Throughout the history of independent Malaysia, the non-*bumiputeras* have had alternative options to constitute their own 'institutions' to compensate discrimination. The supremacy of Malay-Muslim interests in recent decades, however, has apparently made it difficult to sustain this mechanism of compensation.

In the Constitution, the commitment to the Sultan system and royalty is institutionalised, but since the Sultans and the king cannot be said to possess real political power, they do not endanger the plural society model. The notion of royalty and its institutionalisation reflect the *cultural* dimension of the polity rather than an element of real political power. Real political power rests with the elected powers that be, which are dominated by the United Malays National Organisation or UMNO. Hence the capacity to endanger or to preserve a plural society lies with politics.

---

54 J. Lee, *Islamization and Activism in Malaysia*, 2010, pp. 91-93; see also 'Demonstrators cause Article 11 Forum to end abruptly' on the Malaysian Bar's website, http://www.malaysianbar.org.my/bar_news/berita_badan_peguam/demonstrators_cause_article_11_forum_to_end_aburptly.html (retrieved Oct. 6, 2010).

55 See, for instance, http://aliran.com/282.html (retrieved Oct. 6, 2010).

56 See, for instance, Liow, *Piety and Politics*, 2009, or Stark, *Beyond 'Terrorism' and 'State Hegemony'*, 2005.

In education, non-*bumiputeras* have passed the *bumiputeras* in lifting up the level of knowledge, especially in the private institutions of higher learning. Albeit Malay has been declared the national language, the requirements of global international communication lead to increased usage of English. In the internationally oriented business sector, Malay has become relegated to second rank. Affirmative action in the shape of the New Economic Policy has not brought the desired 30% share of the nation's economic wealth for the *bumiputeras*, but it has at least reduced poverty and enabled Malaysia to remain politically stable. Without the economic and business skills and the knowhow of the non-*bumiputeras* though, Malaysia would never have reached growth rates of around 7% during the last three decades (except for the period of the financial crisis mid-1997 to mid-1999).

From the perspective of comparative politics, the case of Malaysia merits attention for several reasons. One of these reasons is the striking antagonism of ethnic discrimination and ethnic integration. Asked about the success or failure of ethnic integration in Malaysia, the people in the street would simply respond that there is no ethnic integration. On the institutional as well as on the policy level, we do not find too much of a devotion towards *equity*, but rather an equity-labelled yet *bumiputera*-biased output of procedures taking place in the black box of the political decision-making. Despite this bias, political stability has remained to a great extent, and upheavals like in Indonesia, Yugoslavia, the Baltic states or elsewhere have been prevented.

I have concentrated on just one realm of institutional frameworks that have contributed to keep tensions from exploding: the provisions of the Constitution and its translation into concrete policies. The translation of constitutional provisions into policies renders the prediction of the actual effects of institutions impossible. As the discussion above has shown, the 'good intention' of a policy can easily shift into shallow waters when certain segments of a society manage to hijack the interpretation of law and order and gain normative authority over others. The constitutionalization of rights of freedom does, therefore, not guarantee the possibility to actually use these rights. Securing the possibility to use the rights that are granted in legal institutions such as the constitution, necessitates the concerted engagement of both judicial, political and civil society actors and authorities.

Works cited

Abdullah, Ahmad, *Tengku Abdul Rahman and Malaysia's Foreign Policy 1963-1970*, Kuala Lumpur: Berita Publishing, 1985.

Andaya, Barbara Watson, and Leonard Y. Andaya, *A History of Malaysia*, Houndmills and others: Macmillan, 1984.

Beyme, Klaus von, *Die politischen Theorien der Gegenwart* [Contemporary Political Theories], 7th ed., Opladen: Westdeutscher Verlag, 1992.

Brown, Michael E., and Sumit Ganguly, eds., *Government Policies and Ethnic Relations in Asia and the Pacific*, Cambridge MA and London: The MIT Press, 1997.

Fischer, Johan, *Proper Islamic Consumption: Shopping among the Malays in Modern Malaysia*, Copenhagen: NIAS Press, 2008.

Ganguly, Sumit, "Ethnic Policies and Political Quiescence in Malaysia and Singapore," in *Government Policies and Ethnic Relations in Asia and the Pacific*, eds. M.E. Brown and S. Ganguly, Cambridge MA and London: The MIT Press, 1997, pp. 233-272.

Hng Hung Yong, *CEO Malaysia: Strategy in Nation-building*, Subang Jaya: Pelanduk Publications, 1998.

Khoo, Boo Teik, *The Paradoxes of Mahathirism*, Kuala Lumpur and New York: Oxford University Press, 1995.

Lau, Albert, *A Moment of Anguish: Singapore in Malaysia and the Politics of Disengagement*, Singapore: Times Academic Press, 1998.

Lee, Julian C.H., *Islamization and Activism in Malaysia*, Singapore: Institute of Southeast Asian Studies, 2010.

Lee, Molly N.N., "Public Policies on Private Education in Malaysia," in *Rethinking Malaysia: Malaysian Studies*, ed. K.S. Jomo, Hong Kong: Asia 2000, 1999, pp. 70-83.

Lee, Molly N.N., "Education Reforms during the Mahathir Era: Global Trends and U-Turns," in *Reflections: The Mahathir Years*, ed. B. Welsh, Washington DC: John Hopkins University Press, 2004, pp. 437-449.

Liow, Joseph Chinyong, *Piety and Politics: Islamism in Contemporary Malaysia*, New York: Oxford University Press, 2009.

Loh Kok Wah, Francis, "Managing Ethnic Conflict and Violence in Malaysia: Development, the Strong Developmental State and Developmentalism," in *The Politics of Death: Political Violence in Southeast Asia*, eds. A. Croissant, B. Martin, and S. Kneip, Berlin: LIT Verlag, 2006, pp. 251-281.

Mahathir Mohamad, *The Malay Dilemma*, Singapore: Asia Pacific Press, 1970.

Mahathir Mohamad, *The Way Forward*, London: Weidenfeld & Nicolson, 1998.

Milne, Robert Stephen, and Diane K. Mauzy, *Malaysian Politics under Mahathir*, London and New York: Routledge 1999.

Milner, Anthony, "Ideological Work in Constructing the Malay Majority," in *Making Majorities: Constituting the Nation in Japan, Korea, China, Malaysia, Fiji, Turkey, and the United States*, ed. D. C. Gladney, Stanford: Stanford University Press, 1998, pp. 151-171.

Ongkili, James P., *Nation-building in Malaysia 1946-1974*, Oxford and others: Oxford University Press, 1985.

Shamsul, A.B., "Debating about Identity in Malaysia: A Discourse Analysis," *Southeast Asian Studies* 24 (1996): 476-499.

Shamsul, A.B., "The Construction and Transformation of a Social Identity: Malayness and Bumiputraness Re-examined," *Journal of Asian and African Studies* 52 (1996): 15-33.

Shamsul, A.B., "The Making of a 'Plural' Malaysia," in *Emerging Pluralism in Asia and the Pacific*, eds. D.Y.H. Wu, H. McQueen, and Y. Yamamoto, Hong Kong: Hong Kong Institute of Asia-Pacific Studies, 1997, pp. 67-83.

Shamsul, A.B., "Identity Construction, Nation Formation, and Islamic Revivalism in Malaysia," in *Islam in an Era of Nation States: Politics and Religious renewal in Muslim Southeast Asia*, eds. R. W. Hefner and P. Horvatich, Honolulu: University of Hawaii Press, 1997, pp. 207-227.

Shamsul, A.B., "Bureaucratic Management of Identity in a Modern State: 'Malayness' in Postwar Malaysia," in *Making Majorities: Constituting the Nation in Japan, Korea, China, Malaysia, Fiji, Turkey, and the United States*, ed. D. C. Gladney, Stanford: Stanford University Press, 1998, pp. 135-150.

Sopiee, Mohamed Noordin, *From Malayan Union to Singapore Separation: Political Unification in the Malaysia Region 1945-1965*, Kuala Lumpur: Penerbit Universiti Malaya, 1974.

Stark, Jan, "Beyond 'Terrorism' and 'State Hegemony': assessing the Islamist mainstream in Egypt and Malaysia," *Third World Quarterly* 26 (2005): 307-327.

Constitutionalization and Rights of Freedom: Implementing International Human Rights Standards as a Contribution to the Constitutionalization of National Criminal Law

Robert Esser

A. Criminal Law as an Element of Constitutionalization

The term "constitutionalization"[1] can be understood in two different ways: In the narrow sense of the word, constitutionalization describes the process of establishing a (written) constitution. In a broader sense, the term "constitutionalization" further refers to the emergence and development of a normative system in general. Therefore, constitutionalization is also possible beyond the limits of a written constitution. Constitutionalization always describes a process of development.[2] In recent times, discussions often centred on the constitutionalization of international law.[3]

Instead of focussing on this international level, however, this article addresses the question of how internationally already established human rights standards (especially those of the European Convention on Human Rights, ECHR) influence national law and specifically constitutional law, thereby contributing to the development of the national normative system and constitutionalization in the broader sense. The focus will thus be on national criminal law.

---

1 The Federal Constitutional Court first used the term in relation to political parties, compare BVerfGE (Official Digest of Rulings of the Federal Constitutional Court) 5, 85, 388 (Prohibition of the Communist Party of Germany).

2 See Wahl, "Konstitutionalisierung," 2002; Bryde, "Konstitutionalisierung des Völkerrechts," 2003, p. 62; Kadelbach and Kleinlein, "Überstaatliches Verfassungsrecht," 2006, p. 236; Emmerich-Fritsche, *Vom Völkerrecht zum Weltrecht*, 2007, p. 705.

3 See amongst others: Bryde, "Konstitutionalisierung des Völkerrechts," 2003, p. 61; Emmerich-Fritsche, *Vom Völkerrecht zum Weltrecht*, 2007, pp. 703 ff.; Frowein, "Konstitutionalisierung des Völkerrechts," 1999, p. 427; Kadelbach and Kleinlein, "Überstaatliches Verfassungsrecht," 2006, p. 235; Klabbers, Peters and Ulfstein, *The Constitutionalization of International Law*, 2009; Wahl, "Konstitutionalisierung," 2002, pp. 199 ff.

The first question to be answered in this context is whether it is even possible for an *internationally* initiated process of constitutionalization to influence *national* criminal law. The question arises because criminal law as such is traditionally understood to be an expression of the state's authority and a stronghold of state sovereignty. Is criminal law therefore a subject matter whose development can and must take place primarily at national level? Would an international constitutionalization of criminal law perhaps even conflict with the national constitution?

B. Constitutional Requirements and the Limits of Developing Criminal Law at International Level – From the Perspective of the German Federal Constitutional Court

A look in the German constitution, the Basic Law, shows that criminal law is explicitly mentioned only in a few places, despite numerous amendments of the constitution since its establishment in 1949. Whilst the charter of basic rights (Articles 1 to 19 of the Basic Law) does not contain criminal law guarantees, Article 74 para. 1 Nr. 1 of the Basic Law stipulates the (concurrent) legislative powers of the Federation for criminal law. Article 102 of the Basic Law abolishes capital punishment; Article 103 para. 2 of the Basic Law provides the criminal law principle of certainty and clarity (*nullum crimen, nulla poena sine lege*); Article 103 para. 3 of the Basic Law further guarantees the principle of *ne bis in idem*, and lastly Article 104 of the Basic Law contains fundamental rights related to the deprivation of liberty of which some are of a criminal law nature.

Further criminal law guarantees with constitutional status also exist outside of written constitutional law. The Federal Constitutional Court for example derives essential requirements concerning criminal justice from the – explicitly nominated – rule of law (Article 20 para. 3 of the Basic Law). These include the procedural **right to a fair criminal trial**[4], the **presumption of innocence**[5] and the requirement that **punishment must always be proportionate to the gravity of the offence**[6]. **The principle of guilt** is also enshrined in so far in the constitution, as the Federal Constitutional Court

4 BVerfGE 54, 277, 292; 78, 88, 99; 89, 347, 356.
5 BVerfGE 19, 342, 348; 74, 358, 370; 82, 106, 114.
6 BVerfGE 54, 100, 109 ff.

holds it to be grounded in the guarantee of human dignity in Article 1 para. 1 of the Basic Law.[7]

It can thus be said that only very elemental criminal law values are explicitly mentioned in the German constitution and thereby formally – even in the narrow sense of the word – constitutionalized. However, most of these guarantees are not even state specific: They can also be found in the later passed human rights treaties: the European Convention on Human Rights (ECHR – 1950) and the International Covenant on Civil and Political Rights (ICCPR – 1966). Their inclusion in the constitution is therefore neither an argument for nor against a resistance of criminal law to constitutionalization in general.

Concerning other fundamental questions, however, such as the **interpretation of the term "penalty"**, the views of national constitutional law and international human rights conventions clearly conflict. What "penalty" means, is not bindingly expressed in the German constitution. Loopholes like this in the constitution open a gateway to international interpretation standards. This is well shown by a case decided in December 2009 by the European Court of Human Rights (ECtHR) against the Federal Republic of Germany (M. against Germany).[8] It originated in the individual application of an imprisoned offender who claimed a breach of Article 5 ECHR (right to liberty) and Article 7 para. 1 ECHR (*nulla poena sine lege*). The case *specifically* concerned the question of whether the sanction of preventive detention (*Sicherungsverwahrung*), which is ordered for preventive reasons *in addition* to a prison sentence and classified as a measure of correction and prevention in German criminal law, could be qualified as a "penalty" within the meaning of Article 7 para. 1 ECHR. Indirectly, such a verdict contains international law standards for a corresponding interpretation of the term "penalty" in the German Basic Law (GG) and the Criminal Code (StGB). The case of M. is of high practical significance for the applicability of the principles of *nulla poena sine lege* (Article 103 para. 2 of the Basic Law) and *ne bis in idem* (Article 103 para. 3 of the Basic Law). We will return to the case later.

---

7 BVerfGE 57, 250, 275; 80, 367, 378; 90, 145, 173; BVerfG NJW 2009, 2267, 2289, § 364 (Treaty of Lisbon).

8 EGMR *M./GER*, judgement of 17 December 2009, JR 2010, 218 = NStZ 2010, 263 = StV 2010, 181 = EuGRZ 2010, 22 (Retrospective extension of preventive detention for the purpose of Article 66 para. 1 of the Criminal Code beyond the maximum of ten years set out by the legal provisions applicable at the time of the offence).

In order to be able to analyse the possibility of international human rights standards influencing German criminal law, a look in the jurisdiction of the Federal Constitutional Court is not only helpful, but also necessary. It must be examined how the Federal Constitutional Court understands criminal law in the constitutional context and in how far it judges the transfer of sovereign rights to international and interstate organizations in the area of criminal law to be constitutionally permissible – hence perhaps incidentally setting limits to the implementation of human rights standards.

In this context, the judgement of the Federal Constitutional Court (BVerfG) of 30 June 2009 concerning the Treaty of Lisbon[9] contains several interesting statements. First of all, the Court emphasises that the Basic Law *"calls for the participation of Germany in international organisations, an order of mutual peaceful balancing of interests established between the states and organised co-existence in Europe".*[10] For that purpose, the Basic Law contains provisions like the empowerment to integrate into the European Union (Article 23 para. 1 of the Basic Law), to participate in intergovernmental institutions (Article 24 para. 1 of the Basic Law) and to join systems of mutual collective security (Article 24 para. 2 of the Basic Law).

However, **as regards criminal law**, the Federal Constitutional Court only allows the transfer of sovereign rights for *"specific cross-border situations on restrictive conditions"* and holds the view that *"substantial freedom of action must remain reserved to the Member States here".*[11] The reason for this restriction is that – in the Court's opinion – the administration of criminal law is the product of a cultural process of previous understanding that is influenced by history and language. The decision which social behaviour should be punished by criminal law can only be derived to a restricted extent from values and moral premises common to all European countries and should rather be left to the democratic decision-making process. The Court regards it as a central duty of state authority that legal peace should be assured by the administration of criminal law.[12] Each criminal provision *"contains a social and ethical judgment of unworthiness on the action which it penalizes."*[13] The Court argues that it is a fundamental decision of a po-

9 BVerfG NJW 2009, 2267; available in English at http://www.bundesverfassungsgericht.de/entscheidungen/es20090630_2bve000208en.html.
10 BVerfG NJW 2009, 2267, 2270, § 222.
11 BVerfG NJW 2009, 2267, 2270, § 253.
12 BVerfG NJW 2009, 2267, 2270, § 355.
13 BVerfG NJW 2009, 2267, 2270, § 355.

litical community whether and to what extent criminal provisions should be installed to carry out social control. It is principally left to the free decision of the legislature whether there are necessities to punish a behaviour by criminal law, as long as the boundaries of the constitution are observed.[14]

However, the freedom of the legislature may be limited by the obligation to enforce supranational law as it may be necessary to penalise certain behaviours such as genocide, crimes against humanity and war crimes.[15] Where a polity cannot decide freely according to its own values if a certain behaviour is to be punished, *"democratic self-determination is [...] affected in a particularly sensitive manner"*, especially if *"these values are connected with historical experience, traditions of faith and other factors essential to the self-esteem of the people and their society"*.[16] Because of this, the Federal Constitutional Court takes up the position that the transfer of competences for criminal legislation in these areas is only permitted to a limited extent and that the requirements of Article 23 para. 1 of the Basic Law have to be strictly preserved.

The Court also emphasizes the importance of the **principle of guilt** on which criminal law is based.[17] In the Court's opinion, *"it forms part of the constitutional identity which is unassailable due to Article 79 para. 3 of the Basic Law and which is also protected against encroachment by supranational public authority"*.[18] Due to this, introducing a so called **corporate sanction** – a criminal sanction for companies – into the German criminal sanctions system would not be in conformity with the constitution: A corporate sanction is not reconcilable with the principle of guilt, as it would apply to a company which lacks the power to act in the criminal sense. As the principle of guilt is protected by the eternity clause in Article 79 para. 3 of the Basic Law, the legislature cannot circumvent it by transferring sovereign rights under Article 23 para. 1 or Article 24 para. 1 of the Basic Law. Therefore, the eternity clause limits the process of constitutionalization.

To conclude, the constitutionalization of criminal law at European Union level, initiated by the formulation and implementation of international standards, is restrained by strict constitutional requirements. This raises the im-

14 BVerfG NJW 2009, 2267, 2270, § 356.
15 BVerfG NJW 2009, 2267, 2270, § 357.
16 BVerfG NJW 2009, 2267, 2270, § 363.
17 BVerfG NJW 2009, 2267, 2270, § 364.
18 BVerfG NJW 2009, 2267, 2270, § 364.

portant question of in how far such a process could take place using international treaties already implemented in national law and the jurisdiction of the judicial bodies responsible for their interpretation – a question which will be answered in the following.

C. Constitutionalization of Criminal Law via the Constitutional Duty to Enforce Human Rights Standards – Illustrated by the ECHR

When examining the influence of the ECHR on national criminal law[19], it must be kept in mind that the ECHR was implemented by Germany with an act of assent within the meaning of Article 59 para. 2 sentence 1 of the Basic Law. In contrast to other Member States of the Council of Europe[20], the ECHR therefore does not have constitutional status in Germany and only represents a simple Act of Parliament.[21] By ratifying the ECHR, the Federal Republic of Germany did not participate in the development of the European Union within the meaning of Article 23 para. 1 of the Basic Law, since the ECHR as an international treaty and the European Court of Human Rights (ECtHR) as its abidance ensuring court are not institutions of the European Union. The accession to the ECHR and the submission under the jurisdiction of the ECtHR further did not transfer sovereign rights within the meaning of Article 24 para. 1 of the Basic Law, as the ECtHR only has judicial power. In contrast to the institutions of the European Union, the ECtHR is not empowered to autonomously create new law.[22] The restrictions established by the Federal Constitutional Court regarding the transfer of sovereign rights in the area of criminal law thereby do not apply to the implementation of human rights standards (jurisdiction of the ECtHR).

A constitutionalizing influence of the ECHR on a national legal order can take place in different ways. For one, the ECHR serves as a role model in the process of developing a new constitution.[23] From the German perspec-

19 In detail to the influence of the ECHR on individual provisions of the Criminal Code, Diehm, *Die Menschenrechte der EMRK*, 2006.

20 For example in Austria.

21 See Herdegen, *Europarecht*, 2010, § 3 margin no. 52; Schweitzer, *Staatsrecht III*, 2010, margin no. 709.

22 See Herdegen, *Europarecht*, 2010, § 3 margin no. 57.

23 See Gerards, *Die Europäische Menschenrechtskonvention*, 2007, pp. 237 ff.; Bryde, "Konstitutionalisierung des Völkerrechts," 2003, p. 68. This aspect is especially important for eastern European states which joined the ECHR.

tive, however, this aspect is of no importance, as the ECHR came into force in 1953, later than the German constitution (1949). In another way, the ECHR as an abstract-general norm can also de facto and normatively influence already existing basic rights guarantees, thereby contributing to constitutionalization.[24] Of particular importance, however, is the influence of the jurisdiction of the ECtHR on the national legal order, the ECtHR being the institution which enforces abidance to the ECHR. In this respect, the ECtHR is partly spoken of as a constitutional court.[25] However, the judgements of the ECtHR do not have the same effects as those of a (national) constitutional court. In particular, they do not have an effect of cassation, but rather are of a declaratory nature only. Nevertheless, the convicted state is obliged to take corrective action (Art. 46 para. 1 ECHR). The concrete manner in which the offending law or practice is remedied is in turn left to the discretion of the state.[26] Corrective action may require a retrial (Article 359 Nr. 6 StPO) or an amendment of the law.[27]

It remains to be examined whether the influence of human rights standards on the national constitution, as especially exerted by the jurisdiction of the ECtHR, could in a given case even exceed the limited possibilities of transferring sovereign rights.

D. Implementing Human Rights Standards in National Criminal Law – Exemplified by the Dispute about the Term 'Penalty'

In order to illustrate such an influence of the ECHR and the jurisdiction of the ECtHR in constitutionalization, the already mentioned dispute about the significance of the term "penalty" serves as a good example. First conflicts in this area already emerged in the 1980 s. German law differentiates between **criminal offences** and **regulatory offences** (so-called *Ordnungswidrigkeiten, regulated by the Administrative Offence Act, OWiG*). The latter do not lead to a criminal conviction; according to the German

24 See Gerards, *Die Europäische Menschenrechtskonvention*, 2007, pp. 249 ff.

25 See Gerards, *Die Europäische Menschenrechtskonvention*, 2007, pp. 284 ff.; Goerlich, "Der Europäische Gerichtshof für Menschenrechte," 2004; Wildhaber, "Ein Überdenken des Zustands und der Zukunft des EuGM, " 2009, pp. 551 ff.

26 See Gerards, *Die Europäische Menschenrechtskonvention*, 2007, pp. 253, 294 ff.

27 For examples see Gerards, *Die Europäische Menschenrechtskonvention*, 2007, pp. 263 ff.

notion therefore a "penalty" is not imposed. For this reason, the procedural safeguards of Article 6 ECHR were deemed not to apply to the proceedings concerning regulatory offences. However, the ECtHR decided in 1984 that the charge of a regulatory offence constituted a "criminal charge" within the autonomous meaning of Article 6 ECHR, just like the charge of a criminal offence.[28] As a result, the Federal Republic of Germany since then also has to ensure the compliance with the guarantees of Article 6 ECHR in proceedings concerning regulatory offences. This example illustrates the development of national law and thereby constitutionalization in the broader sense of the term.

Much more excitement, however, was caused by the recent case of *M.* against Germany.[29] Here, too, a fundamental dogmatic question of German criminal law became significant: Concerning the legal consequences of criminally relevant behaviour, Germany has a so-called *twin-track system of sanctions*. The German Criminal Code distinguishes between **penalties** (Articles 38 *et seq.* of the Criminal Code) on the one hand, and so-called ***measures of correction and prevention*** (Articles 61 *et seq.* of the Criminal Code) on the other hand. One of these measures of correction and prevention is the placement in preventive detention (Articles 66 *et seq.* of the Criminal Code). Preventive detention is imposed on offenders in addition to their punishment, if they represent a danger. Due to this purely preventive character, preventive detention is not regarded as a penalty in Germany, to which the constitutionally enshrined criminal law principle of *nullum crimen, nulla poena sine lege* (Article 103 para. 2 of the Basic Law) would be applicable. Prior to 1998, Article 67 d para. 1 of the German Criminal Code limited the duration of preventive detention to a maximum of ten years. In 1998, however, whilst the applicant was already in preventive detention, the legislator amended this provision, making the termination of the measure depend on the detainee no longer representing a danger. The new rule was to apply without restriction. M.'s preventive detention was therefore retroactively extended from a maximum of ten years to an unlimited period of time. In 2004, the Federal Constitutional Court dismissed M.'s constitutional complaint and held that the amended provisions and thus the prolongation of M.'s preventive detention were compatible with the Basic Law: Preventive

28 ECtHR *Öztürk/GER,* judgement of 21 February 1984, NJW 1985, 1273; see annotation by Schroth, EuGRZ 1985, 557.

29 ECtHR *M./GER*, judgement of 17 December 2009, JR 2010, 218 = NStZ 2010, 263 = StV 2010, 181 = EuGRZ 2010, 22.

detention was not a penalty to which the prohibition of retrospective punishment applied.[30]

When looking at the wording of the guarantee of *nulla poena sine lege* in the Basic Law and the ECHR, a divergent opinion of the ECtHR could not necessarily have been expected. Whilst Article 103 para. 2 of the Basic Law requires that "An act may be punished only if it was defined by a law as a criminal offence before the act was committed", Article 7 para. 1 ECHR contains a corresponding guarantee of *nulla poena sine lege*[31], stating that "No one shall be held guilty of any criminal offence on account of any act or omission which did not constitute a criminal offence under national or international law at the time when it was committed. Nor shall a heavier penalty be imposed than the one that was applicable at the time the criminal offence was committed". Apart from differences in the phrasing, both provisions contain the same guarantees; both focus on the term "penalty". When solely regarding the wording, there was therefore little room for a development and thus constitutionalisation of the German law.

The ECtHR however interpreted the term "penalty" in Article 7 ECHR **autonomously** and classified the German preventive detention as a *penalty*. In contrast to the German courts, the ECtHR did not only focus on the theoretical purpose of preventive detention, but also considered its practical circumstances. The main arguments of the ECtHR were that a substantial difference between the execution of a prison sentence and a preventive detention order does not exist, preventive detention entails a clear deterrent element and constitutes a very severe infringement of rights.

The judgement was cause for significant turmoil in Germany. Since the Basic Law as already mentioned barely contains any criminal law provisions and does not define the term penalty either, the Basic Law would not hinder the legislature from completely abolishing the twin-track system of sanctions. The Federal Ministry of Justice felt compelled to examine the possi-

30 BVerfGE 109, 133. As opposed to the French Constitutional Council, which found that even though preventive detention could not be qualified as a "penalty", it could nevertheless not be ordered retrospectively, see also ECtHR *M./GER*, judgement of 17 December 2009, § 75.

31 Corresponding guarantees can be found in Article 9 of the American Declaration of the Rights and Duties of Man and Article 7 of the African Charter on Human and Peoples' Rights („Banjul Charter").

bilities of fundamentally reforming the preventive detention system.[32] On the 1st of September 2010, the Federal Government presented key points for such a reform. Government proposes consolidating the initial preventive detention (restrict its applicability, specify the decisive time for judging the offender's dangerousness) and expanding the so-called reserved preventive detention ("vorbehaltene Sicherungsverwahrung"), i.e. abandoning the requirement of a "disposition" to commit severe crimes, making it applicable for first offenders and restricting its possibility to the end of imprisonment. These new rules will not (and cannot, due to Article 7 para. 1 ECHR) apply retroactively. At the same time, the supervision of conduct is to be strengthened, especially by the possibility of determining the location of an offender via electronic tags. So-called "parallel cases" to the judgement of the ECtHR, meaning cases in which the preventive detention was retroactively extended from ten years to an unlimited period of time, are to be comprised by the planned "Treatment and Placement of Mentally Disturbed Violent Offenders Act" (Gesetz zur Therapierung und Unterbringung psychisch gestörter Gewalttäter – Therapieunterbringungsgesetz – ThUG). A civil chamber of a regional court, staffed by three professional judges, may under certain circumstances make a placement order for those offenders who would otherwise have had to be released from preventive detention due to the verdict of the ECtHR.

Although the term "penalty" could nevertheless be interpreted differently regarding Art. 103 of the Basic Law and Art. 7 ECHR, the judgement of the ECtHR led to the national comprehension of "penalty", which had characterised German criminal law for many centuries, being reconsidered. The applicability of Article 103 para. 2 of the Basic Law to preventive detention appears to be much broader than traditionally thought. In this respect, the judgement of the ECtHR triggered a process of rethinking and developing new approaches in dealing with dangerous offenders. Therefore, human rights standards can force a state to pass legislation, which due to (false) respect for traditional structures and the urge to preserve a functioning system would not have come into being otherwise. The reason behind such a lack of development of national law in the political process often lies in the fear of losing one's state identity and sovereignty. However, human rights standards are only capable of changing such situations, if a court exists which

32 See the press release of the Federal Ministry of Justice of 9 June 2010, available under http://www.bmj.de/cln_102/DE/Medien/Pressemitteilungen (last visited on 14 March 2011).

can enforce them. In so far, the ECtHR also has to fulfil the important task of providing thought-provoking impulses with its judgements. As the judgements of the ECtHR do not have a cassation effect, the fear of giving up state sovereignty is unfounded. How a judgement is *concretely* executed remains for each state to decide.

The current discussion in Germany however also illustrates a further aspect: It would have sufficed for the legislator to merely apply Article 103 para. 2 of the Basic Law to those measures of correction and prevention in the future constituting penalties in the sense of Article 7 ECHR and especially prohibiting a retroactive order of preventive detention. Instead however, going beyond the few cases to which the ECtHR judgement applies, a discussion was initiated as to a far reaching reform of preventive detention. In particular, the current option of a **subsequent preventive detention** (so-called *nachträgliche Sicherungsverwahrung*, Article 66 b StGB) is to be abolished nearly altogether, although the judgement of the ECtHR did not concern this specific manner of preventive detention. The judgement of the ECtHR has led to a development of the national legal order. The process character of constitutionalization can clearly be seen. However, this process of constitutionalization is still nowhere near completion.

E. Is the Constitutionalization of the Term 'Penalty' Limited by Constitutional Restrictions Manifesting the Positive Obligation to Protect Life? – The Implementation of the ECtHR Judgement in the Case of M. v. Germany by German Jurisdiction

Independent of and especially chronologically prior to a final reaction of the legislative body, it is mainly up to the national courts to implement the jurisdiction of the ECtHR to national law. In his leading "Görgülü" decision of 14th October 2004 the German Federal Constitutional Court (BVerfG) laid down some basic principles how the judgements and decisions of the ECtHR have to be considered by German courts.[33] Firstly, the Constitutional Court stresses that the European Convention on Human Rights has the status of a federal statute in the German legal system.[34] In the Court's view, the binding effect of statute and law according to Article 20 para. 3 of the German Basic Law "includes a duty to take into account the guarantees of the

33 BVerfGE 111, 307 = NJW 2004, 3407.
34 BVerfG, l.c., § 30.

Convention and the judgements of the ECtHR as part of a methodologically justifiable interpretation of the law".[35] Because of that, fundamental rights in conjunction with the rule of law are violated where a national court fails to consider a decision of the ECtHR or tries to enforce a decision in a schematic way in violation of prior-ranking law.[36] The Court defines the term "take into account" as "taking notice of the Convention provision as interpreted by the ECtHR and applying it to the case, provided the application does not violate prior-ranking law, in particular constitutional law. [...] [T]he court must at least duly consider it".[37]

According to an enquiry of the Federal Ministry of Justice, there are about 80 parallel cases in which (initial) preventive detention is being executed retrospectively for more than ten years. However, not all of these offenders have been released immediately "ex officio" since the ECtHR pronounced his judgement on 17 December 2009. Rather, several detainees lodged an application for the termination of their preventive detention, which instituted the following court proceedings.

Already in March 2010, the **Koblenz Court of Appeal** had to decide on the immediate appeal of a detainee. Arguing – inter alia – that the judgement of the ECtHR was not final, the Court declined the release from preventive detention.[38] However, this "excuse" got inapplicable shortly after: On 10 May 2010, the five-judge panel of the Grand Chamber of the ECtHR rejected the referral request in the case of M./Germany submitted by the German Government (Article 43 ECHR). Thereby, the judgement of 17 December 2009 became final (Art. 44 para. 2 *lit.* c ECHR). Since that day, several German Courts of Appeal dealt with the problem, but arrived at extremely different conclusions.

In the case of the applicant M. himself, the **Frankfurt Court of Appeal** confirmed M.'s discharge from preventive detention on 25 June 2010 and quashed the contrarious appeal of the prosecution.[39] Article 2 para. 6 of the German Criminal Code says that measures of correction and prevention –

35 BVerfG, l.c., § 47.
36 BVerfG, l.c., § 47.
37 BVerfG, l.c., § 62.
38 Koblenz Court of Appeal, decision of 30 March 2010 – 1 Ws 116/10; see also Federal Court of Justice, decision of 11 February 2010 – 4 StR 577/09 (concerning a case of subsequent preventive detention); Federal Court of Justice, decision of 14 January 2010 – 1 StR 595/09, § 21 (concerning a case of subsequent preventive detention).
39 Frankfurt Court of Appeal, decision of 24 June 2010 – 3 Ws 485/10.

such as preventive detention – are ruled by the law valid at the time of the decision, if there is ***nothing else provided by law***. The Frankfurt Court of Appeal argued that Article 2 para. 6 of the German Criminal Code should be interpreted in conformity with the Convention. Article 7 para. 1 of the ECHR, as it is currently interpreted by the ECtHR, was to be seen as such differing legal regulation, i.e. *something else provided by law*.[40] Because of that, Article 2 para. 6 of the German Criminal Code was to be interpreted to the effect that – instead of the law valid at the time of the decision – the law valid at the time of the offence was applicable, whereby the first preventive detention was allowed to have a maximum duration of ten years.[41] The binding force of the leading judgement of the Federal Constitutional Court from 2004[42] was – in the Court's view – not opposed to such interpretation, because it was not a question of constitutional law, if the law valid at the time of the offence or of the decision is applicable. Thus, there was no contradiction to the opinion of the Federal Constitutional Court that preventive detention does not fall under the prohibition of retrospective punishment laid down in Article 103 para. 2 of the German Basic Law.[43] A consideration of interests, namely of the detainee's right to liberty and the positive obligation to protect society against prospective offenders, was not possible because the prohibition of retrospective punishment was not capable of consideration.[44]

The **Frankfurt Court of Appeal** later confirmed this reasoning and assigned it to one of the parallel cases because Article 1 of the ECHR obliged the convicted Member State to finish a violation of the Convention also in parallel cases.[45] Thus, Article 2 para. 6 of the German Criminal Code should be interpreted in conformity with the Convention in these cases correspondingly.[46]

---

40 Frankfurt Court of Appeal, l.c., § 12 ff.

41 Frankfurt Court of Appeal, l.c., § 15.

42 BVerfGE 109, 133.

43 Frankfurt Court of Appeal, l.c., § 19.

44 Frankfurt Court of Appeal, l.c., § 20 ff.

45 Frankfurt Court of Appeal, decision of 01 July 2010 – 3 Ws 539/10, § 25; differently in a case where subsequent preventive detention was concerned: Frankfurt Court of Appeal, decision of 01 July 2010 – 3 Ws 418/10 (only resumption according to Article 359 No. 6 of the German Code of Criminal Procedure possible).

46 Frankfurt Court of Appeal, l.c., § 26.

The possibility of such interpretation was already shown by the **Federal Court of Justice** (BGH) in a decision of 12 May 2010.[47] However, this decision did not concern one of the so-called parallel cases, but a case of subsequent preventive detention according to Article 66 b para. 3 of the German Criminal Code. In the Court's opinion this legal norm was – corresponding to the reasoning of the Frankfurt Court of Appeal in the above mentioned cases – according to Article 2 para 6 of the German Criminal Code in conjunction with Article 7 para. 1 of the ECHR not applicable to offences committed prior to 29 July 2004, when Article 66 b para. 3 of the German Criminal Code came into force.[48]

In the first of the parallel cases the **Hamm Court of Appeal** decided with regard to the jurisdiction of the ECtHR that the preventive detention should be finished.[49] The Court argued that the execution of preventive detention for more than ten years constituted a violation of human rights.[50] The Court stresses that the judgement of the ECtHR was only effective *inter partes*; however, governmental bodies were obliged to prevent corresponding violations of the ECHR in parallel cases. In so far, the ECtHR's judgement had the effect of a general role model ("*allgemeine Orientierungswirkung*").[51] Hence, it had to be regarded at least when assessing the principle of proportionality; preventive detention had to be declared finished in these cases.[52] The Court of Appeal confirmed and developed this opinion further in a later decision.[53] As the legislative body had not acted yet, Article 2 para. 6 of the German Criminal Code had to be interpreted in conformity with the Con-

47 Federal Court of Justice, decision of 12 May 2010 – 4 StR 577/09, EuGRZ 2010, 359; postponed until the judgement of the ECtHR becomes final: Federal Court of Justice, decision of 11 February 2010 – 4 StR 577/09.

48 Federal Court of Justice, decision of 12 May 2010 – 4 StR 577/09, EuGRZ 2010, 359, § 7. Different view concerning subsequent preventive detention according to Article 7 para. 2 No. 1 German Code of Juvenile Criminal Procedure because of particularities of Juvenile Criminal Law: Federal Court of Justice, judgement of 09 March 2010 – 1 StR 554/09, NJW 2010, 1539 = NStZ 2010, 381, § 60 ff.; see to this Eisenberg, NJW 2010, 1507, 1508 f. See. also Federal Court of Justice, decision of 06 July 2010 – 5 StR 142/10.

49 Hamm Court of Appeal, decision of 12 May 2010 – 4 Ws 114/10.

50 Hamm Court of Appeal, l.c., § 8.

51 Hamm Court of Appeal, l.c., § 9.

52 Hamm Court of Appeal, l.c., § 9.

53 Hamm Court of Appeal, decision of 06 July 2010 – 4 Ws 157/10, § 8 ff.; decision of 22 July 2010 – 4 Ws 180/10, § 2 ff.

vention.[54] For this interpretation, the Court recalls the reasoning of the Frankfurt Court of Appeal. The **Karlsruhe Court of Appeal** also subscribed to this view.[55]

In contrast, the **Koblenz Court of Appeal**, which was already in March 2010 reluctant to transform the judgement of the ECtHR, was not able to decide finally on the discharge of a detainee in a parallel case on 17 May 2010 and ordered the continuation of the appeal proceedings because it was necessary to examine in detail if the judgement of the ECtHR permitted the interpretation of the law about the length of preventive detention to the effect that the preventive detention had to be declared finished and the detainee had to be released.[56]

Another division of the **Koblenz Court of Appeal** decided on 7 June 2010 not to discharge a detainee from preventive detention.[57] It justified that decision with the reasoning that an interpretation in conformity with the Convention – which would help to transform the judgement of the ECtHR in parallel cases – was not possible under existing law.[58] Particularly, the judgement of the ECtHR did not have the effect of a "differing legal regulation" in terms of Article 2 para. 6 of the German Criminal Code, since it qualifies preventive detention as a "penalty" and hence affects the scope of Article 2 para. 1 of the German Criminal Code, not of Article 2 para. 6.[59] However, the application of Article 2 para. 1 of the German Criminal Code would be opposed to the judgement of the German Federal Constitutional Court which does not regard preventive detention as a "penalty" and is vested with legal force according to Article 31 para. 2 of the Federal Constitutional Court Act.[60] The implementation of the judgement of the ECtHR was incumbent upon the legislative body.[61] Furthermore, the continuation of pre-

54 Hamm Court of Appeal, l.c., § 9 f. („As can be concluded from the statements of the Federal Minister of Justice, the responsibility shall be shifted to the courts.")

55 Karlsruhe Court of Appeal, decision of 15 July 2010 – 2 Ws 458/09; decision of 15 July 2010 – 2 Ws 44/10.

56 Koblenz Court of Appeal, decision of 17 May 2010 – 2 Ws 573/09.

57 Koblenz Court of Appeal, decision of 07 June 2010 – 1 Ws 108/10; explicitly consenting: Cologne Court of Appeal, decision of 14 July 2010 – 2 Ws 428/10, § 25; see also Nuremberg Court of Appeal, decision of 24 June 2010 – 1 Ws 315/10; decision of 07 July 2010 – 1 Ws 342/10.

58 Koblenz Court of Appeal, l.c., § 9.

59 Koblenz Court of Appeal, l.c., § 11.

60 Koblenz Court of Appeal, l.c., § 16 ff.

61 Koblenz Court of Appeal, l.c., § 20.

ventive detention for more than ten years was not disproportional (see Article 62 of the German Criminal Code) because the positive obligation deriving from Article 2 para. 2 in conjunction with Article 1 para. 1 of the German Basic Law to protect life of potential victims especially from unlawful assaults of others prevailed the detainee's right to liberty. Thus, the violation of the right to liberty had to be accepted until a revision of the law or the judgement of the Federal Constitutional Court in the pending principal proceedings.[62]

In another parallel case the **Celle Court of Appeal** also ordered the continuance of preventive detention on the grounds that Article 7 ECHR, as it is interpreted by the ECtHR, cannot be qualified as "differing legal regulation" in terms of Article 2 para. 6 of the German Criminal Code, because this would be contrary to the explicit intention of the legislator as it was expressed in Article 1 a para. 3 of the Introductory Act to the German Criminal Code as amended on 26 January 1998.[63] Moreover, the basic rights of prospective victims preceded the right to liberty of the detainee.[64] With quite similar reasons, the **Stuttgart Court of Appeal** declined the immediate release of a detainee.[65]

Finally, the **Cologne Court of Appeal** subscribed to the view of the mentioned Courts of Appeal, that the implementation of the judgement of the ECtHR is not possible through an interpretation of Article 2 para. 6 of the German Criminal Code, but that an intervention of the legislative body is necessary.[66] As the only one – insofar as apparent – of the Courts of Appeal which decline the discharge in parallel cases, the Cologne Court of Appeal responds to the above mentioned decision of the 4th division of the Federal Court of Justice of 12 May 2010.[67] The decision, which did not have a binding effect, was not compatible with the principles laid down in the "Görgülü" decision of the Federal Constitutional Court[68] whereby the guarantees of the ECHR had only to be taken into account as part of a methodologically jus-

---

62 Koblenz Court of Appeal, l.c., § 21 f.

63 Celle Court of Appeal, decision of 25 May 2010 – 2 Ws 169/10, § 12 ff.

64 Celle Court of Appeal, l.c., § 19.

65 Stuttgart Court of Appeal, decision of 01 June 2010 – 1 Ws 57/10, § 30 ff.

66 Cologne Court of Appeal, decision of 14 July 2010 – 2 Ws 428/10, § 11 ff.; decision of 14 July 2010 – 2 Ws 431/10, § 11 ff., 41.

67 Cologne Court of Appeal, decision of 14 July 2010 – 2 Ws 428/10, § 33 f.; decision of 14 July 2010 – 2 Ws 431/10, § 41.

68 BVerfGE 111, 307 = NJW 2004, 3407.

tifiable interpretation of the law. Thus, the Court could not follow the opinion of the Federal Court of Justice.

It can be concluded that the contrarious decisions of the Courts of Appeal, which partly ordered the continuation, partly the termination of preventive detention, have led to a chaotic situation. Whether detainees in parallel cases could be released from preventive detention eventually depended on the question which Court of Appeal was competent to decide the case. The **legislator** also recognized this chaos which cannot be accepted for reasons of legal certainty. Thus, he made an amendment to the German Judicature Act on 24 July 2010, whereby a Court of Appeal which in his decision on preventive detention wants to deviate from a decision of another Court of Appeal adopted after 1 January 2010 or a decision of the Federal Court of Justice has to refer this case to the Federal Court of Justice (Article 121 para. 2 Nr. 3 of the German Judicature Act). This amendment came into effect on 30 July 2010.

The **Hamm Court of Appeal** already took notice of the upcoming amendment on 22 July 2010 and adhered to its opinion that an interpretation in conformity with the ECHR of Article 2 para. 6 of the German Criminal Code was possible.[69] For want of legal validity of the amendment, there was no duty to refer the case to the Federal Court of Justice. However, the Court stated in an obiter dictum, that even if the amendment had come into effect, there would have been no duty to refer the case: Its opinion was in accordance with the view taken by the 4th division of the Federal Court of Justice in his above mentioned decision of 12 May 2010[70], which concerned the same point of law, that is to say the possibility of an interpretation in conformity with the ECHR of Article 2 para. 6 of the German Criminal Code.[71] The decision of the 2nd division of the Federal Court of Justice of 12 May 2010[72] could not be regarded as diverging decision, because it did not even mention the point of law in question. Thus, it had to be assumed that the 2nd division did not have notice of the fact that the judgement of the ECtHR

69 Hamm Court of Appeal, decision of 22 July 2010 – 4 Ws 180/10, § 11.

70 Federal Court of Justice, decision of 12 May 2010 – 4 StR 577/09, EuGRZ 2010, 359.

71 Hamm Court of Appeal, l.c., § 12.

72 Federal Court of Justice, decision of 12 May 2010 – 2 StR 171/10.

had become final.[73] The **Hamm Court of Appeal** confirmed this decision once again on 29 July 2010.[74]

The question if there is a duty to refer the case to the Federal Court of Justice got crucial when the **Karlsruhe Court of Appeal** had to take its decision of 4 August 2010.[75] Following the reasoning of the Hamm Court of Appeal, the Court, however, denied a duty to refer the case. Yet, the Courts of Appeal which have so far declined release from preventive detention will have to refer an upcoming parallel case to the Federal Court of Justice if they want to adhere to their point of view.

By the end of 2010, there were at least six cases pending with the Federal Court of Justice (BGH).[76] Concerning three of these cases, the 5th division of the Federal Court of Justice decided on 9 November 2010 that an interpretation in conformity with the Convention was not possible, because the application of the law valid at the time of the offence would be contrary to the explicit intention of the legislator.[77] However, this was not a final decision. As this legal opinion clearly conflicts with the above mentioned decision of the 4th division of the Federal Court of Justice of 12 May 2010, the 5th division sent an inquiry to the 4th division: If the 4th division wants to adhere to its opinion, the cases have to be referred to the Grand Chamber of the Federal Court of Justice. Thus, the final decision of the Federal Court of Justice in these cases remains to be seen.

The **Federal Constitutional Court** (BVerfG) declined an interim order already shortly after the ECtHR pronounced its judgement in the case of M. against Germany and told the applicant to await the main proceedings.[78] This decision was confirmed repeatedly even after the judgement of the ECtHR

---

73 Hamm Court of Appeal, l.c., § 12.

74 Hamm Court of Appeal, decision of 29 July 2010 – 4 Ws193/10.

75 Karlsruhe Court of Appeal, decision of 04 August 2010 – 2 Ws 227/10, BeckRS 2010, 18797.

76 Nuremberg Court of Appeal, decision of 04 August 2010 – 1 Ws 404/10, BeckRS 2010, 20614; Cologne Court of Appeal, decision of 12 August 2010 – 2 Ws 488/10, BeckRS 2010, 20734; Stuttgart Court of Appeal, decision of 19 August 2010 – 1 Ws 57/10; Koblenz Court of Appeal, decision of 01 September 2010 – 2 Ws 370/10; decision of 30 September 2010 – 1 Ws 108/10; Celle Court of Appeal, decision of 09 September 2010 – 2 Ws 270/10.

77 Federal Court of Justice, decision of 09 November 2010 – 5 StR 394/10, 5 StR 440/10, 5 StR 474/10.

78 Federal Constitutional Court, decision of 22 December 2009 – 2 BvR 2365/09.

became final.[79] A judgement in the main proceedings has not been rendered yet.

Thus, German jurisdiction is rather reluctant to implement the ECtHR's judgement in the case of M up to now. Many Courts of Appeal are not willing to enforce the judgement in a – from their point of view – schematic way and to release undoubtedly dangerous offenders immediately. They often quote the allegedly conflicting precedent of the Federal Constitutional Court, albeit the question how Article 2 para. 6 of the German Criminal Code can be interpreted evidently is a question of non-constitutional law.[80] In contrast, most Courts of Appeal do not even respond to the decision of the 4th division of the Federal Court of Justice, which made use of the possibility of an interpretation in conformity with the ECHR of Article 2 para. 6 of the German Criminal Code even in a broader sense when deciding on a case of *subsequent* preventive detention. The Koblenz Court of Appeal even takes the view that – because the ECtHR qualified preventive detention as a "penalty" – Article 2 para. 6 of the German Criminal Code was not applicable, but Article 2 para. 1.[81] However, the Court on the one hand mistakes the fact that in this case the law valid at the time of the offence would be applicable anyway. On the other hand, the ECtHR understands the concept of "penalty" in Article 7 of the ECHR autonomously, so that the qualification under national law is irrelevant.[82] Thus, it becomes apparent that human rights standards obviously are not capable to overrule national authority if it does not fit in the framework.

However, Government apparently assumes that offenders in parallel cases have to be released from preventive detention. If there was no such duty, the planned "Treatment and Placement of Mentally Disturbed Violent Offenders Act", which was presented by Government within the key points for the reform of the preventive detention system, would not have been necessary. The twin-track system of sanctions shall thus be retained in the future. The planned placement has to be developed in a way though, that it is clearly

79 Federal Constitutional Court, decision of 19 May 2010 – 2 BvR 769/10 = EuGRZ 2010, 385; decision of 05 August 2010 – 2 BvR 1646/10; decision of 16 August 2010 – 2 BvR 1762/10; see also Federal Constitutional Court, decision of 30 June 2010 – 2 BvR 571/10 (concerning a case of subsequent preventive detention).

80 Federal Court of Justice, decision of 12 May 2010 – 4 StR 577/09, EuGRZ 2010, 359, § 18; consenting *Gaede,* HRRS 2010, 329, 332.

81 Koblenz Court of Appeal, decision of 07 June 2010 – 1 Ws 108/10, § 11.

82 Already mentioned by Karlsruhe Court of Appeal, decision of 15 July 2010 – 2 Ws 458/09, § 6.

distinguishable from imprisonment. Independent of its qualification under national law, it would otherwise again be regarded as "penalty" in terms of Article 7 para. 1 of the ECHR. Thus, it would conflict with the strict prohibition of retrospective punishment comprised in Article 7 ECHR. This follows from the autonomous interpretation of the concept of "penalty" by the ECtHR.

In the meantime it remains to be seen if the Federal Constitutional Court will also qualify the present system of preventive detention as conflicting with the strict prohibition of retrospective punishment comprised in Article 103 para. 3 of the German Basis Law in the pending main proceedings and will thus contribute to the constitutionalization of the concept of "penalty".

F. Conclusion

The constitutionalization process of the concept of "penalty" in Germany has just begun. It has shown that human rights have the power and authority to question and change long established national legal structures, also in criminal law. With the help of nationally implemented convention standards, a powerful international court and a case law which is binding on the member states, it is even possible to constitutionalize fundamental criminal law issues. However, the basis of such a process must usually be established by the national courts. Independent and yet bound by law, national courts are requested to orientate their interpretation on international standards and thereby develop national law in accordance with human rights.

Works cited

Bryde, Brun-Otto, "Konstitutionalisierung des Völkerrechts und Internationalisierung des Verfassungsrechts," *Der Staat* 42 (2003): 61-75.

Diehm, Dirk, *Die Menschenrechte der EMRK und ihr Einfluss auf das deutsche Strafgesetzbuch*, Berlin: Logos Verlag, 2006.

Emmerich-Fritsche, Angelika, *Vom Völkerrecht zum Weltrecht*, Berlin: Duncker & Humblot, 2007

Frowein, Jochen A., "Konstitutionalisierung des Völkerrechts," *Berichte der. Deutschen Gesellschaft für Völkerrecht* 39 (1999): 427-448.

Gerards, Regine, *Die Europäische Menschenrechtskonvention im Konstitutionalisierungsprozess einer gemeineuropäischen Grundrechtsordnung*, Frankfurt and others: Peter Lang, 2007.

Goerlich, Helmut, "Der Europäische Gerichtshof für Menschenrechte in Straßburg als ein europäisches Verfassungsgericht – insbesondere in Fragen der Menschenrechte und darüber hinaus bis in die Rechtspraxis der Europäischen Union," in *Die Bedeutung der EMRK für die nationale Rechtsordnung*, eds. R. Esser, B. Harich, F. Lohse and A. Sinn, Berlin: Berliner Wissenschafts-Verlag, 2004, pp. 101 ff.

Herdegen, Matthias, *Europarecht*, 12th ed., München: C.H. Beck, 2010.

Kadelbach, Stefan, and Thomas Kleinlein, "Überstaatliches Verfassungsrecht: Zur Konstitutionalisierung im Völkerrecht," *Archiv des Völkerrechts* 44 (2006): 235-266.

Klabbers, Jan, Anne Peters, and Geir Ulfstein, *The Constitutionalization of International Law*, Oxford: Oxford University Press, 2009.

Schweitzer, Michael, *Staatsrecht III: Staatsrecht, Völkerrecht, Europarecht*, 10th ed., Heidelberg: C.F. Müller, 2010.

Wahl, Rainer, "Konstitutionalisierung – Leitbegriff oder Allerweltsbegriff?" in *Der Wandel des Staates vor den Herausforderungen der Gegenwart, Festschrift für Winfried Brohm zum 70. Geburtstag*, eds. C.-E. Eberle, M. Ibler and D. Lorenz, München: C.H. Beck, 2002, pp. 191-207.

Wildhaber, Luzius, "Ein Überdenken des Zustands und der Zukunft des Europäischen Gerichtshofs für Menschenrechte," *Europäische Grundrechte-Zeitschrift* (2009): 541-553.

Constitutionalization of Political Rule in Europe: Freedom of Speech, Press and Assembly

Rainer Grote

A. Introduction: The Role of Freedom of Opinion and Assembly in a Democratic Society

The understanding of the role of free speech in any given society and the degree of protection accorded to it depend crucially on the prevailing view of the relationship between those exercising political authority and those who are subject to it. If the ruler is regarded as being by the nature of his position presumably wise and good, then it must necessarily follow that it is wrong to criticize him openly, and such criticism must be stifled and discouraged. If on the other hand the ruler is regarded as the agent of the subjects who have delegated their powers to him to be exercised in their name and in their interest, the right to criticise the ruler would appear as a natural right of the subjects to find fault with their agent.

In Europe, it is the second view which is largely prevailing today and which informs the relevant jurisprudence of national constitutional courts as well as of the European Court of Human Rights on freedom of speech, press and assembly. In its well-known decision in the *Lüth* case which forms the basis of much of its subsequent jurisprudence on freedom of opinion as guaranteed in Article 5 (1) of the German Basic Law, the German Federal Constitutional Court emphasized the central role of free speech in a democratic society by declaring that, in addition to being the most direct expression of human personality in society and one of the foremost human rights of all, it is a constitutive part of any free democratic system since it is only through the free expression of opinions and ideas that the constant intellectual debate, the clash of opinions that is democracy's vital element is made possible.[1] In a later case the Court has stressed that the fundamental right to free expression of opinion grew specifically out of the special need to protect

1 BVerfGE 7, 198 (208) – *Lüth case.*

criticism of power, and continues to find its significance therein.[2] The Court has characterized freedom of assembly in Article 8 of the Basic Law in equally strong terms as an essential element of democratic openness. In the Court's view, the citizens' right to take part actively in the political process by exercising freedom of assembly is among the indispensable functional elements of a democratic community. In a democracy with a representative system of government and very limited influence of citizens during the period between the elections freedom of assembly plays a vital in the stabilization of the representative democratic process by allowing dissatisfaction, discontent and criticism to be brought out openly and by operating as an important element in democracy's early-warning system that points to potential disruption.[3] In particular, the protection of freedom is not diminished by the fact that specifically in demonstrations the argumentational aspect which as a rule characterizes the exercise of freedom of opinion takes second place since the participants in a demonstration primarily express their opinion through their physical presence in community with others. According to the Court, the danger of such manifestations of opinion being demagogically misused and emotionalized in questionable fashion is not decisive for the positive assessment of freedom of assembly in principle, any more than in the area of freedom of opinion and the press.[4]

At the European level, the Court of Human Rights in Strasbourg has adopted a similar approach to the interpretation and application of the rights to freedom of expression and freedom of assembly contained in Articles 10 and 11 of the European Convention on Human Rights. Indeed, freedom of expression is considered to be not only an indispensable means for the individual to express and develop his personality through communication with others, but also as a defining feature and requirement of a democratic society. According to the European Court, freedom of expression "constitutes one of the essential foundations of a democratic society, one of the basic conditions for its progress and for each individual's self-fulfilment."[5] The same

2 BVerfGE 93, 266 (293) – *Tucholsky case*.
3 BVerfGE 69, 315 (347) – *Brokdorf case*.
4 BVerfGE 69, 315 (345).
5 *Handyside v. United Kingdom*, A 24, 7 December 1976, para. 49.

characterization would seem to apply to the freedom of assembly as freedom for the collective manifestation of opinion.[6]

B. Major Issues in the Protection of Speech, Press and Assembly

I. Freedom of Speech under the German Basic Law

1. Freedom of Speech and of the Press

However, the prominent position which freedom of speech enjoys in contemporary democracy in Europe does not give it absolute protection. According to Article 5 (2) of the German Basic Law, freedom of opinion, freedom of the press and freedom of broadcasting shall find their limits in the provisions of the general laws, in provisions for the protection of young persons, and in the right to personal honour.

The Federal Constitutional Court has interpreted the reference to "general laws" in the limitation clause of Article 5 (2) as meaning those laws that are not directed against a specific opinion but rather serve to safeguard individual or collective rights or interests which deserve protection regardless of the opinion in question.[7] As a matter of principle, government shall have no role in deciding as to what views shall be voiced in public debate based on their actual content. A law that restricts opinions is deemed impermissible "special legislation" (*Sonderrecht*) if it is not drafted in a sufficiently open manner and if it is from the outset only directed against certain convictions, attitudes or ideologies. The same applies to provisions for the protection of young persons and for the protection of personal honour pursuant to Article 5.2 alternatives 2 and 3 GG. Both criminal and civil law provisions which aim to protect the dignity and honour of others against defamation or libelous remarks qualify for classification as "general laws" within the meaning of Article 5 (2).

However, the Constitutional Court has accepted the need for certain exceptions to the ban on content-related special legislation contained in Article 5 (2).

---

6 Although the European Court of Human Rights has not expressly addressed the issue, the (now defunct) European Commission has done so, see *Rassemblement jurassien and Unité jurassienne v. Switzerland*, Opinion of 10 October 1979, DR 17, 93, 105.

7 BVerfGE 7, 198 (209 f.); 28, 175 (185 f.).

With a view to the injustice and terror caused by the National Socialist rule, an exception to the ban on special legislation is inherent in Article 5.1 and 5.2 GG for provisions that set limits to the propagandistic approval of the historical National Socialist rule of arbitrary force. To a large extent the Basic Law can virtually be regarded as a counter-concept to the totalitarianism of the National Socialist regime. The experience gained from the destruction of all achievements of civilization by the National Socialist rule of arbitrary force has had a lasting and decisive effect on the entire post-war order and the integration of the Federal Republic of Germany into the international community. A provision in the German Penal Code which provides for the punishment of a person who, publicly or in an assembly, disturbs the public peace by approving, glorifying or justifying the National Socialist rule of violence and arbitrariness in a manner violating the dignity of the victims with imprisonment for up to three years or a fine has thus been held to be compatible with Article 5 (1), (2) of the Basic Law.[8]

However, even if a law qualifies as general law within the meaning of Article 5 (2), this does not mean that it constitutes *per se* a valid justification for every sort of limitation of the right to freedom of expression. Rather the general laws must be interpreted in the light of the importance of that fundamental right in a democratic society and thus in turn be restricted themselves in their effect of limiting the fundamental right. The Federal Constitutional Court which is ultimately called upon to uphold the fundamental rights through the mechanism of the constitutional complaints procedure will check whether the ordinary courts have properly taken into account the specific value of freedom of expression for a free democracy in the application of the relevant criminal or private law provisions, or whether they have misapprehended the fundamental importance of free speech in a democracy and inadmissibly restricted the scope of the right in an individual case.

In practice this means that the protection of free speech takes places through a balancing exercise in which the ordinary judge, subject to final control by the Constitutional Court, must in each case weigh the fundamental importance of free speech for public debate against the interests of the person allegedly injured by the utterance which are protected by the general law. An incorrect balancing exercise will infringe the fundamental right and justify a constitutional complaint to the Federal Constitutional Court. In the context of this balancing exercise, the central role of free speech in a func-

8 Federal Constitutional Court, Decision of 17 November 2009, 1BvR 2150/2008.

tioning democracy must lead to a basic presumption in favour of freedom of opinion in all areas but particularly in public life.[9]

The outcome of this balancing exercise does not lend itself to easy generalizations because of its essential case-relatedness. However, a number of criteria have been developed in the case law of the Constitutional Court which can serve as guidelines for the balancing operation in individual cases. An important distinction applies to the means being used for the dissemination or defense of opinions or ideas. Article 5 (1) is designed to protect the freedom of intellectual debate. It is thus opposed to any forms of communication which aim to impose certain views or opinions by other means than argument or counterargument, namely by force, intimidation or threat. Thus the exercise of economic pressure that leads to severe drawbacks for those concerned and pursues the objective to curtail the free circulation of opinions and ideas undermines the equality of opportunities in the public discussion process and violates the freedom of information of those who are on the receiving end of the views forcefully removed from public debate.[10]

Another important distinction is that between the assertion of facts and the statement of opinions or value judgments. Wrong information is not an object deserving of protection from the viewpoint of freedom of opinion since it cannot promote the constitutionally intended objective of proper formation of opinion. Where expression of opinion is linked to factual assertions, the protection merited can depend on the truth of the underlying factual assumptions. If these assumptions have been proven untrue, freedom of expression will yield to protection of personal honour and dignity.[11] When the press makes use of its right to inform the public it is thus obliged to report truthfully. In particular, it must verify information and assertions which it passes on for their truth content.[12] On the other hand, the Constitutional Court cautions against excessive requirements concerning the duty of truth which could have a crippling effect on freedom of debate, particularly in the media. Thus the media may not be subjected to disproportionate risks which could prevent them from fulfilling their function of providing a public check on the elected politicians.[13]

---

9 BVerfGE 7, 198 (208).

10 BVerfGE 25, 256 (265) – *Blinkfüer Case.*

11 BVerfGE 61, 1 (8); 85, 1 (17).

12 BVerfGE 12, 113 – *Schmidt-Spiegel Case.*

13 BVerfGE 54, 208 – *Böll case.*

By contrast, in the case of value judgments or critical comments, it is in principle irrelevant whether the criticism is justified or the value judgment is "right". This approach leaves ample room for a critical debate on matters of general interest as well as for criticism of the conduct of prominent figures of public life, including politicians. The only limits to freedom of opinion are those resulting from the fundamental rights of others, in particular from the right to human dignity and the personality rights protected by Articles 1, 2 of the Basic Law. Freedom of opinion must yield to the protection of the dignity and honour of another person in cases in which the criticism affects the essential human dignity of the criticised person. Free speech thus took second place in a case in which a prominent German politician was portrayed in a satirical magazine as an animal engaged in sexual activity with another animal wearing a judge's robe. The caricature clearly transgressed the limits of freedom of art protected by Article 5 (3) of the Basic Law as it was intended to devalue the person concerned as a person, to deprive him of his dignity as a human being.[14] This principle, stated in relation to artistic freedom, applies to freedom of opinion as well, because human dignity, as the root of all the basic rights, is not capable of being weighed against any individual basic right. However, not only the individual fundamental rights but also the basic rights taken as a whole are an expression of the principle of human dignity; a careful analysis is therefore necessary in order to establish that the exercise of freedom of expression constitutes indeed a violation of human dignity in a specific case.[15]

Similarly, where disparaging statements are concerned which constitute an insult within the meaning of the applicable criminal law or abusive criticism, freedom of opinion as a rule takes second place to protection of personal honour.[16] But because of its effect in suppressing freedom of opinion, the Federal Constitutional Court has defined narrowly the concept of abusive criticism developed in the specialist courts. According to this approach, an exaggerated or even rude criticism does not of itself turn a statement into abuse. Instead, the dominant feature about the statement must be defamation of the person rather than debate about the issue. The statement must go beyond even polemical and overstated criticism and have personal denigration as its primary object.[17]

14 BVerfGE 75, 369 (425) – *Strauß Caricature Case*.
15 BVerfGE 93, 266 (293).
16 BVerfGE 61, 1 (12).
17 BVerfGE 82, 272 (283); 93, 266 (294).

Against the background of this jurisprudence, public figures in particular may be subjected to sharp, unsparing criticism, as long as it remains issue-related. The limits of legitimate public criticism are only transgressed if the attack degenerates into abusive or defamatory criticism, i.e. the intentional wounding of a person's honour. Such abusive criticism will only exceptionally be present in statements about a question materially affecting the public and will otherwise tend to remain confined to the so-called private feud. If a court qualifies a statement wrongly as defamation with the consequence that a balancing operation taking into account all the circumstances of the individual case does not take place such omission will amount to a constitutionally relevant error and lead to the decision being quashed if it is based on the omission.

If the statement can be classified neither as an attack on human dignity nor as insult or abusive criticism, it will normally enjoy constitutional protection, especially if the statement in question has been made with the purpose of initiating or promoting a public debate on an issue of general concern. If the statement in question represents a contribution to the formation of public opinion, then according to the consistent case law of the Federal Constitutional Court there is a presumption in favour of the freedom of speech. Departures from the presumption require justification which takes account of the constitutive importance of freedom of opinion for democracy in which the presumption is rooted.[18]

2. Freedom of Assembly

The freedom of assembly in Article 8 of the Basic Law has been given a similarly broad interpretation by the German Constitutional Court. The wording of Article 8 (1) itself restricts the right of assembly to "peaceful" and "unarmed" demonstrations, thus clarifying in the Court's view the legal nature of the freedom as a means for intellectual debate and for influencing the process in which public opinion is formed. No longer peaceful is a demonstrator who commits violence against persons or things.[19] By contrast, the Court has held that participants of a sit-down blockade of military installations do not fall outside the scope of the basic right just because they

18 BVerfGE 93, 266 (295).
19 BVerfGE 69, 315 (360).

use elements of coercion in order to manifest their pacifist convictions. As long as participants confine themselves to passive resistance and remain peaceful, sit-down blockades can mainly be treated as peaceful assemblies within the meaning of Article 8 Basic Law, unlike assemblies which proceed with violence or are rebellious in nature.[20] However, this does not necessarily lead to the conclusion that sit-down blockades are lawful. It only means that they are subject to restrictions pursuant to a law referred to in paragraph 2 of Article 8 for outdoors assemblies. Within this power to regulate, the legislature may also order sanctions against deliberate traffic obstructions.[21]

While Article 8 (2) thus seemingly confers wide discretionary powers on the legislature in the regulation of outdoors assemblies, these powers must in the view of the Constitutional Court be interpreted in accordance with the purpose of the provision. The Constitution is thereby taking into account the fact that in view of the manifold contacts with the outside world of open air demonstrations, a particularly regulatory regime is needed, involving organizational and procedural regulation, in order to create the actual conditions for the exercise of the freedom of assembly and simultaneously to protect the conflicting interests of others.[22] Therefore the same principle which has already been explained in relation to freedom of speech also applies with regard to freedom of assembly: The legislature must duly take into account the significance of the freedom of assembly when using its regulatory powers under Article 8 (2) to restrict its exercise. The legislature may thus limit the exercise of the freedom of assembly only to the extent necessary to protect other rights and legal interests of equal value, in strict observance of the principle of proportionality.[23]

Similarly, when the courts and competent state authorities interpret and apply the statutes restricting the freedom of assembly in individual cases, they must conform to the same principles which govern the application of "general laws" in cases concerning freedom of speech. In such a situation, they must always interpret the statute in the light of the fundamental importance of the fundamental right in a democratic society, confining themselves in their measures to what is necessary in order to protect the conflicting rights and interests. Thus the Court has considered measures which impede access to a demonstration by blocking routes, engage in drawn-out identity checks

20 BVerfGE 92, 1.
21 BVerfGE 92, 1.
22 BVerfGE 69, 315 (348).
23 BVerfGE 69, 315 (348/349).

prior to the event or alter its unregulated, state-free character through excessive observation and registration as incompatible with the constitutional requirements for the effective protection of freedom of assembly.[24] The permitted degree of intervention also depends on the cooperation of the organizers of the assembly: The more the organizers are willing to take confidence-building measures or to adopt a cooperative attitude, the higher is the threshold for the authorities to intervene on grounds of danger to public safety.[25]

II. Protection of Freedom of Speech, Press and Assembly under the European Convention of Human Rights

1. Freedom of Speech and the Press

The rulings of the European Court of Human Rights on the freedom of speech, press and assembly under the European Convention of Human Rights follow a similar approach. In its case law the European Court of Human Rights has consistently stressed the importance of these rights as central pillars of a democratic society. The protection granted by Article 10 extends to any form of expression notwithstanding its content and the form of its dissemination.[26] It does not only cover ideas and information which are favourably received or regarded as inoffensive by the majority but also those that offend, shock or disturb the state or any sector of the population.[27] The only content-based restriction applied by the former Commission of Human Rights has dealt with the dissemination of ideas promoting racism and the Nazi ideology, and inciting to hatred and racial discrimination. In these cases the Commission has repeatedly relied on Article 17 of the Convention and held that the freedom of expression may not be used in order to lead to the destruction of the rights and freedoms granted by the Convention.[28] In a

---

24 BVerfGE 69, 315 (349).

25 BVerfGE 69, 315 (357).

26 Including disruptive forms of communication like horn blowing as a means to disturb a fox hunt, see *Hashman and Harrup v United Kingom*, 25 November 1999, Reports 1999-VIII.

27 *Handyside v. United Kingdom*, A 24, 7 December 1976, para. 48.

28 Apps. 8348/78 and 8406/78, *Glimmerveen and Hagenbeek v. Netherlands*, 11 October, (1980) 18 DR 187; App. 12194/86, *Kühnen v. Federal Republic of Germany*, 12 May 1988, (1988) 56 DR 205.

similar vein, the European Court of Human Rights has applied Article 17 from time to time in order to exclude anti-Semitic propaganda and attempts to rehabilitate the Nazi regime from the scope of protection of Article 10.[29]

This does not mean that other offensive material, e.g. obscene publications or speech inciting to violence, will as a rule enjoy the protection of Article 10. But it does mean that States which want to interfere with this speech will be compelled to justify the interference in accordance with the standards laid down in Article 10 (2). "Interferences" within the meaning of Article 10 (2) include censorship and other restricting measures prior to publication as well as all different kinds of post-publication measures, including criminal prosecutions, civil actions and tort claims brought for defamation, libel or breach of confidentiality.

Article 10 (2) establishes stringent standards for the justification of such measures. States have to show that the interference is "prescribed by law" and that it is "necessary in a democratic society" to protect one of the interests or rights referred to in Article 10 (2), namely national security, territorial integrity, public safety, prevention of disorder or crime, protection of health or morals, protection of the reputation or rights of others, the prevention of the disclosure of confidential information, or the maintenance of the authority and impartiality of the judiciary. Within this framework, the European Court examines in each case the type of expression (political, commercial, artistic etc.), the means by which the expression disseminated (personal conversation or letter, press, television etc.) and its audience (adults, children, the public at large, special groups etc.) in order to determine the extent to which a particular form of expression should be protected.

Particularly strong protection is given to the circulation of ideas and informations which contribute to a free public debate on matters of general interest which is at the core of the concept of a democratic society to which Article 10 makes explicit reference. This has led the Court to expressly recognize a "watchdog" role of the press and to develop an extensive body of principles and rules designed to allow the press to effectively discharge this function. While the press must not overstep the boundaries established in Article 10 (2), inter alia, for the protection of the rights of others, in the Court's view it has the task of imparting information and ideas on political issues just as on those in other areas of public interest. Not only does the press have the task of imparting such information and ideas: The public also

29 App. 35222/04, *Ivanov*; App. 65831/01, *Garaudy*.

has a right to receive them. The press affords the public one of the best means of discovering and forming an opinion of the ideas and attitudes of political leaders but it also plays a vital role when other matters of public concern are at stake.

National legislation which blurs the distinction between facts and value judgments and requires the truth proof also with regard to the latter in defamation or libel proceedings makes it excessively hard for the press to effectively discharge its role as watchdog and is therefore per se incompatible with Article 10. In respect of the underlying facts on which the opinion is based the requirement to prove the truth is in principle admissible; but even here the press must be allowed to invoke the defence of good faith so as to allow it some "breathing space for error". Where a journalist or a publication has a legitimate purpose, the matter is of public concern, and reasonable efforts have been made to verify the facts, the journalist or press company shall not be liable, even if the respective facts are proven untrue.[30]

Another consequence of the vital role of the press in a vibrant democratic society is the protection of journalistic sources under Article 10 as one of the basic conditions of press freedom. According to the Court, without such protection sources may be deterred from assisting the press in informing the public on matters of public interest. As a result, the vital public watchdog role of the press would be impaired and the ability of the press to provide accurate and reliable information be adversely affected.[31]

The protection of the reputation and rights of others is by far the legitimate aim most frequently invoked by national authorities for restricting freedom of expression. In numerous cases it has been invoked to protect politicians and civil servants against criticism. The European Court of Human Rights has developed a large body of jurisprudence on the proper balance between the reputation of others and the freedom of expression, and in particular of the press. The media's privileged place derives from the Court's view of the central role of political expression in a democratic society both with respect to the electoral process and to daily matters of public interest. With regard to the type of speech used, the Court has accepted severe and harsh criticism as well as coloured expressions, as they have the advantage of drawing attention to the issues under debate.

---

30 *Dalban v. Romania*, Judgment of 28 September 1999, Reports 1999-VI.

31 *Goodwin v. United Kingdom*, Judgment of 27 March 1996, Reports 1996-II.

According to this jurisprudence, the limits of acceptable criticism are particularly wide with regard to the government. In a democratic society the actions or omissions of the government must be subject to the close scrutiny not only of the legislative and judicial authorities but also of the press and public opinion. The dominant position which the government occupies make it necessary for it to display restraint in resorting to criminal proceedings, particularly when other means are available for replying to the unjustified attacks and criticisms of its adversaries in the media.[32]

Politicians must also display wider tolerance of media criticism than private individuals. Unlike the latter, the former inevitably and knowingly submit themselves to close scrutiny of their every word and deed by both journalists and the public at large, and must consequently show a greater degree of tolerance in dealing with the public scrutiny and criticism.[33]

These criteria for the balancing of freedom of expression with the reputation or rights of others also apply to the criticism of public servants or any other form of public criticism intended to bring about a discussion of other matters of general concern. The Court has expressly rejected to distinguish between political discussion and debate on other matters of public concern. The sentencing of a journalist who had reported on police brutality for defamation was therefore found to be incompatible with Article 10, as was court order directed to a journalist to pay civil damages for having stated that all members of the Water and Forestry Commission except one were corrupt. While the Court accepted that civil servants should not be treated on an equal footing with politicians when it comes to criticism of their conduct, it held that the limits of acceptable criticism are still wider than in the case of private citizens and found the sentences to be contrary to Article 10 since they were capable of discouraging open discussion on matters of public concern.[34]

On the other hand, the European Court of Human Rights draws a more rigid distinction between the different functions or roles of a public figure which is subjected to public scrutiny or debate than some national courts, and in particular the German Constitutional Court. His public role does not automatically justify a close scrutiny by the media or the public of his private

32 *Castells v. Spain*, A 236, 23 April 1992.

33 *Lingens v. Austria*, A 103, 8 July 1986; App. 37698/97, *Lopes Gomes da Silva v. Portugal*, Judgment of 28 September 2000.

34 *Thorgeir Thorgeirson v. Iceland*, A 239, 25 June 1992; App. 38432/97, *Thoma v. Luxembourg*, Judgment of 29 March 2001.

life, at least of those of it aspects which are unrelated to his public functions. If the individual concerned is nevertheless subject to such intrusive forms of media scrutiny, especially those involving photographs from his family life, then the protection of his privacy (guaranteed by Article 8 of the Convention) ought normally to prevail over press freedom.[35]

2. Freedom of Assembly

In comparison to freedom of speech and freedom of the press the freedom of assembly guaranteed in Article 11 of the European Convention has received little attention in the Court's jurisprudence. This is not surprising as this right is closely associated with Article 9 (freedom of religion), and Article 10 and will frequently need to be considered in the light of the rights guaranteed in those Articles. Like Article 8 of the German Basic Law, Article 11 of the European Convention only protects *peaceful* assemblies, a limitation which has been confirmed in the recent case law of the Court.[36] However, a demonstration does not lose its peaceful character just because it violates existing legal rules, e.g. those concerning traffic regulation or the use of public buildings.[37] By contrast, if the organizers of the demonstration are bent on imposing their views on the authorities or the public by using physical violence, they cannot avail themselves of the protection of Article 11.[38]

The European Court of Human Rights has emphasized that the freedom of peaceful assembly does not merely impose a duty on the public authorities not to interfere with public protests. Such a purely negative conception would not be compatible with the object and purpose of Article 11 which sometimes require positive measures to be taken, even in the sphere of relations between individuals. This might require an active intervention of the competent authorities in order to secure conditions permitting the exercise of the right, e.g. by providing the necessary traffic regulation or protecting the demonstration against disruptions or disturbances by violent counter-

35 *Von Hannover v. Germany*, Judgment of 24 June 2004, Reports 2004-XI.

36 Apps. 29221/95 and 29225/95, *Stankov*.

37 App. 51346/99, *Cisse*.

38 App. 8440/78, *Christians against Racism and Fascism*.

demonstrations.[39] This jurisprudence is reminiscent of the statement of the German Constitutional Court, in the *Brokdorf* decision, that the exercise of freedom of assembly in the open air, due to its manifold contacts with the outside world, need a particularly regulatory regime comprising organizational as well as procedural rules which create the actual conditions for the effective exercise of the right,[40] although the German Court did not expressly refer to the concept of positive obligations in this context.

C. Conclusion

The protection of freedom of speech, the press and assembly displays a number of similar features at the national and the European level. It seems therefore possible to speak of a European model of freedom of expression in a functioning democracy. This model stresses the fundamental importance of free speech both as an instrument of the individual to express himself and communicate in a meaningful way with others and as an indispensable precondition for the "clash of opinions and views" which forms the basis of a democratic society.

Both the German and the European Court adopt a broad approach in defining the scope of application of the relevant constitutional guarantees so as not to exclude *a priori* any type or form of speech from their protection. Exceptions to this rule are opinions promoting racism or the rehabilitation of the Nazi ideology which according to both Courts may not be regarded as constitutionally or conventionally protected free speech. Although this restrictive attitude raises some difficult issues with regard to the limits of free speech and the treatment of minority views, it is essentially a sensitive response to the still vivid memories of the havoc wrought by racist and Nazi ideologies in Europe's recent past. By contrast, the limits regarding public criticism on matters of general interest are drawn fairly widely both under the European Convention and the Basic Law. This is protection is not limited to political speech in the narrow sense; it also covers open discussion on other matters of public concern.

---

39 *Plattform 'Ärzte für das Leben' v. Austria*, Judgment of 21 June 1988, Series A, No. 139. In the case at hand, the Court concluded that the Austrian authorities had not failed in their duty to take positive measures to permit the effective exercise of the right.

40 See note 22 above.

Both Courts take into account the vital importance of free speech in a functioning democracy when examining the proportionality of state interference with the right. It leads the German Constitutional Court to a basic presumption in favour of free speech in all areas but particularly in public life; it makes the European Court particularly wary of all practices which are capable of stifling dissent and discussion on matters of public concern. Both Courts accept that there are limits to free speech resulting from the honour and reputation of others. But these limits are narrowly defined, by way of reference to the concept of human dignity in the German case (a concept which is not acknowledged as such by the European Convention, although it may be said to be implicit in Article 3), and by distinguishing carefully between the public and the private aspects of a public figure's life in the case of the European Human Rights Court.

Part IV:

Courts

Interpretations of the Constitutional Court and the Developments of Rule of Law and Democratic Constitutionalism in Taiwan

Yueh-sheng Weng

A. Introduction

The development of constitutional laws depends not only upon their contents but also upon their real practices. Constitutional laws will fall into mere formality if there exists a huge gap between constitutional norms and their practices. Constitutional revisions, constitutional interpretations, and constitutional customs all lead to the developments of constitutional laws in modern constitutional states. Taiwan, a country with a written constitution, has developed its distinctive constitutionalism upon constitutional revisions as well as constitutional interpretations. Constitutional interpretations and constitutional revisions are two distinct concepts. The former illuminates the meaning of the constitution while the latter rewrites what the constitution prescribes. The former is understood as a legal judgment that falls into judicial powers while the latter is regarded as the exercise of political powers by the National Assembly or the Legislative Yuan. Both are important and by no means mutually exclusive.[1] They usually overlap with each other. The requirements to amend a constitution are often difficult to meet as written constitutions usually emphasize stability. Constitutional interpretations, thus, may play a pivotal role and affect substantively the development of democratic constitutionalism and the rule of law for modern states.

This article provides a brief discussion of the Constitutional Court in Taiwan and its changing functions. Next, it further articulates the influences of constitutional interpretations upon the developments of rule of law and democratic constitutionalism in Taiwan.

1 See Weng, "Guardians of the Constitution," 2009, pp. 61-63 (in Chinese).

B. The Development of Constitutionalism in Taiwan and the Changing Functions of the Constitutional Court

I. The Backgrounds of Constitutional Developments

The Constitution of the Republic of China (hereinafter "the Constitution") was promulgated on January 1, 1947, and put into effect on December 25 of the same year.[2] After the World War II, the Nationalist Government invited 38 representatives of all parties in Chongqing and held the Political Consultative Conference. In the conference, they agreed upon 12 principles of the draft constitution and established the Constitution Drafting Committee. These representatives were also compromised with the dissenters against the Kuomintang (hereinafter KMT) and reached three agreements. The National Assembly was held on November 15, 1946, in Nanjing and passed the Constitution on December 25 of the same year. Owing to the failed negotiation between KMT and the Chinese Communist Party (CCP), the CCP boycotted the National Assembly and refused to recognize the Constitution. Intense conflicts burst into flame afterwards.[3] Hence, the Republic of China was factually embroiled in a civil war when the Constitution was promulgated. The National Assembly passed the Temporary Provisions Effective During the Period of Communist Rebellion (hereinafter Temporary Provisions) on April 18, 1948 and authorized the President to issue emergency decrees without the constraints of Article 39 and 40 of the Constitution. The enactment of the Temporary Provisions forced the Republic of China into the era of Mobilization for Suppressing the Communist Rebellion.[4] After that, the Nationalist Government retreated from mainland China to Taiwan in December 1949. The President substantively became the highest administrative officer and the presidential powers were enhanced considerably by the promulgation of the Temporary Provision. The National Assembly also expanded its powers and the original intent of the Constitution was gradually ignored, if not totally discarded.

In addition to the Temporary Provisions, the Nationalist Government issued the Martial Law Decree, which was not lifted until July 14, 1987, in

---

2 See Zhonghua Minguo Xianfa (The Constitution of the Republic of China) (1947) (Taiwan), *available at* http://www.judicial.gov.tw/CONSTITUTIONALCOURT/en/p07_2.asp?lawno=36 (last visited Jan. 15, 2011).

3 See Chen, *Constitutional Law*, 1999, pp. 36-46 (in Chinese).

4 See Hsu, *Law and Government Power*, 1999, pp. 405-406 (in Chinese).

accordance with the martial law after the retreat. The martial law period lasted continuously for almost 40 years, which was rare even compared to histories of other nations. The Temporary Provision came into effect from 1949 and was lifted in 1991, and the period of Mobilization for Suppressing the Communist Rebellion lasted for 43 years. During that time, the Taiwanese people could not exercise their fundamental rights enshrined in the Constitution due to the Martial Law Decree and the Mobilization, notwithstanding that the Constitution ostensibly remained in force.

II. Constitutional Interpretations and Justices of the Constitutional Court

1. The Jurisdictions of the Constitutional Court

According to Article 77 of the Constitution,[5] the Judicial Yuan shall be the highest judicial organ of the State and shall be in charge of civil, criminal, and administrative cases, and over cases concerning disciplinary measures against public functionaries. Article 78 and 173 stipulate that the Judicial Yuan shall interpret the Constitution and shall have the power to unify the interpretation of laws and regulations.[6] Article 79, Paragraph 2 prescribes that the Judicial Yuan shall have a number of Grand Justices [hereinafter Justices] to take charge of matters specified in Article 78 of the Constitution, who shall be nominated and, with the consent of the Control Yuan, appointed by the President of the Republic.[7] Article 5, Paragraph 4 of the Additional Articles of the Constitution of the Republic of China prescribes that the Justices shall, in addition to the discharge of their duties in accordance with Article 78 of the Constitution, form a Constitutional Court to adjudicate matters relating to the impeachment of the president or the vice president, and the dissolution of unconstitutional political parties.[8]

5 See Zhonghua Minguo Xianfa, art 77.

6 See Zhonghua Minguo Xianfa, arts 78 & 173.

7 See Zhonghua Minguo Xianfa, art 79, para. 2.

8 The Additional Articles of the Constitution of the Republic of China (*hereafter The Additional Articles*), art 5, para. 4 (2005) (Taiwan).

2. The Qualifications for the Appointment of Justices

Pursuant to Article 4, Paragraph 1 of the Organic Act of the Judicial Yuan[9], to be eligible for appointment as a Justice of the Constitutional Court, a candidate must: 1) have served as a Justice of the Supreme Court for more than ten years with a distinguished record; or 2) have served as a Member of the Legislative Yuan for more than nine years with distinguished contributions; or 3) have been a professor of a major field of law at a university for more than ten years and have authored publications in a specialized field; or 4) have served as a Justice of the International Court, or have had authoritative works published in the fields of public or comparative law; or 5) be a person highly reputed in the field of legal research and have political experience. In addition, the number of Justices qualifying under any single qualification listed above shall not exceed one third of the total number of Justices.

3. The Procedures of the Appointment of Justices

The Justices should be nominated and, with the consent of the Congress, appointed by the President of the Republic. The "Congress" here referred to the Control Yuan at the very beginning and then the National Assembly when members of the Control Yuan were no longer directly elected by popular votes. After 2003, the Legislative Yuan exercised the power of consent. In early days, there were totally 17 Justices who served for a renewable term of nine years. Beginning in 2003, 15 Justices, including the President and the Vice President of the Judicial Yuan selected from amongst them, served for a non-renewable term of eight years,[10] independent of the order by which each Justice was appointed to office.

9 Organic Act of the Judicial Yuan, art 4, para. 1 (Taiwan), *available at* http://www.judicial.gov.tw/constitutionalcourt/p07_2.asp?lawno=81 (in Chinese) (last visited Jan. 16, 2011).

10 Some scholars suggest that the change may lead to more political-biased justices. See Lee, "The Systematic Change of the Justices and the Constitutional Role of Judicial Yuan," 2003, p. 553 (in Chinese).

III. The Revisions of the Procedure Act and Changing Functions of the Constitutional Court

After the implementation of the Constitution, the Judicial Yuan was established on July 1, 1948. The President nominated 17 Justices of the first term in accordance with the Organic Act of the Judicial Yuan. Only twelve of them were consented by the Control Yuan and served as Justices in early August of the same year. They convened formally on September 15 and enacted the Regulations Governing the Adjudication of Grand Justices Council for their handling of cases.

The Constitutional Court, known as the Council of Grand Justices then, promulgated Interpretations No. 1 and No. 2 on January 6, 1949. After the retreat, only two Justices came to Taiwan and the President re-nominated 7 Justices with the consent of the Control Yuan to meet the quorum. On April 5, 1952, the Constitutional Court functioned for the first time in Taiwan and has since issued more than 680 interpretations by the end of 2010.

In respect to changing functions of the Constitutional Court, we can distinguish roughly each stage in pursuant to their terms:

1. Era of Legal Counsel: The First Term (1948~1958, Interpretation No. 1 – No. 79)

During the first term, only national and local government agencies could petition to the Constitutional Court, which was known as the Council of Grand Justices, due to the Regulations Governing the Adjudication of Grand Justices Council. A constitutional interpretation should be made with the concurrence of more than half of the Justices present at the meeting having a quorum of more than half of the total number of the Justices. Since the Constitution was barely promulgated and implemented, the Constitutional Court usually played the role of a legal counsel: They unified different interpretations of laws and regulations by lower courts and provided constitutional interpretations if government agencies had constitutional concerns with various laws and regulations.

2. Era of Functional Decline: The Second and Third Terms (September, 1958~September 1976, Interpretation No. 80 – No. 146)

Interpretation No. 76[11], made by the Justices of the first term, declared that the National Assembly, the Legislative Yuan, and the Control Yuan should all be considered en masse as equivalent to parliaments of other democratic nations. The Legislative Yuan was irritated by this Interpretation and enacted the Grand Justices Council Adjudication Act which noticeably limited the function of the Justices. The Act stipulated that a constitutional interpretation should be made with the concurrence of three quarters of the Justices present at the meeting having a quorum of three quarters of the total number of the Justices. The function of the Constitutional Court was, thus, profoundly affected and went gradually in decline. Nevertheless, the Act had three merits worthy of mentioning: 1) the separation of reasoning of the interpretation from its holding; and 2) allowing individuals to petition to the Council; and 3) the permission of issuing dissenting opinions. However, during this period, the Constitutional Court rendered only one case filed by individuals.[12]

3. The Beginning of Protecting Human Rights: The Fourth Term (October, 1977~ September, 1985, Interpretation No. 147 – No. 199)

Beginning with the fourth term, the Constitutional Court emphasized the protection of human rights instead of solving legal or institutional disputes between government agencies, which was a cardinal and correct shift. As aforementioned, Justices of the second and the third terms adjudicated only one case appealed by individuals. During the fourth term, more than half of the interpretations that Justices made were appealed by individuals.[13]

In the past, the effect of interpretations made by the Constitutional Court was not clearly prescribed. However Interpretation No. 177 declared that "[a]n Interpretation given by this Yuan in response to a petition shall also

---

11 Judicial Yuan Interpretation *(hereafter J.Y. Interpretation)* No. 76, *available at* http://www.judicial.gov.tw/CONSTITUTIONALCOURT/en/p03_01.asp?expno=76 (last visited Jan. 16, 2011).

12 See Weng, "Die Verfassungskontrolle durch richterliche Fortbildung," 2004, pp. 1224-1226.

13 See Chang, "The Role of Judicial Review in Consolidating Democracies," 2005, p. 79.

be applicable with respect to the legal action of the petitioner, for which the original petition was made."[14] Thus the interpretations made by the Constitutional Court have a retrospective effect insofar as the petitioned case is concerned. In addition, Interpretation No. 185 confirmed that "[t]he interpretations of the Judicial Yuan shall be binding to every institution and person in the country... the party against whom such final and irrevocable judgment is entered shall be entitled to file for a retrial or an extraordinary appeal on the basis of said interpretation."[15] Moreover, the Constitutional Court began to review the constitutionality of precedents and expanded the meaning of administrative actions (also known as administrative disposition), making it easier for individuals to file administrative litigation against government agencies.[16] The Constitutional Court also fired the first shot to the theory of "special power relationship *(Das besondere Gewaltverhältnis)*" in Interpretation No.187 by permitting a civil servant to file administrative litigation against the government.[17]

4. Era of Democratic Transition: The Fifth Term (October, 1985~ September, 1994, Interpretation No. 200 – No. 366)

During the fifth term, the Martial Law Decree was lifted on July 14, 1987. The Temporary Provisions and the period of Mobilization for Suppressing the Communist Rebellion were also terminated on May 1, 1991. The national representatives of the first term ceased to exercise their power on December 31, 1991, and the second-term election of national representatives was held. The Grand Justices Council Adjudication Act was revised as Constitutional Interpretation Procedure Act on February 3, 1993.[18] Several progresses merit discussions here. First, the requirements for petitions to the Constitutional

---

14 J.Y. Interpretation No. 177, *available at* httpww://w.judicial.gov.tw/CONSTITUTIONALCOURT/en/p03_01.asp?expno=177 (last visited Jan. 16, 2011).

15 J.Y. Interpretation No. 185, *available at* http://www.judicial.gov.tw/CONSTITUTIONALCOURT/en/p03_01.asp?expno=185 (last visited Jan. 16, 2011).

16 See Weng, "Research on Recent Interpretations of the Council of Grand Justices, Judicial Yuan," 2009, p. 387 (in Chinese).

17 Judicial Yuan Interpretation No. 187, *available at* http://www.judicial.gov.tw/CONSTITUTIONALCOURT/en/p03_01.asp?expno=187 (last visited Jan. 16, 2011).

18 Constitutional Interpretation Procedure Act (1993) (Taiwan), *available at* http://www.judicial.gov.tw/CONSTITUTIONALCOURT/en/p07_2.asp?lawno=73 (last visited Jan. 16, 2011).

Court were loosened; one-third of the Legislators or more, the Supreme Court or the Supreme Administrative Court may petition the Constitutional Court to interpret the Constitution. Second, the Constitutional Court was established to adjudicate cases concerning the dissolution of a political party. Third, it requires a majority of two-thirds of the Justices present at a session having a quorum of two-thirds of total number of the Justices for passing an interpretation of the Constitution. Fourth, in addition to dissenting opinions, Justices were entitled to issue concurring opinions. Fifth, on petitioner's motion, or sua sponte, the Justices may order the petitioners, the pertinent parties or agencies to brief – in written or orally – to the Justices. The Justices may also conduct its own investigation. Oral arguments may be held in an open court when necessary. Last but not the least, in its interpretations, the Constitutional Court may designate an agency to execute the judgment and specify the means for execution.

With the emphasis on the protection of human rights, the Constitutional Court now plainly invalidated unconstitutional laws. Many constitutional disputes were solved, including but not limited to the reelection of national representatives (Interpretation No. 261),[19] the constitutionality of budgetary augmentation (Interpretation No. 264),[20] the limit of the investigative power of the Legislative Yuan (Interpretation No. 325),[21] and the independence of the Auditor-General (Interpretation No. 357).[22]

The Justices of the fifth term were in session three times per week and made 167 interpretations during their term of nine years. It was a highly valuable performance under the strict three-quarters voting quorum.

5. Era of Full-fledged Functions: The Sixth Term (October, 1994~ September, 2003, Interpretation No. 367 – No. 566)

Beginning with the sixth term, the nomination of the Justice no longer took their respective provincial origins into account. The revision of the Consti-

---

19 J.Y. Interpretation No. 261, *available at* http://www.judicial.gov.tw/CONSTITUTIONALCOURT/en/p03_01.asp?expno=261 (last visited Jan. 16, 2011).

20 J.Y. Interpretation No. 264, *available at* http://www.judicial.gov.tw/CONSTITUTIONALCOURT/en/p03_01.asp?expno=264 (last visited Jan. 16, 2011).

21 J.Y. Interpretation No. 325, *available at* http://www.judicial.gov.tw/CONSTITUTIONALCOURT/en/p03_01.asp?expno=325 (last visited Jan. 16, 2011).

22 J.Y. Interpretation No. 357, *available at* http://www.judicial.gov.tw/CONSTITUTIONALCOURT/en/p03_01.asp?expno=357 (last visited Jan. 16, 2011).

tutional Interpretation Procedure Act contributed to the full-fledged functions of the Constitutional Court. During the nine years, the Constitutional Court made 200 interpretations which included some cardinal interpretations that protected the human rights. To name a few, the Gangster Prevention Act was declared unconstitutional twice (Interpretation Nos. 384 & 523).[23] The power to detain was transferred to judges from prosecutors in Interpretation No. 392.[24] In respect to equal protection, Interpretation No. 410 declared that marital property regulations stipulated in the Civil Code violated the gender equality.[25] Interpretation No. 452 struck down Article 1002 of the Civil Code regulating a wife's domicile on the same reason.[26] As to the right of instituting legal proceedings, Interpretation Nos. 224, 321 and 434 declared that Article 23 of the Customs Act was unconstitutional since it deprived a taxpayer, who failed to make full payment of the customs duties, of the opportunity in seeking administrative remedy.[27] In Interpretation No. 462, a faculty member who was dissatisfied with his evaluation committee's decision over his career advancement should be entitled to bring an administrative appeal and later an administrative litigation to challenge the decision. In addition, there were many other interpretations that protected the freedom of teaching, freedom of religious belief, and freedom of assembly and association.

In respect to the rule of law and separation of powers, Interpretation No. 436 declared that a defendant sentenced by the military tribunal should be

23 J.Y. Interpretation No. 384, *available at* http://www.judicial.gov.tw/CONSTITUTIONALCOURT/en/p03_01.asp?expno=384 (last visited Jan. 16, 2011); J.Y. Interpretation No. 523, *available at* http://www.judicial.gov.tw/CONSTITUTIONALCOURT/en/p03_01.asp?expno=523 (last visited Jan. 16, 2011).

24 J.Y. Interpretation No. 392, *available at* http://www.judicial.gov.tw/CONSTITUTIONALCOURT/en/p03_01.asp?expno=392 (last visited Jan. 16, 2011).

25 J.Y. Interpretation No. 410, *available at* http://www.judicial.gov.tw/CONSTITUTIONALCOURT/en/p03_01.asp?expno=410 (last visited Jan. 16, 2011).

26 J.Y. Interpretation No. 452, *available at* http://www.judicial.gov.tw/CONSTITUTIONALCOURT/en/p03_01.asp?expno=452 (last visited Jan. 16, 2011).

27 J.Y. Interpretation No. 224, *available at* http://www.judicial.gov.tw/CONSTITUTIONALCOURT/en/p03_01.asp?expno=224 (last visited Jan. 16, 2011); J.Y. Interpretation No.321, *available at* http://www.judicial.gov.tw/CONSTITUTIONALCOURT/en/p03_01.asp?expno=321 (last visited Jan. 16, 2011); J.Y. Interpretation No.434, *available at* http://www.judicial.gov.tw/CONSTITUTIONALCOURT/en/p03_01.asp?expno=434 (last visited Jan. 16, 2011).

permitted to appeal directly to a civilian regular court.[28] Interpretation No. 371 articulated that in trying a case where a judge, with reasonable assurance, had suspected that the statute applicable to the case was unconstitutional, he or she should be allowed to petition for interpretation of its constitutionality (concrete review).[29] Moreover, the constitutional amendments were under judicial review in Interpretation No.499.[30] After this Interpretation, the National Assembly was abolished and constitutional amendments would be sanctioned by electors from then on. As a general assessment, the interpretations made during the sixth term were better in term of quality and the reasoning was much more elaborative.

6. Era of Stable Development: Beginning October, 2003, Interpretation No. 567 to date

In 2003, an important aspect of reforms for the Constitutional Court was put into place. Among the justices nominated by the President in the year of 2003, eight members served for four years, while seven others served a term of eight years to facilitate subsequent staggered terms of Justices, each having a nonrenewable term of eight years. The Justices serving as President and Vice President of the Judicial Yuan however do not enjoy the guarantee of an eight-year tenure. Since 2003, the Constitutional Court has 15 justices, and the President and the Vice President of the Judicial Yuan shall be selected from amongst them.[31]

The following three characteristics must be noted for the practice by the Constitutional Court in the past 7 years. First, the holding was shorter while the reasoning was longer.[32] Second, the number of concurring and dissenting opinions and the number of words in each opinion increased multiply. Thirdly, there were respectively 6 Justices with American academic back-

28 J.Y. Interpretation No.436, *available at* http://www.judicial.gov.tw/CONSTITUTIONALCOURT/en/p03_01.asp?expno=436 (last visited Jan. 16, 2011).

29 J.Y. Interpretation No.371, *available at* http://www.judicial.gov.tw/CONSTITUTIONALCOURT/en/p03_01.asp?expno=371 (last visited Jan. 16, 2011).

30 J.Y. Interpretation No.499, *available at* http://www.judicial.gov.tw/CONSTITUTIONALCOURT/en/p03_01.asp?expno=499 (last visited Jan. 16, 2011).

31 See Weng, *Auf dem Weg zu einer ausgereiften Verfassungsgerichtsbarkeit*, 2007, pp. 1061 et seq.

32 See Lee, "The Preventive Proceeding in Judicial Review II," 2007, p. 114 (in Chinese).

ground and 7 Justices with German academic background. The influence of Anglo-American jurisprudence was in gradual increase. Currently, 7 Justices obtained their Ph.D. degree in Germany and 2 Justices who obtained their Ph.D. degree in Taiwan had spent one or two years for study in Germany. Not surprisingly, therefore, the arguments elaborated by the Federal Constitutional Court of Germany (Bundesverfassungsgericht) and the European Court of Human Rights have had some significant influence upon the Constitutional Court and their interpretations.

C. The Influences of Interpretations upon Democratic Politics in Taiwan

There were three waves of constitutional transition that had momentous impact on democratic politics in Taiwan. The Constitutional Court played an essential role in these three waves of transformation.

I. Interpretation Nos. 31 and 85

The first constitutional issue after the retreat was to make the Constitution designed for mainland China suitable to apply to Taiwan. No constitutional revision by the National Assembly was available at that time. The only way to make this happen was by judicial interpretations. Accordingly, the Constitutional Court, which was known as the Council of Grand Justices, made Interpretation No. 31 on January 29, 1954, and contended that all of the first-term members of both the Legislative and Control Yuan should continue to exercise their respective powers since the state had undergone a severe calamity that made re-election of the second term of both Yuan de facto impossible.[33]

For the same reason, the Constitutional Court made Interpretation No. 85 on February 12, 1960, and argued that under the circumstances, the "total number of National Assembly Delegates" as provided for in the Constitution should be calculated based on the number of those delegates who were

33 J.Y. Interpretation No.31, *available at* http://www.judicial.gov.tw/CONSTITUTIONALCOURT/en/p03_01.asp?expno=31 (last visited Jan. 16, 2011).

elected in accordance with the laws and were still able to convene. Only by this could it exercise its powers in Taiwan.[34]

The extension of the term, though tolerable in extraordinary situations, such as wartime, should not be prolonged indefinitely. Interpretation No. 31 permitted the first-term members to exercise their powers continually and resulted consequently in a constitutional crisis which might not be anticipated by the Constitutional Court.

II. Interpretation No. 261

1. The Background and the Content

This Interpretation contributed to the termination of the first-term national representatives and gave birth to the second-term election. In 1980 s, the economy developed miraculously and the national income multiplied in Taiwan. People became conscious of their rights and could not tolerate the extension of the first-term representatives any longer after the repeal of the martial law on July 14, 1987. The Legislative Yuan, by resolution of its plenary session which was proposed by 26 legislators, petitioned to the Constitutional Court. The Constitutional Court made Interpretation 261 on June 21, 1990, contending that:[35] first, the regular election of representatives was the only approach to entrench the democratic constitutionalism, and second, Interpretation No. 31 did not intend to permit the indefinite exercise of powers by those first-term national representatives who were not reelected periodically; third, since 1969, the national government had held regular elections of the national representatives to reinforce our national representative bodies incrementally; fourth, the first-term representatives who had not been reelected on a periodical basis should cease exercising their powers no later than December 31, 1991; and finally, the national government was mandated to hold, in due course, a nationwide second-term election of the national representatives, in accordance with the spirit of the Constitution, the essence of this Interpretation and the relevant regulations, so that democratic constitutionalism would be put in place properly.

34 J.Y. Interpretation No.85, *available at* http://www.judicial.gov.tw/CONSTITUTIONALCOURT/en/p03_01.asp?expno=85 (last visited Jan. 16, 2011).

35 J.Y. Interpretation No.261, *available at* http://www.judicial.gov.tw/CONSTITUTIONALCOURT/en/p03_01.asp?expno=261 (last visited Jan. 16, 2011).

2. The Analysis

After the revocation of the martial law, Taiwanese people were dissatisfied with the extension of the first-term representatives and demonstrated their anger publicly. Interpretation No. 261 articulated that regular elections were the foundation of democratic constitutionalism and the national government had indeed held regular elections for supplementary or additional seats in the national representatives. There was no reason, theoretical or practical, to prolong the term of the representatives. This Interpretation was pivotal since it alleviated the political conflict and tension resulting from the indefinite extension of terms for national representatives.

Although Justice Chih-Peng Lee issued his dissenting opinion, he still agreed that the first-term representatives should cease exercising their powers as soon as possible. His dissenting opinion argued that the government should enact the Election and Recall Act first in order to hold the second-term election of the national representatives. The first-term representatives should not cease to exercise their power until the second-term representatives to be elected.[36] On the other hand, the majority opinion maintained that the first-term representatives had exercised the power for more than 40 years and should cease exercising their powers before the end of 1991. This void-with-deadline ruling was rendered for the first time by the fifth term of Justices.

When nominating the Justices of the fifth term, the "provincial origin" was still a factor that needed to be taken into consideration. A four-fifths of the Justices of the Constitutional Court, like the first-term national representatives who had to be replaced, came from mainland China. However, when interpreting the Constitution, the Justices rationally and disinterestedly made a fair interpretation without taking this political affinity into account. It was indeed a merit worthy of our praise.

3. The Impact

Interpretation No. 261 solved the constitutional dispute of the first-term national representatives and led to the termination of the Mobilization for Suppressing the Communist Rebellion, a watershed development in the process

36 J.Y. Interpretation No.261 (Lee, J., dissenting) (in Chinese).

of constitutional reforms in Taiwan. Without this Interpretation, it was impossible for the National Assembly to voluntarily abolish the Temporary Provisions or amend the Constitution. After Interpretation No. 261, the National Assembly passed the Additional Articles of the Constitution of Republic of China and abolished the Temporary Provisions. President Teng-hui Lee declared the termination of the forty-year Mobilization era on May 1, 1991, which was another major step towards the development of constitutionalism in Taiwan.

In addition, Interpretation No. 261 reviewed the constitutionality of the Article 6, Paragraph 2 of the Temporary Provisions and declared it unconstitutional regardless of its constitutional status. It was the first precedent that provisions with constitutional status were subject to judicial review.

III. Interpretation No. 499

1. The Background and the Content

The National Assembly was mainly in charge of the election of the president and the vice president, and amendments of the Constitution. After the implementation of the Constitution, the National Assembly gradually expanded its own powers since it monopolized the power to revise the Constitution. Its expansion became another constitutional crisis that needed to be carefully addressed.

On September 3, 1999, the National Assembly passed anonymously a constitutional amendment that prolonged the tenure of the National Assembly itself and the fourth-term legislators. This amendment immediately resulted in a constitutional controversy and opposition to the amendment voiced out. Some legislators petition the Constitutional Court and the Justices made Interpretation No. 499, elaborating the following:[37] First, the Constitution not only provided Articles 78 and 79 in Chapter 7, but also preserved the language "[t]he Constitution shall be interpreted by the judicial Yuan" as Article 173 in Chapter 14, “Implementation and Amendment of the Constitution.” Thus, it is clear that Article 173 was not designed only for general interpretation of the Constitution or unifying the meaning of laws, but it was also to entail the power of the Constitutional Court to cover any

37 J.Y. Interpretation No.499, *available at* http://www.judicial.gov.tw/CONSTITUTIONALCOURT/en/p03_01.asp?expno=499 (last visited Jan. 16, 2011).

issues or doubts on the implementation and amendment of the Constitution. Second, because the process of amending the Constitution is the most direct action that reflects and realizes sovereignty, it must be conducted openly and transparently in order to satisfy the condition of rational communication and, hence, lay the proper foundation for a constitutional state. Third, among the constitutional provisions, principles such as establishing a democratic republic under Article 1, sovereignty of and by the people under Article 2, protection of the fundamental rights of the people under Chapter 2 as well as checks and balances of government powers are some of the most critical and fundamental tenets of the Constitution as a whole. The democratic constitutional process derived from these principles forms the foundation for the existence of the current Constitution and all [government] bodies installed hereunder must abide by this process.

Fourth, both provisions at issue allocated the seats of delegates by relying upon the election result of the Legislative Yuan and the votes received by independent candidates or candidates recommended by respective political parties. Unlike representation by majority or minority, proportional representation based the allocation of delegate seats upon the share of votes received by a certain political party or candidate, and, therefore, violated the constitutional order of democracy. Fifth, the self-granted term extension for National Assembly delegates further violates the principle of disqualification in light of conflict of interests, and is not in conformity with the freedom and democratic state of constitutional rule of law. Last but not the least, the anonymous balloting by which the Third National Assembly adopted to vote on the proposed amendments to Articles 1, 4, 9 and 10 of the Amendment to the Constitution in its 4th Session, 18th Conference on September 4, 1999, violated the principle of openness and transparency and the then-applicable Article 38, Paragraph 2, of the Regulations of the National Assembly Proceedings. The process was clearly and grossly flawed and in violation of the fundamental principles based upon which the provisions of the Constitution would take effect. The aforementioned Articles 1, 4, 9, and 10 should immediately become null and void as of the date this Interpretation was announced, and the text of the Amendment to the Constitution promulgated on July 21, 1997, continued to be effective.

2. The Analysis

a) Procedural Analysis

Interpretation No. 499 averred that the amendment violated the Article 174 of the Constitution as well as the Regulations of the National Assembly Proceedings. However, Article 174, paragraph 1 stipulated that "Upon the proposal of one-fifth of the total number of delegates to the National Assembly and by a resolution of three-fourths of the delegates present at a meeting having a quorum of two-thirds of the entire Assembly, the Constitution may be amended." None of these was literally violated. The violation of Regulations of the National Assembly Proceedings could not be labeled as major constitutional flaw since it was in the realm of what was jurisprudentially called self-regulation or parliamentary autonomy. Anonymous balloting per se was not unconstitutional. "Open balloting" is neither the only way to supervise members of the National Assembly nor a universal principle around the globe when amending constitutional laws.[38] In other words, the existence of procedural flaws in this case would not necessarily render the unconstitutional declaration. And this was also known by the Justices, and that was why they continued to review this case into its substantial violation of the Constitution.

b) Substantive Analysis

Scholars have been debating if there is any limit to constitutional revision and if there is any difference between constitutional revision and constitutional making.[39] In Interpretation No. 499, Justices of the Constitutional Court were deeply influenced by Article 79, Paragraph 3 of the German Basic Law (Grundgesetz) and believed that there was a limit to constitutional revision.[40] It is inadmissible to "alter the existing constitutional provisions concerning the fundamental nature of governing norms and order and, hence, the foundation of the Constitution's very existence destroys the integrity and

---

38 J.Y. Interpretation No.499 (Chen, J., dissenting) (in Chinese); see Lee, "The Anatomy of the 1999 Constitutional Amendments," 2000, pp. 493-533 (in Chinese).

39 See Lin et al., *Constitutional Law*, 2008, pp. 570-76 (in Chinese).

40 Grundgesetz für die Bundesrepublik Deutschland, May 23, 1949, BGBI. I (in German).

fabric of the Constitution itself."[41] This interpretation was beneficial to the entrenchment of human rights and conformed to the development of modern constitutional theories after World War II.[42]

3. The Impact

The National Assembly was frustrated by Interpretation No. 499 and held the sixth conference for constitutional amendments on April 8, 2000. During the conference, the National Assembly was replaced with the mission-oriented National Assembly, and most of its power and authorities were transferred to the Legislative Yuan. It was stipulated that the mission-oriented National Assembly would be composed by three hundred members appointed from among different political parties and proportioned in accordance with the ratio of votes received by each such political party and independent candidates in the election for members of the Legislative Yuan. The power to ratify bills of constitutional amendments proposed by the Legislative Yuan was still retained by the National Assembly. In addition, as a revengeful response to Interpretation No. 499, it added Article 5, Paragraph 1 to the Additional Articles of the Constitution of the Republic of China, which regulated that "the provisions of Article 81 of the Constitution and pertinent regulations on the lifetime holding of office and payment of salary should not apply to justices of the Constitutional Court who were not transferred from the post of a judge."

On June 7, 2005, the Constitution underwent its seventh revision. The emphasis was placed at the reform of the Congress. The mission-oriented National Assembly was nullified thoroughly and "amendment of the Constitution shall be initiated upon the proposal of one-fourth of the total members of the Legislative Yuan, passed by at least three-fourths of the members present at a meeting attended by at least three-fourths of the total members of the Legislative Yuan, and sanctioned by electors in the free area of the Republic of China at a referendum held upon expiration of a six-month period of public announcement of the proposal, wherein the number of valid votes in favor exceeds one-half of the total number of electors."[43] The de-

41 J.Y. Interpretation No.499.

42 See Wu, *The Interpretation and Application of the Constitution*, 2003, pp. 572-76 (in Chinese).

43 The Additional Articles, art. 12.

velopment of constitutionalism in Taiwan has entered a new stage and the task that Justices faced with will be even more challenging than before.

D. The Influences of Interpretations upon the Rule of Law in Taiwan

I. The Protection of Human Rights

No matter there are three or five powers, judicial power has always been the least dangerous. After World War II, the protection of human rights has become a universal value. The first and foremost duty of the judiciary in modern rule of law countries is to protect human rights.

The changing functions of the Constitutional Court have been discussed above. Before the annulment of the Martial Law Decree, the jurisdiction of the Justices was strictly constrained. During that era, Justices rendered interpretations regarding the protection of personal freedom (Interpretation No. 166) and the right of instituting legal proceeding (Interpretation Nos. 89, 115, 128, 156, 177, 185, and 187). After the annulment, cases concerning the protection of human rights became the major part of the Court's docket. In addition to equal protection, enumerated rights or liberties were gradually indicated and entrenched in interpretations, such as personal freedom (Interpretation Nos. 384, 392, 523, 535, 588, and 636), freedom of speech and freedom of express (Interpretation Nos. 407, 417, 445, and 509), freedom of residence and of change of residence (Interpretation Nos. 454, 497, 517, and 535), freedom of teaching (Interpretation Nos. 380 & 450), freedom of religious belief (Interpretation Nos. 460 & 490), freedom of assembly and association (Interpretation Nos. 303, 445, and 479), right of property (Interpretation Nos. 400, 437, 440, and 516), principle of taxation by law (Interpretation Nos. 367, 397, 420, 458, 508, and 515), right to work (Interpretation Nos. 373, 411,456, and 514), and right of instituting legal proceeding (Interpretation Nos. 416, 418, and 442). Furthermore, rights not clearly enumerated in the Constitution were protected as well, including but not restricted to freedom of marriage (Interpretation No. 242), privacy (Interpretation Nos. 393, 509, 535, 585, and 603), and human dignity (Interpretation Nos. 372, 490, 550, 567, and 603). The following briefly discusses major doctrines or principles that Justices used to strike down statutes or regulations that infringed human rights.

1. Principle of Constitutional Reservation (Verfassungsvorbehalt)

Article 8 of the Constitution articulates the protection of personal freedom thoroughly by stipulating "except in case of flagrante delicto as provided by law, no person shall be arrested or detained otherwise than by a judicial or a police organ in accordance with the procedure prescribed by law. No person shall be tried or punished otherwise than by a law court in accordance with the procedure prescribed by law. Any arrest, detention, trial, or punishment which is not in accordance with the procedure prescribed by law may be resisted. When a person is arrested or detained on suspicion of having committed a crime, the organ making the arrest or detention shall in writing inform the said person, and his designated relative or friend, of the grounds for his arrest or detention, and shall, within 24 hours, turn him over to a competent court for trial. The said person, or any other person, may petition the competent court that a writ be served within 24 hours on the organ making the arrest for the surrender of the said person for trial."[44]

This article discloses many constitutional principles including non-delegation doctrine, due process of law, and judicial reservation. The judicial reservation and the 24-hour limit fall in the realm of constitutional reservation, which means that it is unalterable except by a constitutional amendment. Due to this provision, the Constitutional Court declared that the Act Governing the Punishment of Police Offences unconstitutional in Interpretation Nos. 166 and 251. In addition, the Justices also declared that the detention power should be vested exclusively to the judges, but not the prosecutors in Interpretation No. 392.

2. Non-Delegation Doctrine (Vorbehalt des Gesetzes/Gesetzesvorbehalt)

Non-delegation doctrine is the basic principle of rule of law, which requires that a government cannot limit any person's rights without a statute enacted by legislature. Article 23 of the Constitution stipulates that "All the freedoms and rights enumerated in the preceding Articles shall not be restricted by law except such as may be necessary to prevent infringement upon the freedoms of other persons, to avert an imminent crisis, to maintain social order or to

44 Zhonghua Minguo Xianfa, art 8.

advance public welfare."[45] Article 5 of the Central Regulation Standard Act enumerates the objects that shall be stipulated by a statute.

However, the statute may authorize a government to limit individual freedoms or rights by enacting administrative regulations. In the reasoning of the Interpretation No. 443, the Constitutional Court elaborated that "the determination of which freedom or right shall be regulated by law or by rules authorized by the law shall depend on regulated intensity. Reasonable deviation is allowed considering the party to be regulated, the content of the regulation, or the limitations to be made on the interests or freedom. For instance, depriving people's lives or limiting their physical freedom shall be in compliance with the principle of definitiveness of crime and punishment and stipulated by law; limitations concerning people's other freedoms shall also be stipulated by law, in the case where there is authorization by the law to the administrative institutions to make supplemental rules, the authorization shall be specific and precise. The competent authority, on the ground that such limitations shall not be inconvenient for the people, may make only those limitations concerning details and technical matters of law enforcement. For policies concerning benefits to the people, the law governing such policies may be constructed more loosely compared to laws governing limitations on people's rights. Nevertheless, in the case where such policies are related to major public interests, they shall be made by law or rules authorized by law."[46]

3. Principle of Proportionality (Verhältnismäßigkeitsprinzip)

The principle of proportionality can be further divided into three sub-principles which are prescribed in Article 7 of the Administrative Procedure Act: first, the method adopted must be helpful to the achievement of the objectives; second, where there are several alternative methods which will lead to the same result in achievement of the objectives, the one with the least harm to the rights and interest of the people shall be adopted; and finally, the harm that may be caused by the method to be adopted shall not be clearly out of balance against the interest of the objectives anticipated to be

---

45 Zhonghua Minguo Xianfa, art 23.

46 J.Y. Interpretation No.443, *available at* http://www.judicial.gov.tw/CONSTITUTIONALCOURT/en/p03_01.asp?expno=443 (last visited Jan. 16, 2011).

achieved.[47] In the past fourteen years, the principle of proportionality became the most frequently cited criterion by the Constitutional Court in judging if a statute or regulation was unconstitutional.

4. Due Process of Law

Article 8 of the Constitution originates from the concept of "due process of law" embedded in the Anglo-American jurisprudence. In Interpretation No. 384, the Justices articulated that "the contents of the law must be proper in substance…The above substantive due process of law covers substantive law as well as procedural law. In substantive law, it must comply with the principle of legality. In procedural law, examples are as follows: except in the case of flagrante delicto, the arrest of a suspect shall follow necessary judicial process; the accused's confession shall be voluntary; a conviction shall be based upon evidence; no person shall be subject to punishment for the same offence twice; the parties have the right to confront and cross-examine their witnesses; the separation of the judiciary and prosecution; trials shall be public in principle; and the right to appeal the lower court's decision. Unless in the permissible exception that martial law is declared in accordance with the law, or when the state or the people are in a state of emergency, all statutory provisions are deemed to contradict the substantive due process of law if they are inconsistent with the above said principles."[48] In accordance with Article 8 of the Constitution, the Constitutional Court declared the Act for Eliminating Hoodlums partly unconstitutional because it violated substantive due process of law (Interpretation Nos. 384, 523, and 636). The Act for Eliminating Hoodlums was finally repealed on January 21, 2009.

In addition, the Constitutional Court also elaborated in many interpretations that all constraints upon fundamental rights and freedoms should be subject to review in accordance with due process of law (for example, Interpretation Nos. 418, 436, 446, 488, 491, 523, 574, 582, 585, 610, 631, 636, 639, and 653).

---

47 Administrative Procedure Act, art. 7 (Taiwan), *available at* http://law.moj.gov.tw/Eng/LawClass/LawAll.aspx?PCode=A0030055.

48 J.Y. Interpretation No.384, *available at* http://www.judicial.gov.tw/CONSTITUTIONALCOURT/en/p03_01.asp?expno=384 (last visited Jan. 16, 2011).

5. Principle of Reliance Protection/Principle of Legitimate Expectation (Vertrauenschutzprinzip)

Rule of law is one of the prime principles in constitutional law. A constitutional state emphasizes primarily on the protection of human rights, the stability of legal order, and the principle of reliance protection. People believe what the government does is legal and effective and the government must in turn protect this belief. This is the legal foundation for the principle of reliance protection. In Interpretation No. 362, the Constitutional Court articulated that "where a person's first marriage is dissolved by a final court decision, and a third party, in good faith and without negligence, trusting in the validity of such final court decision, enters into marriage with a party of the previous marriage, and subsequently such final and binding judgments reversed, the latter marriage (between that person and the third party), thus becomes bigamous. This situation differs from general bigamy, and thus, according to the principle of legitimate expectation, the validity of the latter marriage should be maintained."[49]

Furthermore, Article 8 of the Administrative Procedure Act, which was implemented on January 1, 2000, prescribes that "all administrative acts shall be performed in good faith and shall be aimed at the protection of the legitimate and reasonable reliance of the people." Chapter II of the Act also specifies the circumstances under which a beneficiary deserves or loses the protection of reliance when an administrative disposition is withdrawn or annulled. Moreover, the Constitutional Court elaborated that the principle of reliance protection should be applicable when a law was revoked or revised. In Interpretation No. 525, the Constitutional Court argued that "once an administrative ordinance is proclaimed effective, the authority responsible for drafting or proclaiming such regulation shall protect the legitimate expectations of subjects affected by the regulation when seeking to amend or abolish such regulation pursuant to legal procedures. So unless the regulation has a predetermined period for application or there is a change of circumstance which leads to its ineffectiveness, in which instance there is no legitimate expectation, authorities seeking to abolish or amend the regulation for public interest, to the effect that such action abridges the privileges of those who had a legitimate expectation of enjoying these privileges, shall

---

49 J.Y. Interpretation No.362, *available at* http://www.judicial.gov.tw/CONSTITUTIONALCOURT/en/p03_01.asp?expno=362 (last visited Jan. 16, 2011).

provide reasonable measures of remediation or transition period clauses with a view to minimize loss, thus complying with the Constitution's objective to protect the people's rights."[50]

After that, the principle of reliance protection has become one of the cardinal principle in the protection of constitutional rights. It has been continuously emphasized in other interpretations, such as Interpretation Nos. 529, 547, 574, 577, 580, 589, 605, 620, 629, among others.

II. Separation of Powers

During the authoritarian regime, the Constitutional Court, known as the Council of Grand Justices then, made interpretations elaborating the equal status of the five powers in the Constitution and that each Yuan should have the power to propose and present statutory bills in Interpretation Nos. 3 and 175.[51] At the time, the Constitutional Court emphasized little, if any, on checks and balances between the powers. After the democratization, the Constitutional Court began to stress checks and balances among the powers. In Interpretation No. 264, the Constitutional Court asked the Legislative Yuan to fulfill its role of supervising government finance. In Interpretation No. 391 when the Legislative Yuan would add, delete or adjust the amount of individual items within each or among different government agencies without changing the total amount of the general budget, the Justices said "it involves the revision and adjustment of the contents of policy implementation and planning, which can easily result in the successfulness or failure of a policy being unaccounted for, and politics of accountability being difficult to establish, hence violating the separation of Executive and Legislative power and the principle of checks and balances, which shall not be permitted by the Constitution."[52] From then on, we may conclude that the Justices no longer resisted interpreting the separation of powers from the perspective of checks and balances.

---

50 J.Y. Interpretation No.525, *available at* http://www.judicial.gov.tw/CONSTITUTIONALCOURT/en/p03_01.asp?expno=525 (last visited Jan. 16, 2011).

51 J.Y. Interpretation No. 3, *available at* http://www.judicial.gov.tw/CONSTITUTIONALCOURT/en/p03_01.asp?expno=3 (last visited Jan. 16, 2011); J.Y. Interpretation No. 175, *available at* http://www.judicial.gov.tw/CONSTITUTIONALCOURT/en/p03_01.asp?expno=175 (last visited Jan. 16, 2011).

52 J.Y. Interpretation No. 391, *available at* http://www.judicial.gov.tw/CONSTITUTIONALCOURT/en/p03_01.asp?expno=391 (last visited Jan. 16, 2011).

There are plenty of interpretations with regard to separation of powers and some are much more eye-catching than others, such as:

(1) Interpretation No. 342 (April 8, 1994)
The Constitutional Court argued that "whether the review of the bills of act that are submitted by the Legislative Yuan to the President for promulgation follows the review procedures shall not be subject to scrutiny by the authority responsible for interpretation of the Constitution unless it is in clear contravention to the Constitution since it is an internal matter which falls within the scope set by the Legislative Yuan by virtue of the principle of parliamentary autonomy."[53]

(2) Interpretation No. 387 (Oct. 13, 1995)
The Constitutional Court reasoned that "since the premier has to receive consent from and be politically accountable to the Legislative Yuan, the premier has to resign before the first session of each new Legislative Yuan so as to fulfill the doctrine of government by the people and his/her political accountability."[54]

(3) Interpretation No. 419 (Dec. 31, 1996)
The Constitutional Court ruled that "while the nature of the duties of the two offices is not apparently incompatible, in case the office of the President should become vacant or the President is incapable of carrying out his/her duties, the situation [of the same individual holding two offices] will affect the very design of power acting or succession under the Constitution, hence it will not be completely in conformity with the Constitution's objective of having separate individuals assume the duties of the offices of Vice President and Premier, respectively."[55]

(4) Interpretation No. 461 (July 24, 1998)
The Constitutional Court interpreted that "the Chief of the General Staff, who is the chief staff member for, and reports directly to the Minister of National Defense in the administrative system, is not a head of ministry under the Constitution." Therefore, he did not have the duty to present

---

53 J.Y. Interpretation No. 342, *available at* http://www.judicial.gov.tw/CONSTITUTIONALCOURT/en/p03_01.asp?expno=342 (last visited Jan. 16, 2011).

54 J.Y. Interpretation No. 387, *available at* http://www.judicial.gov.tw/CONSTITUTIONALCOURT/en/p03_01.asp?expno=387 (last visited Jan. 16, 2011).

55 J.Y. Interpretation No. 419, *available at* http://www.judicial.gov.tw/CONSTITUTIONALCOURT/en/p03_01.asp?expno=419 (last visited Jan. 16, 2011).

to the Legislative Yuan a statement on its administrative policies and a report on its administration.[56]

(5) Interpretation No. 520 (Jan. 15, 2001)
The Constitutional Court decided that "in light of its effect on energy reserves, the environment, and related industries … the present statutory budget item that the Executive Yuan meeting resolved to withhold is indeed a change of a critical national policy that the … Having received the above report from the Executive Yuan, the Legislative Yuan is obligated to listen [to it]. ... It should also be pointed out that if the Legislative Yuan should decide to oppose or form other resolutions, depending upon the contents of the resolution, all related agencies should then negotiate a solution based upon the meanings and purpose of this Interpretation, or to select a proper channel within the current constitutional mechanism to end the stalemate."[57]

(6) Interpretation No. 585 (Dec. 15, 2004) and No. 633 (Sep. 28, 2007)
In Interpretation No. 585 which was filed by a number of legislators, the Constitutional Court declared that part of the Act of the "Special Commission on the Investigation of the Truth in Respect of the 319 Shooting" were unconstitutional and thus void.[58] The Legislative Yuan revised the Act on April 11, 2006. Some legislators still thought that it violated the separation of powers and petitioned to the Constitutional court again. The Constitutional Court made Interpretation No. 633 and declared some articles were still "contrary to the principle of separation of powers and checks and balances, and shall become null and void as of the date of the promulgation hereof."[59]

(7) Interpretation No. 613 (July 21, 2006) and No. 645 (July 11, 2008)
The Executive Yuan believed that the Organic Act of the National Communications Commission was unconstitutional and petitioned to the Constitutional Court. In Interpretation No. 613, the Constitutional Court argued that the provisions at issue "practically deprive the Executive

56 J.Y. Interpretation No. 461, *available at* http://www.judicial.gov.tw/CONSTITUTIONALCOURT/en/p03_01.asp?expno=461 (last visited Jan. 16, 2011).

57 J.Y. Interpretation No. 520, *available at* http://www.judicial.gov.tw/CONSTITUTIONALCOURT/en/p03_01.asp?expno=520 (last visited Jan. 16, 2011).

58 J.Y. Interpretation No.585, *available at* http://www.judicial.gov.tw/CONSTITUTIONALCOURT/en/p03_01.asp?expno=585 (last visited Jan. 16, 2011).

59 J.Y. Interpretation No. 633, *available at* http://www.judicial.gov.tw/CONSTITUTIONALCOURT/en/p03_01.asp?expno=633 (last visited Jan. 16, 2011).

Yuan of substantially all of its power to decide on personnel affairs, which transgresses the limits on the checks and balances exercisable by the legislature on the Executive Yuan's power to decide on personnel affairs, thus violating the principles of politics of accountability and separation of powers ... shall become void no later than December 31, 2008."[60]

By the same token, in Interpretation No. 645, the Constitutional Court again declared that "the provision with respect to the appointment of such members has virtually deprived the Executive Yuan of its power to make decisions on personnel appointment under the Constitution and has obviously transgressed the limit of check and balance of powers, it is clearly contrary to the principles of separation of powers and must be made inoperative not later than one year as of the date of issuance of this Interpretation."[61]

(8) Interpretation No. 632 (August 15, 2007)

The Constitutional Court elaborated that "given that the Chief Commissioner, Deputy-Chief Commissioner and Commissioners are all legal positions preserved by the Constitution, it behooves all constitutional agencies, as regards their respective duties, to maintain the functional existence and normal operations of the Control Yuan ... the President should nominate candidates to fill these positions in a timely manner and seek the Legislative Yuan's consent. The Legislative Yuan, in turn, should exercise such consent power in a timely manner to maintain the normal operations of the Control Yuan. The Constitution does not allow for the event in which either the President or the Legislative Yuan fails to nominate or consent to the nomination of candidates so that the Control Yuan cannot exercise its power or function, thereby jeopardizing the integrity of the constitutional system."[62]

Based upon the aforementioned interpretations, it is clear that the Constitutional Court tried hard to strike a delicate balance in making decisions relating to the Executive Yuan, the Legislative Yuan, and all political parties. This attitude, however, was often criticized. To mention a few, many critics

---

60 J.Y. Interpretation No. 613, *available at* http://www.judicial.gov.tw/CONSTITUTIONALCOURT/en/p03_01.asp?expno=613 (last visited Jan. 16, 2011).

61 J.Y. Interpretation No. 645, *available at* http://www.judicial.gov.tw/CONSTITUTIONALCOURT/en/p03_01.asp?expno=645 (last visited Jan. 16, 2011).

62 J.Y. Interpretation No. 632, *available at* http://www.judicial.gov.tw/CONSTITUTIONALCOURT/en/p03_01.asp?expno=632 (last visited Jan. 16, 2011).

contended the issue of whether the Vice-President could constitutionally assume the duties of Premier was not clearly declared in Interpretation No. 419.[63] While the Constitutional Court did advise the Vice President not to concurrently serve as Premier, it expressed it in a rather cautioned way. Eventually, the then Vice President Lien Chan resigned as Premier after this interpretation. Another example was Interpretation No. 520.[64] Both the two parties, the Legislative Yuan and the Executive Yuan, thought they won. Despite a certain degree of ambiguity, this interpretation nevertheless solved the conflict between the government and the legislature.

The challenges faced by the Constitutional Court have become more and more severe owing to the escalating political conflicts between political parties. After 2000, the Premier and the majority of the Legislative Yuan belonged to different parties, and this discord resulted in many interpretations, such as Interpretation Nos. 520, 585, 613, 632, 633, and 645. Notwithstanding the judicial prudence, the Constitutional Court was still retaliated by the Legislative Yuan. After the Interpretation No. 585, the Legislative Yuan suspended the budget appropriated as a specialty premium for the Justices. Petitioned by some legislators, the Justices made Interpretation No. 601 and declared the suspension unconstitutional.[65] Four concurring opinions were issued in this interpretation.

III. Judicial Independence

Judicial independence is part of the cardinal principles in checks and balances among powers in constitutional democracies. Article 80 of the Constitution prescribes "judges shall be above partisanship and shall, in accordance with law, hold trials independently, free from any interference."[66] Article 81 guarantees that "judges shall hold office for life. No judge shall be removed from office unless he has been guilty of a criminal offense or subjected to disciplinary measure, or declared to be under interdiction. No

63 J.Y. Interpretation No. 419, *available at* http://www.judicial.gov.tw/CONSTITUTIONALCOURT/en/p03_01.asp?expno=419 (last visited Jan. 16, 2011).

64 J.Y. Interpretation No. 520, *available at* http://www.judicial.gov.tw/CONSTITUTIONALCOURT/en/p03_01.asp?expno=520 (last visited Jan. 16, 2011).

65 J.Y. Interpretation No. 601, *available at* http://www.judicial.gov.tw/CONSTITUTIONALCOURT/en/p03_01.asp?expno=601 (last visited Jan. 16, 2011).

66 Zhonghua Minguo Xianfa, art 80.

judge shall, except in accordance with law, be suspended or transferred or have his salary reduced."[67] The constitutional status of judicial power in Taiwan is no less venerable than that of other countries. However, after the promulgation of the Constitution, Taiwan entered into the era of Mobilization and Martial Law Decree. Whether the current judicial system has conformed to the essence of the Constitution still merits further discussion. In the following, I would analyze this issue from the perspective of some interpretations rendered by the Constitutional Court.

1. The Establishment of Judicial Independence (Grundsatz des Richtervorbehaltes)

a) Interpretation No. 86

This interpretation was the greatest contribution that the Constitutional Court made to the judicial reform in Taiwan. This case was appealed by 51 members of the Control Yuan. On August 15, 1960, the Justices made Interpretation No. 86, elaborating that "in view of the fact that different levels of courts and subsidiary courts below the High Court inclusively hold the judicial power over trials of civil and criminal litigation, these courts shall be subordinate to the Judicial Yuan."[68] In its reasoning, the Constitutional Court further demanded that "all relevant acts and regulations shall respectively be amended to comply with the concept of Article 77 of the Constitution."[69] The Constitutional Court implicitly declared the judicial system operated at the time as unconstitutional because an explicit declaration was almost not possible given the background of authoritarian regime. In response, the Judicial Yuan and then Ministry of Judicial Administration negotiated several times for the implementation of this interpretation. On July 1, 1980, all different levels of courts and subsidiary courts below the High Court became subordinate to the Judicial Yuan. It was 20 years after the

67 Zhonghua Minguo Xianfa, art 81.

68 J.Y. Interpretation No. 86, *available at* http://www.judicial.gov.tw/CONSTITUTIONALCOURT/en/p03_01.asp?expno=86 (last visited Jan. 16, 2011).

69 J.Y. Interpretation No. 86, *available at* http://www.judicial.gov.tw/CONSTITUTIONALCOURT/en/p03_01.asp?expno=86 (last visited Jan. 16, 2011).

release of Interpretation No. 86. The difficulty of the judicial reform was evident.[70]

b) Interpretation No. 436

On October 3, 1997, the Constitutional Court made this interpretation, arguing that "the initiation and operation of the military trial, which is within the power of punishment of the nation, shall meet the minimum requirement of the due process of law, which requirement includes an independent and just tribunal and procedure and the compliance with constitutional principles as stated in Articles 77 and 80 of the Constitution…In light of the spirit of protecting physical freedom and the right of instituting legal proceedings and the provision of Article 77, the defendant receiving the sentence of imprisonment in a final and conclusive judgment made by the military tribunal in peacetime shall be permitted to appeal directly to a normal court on the ground that the judgment received is in violation of the law."[71] This interpretation led to the reform of military trials and military courts, which was meaningful to the protection of human rights.

c) Interpretation No. 530

The Control Yuan believed that the Judicial Yuan and the Ministry of Justice did not have the authority to enact subsidiary judicial rules or supervisory regulations and thus petitioned to the Constitutional Court. The Justices made Interpretation No. 530 on October 5, 2000, arguing that "to realize the principle of judicial independence, the judiciary shall preserve judicial autonomy. Based on judicial autonomy, the highest judicial organ shall retain the power of rulemaking governing its practice and judicial matters … Based upon judicial autonomy, the highest judicial organ may prescribe and amend rules governing the details and technical matters of judicial procedures … judicial rules shall not be inconsistent with laws and these rules shall not add

---

70 See Weng, "Die neuere Entwicklung des national-chinesischen Verfassungsrechts," 1978, pp. 561 et seq.

71 J.Y. Interpretation No. 436, *available at* http://www.judicial.gov.tw/CONSTITUTIONALCOURT/en/p03_01.asp?expno=436 (last visited Jan. 16, 2011).

any further restrictions on the people's freedoms and substantive rights without the concrete and detailed delegation of law."[72]

Following that, the Constitutional Court continued to criticize that "the Judicial Yuan, other than Justices with the aforesaid adjudicative powers, has become merely the highest judicial administrative organ, resulting in the separation of the highest adjudicative organ from the highest judicial administration. In order to be consistent with the intent of the framers of the Constitution that considered the Judicial Yuan as the highest judicial adjudicative organ, the Organic Act of Judicial Yuan, the Court Organic Act, the Organic Act of Commission on the Disciplinary Sanction of Public Functionaries must be reviewed and revised in accordance with the designated constitutional structure within two years after the date of this Interpretation." In response to this constitutional demand, the Judicial Yuan proposed the draft amendments of the Organic Act of Judicial Yuan twice, but none was passed. Consequently, Interpretation No. 530 has not been implemented fully and became problematic.[73]

2. The Role of Judges and the Principle of Judicial Reservation (Grundsatz des Richtervorbehaltes)

Judicial independence will not be achieved without judges. Who is the "judge" stipulated in the Constitution? Article 8 of the Constitution plainly protects personal freedom and elaborates parameters of such protection including especially the principle of judicial reservation. The definition of a "court" in Article 8 has been deeply connected with the implementation of the principle of judicial reservation. The followings are some important interpretations on this issue.

a) Interpretation No. 13

Some members of the Control Yuan doubted whether the judge specified in Article 81 of the Constitution included the prosecutor and petitioned to the

---

72 J.Y. Interpretation No. 530, *available at* http://www.judicial.gov.tw/CONSTITUTIONALCOURT/en/p03_01.asp?expno=530 (last visited Jan. 16, 2011).

73 See Lee, "An Analysis of the Relationship between the Judicial Independence and the Supervisory Power of Judicial Administration," 2002 (in Chinese).

Constitutional Court, known as the Council of Grand Justices at the time. The Justices made Interpretation No. 13 on January 31, 1953, arguing that "the Judge referred to in Article 81 of the Constitution means the Judge that Article 80 of the Constitution refers to and does not include the Prosecutor. However, the guarantee of tenured prosecutors, according to Article 82 of the Constitution and Article 40, Paragraph 2, of the Court Organic Act, apart from their transfer, is the same as that of tenured judges."[74] Based on the separation of powers in a constitutional state, a judge should be passive, independent, disinterested while a prosecutor must actively investigate in each case and be subject to orders of the Prosecutor General and chief prosecutors. This interpretation not only correctly distinguished the differences between the judicial power and the executive power but also conformed to constitutional rule of law and separation of powers given that it was made in an authoritarian regime and the Constitution was still in its infancy.

b) Interpretation No. 162

Just like Interpretation No. 13, Interpretation No. 162 was appealed by the Control Yuan. The Control Yuan held doubts as to whether the President of the Administrative Court and the Chief Commissioner of the Public Functionaries Disciplinary Commission should be considered to be judges under the Constitution. The Constitutional Court made Interpretation No. 162 on April 25, 1980, arguing that "the President of the Administrative Court and the Chief Commissioner of the Public Functionaries Disciplinary Commission are the administrative heads of the respective agencies. Therefore, the provisions set forth in Article 81 of the Constitution are not applicable to the President of the Administrative Court or the Chief Commissioner of the Public Functionaries Disciplinary Commission. The adjudicator of the Administrative Court and the commissioner of the Public Functionaries Disciplinary Commission have authority to adjudicate or deliberate administrative cases independently and impartially pursuant to the law without political interference. Therefore, the adjudicator of the Administrative Court and the commissioner of the Public Functionaries Disciplinary Commission should

74 J.Y. Interpretation No. 13, *available at* http://www.judicial.gov.tw/CONSTITUTIONALCOURT/en/p03_01.asp?expno=13 (last visited Jan. 16, 2011).

be considered as judges under the Constitution in accordance with Articles 78 and 80 of the Constitution."[75]

The Constitutional Court hesitated to make this decision since many adjudicators of the Administrative Court and commissioners of the Public Functionaries Disciplinary Commission were government officials rather than judges. In fact, what really mattered was the function of a judge under Articles 78 and 80 of the Constitution. The principle of judicial reservation entrenched the protection of human rights by assuring a fair and transparent judicial process.

c) Interpretation No. 392

On October 19 and November 2, 1995, the Justices held oral arguments twice in the Constitutional Court and made Interpretation No. 392 on December 22, 1995, declaring that "the Code of Criminal Procedure ... which empowers a prosecutor to withdraw, suspend, resume, continue detention, or to take any other measures in conjunction with a detention ... violates the aforementioned Article 8, Paragraph 2, of the Constitution. ... the abovementioned unconstitutional provisions of the Code of Criminal Procedure and the Habeas Corpus Act shall lose effect within two years from the date of promulgation of this Interpretation."[76]

This was a cardinal interpretation pertaining to the protection of human rights. In its reasoning, the Constitutional Court elaborated that "judiciary of a restrictive definition is the common meaning for the judiciary. It refers to state functions in civil and criminal trials, and the capacity to carry out this function is called judicial power or adjudicative power ... Whereas in this state, the administrative litigation, the disciplinary measures against public functionaries, judicial interpretation, the trial for dissolution of unconstitutional political parties and any sort of "state functions of adjudication" shall also be included ... As to those state functions to further the purpose of the judiciary of a restrictive definition (i.e., state functions with a judicial nature), they are included in the category of the judiciary of an

75 J.Y. Interpretation No. 162, *available at* http://www.judicial.gov.tw/CONSTITUTIONALCOURT/en/p03_01.asp?expno=162 (last visited Jan. 16, 2011).

76 J.Y. Interpretation No. 392, *available at* http://www.judicial.gov.tw/CONSTITUTIONALCOURT/en/p03_01.asp?expno=392 (last visited Jan. 16, 2011).

expansive definition ... Therefore, in a procedural sense, a court (a court of a restrictive definition) is equated with a judge."[77]

In addition, this was the first time that Justices of the Constitutional Court were evidently regarded as the judge under the Constitution in interpretations.

d) Interpretation No. 601

As aforementioned, this interpretation discussed whether it was unconstitutional for the Legislative Yuan to suspend the budget appropriated as a specialty premium for the Justices of the Constitutional Court. The Constitutional Court maintained that "in order to realize the people's right of instituting legal proceedings, to protect their constitutional or legal rights, and to preserve the constitutional order, the Justices, based on the petitions made by the people or the governmental agencies in respect of individual cases, will render final and conclusive judgment on the constitutional dispute or doubt as to such cases, whose interpretations will bind all the agencies, as well as all the people, of the State. The effects are, in nature, the adjudicative function of the State, which is the core area of the judicial power. Therefore, the Justices, like ordinary judges, are judges in the constitutional context, as has been made clear by this Court in J.Y. Interpretations Nos. 392, 396, 530 and 585."[78] This interpretation best elucidated the characteristics of the judge under the Constitution.

e) Interpretation No. 631

The appellant of this case, after exhausting all legal remedies, argued that the Communication Protection and Monitoring Law infringed the freedom of privacy of correspondence and petitioned to the Constitutional Court. The Constitutional Court made this decision on July 20, 2007, confirming that "Article 5-II of the Communication Protection and Monitoring Law ... did not require that the writ of communication monitoring be in principle issued

---

77 J.Y. Interpretation No. 392, *available at* http://www.judicial.gov.tw/CONSTITUTIONALCOURT/en/p03_01.asp?expno=392 (last visited Jan. 16, 2011)..

78 J.Y. Interpretation No. 601, *available at* http://www.judicial.gov.tw/CONSTITUTIONALCOURT/en/p03_01.asp?expno=601 (last visited Jan. 16, 2011).

by an impartial and independent judge. It charged the prosecutor and judicial police officers, who are responsible for criminal investigations, with the concurrent duties of applying for and issuing the writ of communication monitoring. Such provision cannot be regarded as reasonable and legitimate and is in violation of Article 12 of the Constitution that guarantees the freedom of privacy of correspondence."[79] Here the Constitutional Court emphasized the differences between a judge and a prosecutor again.

3. The Independence of Judges

a) Constitutional Review of Administrative Regulations and Judicial Precedents

1) Interpretation No. 38

On August 27, 1954, the Constitutional Court, known as the Council of Grand Justices at the time, explained in Interpretation No. 38 that "the aim of Article 80 of the Constitution is to ensure independent adjudication of judges, free from any interference. The term 'in accordance with law' denotes that statutes are the primary basis of adjudication. It does not exclude ordinances and regulations that do not contradict the Constitution and statutes as a source of law."[80] In other words, the Constitutional Court thought what the "law" was should be interpreted substantively. Regulations enacted by local governments should be applied if they were held consistent with the Constitution or statutes. However, if the regulations contradicted the Constitution or statutes, a judge should decline to apply them.

2) Interpretation No. 137

After the Interpretation No. 38, the Control Yuan still held doubts as to whether a judge was bound by administrative orders issued by government agencies in accordance with their respective authorities. The Constitutional

79 J.Y. Interpretation No. 631, *available at* http://www.judicial.gov.tw/CONSTITUTIONALCOURT/en/p03_01.asp?expno=631 (last visited Jan. 16, 2011).

80 J.Y. Interpretation No. 38, *available at* http://www.judicial.gov.tw/CONSTITUTIONALCOURT/en/p03_01.asp?expno=38 (last visited Jan. 16, 2011).

Court made Interpretation No. 137 on December 14, 1973, arguing that "with regard to the administrative orders of statutory interpretation handed down by the government agencies in accordance with their respective authorities, the court may not refuse to apply them if they are applicable to the case. However, a judge shall, based on his or her fair and honest belief in the accurate interpretation of the law, give a lawful and legitimate legal opinion on a controversy which requires an accurate judicial interpretation."[81]

This conclusion may be worthy of further debate since the fourth-term Constitutional Court believed that a judge was obligated to apply administrative orders in principle, a conclusion that was consequently not strictly followed.

3) Interpretation No. 216

During the fifth term, several young scholars with learned legal backgrounds were appointed and became Justices of the Constitutional Court. The authoritarian environment gradually became open and democratized. On June 19, 1987, the Constitutional Court made Interpretation No. 216, the last interpretation made before the annulment of the Martial Law Decree. In this interpretation, the Constitutional Court articulated that "administrative rules adopted under the duty of seeking proper construction of laws by various government agencies may be applied by judges in the course of adjudication, who, not being bound thereby, may in a proper manner, express their opinion in light of the law, as stated in Interpretation No. 137 of this Court. Ordinances issued by a judicial administration involving legal issues in the business of adjudication are merely references for judges, who again, are not bound thereby in the course of adjudication."[82]

In its reasoning, the Constitutional Court emphasized that "the provision that administrative ordinances issued by a judicial administration shall not intervene in adjudication is specifically prescribed in Article 90 of the Court Organic Act. Judicial administrations shall not put forth their own legal

81 J.Y. Interpretation No. 137, *available at* http://www.judicial.gov.tw/CONSTITUTIONALCOURT/en/p03_01.asp?expno=137 (last visited Jan. 16, 2011).

82 J.Y. Interpretation No. 216, *available at* http://www.judicial.gov.tw/CONSTITUTIONALCOURT/en/p03_01.asp?expno=216 (last visited Jan. 16, 2011).

views and order judges to follow such views in the course of adjudication."[83] Some criticized that it violated the prohibition of ultra petita rulings.[84] Nevertheless, after this interpretation, the Judicial Yuan no longer issued any of these kinds of interpretive ordinances.

b) Constitutional Review of Legislative Statutes Without the Power of Invalidation

1) Interpretation No. 371

After the Justices of the sixth term took office on October 1, 1994, they made Interpretation No. 371 on January 20, 1995, arguing that "a judge shall have no capacity to hold a statute unconstitutional, and shall not refuse to apply a statute for that reason. Nonetheless, since the Constitution's authority is higher than the statute's, judges have the obligation to obey the Constitution over any other statutes. Therefore, in trying a case where a judge, with reasonable assurance, has suspected that the statute applicable to the case is unconstitutional, he shall surely be allowed to petition for interpretation of its constitutionality. In the abovementioned situation, judges of different levels may suspend the pending procedure on the ground that the constitutionality of the statute is a prerequisite issue. At the same time, they shall provide concrete reasons for objectively believing the unconstitutionality of the statute, and petition to the Grand Justices of the Yuan to interpret its constitutionality."[85]

This interpretation was the borrowing of "concrete review" stipulated in Article 100, Paragraph1 of the German Basic Law. Nevertheless, in Taiwan, the Constitutional Court introduced it in Interpretation No. 371 by relying on the principle of judicial independence.

---

83 J.Y. Interpretation No. 216, *available at* http://www.judicial.gov.tw/CONSTITUTIONALCOURT/en/p03_01.asp?expno=216 (last visited Jan. 16, 2011).

84 But see Lin, "Judicial Independence and Administrative Interpretations ?," 2009, p. 55 (in Chinese).

85 J.Y. Interpretation No. 371, *available at* http://www.judicial.gov.tw/CONSTITUTIONALCOURT/en/p03_01.asp?expno=371 (last visited Jan. 16, 2011).

2) Interpretation No. 572

After the Interpretation No. 371, judges of district courts began to petition to the Constitutional Court. However, lower court judges have not understood fully relevant requirements in making such requests. The Constitutional Court made Interpretation No. 572 on February 6, 2004 as a supplementary interpretation to Interpretation No. 371. In this interpretation, the Constitutional Court mentioned that the "prerequisite issue" was the matter "when the court presiding over the pending case believes that the law at issue violates the Constitution and may clearly affect the ruling of the case."[86] And "to provide concrete reasons for objectively believing the unconstitutionality of the statute" meant that "in the petition, the petitioning court is required to describe in detail its interpretation of the statute that violates the Constitution, explain the standard used to interpret the Constitution, and accordingly, provide evidence that it believes the statute is unconstitutional and is objectively without obvious mistakes. If the petitioner only has doubts about whether the statute is unconstitutional or the statute may possibly be reconciled with the requirement for requesting a constitutional interpretation, this is not sufficient to constitute concrete reasons for objectively believing that the statute is unconstitutional."[87] After this Interpretation, the requirements for judges to petition to the Constitution Court became more perspicuous.

3) Interpretation No. 590

After the Interpretation No. 572, a judge of Miaoli District Court petitioned to the Constitutional Court, requesting whether it was allowed for judges to take some preventive measures during the suspension of a trial when petitioning to the Constitutional Court. The Constitutional Court made Interpretation No. 590 on February 25, 2005, complementing that "after the suspension of a trial or non-trial procedure, a judge shall, in urgent circumstances, look into legislative purposes, balance the rights and welfare of parties with public interests, and consider all related matters of the case so as to maintain necessary safeguards, protection or take other appropriate

86 J.Y. Interpretation No. 572, *available at* http://www.judicial.gov.tw/CONSTITUTIONALCOURT/en/p03_01.asp?expno=572 (last visited Jan. 16, 2011).

87 J.Y. Interpretation No. 572, *available at* http://www.judicial.gov.tw/CONSTITUTIONALCOURT/en/p03_01.asp?expno=572 (last visited Jan. 16, 2011).

measures."[88] Hence, the function of a court will not be influenced during the petition.

In the past decades, this concrete review system has developed stably. If a petition is filed by a judge who is undoubtedly a legal expert, the provision at issue will be more likely to be held unconstitutional by the Constitutional Court. The establishment of the system is advantageous to the development of constitutionalism in Taiwan.

E. Conclusion

Taiwan is a country with a written constitution. However, the Constitutional Court has from time to time exercised its power without clear constitutional or statutory authorization. For example, as discussed before, the legal effect of the interpretations rendered by the Constitutional Court has not been stipulated clearly in any statute. The Constitutional Court had to render interpretations pertaining to the legal effect of its own interpretations.[89] The situations concerning other disputes, such as the concrete review system (Interpretation No. 371), the preliminary injunction (Interpretation No. 599),[90] the limit of constitutional revision (Interpretation No. 499), are also similar. Has the Constitutional Court transgressed the boundary of judicial power and infringed upon the legislative realm? Should the Constitutional Court be self-restraint or embrace a certain degree of judicial minimalism?[91] Without any doubt, the Constitutional Court recognized the boundary of judicial power.[92] In Interpretation No. 328, for instance, the Constitutional Court contended that the issue of national territory was a political question with which the Justices had no jurisdiction. With the changing political environment, more and more political disputes are appealed to the Constitutional Court. From the early party-state era to a new democracy, from indirect democracy to direct referendum, Taiwan has experienced a major transition

88 J.Y. Interpretation No. 590, *available at* http://www.judicial.gov.tw/CONSTITUTIONALCOURT/en/p03_01.asp?expno=590 (last visited Jan. 16, 2011).

89 See Weng, "Research on the Validity of the Interpretations," 2004, pp. 1-36 (in Chinese).

90 See R.-M. Lee, "The Preventive Proceeding in Judicial Review I," 2006, p. 1 (in Chinese); R.-M. Lee, "The Preventive Proceeding in Judicial Review II," 2007, p. 91.

91 See Hwang, "The Practice of Judicial Passivism," 2002, p. 875 (in Chinese).

92 See Weng, *Guardians of the Constitution*, 2009, p. 51.

in democratic constitutionalism, a velvet revolution.[93] It will be difficult, if not impossible, for the Constitutional Court Justices to embrace the judicial minimalism or insulate themselves from the changing dynamics. Undoubtedly, the judiciary has its own limit and the Constitutional Court must exercise more cautions to highly political issues after the democratization. Unanimous decisions may be required in these cases to maintain the authority of the Constitutional Court and win the confidence of the people.[94] In respect to the protection of human rights, a sacred duty of the judiciary, the Constitutional Court must function actively as the cardinal realm of fundamental rights should not be violated by the majority.

The Constitutional Court has functioned for more than sixty years and is closely connected with the constitutional development in Taiwan. There are 683 interpretations rendered till January 15, 2011. Each of these interpretations is a collective work of all Justices. Some interpretations are opposed while others are appraised by citizens. Having worked hard on its own, the Constitutional Court as the guardian of the Constitution and human rights has gradually won the respect of the people. History will tell if it will continue to be so in the future.

Works cited

Chang, Wen-Chen, "The Role of Judicial Review in Consolidating Democracies – The Case of Taiwan," *Asia Law Review* 2 (2005): 73-88.

Chen, Shin-Min, *Constitutional Law* [in Chinese], 3rd ed., Taipei: San Min Book Co., 1999.

Hsu, Tzong-Li, *Law and Government Power* [in Chinese], Taipei: Angle Publishing Co., 1999.

Hwang, Jau-Yuan, "The Practice of Judicial Passivism – Reflection on Prof. Sunstein's Judicial Minimalism," [in Chinese], in *Modern Theories of Public Law I*, 2002, pp. 875-917.

Lee, Chien-Liang, "The Anatomy of the 1999 Constitutional Amendments," [in Chinese] in *Constitutional Theory and Practice II*, 2000, pp. 493-533.

Lee, Chien-Liang, "An Analysis of the Relationship between the Judicial Independence and the Supervisory Power of Judicial Administration," [in Chinese], *Taiwan Law Journal* 32 (2002): 43-59.

---

93 See Yeh and Chang, *The Changing Landscape of Modern* Constitutionalism, 2009.

94 See Weng, "The Expectation of the Constitutional Litigation System in Taiwan," 2007, pp. 36-40 (in Chinese).

Lee, Chien-Liang, "The Systematic Change of the Justices and the Constitutional Role of the Judicial Yuan," [in Chinese] in *Constitutional Theory and Practice I*, 2nd ed., Taipei: New Sharing Publishing Co., 2003.

Lee, Ren-Miau, "The Preventive Proceeding in Judicial Review I," [in Chinese] *National Chengchi University Law Review* 94 (2006): 1-28.

Lee, Ren-Miau, "The Preventive Proceeding in Judicial Review II," [in Chinese] *National Chengchi University Law Review* 95 (2007): 91-126.

Lin, Tzu-Yi et al., *Constitutional Law: Separation of Powers* [in Chinese], 2008.

Lin, Tzu-Yi, "Judicial Independence and Administrative Interpretations – Should A Judge be Bound by Administrative Interpretations Issued by Government Agencies?," [in Chinese] in *The Development and The Inheritance of Rule of Law*, 2009, pp. 55 ff.

Weng, Yueh-sheng, "Die neuere Entwicklung des national-chinesischen Verfassungsrechts," *Jahrbuch des öffentlichen Rechts, Neue Folge* 27 (1978): 535-576.

Weng, Yueh-sheng, "Research on the Validity of the Interpretations," [in Chinese] in *The Public Law and the Political Theories*, 2004, pp. 1-36.

Weng, Yueh-sheng, "Die Verfassungskontrolle durch richterliche Fortbildung, die Geschichte von Taiwans Judicial Activism," in *Der Staat des Grundgesetzes – Kontinuität und Wandel: Festschrift für Peter Badura zum siebzigsten Geburtstag*, eds. Michael Brenner, Peter M. Huber and Markus Möstl, Tübingen: Mohr Siebeck, 2004, pp. 1219-1243.

Weng, Yueh-sheng, "The Expectation of the Constitutional Litigation System in Taiwan," [in Chinese] *Academia Sinica Law Journal* 1 (2007): 36-40.

Weng, Yueh-sheng, "Auf dem Weg zu einer ausgereiften Verfassungsgerichtsbarkeit, Neue Entwicklungen der Verfassungsgerichtsbarkeit in der Republik China (Taiwan) zu Anfang des 21. Jahrhunderts," in: *Die Ordnung der Freiheit, Festschrift für Christian Starck zum siebzigsten Geburtstag*, eds. Rainer Grote et al., Tübingen: Mohr Siebeck, 2007, pp. 1053-1072.

Weng, Yueh-sheng, "Guardians of the Constitution – Reflection and Expectation," [in Chinese] in *Constitutional Interpretation: Theory and Practice*, Vol. 6, Taipei: Academia Sinica, 2009, pp. 1-169.

Weng, Yueh-sheng, "Research on Recent Interpretations of the Council of Grand Justices, Judicial Yuan," [in Chinese] in *The Administrative Law and the Judiciary in Rule of Law Countries*, 2009, pp. 387 ff.

Wu, Geng, *The Interpretation and Application of the Constitution* [in Chinese], Taipei: San Min Book Co., 2003.

Yeh, Jiunn-Rong, and Wen-Chen Chang, "The Changing Landscape of Modern Constitutionalism: Transitional Perspective," National Taiwan University Law Review 4 (2009): 145-183.

Democracy, Elections and the Constitutional Governance*

Hassavut Vititviriyakul

A.

In my capacity as an instructor of law and a committed legal scholar charged with tasks relating to the public law as well as certain administrative duties, it is inevitable that I have devoted substantial interest to public policies and good governance. Therefore, I am thrilled by this conference and would like to congratulate Thammasat University and the three universities from Germany for their collaboration in organizing it. My praises go especially to the collaboration between academics in Germany and Thailand that have been taken a step further. If the law is to be regarded as an integral part of culture, then there has been an elevation of the level of cultural cooperation, for which the German Academic Exchange Service (DAAD) should be thanked for its essential role in promoting this agenda.

Thirty years ago, the Thai educators and scholars acquired academic inspiration from Germany through Dr. Pridi Kasemsap of Thammasat University. He introduced the younger generation to the struggles for justice by means of intellect, the protection of rights and liberties and the limitation of state powers by way of principles rather than by force. These were changes which permeated from surface to roots, and not through the uprooting of foundations.

The attempts to instill these principles and to foster a network of knowledge amongst youths were achieved by the determined infusion of an understanding on legal methods, jurisprudence and administrative law principles. This could be regarded as another way to combat injustice. The battle was protracted and relied on serious attempts over long periods until they were passed on from one generation to another, and until the public acquired a proper understanding. Thirty years later, those attempts are now manifest in the Administrative Courts and the Constitutional Court.

---

* Keynote speech, delivered at the first annual conference "Constitutionalism and Good Governance" of the German-Southeast Asian Center of Excellence for Public Policy and Good Governance, 15-17 November 2010, Bangkok, Thailand.

The focus on promoting the knowledge of the younger generation is admirable and promising. I hope that youths in Southeast Asia will receive the same opportunity. At present, we have the Asian Institute of Technology, which trains engineers for this region, and has been situated adjacent to Thammasat University's Rangsit Campus for 40 years. Our physical progress has been substantial, but lopsided when compared with society. We have built impressive roads and dams, but we have not yet achieved a well ordered society. In the future, I hope that we will also have an Asian institute for legal and public policy studies, and that we will have social engineers through academic collaborations, not less than the construction of dams in the past.

B.

Even though the accomplishments at this time could not be said to be perfect, clear progress has been made. We have travelled a long distance from the time when every matter was determined by the policies of unaccountable and powerful authorities to a time when decisions are now increasingly made in accordance with transparent rules and reasons. Even pure policy matters have relaxed from being unilateral decisions that could not be disputed to reasoning that has increasingly taken account of the wider difference in opinions. Despite the fact that the differing opinions have been expressed in a critical and forceful manner, they were still acceptable to the extent that such opinions were based on reasons provided for motivation, and not in order to insult one's human dignity, incite hate or fear or threaten the use of violence.

It is hoped that German academics will disseminate works on their reflections and the search for fairness on the basis of rules and consistency with reasons throughout Southeast Asia. Academics in this region will benefit from the development of an understanding on the rights and liberties, and the balance of interests for the determination of proportionality and a structured approach to the protection of rights and liberties, as well as efficiency in the systematic, fair and appropriate administration of the state.

The mutual benefit obtained by academics residing on opposite ends of the world would emanate to the public in the form of developments in public policy and good governance, or as it is known in Sanskrit, "Thammaphiban".

Thailand has entered into a major transition ever since the end of the Cold War and has adapted a system of democratic governance with the participation of the people and supremacy of the law. These changes have occurred alongside the trends of free and fair competition, and were initiated by the people's movement in 1992 in order to reject the quasi-military governments which had held power throughout the preceding Cold War era.

Concurrent with the promulgation of the Constitution of the Kingdom of Thailand B.E. 2540 (1997), whilst facing a severe financial crisis which reflected the existence of a variety of conflicts and a number of disputes which remain unresolved, Thailand established judicial institutions in addition to the Courts of Justice, namely the Constitutional Court and the Administrative Courts. These institutions performed functions as protectors of the people's rights and liberties, and imposed limitations on the exercise of state powers under the Constitution and the law. Other independent agencies, such as the Election Commission, the National Anti-Corruption Commission, the Ombudsman and State Audit Commission, were also established as specialized agencies exercising scrutiny functions.

It is perceivable that the concepts of a Constitutional Court and Administrative Courts in the Thai legal system were influenced by German and French jurisprudence that had accumulated since the post-14th October 1973 incident[1] and subsequently proliferated throughout the country. The concepts of independent commissions were derived from the United States of America. Nevertheless, they were all implemented under the principle of the rule of law. At the same time, Thai society emerged from a time where the ruling authority prescribed rules of conduct and advanced planning and controls, to one where the ruling authorities were made accountable, and there were rules for retrospective review and remedy with the law as the adjudicating principle.

This process necessarily requires knowledge of academic principles and the freedom of action for bodies tasked with oversight as a foundation, as well as the performance of government functions in a fair, expeditious, comprehensive and economical manner. These are key aspects of the administration of justice. However, knowledge in this area is still insufficient.

---

1 The *14th October 1973 Incident* refers to the crashing of the student-led uprising against the military dictatorship under Prime Minister Thanom Kittikachorn on 14 October 1973. (Editors' remark)

C.

Along with the expansion of democracy and free and fair competition that have occurred in parallel to the advancements in telecommunications technology, we have also found that in this new era, while the traditional business sectors, whether the real estate sector or the financial sector, are still reeling from the economic crisis, new operators have arisen and acquired political influence widely and quickly and hence have become the hope of many people.

The popularity of this third wave of knights[2] in shining armor has resulted in political changes and the undertaking of economic and profit-seeking activities which relates to and affects the implementation of public policies and good governance in both desirable and fraudulent ways.

It is certainly the case that the scrutinizing authorities have exercised their functions. However, when there was a trend in favour of scrutiny, there were also attempts by political powers to exert their influences to control the judiciary and independent agencies in order to lessen the burdens associated with the scrutiny on the exercises of powers. In the initial stage, there was widespread tendency toward leniency or to allow the exercise of discretion by the executive branch, and judges were reluctant to scrutinize or control the exercise of such powers by law, unless there was clear evidence requiring such action. This was especially true in the case of corruption by policy. There was a due recognition for democratic principles and the legitimacy of decisions made by representatives of the people's majority. In the consequence, the judiciary was criticized for its failure to curb corruption and for being submissive to political influences.

In the following period, when the judiciary exercised extensive scrutinizing powers over the executive without regard to the majority status, a number of politicians, lawyers and political scientists joined in criticizing the judiciary for over-interference with the executive, or for not paying due respect to the majority, which was contrary to democratic governance, contrary to the principles of the legal state, being a state of rule by the judiciary, sometimes also referred to as judicial activism.

An example may be cited in the case where the Administrative Court invalidated the general election on 2nd April B.E. 2549 (2006) because the

2 The notion of "third wave of knights" is unsually used with reference to outsted former Prime Minister Thaksin Shinawatra. (Editors' remark)

election had proceeded in a manner contrary to the principles of votes by secret ballot. In such a case, there were numerous criticisms that the court should not interfere with the powers of the Election Commission which derived exclusive and absolute powers under the Constitution. Those powers should not be subject to review by the judiciary since the Election Commission's discretion in the administration of an election was a "Political Element – Technical Element", and not a "Legal Element".

In the case where the Constitutional Court ruled on the removal of the Prime Minister from office due to benefits obtained from a private business operator in September 2008, criticisms were directed at the court's use of the "dictionary" as a decision-making tool without regard to the law. It was said that the constitutional prohibition from being an "employee" did not include "hire for services". The court, however, gave a wider interpretation, arguing that the dictionary definition of an employee also included hire for services.

If the Constitutional Court actually explained that the interpretation of the Constitution had to be made in accordance with the perceptions of a reasonable person, and not restricted to the legal definition, then the constitutional prohibition on the Prime Minister from becoming an employee was essentially a prohibition from obtaining benefits from private parties. In this sense, the term "employee" would also include hire for services. Such an interpretation would be consistent with the principles of teleological interpretation, and would not be a departure from the common understanding of reasonable persons.

In December 2008, the Constitutional Court ruled on the dissolution of the People's Power Party, and revoked the election rights of party executives for a period of five years due to evidence of hire to commit election fraud. In this instance, there were also criticisms that the decisions were more politically motivated than based on legal reasoning and in effect replacing the parliamentary system and censure system by the judiciary.

As for the case of the conversion of obligations under a concession into excise tax, the Supreme Court Criminal Division for Political Office Holders later held in a judgment that although the Constitutional Court had previously ruled that the enactment of the Emergency Decree was constitutional, the Prime Minister, however, continued to retain management powers in the mobile telephone business through family members. As such, the Council of Ministers, which was under the *de facto* control of the Prime Ministers, by passing a resolution to allow deductions of those taxes from concession fees, had acted in conflict of interest with the office. The act was held as wrongful by the Supreme Court Criminal Division for Political Office Holders. The decision also constituted one of the causes leading to the judgment that the Prime Minister was unusually wealthy, which was subsequently followed by a court order to seize the Prime Minister's assets.

A number of academics, especially the younger generation, were concerned that the judiciary was engaging in political decisions, and that trust in the judiciary would deteriorate and the judiciary would be viewed as exercising judicial powers for political reasons. Such instances could be a result of imitation of other countries or subservience to politics or influential persons in society.

Nevertheless, I can affirm that the exercise of judicial powers of scrutiny and remedy as it exists in Thailand, despite its novelty, is the product of an accumulation of academic principles and a conscience of right and wrong embedded within the judges themselves. Defects can be criticized under academic principles. The decisions of judges are in any event taken independently, free from any influence. This is a phenomenon in all countries. Even though the democratic form of governance makes a presumption that the average person is reasonable, there are no guarantees that the majority will not exercise their powers wrongfully.

In August this year, i.e. on 4th August 2010, the United States Supreme Court gave a decision in the case of *Perry v. Schwarzenegger* which went against the majority opinion expressed in a referendum of the people of California, stating that the prohibition on same-sex marriage and co-habitation as spouses was contrary to the principles of equality under the Constitution.

In actual fact, judicial powers are the powers which balance the sovereign powers of the people. A majority opinion cannot be claimed as the correct opinion at all times. A government elected by the people should be regarded as representatives of the people, but not as the exclusive holder of rightfulness.

Moreover, there were also several cases giving rise to political conflicts in such a way that political mechanisms fail, or lead to political impasse. In such a state of affairs, the judiciary will naturally have an increasing role in the resolution of political dispute.

Rightfulness and justice must be decided on intellectual and academic principles without any prejudice. Decisions must be made in accordance with reasons embedded in the legal principles without bias. Judges are not prescribers of the law, but they are the ones who are legitimately entitled to search for legal principles and interpret those legal principles to the case at hand. Even though the legal principle has not yet been perceived by the general public, judges, in their capacity as holders of knowledge and a conscience of rightfulness in society, are under a duty to discover those legal principles and apply the same to cases. These are the academic tasks of judges.

For these reasons, court judgments, although final, can be criticized using reason and academic principles. Judicial powers must listen to academics. This must be promoted as a legal culture of the country. At the same time, however, criticisms have to be made with care and in a courteous manner. Defamatory or derogatory remarks made without good faith reasons cannot be allowed. Also, political reasons also should not form part of the motivation or interference.

D.

Nowadays, legal principles have greatly advanced. The reasons existent in the factual relationships of society have become increasingly complex. Legal principles and trial procedures have also become more detailed and incomprehensible. News exchanges are quick with little time for review. The tasks of lawyers in managing knowledge have therefore become more important. How do we develop a legal understanding amongst lawyers and the public in line with changes? How do we effect communicative actions in order to advance knowledge networks and understanding networks in line with the needs of society?

In my opinion, I find the academic tasks of jurists in universities to be an important one that should be promoted in order to produce lawyers who possess knowledge as well as faith in the law and reasons. This is important, and indeed more necessary than engineers who construct buildings, roads, bridges and dams. Lawyers are the invisible creators of the world in which we all co-exist. Jurists are the ones who cast light on rules that would otherwise be invisible to the naked eye, and they are the ones who foster a better understanding for us to co-exist peacefully and happily.

A good lawyer in the future should not only "know the law and be able to apply the law," but they should have proficiency of expression so as to secure the understanding of the public, and proficiency in fostering networks of knowledge in line with the changes and demands of society.

Transformation of Constitutionalism in Asia: The Role of the Judiciary

Björn Dressel

A. Introduction

Courts have become highly visible in the Asian political landscape. The regular intervention of the Philippine Supreme Court in that country's deadlocked politics was long considered an exception in the region, but no longer. In Korea, Taiwan, and Indonesia, new constitutional courts have assumed crucial roles in diffusing political crisis and consolidating democratic practice. The Malaysian High Court has been embroiled in several politically charged cases, and in Thailand decisions of the Constitutional Court since 2006 have drastically altered the political landscape. Even in more conservative venues like Cambodia, Japan, and Singapore there are occasional hints of judicial assertiveness, though so far those courts have avoided high-profile political cases.

This trend towards what has been called the "judicialization of politics" – which Hirschl describes as "the ever-accelerating reliance on courts and judicial means for addressing core moral predicaments, public policy questions, and political controversies"[1] – has been well-documented for the United States, Europe, and Latin America[2], but the circumstances surrounding its emergence in Asia have largely been unexplored, perhaps because the region continues to battle with legacies of executive dominance, weak rule of law, and an unusual degree of regime diversity that prompted a leading scholar to claim 15 years ago that "a majority of Southeast Asian coun-

---

1 Hirschl, "The New Constitutionalism and the Judicialization of Pure Politics Worldwide," 2006, p. 721.

2 See Sieder et al., *The Judicialization of Politics in Latin America*, 2005; Tate and Vallinder, *The Global Expansion of Judicial Power*, 1995; Epp, *The Rights Revolution,* 1998; Stone Sweet, *Governing with Judges*, 2000; Feeley and Rubin, *Judicial Policy Making and the Modern State*, 1998; Shapiro and Stone Sweet, *On Law, Politics, and Judicialization*, 2002.

tries are unlikely candidates for the judicialization of politics"[3] because so many regimes were neither democratic nor constitutional.

But there has been considerable change in the region over the last two decades. As political and economic liberalization advance – though hardly in a linear fashion and with many throwbacks – many regimes have become more concerned about the rule of law, accountability, and rights issues. Indeed, promoting the rule of law has gained considerable traction in the region, whether as part of state and constitutional reforms initiated by many new democracies to deepen their recent democratic gains or as part of efforts of illiberal regimes to strengthen social control, enhance legitimacy, and ensure credible policy. In both cases, a regional discourse about what constitutes 'good governance' has reinforced the trend. As a result, courts have acquired an unprecedented centrality in the political life of many countries, and the perception has emerged that the region is undergoing a process of judicialization.[4]

Yet the effects of this new trend for governance have been neither clear-cut nor consistent. For instance, while the judiciary has often been empowered by a quest for good governance, the effects of growing judicial involvement in promoting the rule of law and making government more accountable, responsive, and stable have been at best ambiguous. Some courts have actively intervened in politics to strengthen constitutional governance dynamics, for instance providing checks and balances on executive abuse, upholding the supremacy of law, and protecting the rights of citizens. Others, however, have actively subverted the rule of law and undermined mechanisms of accountability in favor of narrow interests. Still others have been deliberately muted or highly restrained when engaging with core issues of political governance, raising questions about their own functioning.

The dramatic variations in judicial behavior raise important questions, both empirical and theoretical, about the nexus between judicialization and constitutional governance – most obviously, what is driving judicial politics along such different tracks? And what effects is the judicialization trend actually having on constitutional governance? More specifically, to what extent does judicialization improve prospects for the rule of law and more accountability to society? In what circumstances, also, does it lead to more

3 Tate, "The Judicialization of Politics in the Philippines and Southeast Asia," 1994.

4 See Ginsburg and Chen, *Administrative Law and Governance in Asia*, 2009; Dowdle, "On the Regulatory Dynamics of Judicialization," 2009.

political interference with the judiciary and even reinforce tendencies towards rule *by* law, if not outright illiberal *un*-rule of law?

To begin answering these questions, this paper extracts from the literature a basic typology of judicial politics and then applies it to the region. The emphasis is on 'mega-politics'– the involvement of constitutional or supreme courts in particular in matters of utmost political significance. These situations, in which courts go beyond ordinary adjudication and take an active role in the political process, bring into tight focus the nexus between judicialization and core aspects of governance. The purpose of the exercise is thus twofold: In providing an analytical framework, the paper will first offer a needed nuanced view of the unfolding judicialization phenomenon itself and its effects on governance. Second, in drawing attention to the different paths the phenomenon has taken, the paper also hopes to inspire closer attention to variations in the structural and political contexts in which courts in the region operate to help elicit new insights for debate.

The paper is structured as follows: First we briefly survey the literature to identify basic concepts and debates, from which we then extract a basic typology of judicial politics. To explore this typology we provide empirical evidence to delineate within the region critical trajectories of judicial involvement in mega-politics and its impact on governance. The paper concludes with a discussion of the nexus between judicialization and governance and what it means for both theoretical debates and practical concerns with rule of law reform and judicial strengthening in the region.

B. Judicialization and Constitutional Governance

The nexus between judicialization and governance seems at first almost too obvious: Governance describes the process by which power is exercised in a polity, and judicialization refers to the process through which the rulings and modes of court reasoning come to influence the decision-making of those in power beyond the courts. But there is little agreement on how this engagement is best conceptualized, what is driving it, and what its effects are.

The idea of the judicialization of politics has often suffered from conceptual stretching that lumps together different, though sometimes interrelated, processes.[5] Deserving of thoughtful separation, for instance, are the abstract capture of social relations and popular culture by law due to the growing complexities of modern societies – a process perhaps better described as 'juridification'[6]; the more concrete and much analyzed expansion of the courts into public policy as part of 'ordinary' constitutional rights jurisprudence (positive rights, procedural justice) and the redrawing of boundaries between state organs (separation of powers, federalism); and the even narrower though highly salient reliance on courts and judges for dealing with 'mega politics' – core political controversies and deep moral dilemmas related to areas of pure politics, such as executive branch prerogatives, electoral politics, and regime change.[7]

I believe that essentially two notions of the judicialization of politics can be identified. Narrowly, judicialization refers to the way judges in exercising judicial review contribute to or at least influence public policy – the process by which courts and judges, especially constitutional or supreme courts, come increasingly to dominate the making of public policy which had previously been the prerogative of legislatures and executives.[8] More broadly, though, judicialization is not limited to the expanded scope of 'judge-made law'; it also encompasses the increased presence of judicial processes and court rulings in political and social life, for instance when social actors use the courts and law to advance their own interests, political actors become more attuned to court actions, and state legitimacy is constructed increasingly in terms of delivering rule of law.[9]

Considering these two notions together, judicialization is thus marked by more deference to the courts, which transforms national high courts into bodies making major political decisions. Thus courts become active political players, with more influence on aspects of governance than their traditional adjudication role would allow.

So far, most relevant research has concentrated on the phenomenology of the judicialization trend and what might be driving it from regional and the-

5 See Hirschl, "The Judicialization of Mega-Politics and the Rise of Political Courts," 2008.

6 See for a good overview Teubner,"Juridification," 1987.

7 See Hirschl, "The Judicialization of Mega-Politics and the Rise of Political Courts," 2008.

8 See Sieder et al., *The Judicialization of Politics in Latin America,* 2005, p. 3; Tate and Vallinder, *The Global Expansion of Judicial Power,* 1995.

9 See Domingo, "Judicialization of Politics or Politicization of the Judiciary?," 2004, pp. 108-110.

oretical angles. The trend towards constitutional transformation and judicialization has been said to be anchored in macro-level processes of democratization and modernization[10]; in a tendency to greater system efficiency, from the functionalist and neo-institutional point of view; or in the search for solutions to systemic collective action problems.[11] Drivers of the trend have been expanded to the global spread of rights consciousness and legal support structures for mobilization by civil society.[12] Despite differences in approach and detail, what all these scholars share is a view that the proliferation and growing assertiveness of judicial and quasi-judicial agencies are an expression of a universal modernization that embraces the rule of law and separation of powers as constructs of viable democratic government that are consistent with a judicialization from 'below' or even 'abroad'.

More recently, however, scholarship has drawn attention to the structural dynamics and actors in the process as part of a process of judicialization from 'above'. Anchoring the process at the structural level, these micro-level theories emphasize its political drivers, arguing that self-interested strategic actors might have political reasons for empowering judges. Such reasons may be dysfunctional institutions[13]; the wish to delegate authority to courts as a means to shift responsibility[14] and build legitimacy for contested policies[15]; or the personal motivations of judges.[16] The effort to embed human agency more comprehensively within the structural context can also be seen in the two theoretical models that are currently dominant: the 'insurance model' that views judicial empowerment as a means of strategic insurance

---

10 See Shapiro, "The Success of Judicial Review," 1999; Sunstein, *Designing Democracy,* 2001.

11 See Feeley and Rubin, *Judicial Policy Making and the Modern State*, 1998; North and Weingast, "Constitutions and Commitment," 1998; Shapiro and Stone Sweet, *On Law, Politics, and Judicialization*, 2002; Weingast, "Constitutions as Governance Structures," 1993, p. 286.

12 See Tate and Vallinder, *The Global Expansion of Judicial Power*, 1995; Epp, *The Rights Revolution*; Slaughter, "Judicial Globalization," 2000.

13 See Guarnieri and Pederzoli, *The Power of Judges*, 2002; Ferejohn, "Judicializing Politics, Politicizing Law, " 2002.

14 SeeVoigt and Salzberger, "Choosing not to Choose," 2002.

15 See Morton, "The Effect of the Charter of Rights on Canadian Federalism," 1995; Goldstein, *Constituting Federal Sovereignty*, 2001.

16 See Baum, *Judges and their Audiences,* 2006; Waldron, *Law and Disagreement*, 1999; Tushnet, *Taking the Constitution Away from the Courts*, 1999; Bork, *Coercing Virtue,* 2003.

in times of growing electoral competition[17]; and the 'hegemonic preservation model' that sees growing judicial empowerment as a means for elites to preserve their power as they become more vulnerable to majoritarian politics.[18]

Not surprisingly, different theories about what is driving the judicialization trend have also generated a variety of views about how the trend affects governance. For instance, while scholars in the macro-level tradition have often enthusiastically embraced the rise of constitutionalism globally and praised the expansion of judicial review as offering greater protection of citizens and deepening democracy[19], authors of the structural school have been far more cautious. For instance, while authors like Ginsburg see the growing role of the judiciary as conducive to the deepening of democratic governance – by transforming political conflict into constitutional dialogue, providing a nonpartisan forum for grievances, and expressing fundamental democratic values – others have been skeptical about what the trend implies for governance, for instance decrying the "rise of unelected, unrepresentative, unaccountable committees of lawyers"[20]; reliance on "court room politics [that are] authoritarian in both process and spirit"[21]; and the possibility that it may reflect what one author described as a move towards 'juristocracy'.[22]

While it is perhaps true that the debate has often been empirically weak, if not outright normatively charged[23], it does highlight the inherent tension between judicial empowerment and areas of governance. For instance, while at the regime level it would be relatively easy to view judicial actors and processes acting in support of the rule of law as part of a general process of legalization, the relationship to aspects of political accountability and representation are often far more complex. This is evidenced in long-standing debates within constitutional theory about the balance between judicial guardianship of constitutional principles and majoritarian rule – the counter-

---

17 See Ginsburg, *Judicial Review in New Democracies*, 2003; Ramseyer, "The Puzzling (In)Dependence of Courts," 1994.

18 See Hirschl, "The New Constitutionalism and the Judicialization of Pure Politics Worldwide," 2006; Hirschl, "The Judicialization of Politics," 2008.

19 See Ackerman, "The Rise of World Constitutionalism," 1997; Dworkin, *A Bill of Rights for Britain*, 1990.

20 Bork, *Coercing Virtue*, 2003, 22.

21 Morton and Knopff, *The Charter Revolution and the Court Party*, 2000.

22 See Hirschl, *Towards Juristocracy*, 2004.

23 See Hilbink, "Assessing the New Constitutionalism," 2008.

majoritarian dilemma – and related debates about who guards the guardians[24]. Meanwhile, a growing empirical literature related to countries in transition is also revealing the pitfalls that emerge when the judiciary is repositioned. It reminds us that judicial self assertion is hardly a linear process – judicial actors are often deeply embedded in an ill-liberal past[25] – and exposes the danger that as judicial systems become more salient, policy-makers may also seek to influence the judiciary. This 'politicization' of the judiciary was recognized early on by such constitutional and legal scholars as Carl Schmitt.[26]

There is not enough room here to comprehensively parse these debates. What we hope to do is simply highlight two dimensions of the debate so far:

1. Judicialization of politics is a complex process driven by factors at several analytical levels, depending to at least some degree on court structural independence (institutional); the willingness of judges to intervene (behavioral); and support from the political elites to facilitate this process (structural). For simplicity's sake, these aspects could be collapsed into dimensions of de facto independence.
2. The involvement of judges in areas of politics can best be understood as a continuum ranging from minimal to extensive involvement in such areas as mega-politics.

If we draw up a simple typology of judicial politics along the two dimensions of (a) judicial de facto independence and (b) engagement in mega-politics, we can then build a matrix with representative examples from Asia (see Figure 1).

24 See Friedman, "The Counter-Majoritarian and the Pathology of Constitutional Scholarship," 2001; Graber, "The Countermajoritarian Difficulty," 2008; Bickel, *The Least Dangerous Branch*, 1962.

25 See Domingo, "Judicialization of Politics or Politicization of the Judiciary?," 2004.

26 See Schmitt, *Verfassungsrechtliche Aufsätze aus den Jahren 1924-1954*, 1958.

Figure 1. Typology of Judicial Politics

Degree of De Facto Judicial Independence		
H	**Judicial Restraint**	**Judicial Activism**
L	**Judicial Co-optation/ Muteness**	**Politicization of the Judiciary**
	L	H
	Degree of Judicial Involvement in Mega-Politics	

The relationship between judicial systems, law, and politics is highly fluid, and the degree of judicial involvement often varies greatly not only from country to country but within a country over time. Indeed, judicial engagement in mega-politics may at times be temporary, whether because judges are propelled into the political fray in reaction to exceptional events (political crisis, deadlock), or because political actors respond to judicial activism with institutional changes that curb judicial powers. However, it is clear that as institutional practices become more engrained, the more stable patterns of judicial governance that emerge allow us to characterize the behavior of a country's courts more consistently.

The suggested typology is thus meant to bring greater analytical rigor to the study of judicialization and its effects on governance, above all by providing a more nuanced view of the phenomenon. It allows us to identify the trajectories of distinct patterns of judicial politics and analyze their drivers. It also allows us to explore more clearly how the trend affects areas of governance as we use the typology to generate hypotheses about what may be conducive to good governance and what more problematic. For instance, does politicization of the judiciary blur the lines between branches of government and undermine the universal application of law, transforming judges into outright political actors with narrow interests? Or does the activism of an independent judiciary strengthen dynamics of good governance because judges act as veto players, societal representatives, or policy makers? And have judges become more active simply because other institutions are unable to solve critical political issues?

To explore our arguments we now turn to actual cases, partly to highlight the nuances of the trend as it plays out in the region and partly to explore the structural contexts in which courts operate.

C. Pathways of Judicialization in Asia

In exploring the diverse trajectories of judicialization in Asia, we look most closely at the behavior of Supreme or Constitutional Courts. Because these are the courts most likely to be involved in mega-politics, they showcase nuances in the trend and their varied effects on governance.

I. Korea: Judicial Activism

The Korean Constitutional Court illustrates growing judicial activism in areas of mega-politics in direct support of democratic governance and constitutionalism. After Korea's Sixth Republic was established in 1987, the Korean Constitutional Court was created in 1988. Gradually moving beyond the quiescent institution envisioned by the creators, it has become one of the most respected institutions in the country, and one of the most active courts within the region.[27]

Indeed, despite pockets of authoritarianism, transitional uncertainties, and occasional open political conflict, the court has regularly been called upon to resolve major political conflicts and address such issues of mega-politics as electoral disputes, executive prerogatives, and restorative justice. In addressing these issues, the court has carefully crafted rulings that have not only been perceived as neutral and legitimate but also expressed a consistent preference for such good governance principles as rule of law, representation, and accountability.

---

27 See Ginsburg, "The Constitutional Court and the Judicialization of Korean Politics," 2010.

Underpinning this common trajectory are similar structures and powers.[28] Created as courts of a Kelsian type, in which power of constitutional review is reserved for a designated court rather than shared, the bench of both courts consists of nine judges who serve renewable terms of six years in Korea. Their members are appointed by a multiple-track system involving different branches of government that allows for candidates from different professional backgrounds to serve. Institutional safeguards of independence (budget autonomy, tenure, etc.) are strong by international standards, and the powers of both courts extend well beyond judicial review into such areas as impeachment, constitutionality of parties, electoral politics, and jurisdictional conflict between branches of government. All these institutional arrangements have allowed the courts to emerge as highly effective and legitimate institutions, often in contrast to courts in the ordinary judicial hierarchy.

Several cases illustrate the growing involvement of the two courts in areas of mega-politics, often with far-reaching consequences for governance. For instance, on several occasions problems related to electoral politics have propelled the courts into action.

Since the 1990 s the Korean Constitutional Court has in a string of high-profile decisions struck down legal provisions that required large registration fees for minority candidates[29]or a higher deposit from independent than party-affiliated candidates[30] and gave party-based candidates advantages over independents in campaigning and leafleting[31]. The court has also rectified disproportional representation of rural against urban districts[32]. Ruling that the constitutional guarantee of equality of opportunity and the right to run for or hold office is a core democratic freedom, the court has not only addressed electoral distortions and leveled the democratic playing field, it has

---

28 In fact, the Indonesian Constitutional Court was partly modeled after the Korean court, see Hendrianto, "Institutional Choice and the New Indonesian Constitutional Court," 2010.

29 One-Person One-Vote Case, 13-2 KCCR 77; 2000Hun-Ma91; 2000Hun-Ma112; 2000Hun-Ma134 (Consolidated) July 19, 2001.

30 National Assembly Members Act Case, 89 HonKa 6, 1 KCCR 199, 249 (Sep. 8, 1989).

31 National Assembly Members Act Case, 92 HonMa 37, 39, 4 KCCR 137 (Mar. 13, 1992).

32 Electoral District Disproportionality Case, 95 HonMa 224, 7-2 KCCR 760 (Dec. 17, 1995).

also lent active support to a more representative and competitive democratic process.[33]

The court also waded into issues of political stalemate and potential political crisis. Consider the involvement of the Korean Constitutional Court in the attempted impeachment of President Roh Moo-Hyun in 2004.[34] Asked whether the president had violated the law by what appeared to be campaigning for his own party during contested mid-term elections, the court took a very measured approach: It found grounds for a violation but rejected removal of the president as disproportionate. By the time the ruling was released, Roh's party had already won an overwhelming election victory.[35] In taking on the case, the court maneuvered itself into becoming final arbiter in charged political cases, often at the expense of other institutions, such as parliament: the trend continued in subsequent cases involving Roh and then his successor, president Lee Myung-bak.[36]

In establishing themselves as an active player in the political process, the court has also made a positive contribution more generally to the democratic constitutional order, for instance when acting as an independent arbiter in times of political crisis, ensuring fairness in the electoral process, and functioning as a critical veto player role in the constitutional process. Building on a solid foundation for independence and careful strategic respect for other branches of government, the court has not only been able to enhance their reputation and legitimacy but have also helped stabilize the political transition and deepen the quality of the democratic process.

II. Thailand: Politicization of the Judiciary

The activist stance of the Thai Constitutional Court since 2006 offers an alternative trajectory for judicialization in Asia. Rather than being driven by independent judicial assertiveness, Thai judicial activism in areas of megapolitics seems to reflect a general politicization of the judiciary. This has undermined not only the legitimacy and reputation of the judiciary itself but

---

33 See Ginsburg, *Judicial Review in New Democracies*, 2003, pp. 226-246.

34 Impeachment of the President Case, 16-1 KCCR 609, 2004Hun-Na1 (May 14, 2004).

35 See Lee, "Law, Politics, and Impeachment," 2005.

36 See Ginsburg, "The Constitutional Court and the Judicialization of Korean Politics," 2010, p. 149.

also principles of good governance in Thailand, particularly in the areas of rule of law, accountability, and inclusive governance.

The first decade of Thailand's Constitutional Court can at best be described as tumultuous.[37] Established in 1998 as part of Thailand's 1997 "People's Constitution", the court was criticized early on for its conservatism under the government of Prime Minister Thaksin Shinawatra (2001–2006). It was then dissolved during the 2006 military coup that revoked the 1997 constitution, replaced by a Constitutional Tribunal appointed by the military, but reconstituted by the 2007 constitution with modified structures, powers, and bench. Throughout, against a background of growing political polarization and intra-elite conflict, this and other Thai courts have increasingly intervened in areas of mega-politics, drawing accusations of at best a lack of impartiality, at worst outright political bias.

Few would have predicted such a trajectory. Taking the French and German constitutional courts as models, the Thai version is in many ways similar to others in the region. Envisioned as the guardian of the new liberal architecture and hub of a network of oversight agencies to strengthen rule-based governance[38], the court has enjoyed comparatively broad jurisdiction and (at least formally) solid safeguards for its independence. Its bench, originally 15 judges, now 9, is chosen through an elaborate multi-track appointment allowing for a professionally diverse bench of judges sitting for a single nonrenewable term of nine years. The 2007 constitution significantly enlarged the political role of the court by involving it in the selection of senators and candidates for the independent agencies; allowing it to propose bills and laws directly to the House of Representatives; and, most controversially, giving it the power to dissolve a political party if one of its leaders is found guilty of election fraud.[39] Not surprisingly, the Court has become ever more prominent in areas of mega-politics.

Perhaps the first manifestation of a new judicial assertiveness was the Constitutional Court's decision to annul the April 2006 general elections.[40] The Thaksin government had decided to call snap elections to

---

37 See Klein, "The Battle for the Rule of Law in Thailand," 2003; Dressel, "Judicialization of Politics or Politicization of the Judiciary?," 2010; Harding, "The Constitutional Court of Thailand," 2010.

38 See Harding, "The Constitutional Court of Thailand," 2010; Leyland, "Thailand's Constitutional Watchdogs," 2008.

39 See Dressel, "Thailand's Elusive Quest for a Constitutional Equilibrium," 2009.

40 Constitutional Court Decision No. 9/2549 (2006).

counter growing public protest about allegations of its disloyalty to the monarchy, corruption, and conflicts of interest; the election went ahead despite a boycott by the opposition. The court's decision to nullify the elections was remarkable not only in itself but even more so for how the case was handled. The unusually broad legal reasoning of the verdict directly challenged the legal opinions of the Election Commission of Thailand (ECT), which many experts considered valid, and there seemed to be an unusual degree of coordination among several courts: The Administrative Court had decided in April to cancel the rerun election of parliamentarians, the Constitutional Court annulled the general election, and the Criminal Court brought actions against the Election Commissioners – actions that many linked to an earlier speech to the judiciary in which the revered monarch directly urged his audience to find a solution to the political impasse.

Then in May 2007 the Constitutional Tribunal issued a decision that dissolved the Thai Rak Thai (TRT) party and barred 111 of its members from public office for five years.[41] It was the first case heard by the military-appointed court, many of whose members were overtly critical of the Thaksin government. The decision came only days after another royal speech to members of the Administrative Court in which the king urged the judiciary to continue working towards a solution to the political crisis (stating "I have the answer in my heart, but have no right to say it"). In finding TRT and its allies Pattana Chart Thai and Paen Din Thai guilty of election violations, it effectively decapitated Thailand's largest and most popular political party, which had won landslide victories in 2001 and 2005. Not only was the popular Thaksin Shinawatra now ineligible to run for office, so was virtually anyone else who had risen in his party or cabinet. In the same ruling the military-favored Democrat Party was unanimously acquitted of all charges, despite similar evidence of illicit activities. Later the court decided to seize almost US$1.7 billion in Thaksin family assets. Concerns grew that the judges were lending implicit support to the junta's agenda. The unusually laborious verdict took more than 11 hours to read out and showed the judges at great pains to downplay procedural concerns about retroactivity. Since some justices also had unusually harsh words for the former Prime Minister, there were grounds for the impression that the tribunal did bend legal rules to achieve a politically desired outcome.

41 Constitutional Tribunal Decision No. 3-5/2550 (2007).

Two Constitutional Court cases in late 2008 suggest that its earlier electoral interventions were not aberrations. The first found Prime Minister Samak Sundaravej guilty of a conflict of interest for hosting a popular cooking show on TV[42]; the second dissolved the People's Power Party (PPP), the political successor of the TRT.[43] Both were heard after a landslide win by the PPP in junta-organized general elections in December 2007 and as a political stand-off between the anti- and pro-Thaksin political camps was growing. The decisions again had bold political implications – forcing Prime Minister Samak to resign for what many considered a minor abuse of power and successor Prime Minister Somchai to resign after PPP leader Yongyut Tiyapairat was found guilty of vote buying; they also cleared the path for a Democrat-led government. Both are notable for the court's judicial creativity in constitutional interpretation and breach of procedural due process, which looked suspiciously like the *un*-rule of law.

These and other court decisions have profoundly altered governance in Thailand: The judges have taken a central role in politics by destroying the country's largest and most successful political party, forcing the resignation of two prime ministers, and keeping pressure on popular former Prime Minister Thaksin to remain in exile. Moreover, other courts are following the Constitutional Court's lead; both the Supreme Administrative Court and the Supreme Court have recently released rulings that directly interfere with government policy.[44]

Yet the growing involvement of the courts in areas of mega-politics has less to do with asserting judicial independence than with a more general politicization of the courts by critical elites, such as the monarchy network. The situation in Thailand warns that a growing judicialization of politics also carries a risk of politicizing the courts as policy makers and elites seek greater influence over court decisions. Politicization undermines not only the legitimacy of the court itself but also basic principles of good governance, such as accountability to society.

---

42 Constitutional Court Decision No. 12-13/2551 (2008).

43 Constitutional Court Decision No. 20/2551 (2008).

44 See for instance, the Supreme Administrative Court's temporary injunction against 76 major investment projects worth Bt400bn (US$12 billion) at and around the Map Ta Phut industrial estate (Court Order 592/2552 (2009)).

III. Japan: Judicial Restraint

The Japanese Supreme Courts illustrate a trajectory in which courts, despite high degrees of nominal independence, decide not to engage with mega-politics, exhibiting a general pattern of judicial restraint.

The Supreme Court of Japan, although "among the most honest, politically independent, and professionally competent [judiciaries] in the world today",[45] is also widely considered one of the most conservative. Since its founding in 1947 the court has struck down only eight statutes on constitutional grounds (over the same period the German Constitutional Court struck down more than 600), and many of its rulings of unconstitutionality have been less than momentous. Perhaps equally important, in some cases of significant political impact it has steadfastly avoided any ruling on the constitutional merits.

The unusual restraint of the two courts in areas of mega-politics has drawn considerable comment. Some authors have questioned how independent of the political realm the 15-member Supreme Court of Japan can be considering the single-party dominance of Japan by the LDP.[46] Others have found evidence of an "extraordinary record of integrity and its equally remarkable record of political independence".[47] More recent studies have tended to fall somewhere in the middle, arguing that the court as an *institution* enjoys a high degree of independence, but that *individual judges* face considerable pressures for restraint from the firm hierarchical control exerted by the General Secretariat of the Supreme Court over selection, training, and career trajectories; and the common practice of appointing judges to the Supreme Court shortly before mandated retirement age.[48]

Thus instead of direct political interventions against liberal-activist judges[49], it is the internal organizational structure and the related internal legal culture that have kept the court from activism.[50] Among the few rulings

---

45 Haley, *The Spirit of Japanese Law*, 2006, p. 99.

46 See Ramseyer and Rasmusen, *Measuring Judicial Independence*, 2003.

47 See Haley, *The Spirit of Japanese Law*, 2006.

48 See Upham, "Political Lackeys or Faithful Public Servants?," 2005; Law, "The Anatomy of a Conservative Court," 2009.

49 A widely debated exception have been the cases against judge Fukushima, a member of the leftist Young Jurist League (YJL) in the 1960 s, or the case of Judge Yasuaki Miyamoto's non renewal in 1971, see Haley, *The Spirit of Japanese Law*, 2006, p. 103.

50 See O'Brian and Ohkoshi, "Stifling Judicial Independence from Within," 2001.

of the Japanese court on constitutionality, hardly any would meet the criterion of mega-politics[51] except, perhaps, the 1976 decision to reject a legislative apportionment scheme that weighted the votes of rural votes five times more heavily than those of urban voters. However, although some saw the decision as a 'high point of over fifty years of judicial review', the court refrained from ordering any remedy.[52] On perhaps the most politically charged question – challenges to Japan's military activities and security arrangements under Article 9 of the postwar constitution, which prohibits the maintenance of armed forces or other 'war potential' – the court has steadfastly refused to rule, citing the political question doctrine.[53]

Japan thus demonstrates that judicial autonomy and independence do not necessarily lead to greater judicial activism. In fact, for internal organizational as well as legal culture reasons, high courts may deliberately decide to exercise judicial restraint in certain cases. Whether that strategy is sustainable in the long run, however, also depends on structural factors outside the court itself.

IV. Singapore: Judicial Cooptation and Muteness

The Singapore Supreme Court clearly illustrates a trajectory marked by limited judicial independence and limited engagement in mega-politics. Operating within the soft authoritarian rule of the People's Action Party (PAP), the court draws attention not only to the limits of judicial autonomy in settings of executive dominance but also to the complexities of judicial behavior in these settings with respect to areas of governance.

---

51 The majority of the cases have involved the Court striking down: a law punishing patricide more severely than other forms of homicide (Aizawa v. Japan, 27KEISHU 265 (Sup. Ct., April 1973); a law restricting the abilities of pharmacies to operate within close physical proximity of one another (Sumiyoshi K.K. v. Governor, Hiroshima-ken, 29 MINSHU 572 (Sup. Ct. April, 1975); a rule limiting the liability of the postal service for the loss of registered mail (Shichifuku Sangyo K.K. v. Japan, 56 MINSHU 1439 (Sup. Ct., Sept. 11, 2002); a law restricting the co-owners of forest land to subdivide their property (Hiragushi v. Hiragushi, 41 MINSHU 408 (Sup. Ct., Sept. 22, 1987); a statutory provision that distinguished for purposes of eligibility between illegitimate children of Japanese fathers who acknowledged paternity prior to birth and those whose fathers acknowledged paternity only subsequent to birth (Jane Doe v. Japan, 62 MINSHU 1367 (Sup. Ct., June 4, 2008).

52 See Law, "The Anatomy of a Conservative Court," 2009, pp. 1547-1548.

53 See Law, "The Anatomy of a Conservative Court," 2009, p. 1548.

Singapore's judicial and legal system is regularly ranked among the best-functioning in the world, and the government has gone to great lengths to stress the role of the judiciary in ensuring good governance. But independent reports over the years have raised serious questions about the impartiality and independence of the judiciary, particularly in politically sensitive cases.[54] As one observer remarked, in light of PAP dominance "separation of powers is observed in work only; the legislature and the judiciary are disenfranchised by the executive, and the legal profession has no capacity to challenge or even advise the executive".[55] Hence, as a result of considerable government control and pervasive corporatist ideology rather than voluntary restraint, courts in Singapore have shown few signs of judicial activism and have had virtually no engagement in areas of mega-politics.

The Singapore Supreme Court is a good illustration. Since it was founded in 1957 the court has exercised its judicial review powers cautiously[56]; virtually none of its cases address substantive constitutional or political issues. In fact, the five-year reviews of developments in Singapore law published by the Singapore Academy of Law provide not a single chapter dedicated to constitutional and administrative law, as the Chief Justice himself pointed out ironically in a recent speech to law students.[57] While this judicial muteness in areas of mega-politics partly reflects the lack of open contestation in a tightly controlled political system, it also illustrates efforts by the government to exert subtle control over the judiciary, the Supreme Court in particular, through such means as removal of external review of Singapore's courts (appeals to the Privy Council ceased in 1994); using legislation to curtail court sentencing prerogatives; direct influence over the terms of appointments through exercise of executive discretion in appointing Supreme Court judges (many of whom have links to the PAP inner circle); rotation of judges with legal service positions; lack of tenure for many judges; and the extension of contracts at the Supreme Court beyond legal retirement age at the will of the prime minister. These are in addition to firm regulation of judges

54 See Worthington, "Between Hermes and Themis," 2001; International Bar Association, *Prosperity versus Individual Rights?*, 2008; Frank, *The Decline of the Rule of Law in Singapore and Malaysia*, 1991; Littlemore, *Report to the International Commission of Jurists*, 1997.

55 See Worthington, *Governance in Singapore*, 2003.

56 Between 1957 and 2010, there have been 79 cases of judicial review, of which 27.8% went in favor of the applicants.

57 See Keong, "Judicial Review," 2010.

in the form of corporatist control over such professional organizations as the Singapore Law Society and over institutions of higher legal education – gateways to the bench. Given the intimate ties of judges to the ruling class in Singapore and the parameters of its corporatist ideology, it is not surprising that courts have done little to address core political issues.

This is not to say that in Singapore the judiciary is without relevance. The government has been careful to maintain the image of a professional and efficient judiciary, and certainly the Supreme Court has done a great deal to sustain the confidence of the international business community in its commercial decisions. But more politically sensitive cases often reveal very different dynamics. For instance, in cases against prominent opposition members the courts suddenly deviated from long held principles of English law,[58] and there has been widespread use of defamation cases against regime critics, with the damages awarded being drastically different in political and nonpolitical cases.[59] In fact, it has been suggested that because the courts have been used blatantly for political purposes, the Supreme Court has had difficulties in filling its bench, with some judges accepting appointment only on the condition that they not be involved in political cases. The bench is thus divided between 'technical' and 'political judges'.[60] Lacking the bureaucratic autonomy of the Japanese court, and with some judges actively supporting the corporatist and communal ideology that seeks to keep political conflict out of the courts[61], Singapore's Supreme Court has shown little inclination to engage with areas of mega-politics.

---

58 See for instance a comment by ICJ observer, Canadian Judge Paul Bentley, in the Jeyaratnam trial: 'The logic escapes me! (Judge) Rajendran indicated that he was adopting the reasoning of the English House of Lords in Rubber Improvements Ltd. v Daily Telegraph Ltd […] as the correct interpretation of the law of defamation […] On this reasoning, Jeyaratnam's words to the crowd could not be defamatory. Yet the conclusion of Judge Rajendran runs in clear opposition to the rationale in the 'Lewis' case.', cited in Worthington, "Between Hermes and Themis," 2001, p. 491.

59 See Worthington, *Governance in Singapore*, 2003, p. 126.

60 See Worthington, "Between Hermes and Themis," 2001, p. 516.

61 A good example here is the recent speech by Chief Justice Chan Sek Keong to law students, in which he advocated a 'green light approach' which views courts not as "first line of defence against administrative abuses of power: instead, control can and should come internally from Parliament and the Executive itself…" thus leaving the role of courts to one of support in 'articulating clear rules and principles by which government may abide one and conform to the rule of law'; cited from Keong, "Judicial Review," 2010, pp. 480-481.

The Singaporean court demonstrates how deeply embedded courts are in such a political system and the difficulty of constructing judicial assertiveness where on party has hegemony and the executive is dominant. A similar trajectory is unfolding in Cambodia and within socialist regimes in the region. Yet the government's ability to sustain a public image of judicial impartiality and independence in nonpolitical cases also reveals the complexities of the relationship between judicialization and governance in such settings – a nexus that might be described as cooptation and muteness of the judiciary.

D. Conclusion

This paper has not only questioned some common assumptions about the role of the judiciary in governance but also drawn attention to variations in the structural and political contexts in which courts in the region operate, thus hopefully providing new insights for the theoretical and empirical debates.

At a macro-level, democratization and constitutionalization in Asia have often been the foundation for growing judicial assertiveness and activism. Yet soft authoritarian regimes like that of Singapore have also begun to see the benefits of having a well-functioning and at least partially autonomous judiciary, though setting clear limits to the involvement of courts in mega-politics.

In their diversity, the cases presented highlight the need for more attention to the complex interplay between institutional, cultural, and structural factors in shaping judicial behavior. Court powers and scope, as well as more general arrangements for enhancing judicial independence (tenure, budget autonomy, and appointment procedures), have often triggered greater judicial assertiveness. Yet, as Japan illustrates, nuances in these arrangements might also reinforce an internal judicial culture that makes it less likely that courts will take on a policy-making role. In fact, the legal traditions in which judges are trained and socialized have often provided a 'stickiness' that leads to strong path dependencies for judicial activity. Finally, there is the structural context itself. All the cases presented illustrate that courts cannot but be deeply embedded within the political realm, which sets the general parameters in which courts can operate and also critically determines whether they will be propelled into the political fray.

The borders between the trajectories described here are often fluid, responding to changes in the environment and the strategic behavior of the judiciary itself. For instance, as illustrated by the Thai court, a danger of growing politicization may accompany growing judicial activism, particularly in times of exceptional political crisis. Similarly, a judiciary that is muted by executive control, as in Singapore, is at permanent risk of being instrumentalized should the political elites so decide. And whether judicial restraint that is self-imposed despite formal independence might ultimately lead to greater activism might be reasonably questioned, as illustrated by the case of Japan. The typology suggested should thus be seen primarily as a starting point for analysis. Because it allows classification for comparative purposes, it can be tremendously useful in drawing inferences about the drivers and effects of judicialization.

The effects of judicialization in areas of governance are a case in point. Assumptions about how greater judicial independence and assertiveness will necessarily lead to improvements in rule of law, constitutional practice, and dynamics of good governance, however appealing, are not easily justifiable given the variety of experiences in the region. Certainly, politicization of the judiciary is likely to be detrimental to many aspects of governance, particularly when courts are used to advance partisan interests. Yet judicial activism may also lead to policy deadlock and paralysis, and judicial restraint may promote political inertia, particularly if other institutions are weak. Ultimately the effects on governance will depend, as the Korean and Indonesian courts illustrate, on the careful strategic behavior of the courts themselves and on the constitutional dialogue that evolves among branches of government. Only meaningful dialogue on critical issues in which all institutions engage will transform political conflict into constitutional politics that lead to truly good governance.

Statements about the unfettered benefits for good governance of an active independent judiciary thus need to be carefully qualified. This is particularly true in Asia, a region that continues to struggle with authoritarian enclaves, legacies of executive dominance, and an often technocratic understanding of the judicial process and the rule of law. Foreign transplants like constitutional courts and broad assumptions about how the rule of law is created need to be analyzed in context. That is why the complexities in Asia need, and deserve, a more comprehensive agenda of empirical research and theoretical abstraction.

Works cited

Ackerman, Bruce, "The Rise of World Constitutionalism," *Virginia Law Review* 83 (1997): 771-797.

Baum, Lawrence, *Judges and their Audiences: A Perspective on Judicial Behavior*, Princeton: Princeton University Press, 2006.

Bickel, Alexander, *The Least Dangerous Branch: The Supreme Court at the Bar of Politics*, New Haven: Yale University Press, 1962 (1986).

Bork, Robert, *Coercing Virtue: The Worldwide Rule of Judges*, Washington, DC: American Enterprise Institute, 2003.

Domingo, Pilar, "Judicialization of Politics or Politicization of the Judiciary? Recent Trends in Latin America," *Democratization* 11 (2004): 104-126.

Dowdle, Michael W., "On the Regulatory Dynamics of Judicialization: the Promise and Perils of Exploring 'Judicialization' in East and Southeast Asia," in *Administrative Law and Governance in Asia*, eds. T. Ginsburg, and A. H. Y. Chen, London and New York: Routledge, 2009: pp. 23-37.

Dressel, Björn, "Thailand's Elusive Quest for a Constitutional Equilibrium, 1997-2007," *Contemporary Southeast Asia* 31 (2009): 296-325.

Dressel, Björn, "Judicialization of Politics or Politicization of the Judiciary?: Considerations from Recent Events in Thailand," *The Pacific Review* 23 (2010): 671-691.

Dworkin, Ronald, *A Bill of Rights for Britain*. London: Chatto & Windus, 1990.

Epp, Charles R., *The Rights Revolution: Lawyers, Activists and Supreme Courts in Comparative Perspective*, Chicago: University of Chicago Press, 1998.

Feeley, Malcolm M., and Edward L. Rubin, *Judicial Policy Making and the Modern State: How the Courts Reformed America's Prisons*, Cambridge: Cambridge University Press, 1998.

Ferejohn, John, "Judicializing Politics, Politicizing Law," Journal of *Law* and *Contemporary Problems* 61 (2002): 41-68.

Frank, Beatrice S., *The Decline of the Rule of Law in Singapore and Malaysia*, New York: The Association of the Bar of the City of New York, 1991.

Friedman, Barry, "The Counter-Majoritarian and the Pathology of Constitutional Scholarship," *Northwestern University Law Review* 95 (2001): 933-954.

Ginsburg, Tom, *Judicial Review in New Democracies: Constitutional Courts in Asian Cases*, Cambridge: Cambridge University Press, 2003.

Ginsburg, Tom, "The Constitutional Court and the Judicialization of Korean Politics," in *New Courts in Asia*, eds. A. Harding and P. Nicholson, Oxon and New York: Routledge, 2010, pp. 145-157.

Ginsburg, Tom, and Albert H.Y. Chen, eds., *Administrative Law and Governance in Asia: Comparative Perspectives*, New York: Routledge, 2009.

Goldstein, L., *Constituting Federal Sovereignty: The European Union in Comparative Context*, Baltimore: Johns Hopkins University Press, 2001.

Graber, Mark A, "The Countermajoritarian Difficulty: From Courts to Congress to Constitutional Order," *Annual Review of Law and Social Science* 4 (2008): 361-384.

Guarnieri, Carlo, and Patrizia Pederzoli, eds., *The Power of Judges*, New York: Oxford University Press, 2002.

Haley, John Owen, *The Spirit of Japanese Law*, Athens GA: University of Georgia Press, 2006.

Harding, Andrew, "The Constitutional Court of Thailand 1998-2006: A Turbulent Innovation," in *New Courts in Asia*, ed. A. Harding and P. Nicholson, Oxon and New York: Routledge, 2010, pp. 121-144.

Hendrianto, "Institutional Choice and the New Indonesian Constitutional Court," in *New Courts in Asia*, eds. A. Harding and P. Nicholson, Oxon and New York: Routledge, 2010, pp. 158-177.

Hilbink, Lisa, "Assessing the New Constitutionalism," *Comparative Politics* 40 (2008): 227-245.

Hirschl, Ran, *Towards Juristocracy: The Origins and Consequences of the New Constitutionalism*, Cambridge MA: Harvard University Press, 2004.

Hirschl, Ran, "The New Constitutionalism and the Judicialization of Pure Politics Worldwide," *Fordham Law Review* 75 (2006): 721-754.

Hirschl, Ran, "The Judicialization of Mega-Politics and the Rise of Political Courts," *Annual Review of Political Science* 11 (June 2008): 93-118.

Hirschl, Ran, "The Judicialization of Politics," in *The Oxford Handbook of Law and Politics*, eds. K. E. Whittington, D. R. Kelemen, and G. A. Caldeira, Oxford and New York: Oxford University Press, 2008.

International Bar Association, *Prosperity versus Individual Rights? Human Rights, Democracy and Rule of Law in Singapore*, London, 2008.

Keong, Chan Sek, "Judicial Review – From Angst to Empathy," *Singapore Academy of Law Journal* 22 (2010): 469-489.

Klein, James R., "The Battle for the Rule of Law in Thailand: The Constitutional Court of Thailand," in *The Constitutional Court of Thailand: The Provisions and the Working of the Court*, eds. Amara Raksasataya and J. R. Klein, Bangkok: Constitution for the People Society, 2003, pp. 34-90.

Law, David, "The Anatomy of a Conservative Court: Judicial Review in Japan," *Texas Law Review* 87 (2009): 1545-1593.

Lee, Youngjae, "Law, Politics, and Impeachment: The Impeachment of Roh Moo-Hyun from a Comparative Constitutional Perspective," *American Journal of Comparative Law* 53 (2005): 403-432.

Leyland, Peter, "Thailand's Constitutional Watchdogs: Dobermans, Bloodhounds or Lapdogs?," *Journal of Comparative Law* 2 (2008): 151-177.

Littlemore, Stuart, *Report to the International Commission of Jurists, Geneva, Switzerland on a Defamation Trial in the High Court Of Singapore: Goh Chok Tong vs J. B Jeyaretnam, August 18-22, 1997.*

Morton, Frederick Lee, "The Effect of the Charter of Rights on Canadian Federalism," *Publius* 25 (1995): 173-188.

Morton, Frederick Lee, and Rainer Knopff, *The Charter Revolution and the Court Party*, Peterborough ON: Broadview Press, 2000.

North, Douglass C., and Barry R. Weingast, "Constitutions and Commitment: The Evolution of Institutions Governing Public Choice in Seventeenth-century England," *Journal of Economic History* 44 (1998): 803-832.

O'Brian, David M., and Yasuo Ohkoshi, "Stifling Judicial Independence from Within: The Japanese Judiciary," in *Judicial Independence in the Age of Democracy: Critical Perspectives from Around the World*, eds. P. H. Russel and D. M. O'Brian, Charlottesville and London: University of Virginia Press, 2001, pp. 37-61.

Ramseyer, Mark J., "The Puzzling (In)Dependence of Courts: A Comparative Approach," *Journal of Legal Studies* 23 (1994): 721-747.

Ramseyer, Mark J., and Eric B. Rasmusen, *Measuring Judicial Independence: The Political Economy of Judging in Japan*, Chicago: University of Chicago Press, 2003.

Schmitt, Carl, *Verfassungsrechtliche Aufsätze aus den Jahren 1924-1954: Materialien zu einer Verfassungslehre*, Berlin: Duncker & Humblot, 1958.

Shapiro, Martin, "The Success of Judicial Review," in *Constitutional Dialogues in Comparative Perspective*, ed. S. Kenney, New York: Palgrave Macmillan, 1999.

Shapiro, Martin, and Alec Stone Sweet, *On Law, Politics, and Judicialization*, New York: Oxford University Press, 2002.

Sieder, Rachel, Line Schjolden, and Alan Angell, eds., *The Judicialization of Politics in Latin America*, New York and Houndsmills: Palgrave Macmillan, 2005.

Slaughter, Anne Marie, "Judicial Globalization," *Virginia Journal of International Law* 40 (2000): 1103-1124.

Stone Sweet, Alec, *Governing with Judges: Constitutional Politics in Europe*, Oxford: Oxford University Press, 2000.

Sunstein, Cass R., *Designing Democracy: What Constitutions Do*, Oxford: Oxford University Press, 2001.

Tate, Neal C., "The Judicialization of Politics in the Philippines and Southeast Asia," *International Political Science Review* 15 (1994): 187-197.

Tate, Neal C., and Torbjörn Vallinder, eds., *The Global Expansion of Judicial Power*, New York: New York University Press, 1995.

Teubner, Gunther, "Juridification – Concepts, Aspects, Limits, Solutions," in *Juridification of Social Spheres: A Comparative Analysis in the Areas of Labor, Corporate, Antitrust and Social Welfare Law*, ed. G. Teubner, Berlin and New York: de Gruyter, 1987.

Tushnet, Mark, *Taking the Constitution Away from the Courts*, Princeton: Princeton Univ. Press, 1999.

Upham, Frank K., "Political Lackeys or Faithful Public Servants? Two Views of the Japanese Judiciary," *Law & Social Inquiry* (2005): 421-455.

Voigt, S., and E. Salzberger, "Choosing not to Choose: When Politicians Choose to Delegate Powers," *Kyklos* 55 (2002): 289-310.

Waldron, Jeremy, *Law and Disagreement*, Oxford: Clarendon Press, 1999.

Weingast, Barry R., "Constitutions as Governance Structures: The Political Foundations of Secure Markets," *Journal of Institutional & Theoretical Economics* (1993): 286-311.

Worthington, Ross, "Between Hermes and Themis: An Empirical Study of the Contemporary Judiciary in Singapore," *Journal of Law and Society* 28 (2001): 490-519.

Worthington, Ross, *Governance in Singapore*, London and New York: RoutledgeCurzon, 2003.

List of Contributors

J. W. F. Allison
University Senior Lecturer at the Centre for Public Law, Queens' College, University of Cambridge

Albert H.Y. Chen
Chan Professor in Constitutional Law, Faculty of Law, The University of Hong Kong

Björn Dressel
Senior Lecturer at the Crawford School of Public Policy, College of Asia & the Pacific, Australian National University

Claudia Derichs
Professor of Comparative Political Science and International Development Studies, University of Marburg

Ingwer Ebsen
Professor emeritus of Public Law, University of Frankfurt, Member of the Supervisory Board of the German-Southeast Asian Center of Excellence for Public Policy and Good Governance

Dirk Ehlers
Director of the Institute of Public Economic Law, University of Münster, Chairman of the Association of German Constitutional Law Professors 2010-2012, Member of the Supervisory Board of the German-Southeast Asian Center of Excellence for Public Policy and Good Governance

Robert Esser
Chair of German, European and International Criminal Law, Criminal Procedure and White-Collar Crime and Head of the Research Centre for "Human Rights in Criminal Proceedings" (HRCP), University of Passau, coordinating professor of the German-Southeast Asian Center of Excellence for Public Policy and Good Governance at the University of Passau

Andreas Føllesdal
Professor of Political Philosophy, PluriCourts – Centre for the Study of the Legitimate Roles of the Judiciary in the Global Order, University of Oslo

Henning Glaser
DAAD Expert-Lecturer at the Faculty of Law, Thammasat University, Head of the German-Southeast Asian Center of Excellence for Public Policy and Good Governance

Dieter Grimm
Professor emeritus at the Faculty of Law, Humboldt University Berlin, former Justice of the Federal Constitutional Court of Germany

Rainer Grote
Associate Professor at the Department of International Law, University of Göttingen

Warawit Kanithasen
Advisor to the Chief Ombudsman of the Kingdom of Thailand, Senior Research Fellow at the German-Southeast Asian Center of Excellence for Public Policy and Good Governance, former Thai Ambassador

Rudolf Mellinghoff
President of the Federal Fiscal Court of Germany, former Justice at the Federal Constitutional Court of Germany, Honorary Professor at the University of Tübingen

Jörg Menzel
Associate Professor at the Institute of Public Law, University of Bonn

Boonsri Mewongukote
Professor of Public Law at the Faculty of Law, Thammasat University, Bangkok

Bodo Pieroth
Professor emeritus, Director of the Institute of Public Law and Politics, University of Münster

Son Soubert
Privy Councillor to His Majesty the King of Cambodia, former Member of the Constitutional Council of Cambodia, former Vice-President of the Cambodian National Assembly

Hassavut Vititviriyakul
President of the Supreme Administrative Court of Thailand

Yueh-sheng Weng
Professor emeritus at the College of Law, National Taiwan University, former President of the Judicial Yuan and Chairman of the Council of the Grand Justices (Constitutional Court) of the R.O.C. (Taiwan)